Sport in the Global Society

General Editor: J.A. Mangan

FOOTBALL CULTURE

SPORT IN THE GLOBAL SOCIETY

General Editor: J.A. Mangan

The interest in sports studies around the world is growing and will continue to do so. This unique series combines aspects of the expanding study of *sport in the global society*, providing comprehensiveness and comparison under one editorial umbrella. It is particularly timely, with studies in the cultural, economic, ethnographic, geographical, political, social, anthropological, sociological and aesthetic elements of sport proliferating in institutions of higher education.

Eric Hobsbawm once called sport one of the most significant practices of the late nineteenth century. Its significance was even more marked in the late twentieth century and will continue to grow in importance into the new millennium as the world develops into a 'global village' sharing the English language, technology and sport.

Other Titles in the Series

FOOTBALL CULTURE

Local Contests, Global Visions

Editors

GERRY P.T. FINN
University of Strathclyde

and

RICHARD GIULIANOTTI
University of Aberdeen

FRANK CASS
LONDON • PORTLAND, OR

First published in 2000 in Great Britain by
FRANK CASS PUBLISHERS
2 Park Square, Milton Park, Abingdon, Oxon, OX14 4RN

and in the United States of America by
FRANK CASS PUBLISHERS
270 Madison Ave, New York NY 10016

Transferred to Digital Printing 2006

Website: www.frankcass.com

British Library Cataloguing in Publication Data

Football culture : local contests, global vision. – (Sport
in the global society ; no. 14)
1. Soccer – Social aspects – Case studies
I. Finn, Gerry P. T. II. Giulianotti, Richard, 1966–
306.4'83

ISBN 0-7146-5041-2 (cloth)
ISBN 0-7146-8100-8 (paper)
ISSN 1368-9789

Library of Congress Cataloging-in-Publication Data

Football culture : local contests, global visions / editors, Gerry
P.T. Finn and Richard Giulianotti.
    p.   cm. – (Sport in the global society, ISSN 1368-9789)
    "This group of studies first appeared as a special issue of
Culture, sport, society ... vol. 2, no. 3." – T.p. verso.
    Includes bibliographical references and index.
    ISBN 0-7146-5041-2. – ISBN 0-7146-8100-8 (paper)
    1. Soccer – Social aspects Cross-cultural studies. 2. Nationalism
and sports Cross-cultural studies. 3. Soccer fans Cross-cultural
studies. I. Finn, Gerry P. T., 1949–   . II. Giulianotti,
Richard, 1966–   . II. Culture, sport, society. Vol. 2, No. 3.
IV. Series: Cass series – sport in the global society.
GV943.9.S64F66   1999
306.4'83 – dc21   99-40498
                                                                          CIP

This group of studies first appeared as a special issue of *Culture, Sport, Society*
(ISSN 1461-0981), Vol.2, No.3, Autumn 1999, published by Frank Cass

Publisher's Note
The publisher has gone to great lengths to ensure the
quality of this reprint but points out that some
imperfections in the original may be apparent

Contents

Series Editor's Foreword

J.A. MANGAN

Soccer will be receiving close attention in the Cass series Sport in the Global Society and in the Cass sports studies journals in the post-Millennium period. In addition to G. Finn and R. Guilianotti (eds.), *Football Culture: Local Conflicts, Global Visions*, Cass will also publish in the Spring of 2000 J. Garland, D. Malcolm and M. Rowe (eds.), *The Future of Football: Challenges for the Twenty-First Century*[1] as the launch number of the new international journal, *Soccer and Society* and as a volume in Sport in the Global Society. Various articles on soccer will also appear in *The International Journal of the History of Sport, Culture, Sport and Society* and *The European Sports History Review*. Soccer merits extensive consideration. This is how it should be. It is the world's game. While John Betjeman's famous city trio of

> ...father, son and clerk join up
> To talk about the football cup

they are now joined across the globe by literally thousands of millions from state presidents to supermarket packers.

Football Culture: Local Conflicts, Global Visions has much to offer the student of international soccer. It is fascinatingly global – geographically and culturally. In view of a recent plethora of monographs and collections on nationalism and the recent creation of a new journal on the subject – *National Identities*, the chapters on soccer and nationalism in Africa are of special interest and importance. The role of soccer, as an agent of rehabilitation of the traumatized and dispossessed and of a secure and confident identity, *at least to an extent*, is good news from a tragic continent. Of course, as *Football Culture* makes quite clear, Africa does not have exclusive ownership of soccer as a 'cement' of nationhood. Also of special interest in this volume is the political and cultural symbolism of soccer as interpreted by the media, and the media's fixation with national images, psyches and stereotypes. *Football Culture* calls for further explanations of such media manifestations beyond this collection, and appropriately, the call will shortly be answered by David Hand and his colleagues in a volume to be published by Cass in Sport in the Global Society entitled *Imagined Identities? Football, Europe and the Press.*[2]

Another theme of some importance only marginally touched on in *Football Culture* is the semiotics of soccer 'songs', and by extension the chants, lyrics and doggerel of sport in general. This has recently been, and will continue to be, a focus of Cass publications with the re-issue of the seminal study in this area of *Athleticism in the Victorian and Edwardian Public School*[3] and the articles both published and forthcoming on the subject in *Culture, Sport, Society* by Keith Gregson and Mike Huggins,[4] Jeff Hill,[5] and Sebastiao Votre.[6] *Football Culture* clearly catches the academic mood of the moment.

Without any doubt, mention should certainly be made of the discussion in *Football Culture* of myopia, 'sectarianism' and prejudice. It is a seminiferous discussion. The careful attention to detail, the thorough compilation of evidence in support of assertion, the delicate comprehensiveness of the conceptual arguments are surely an object lesson to earlier commentators and unquestionably advance the quality of reflection on sectarianism, prejudice and sport in society. The difference in quality of analysis between past commentators and the current commentator in *Football Culture* is marked. It resembles the difference between the furniture of a penthouse and a rented house or between the Glasgow Burrell (international museum) and the Barrows (city flea market). Edmund Burke observed, in a speech on American taxation, that it is the nature of all greatness *not* to be exact. The suspicion must be that before the speech he dined and wined rather too well. The specificity of the arguments in the chapter on 'sectarianism', prejudice and sport constitutes a compelling *tour de force*, if not to greatness. With the significance of the subject so clearly illustrated, and the limitations of previous analyses so clearly demonstrated, a framework for sophisticated consideration is now available, Surely a global study of sectarianism and sport is now due.

Football Culture lays stress on the relative autonomy of sport as a manifestation of indigenous popular culture, and local, regional and national negotiation and resistance in the face of global movements. This is to be welcomed. It was true of sport in the time of British imperialism as was made clear in an earlier Cass publication, *The Cultural Bond:*

Sport, Empire, Society.[7] It is as true as ever today. Incidentally, in this context perhaps a better conceptual term is 'hybridity' rather that 'creolization'![8] Furthermore, if the history of sport 'reveals a continuing dialectic', it also reveals a continuing process of balance and imbalance and adjustment and maladjustment with regard to indigenous cultural customs and their permanence and impermanence. Cultures are complex, changing and invariably challenged. Soccer offers a superb case-study of cultural complexity, change and challenge *on a global scale.*

Much else of topicality and importance is discussed in *Football Culture*: social differentiation and stratification 'within the football nation'; universalism and multiculturalism and their relationship to the complexity of power; gender and modern soccer – perhaps less well considered than other aspects of the modern global game with aggression seen inappropriately as a male prerogative;[9] the future gerontological profile of the spectator; commercialism, globalization and transnationalism and putative and actual outcomes; hooliganism, violence and spectator culture; post-millennium post-industrialism and the impact on the demographics and culture of football crowds; the relationship between national associations, transnational clubs and media companies: the changing nature of Cups and Championships and the visible consequences; *Bosman*, contracts and transfers; communities; commodification and change.

The comprehensiveness and incisiveness of its coverage of contemporary issues ensure that *Football Culture* is invariably stimulating and frequently illuminating.

J. A. MANGAN
International Research Centre for Sport, Socialisation, Society
University of Strathclyde
February 2000

NOTES

1. J. Garland, D. Malcolm and M. Rowe (eds.), *The Future of Football: Challenges for the Twenty-First Century* (London and Portland, OR: Frank Cass, 2000).
2. D. Hand, L. Crolley and R. Jeutter (eds.), *Imagined Identities? Football, Europe and the Press* (London and Portland, OR: Frank Cass, forthcoming).
3. J.A. Mangan, *Athleticism in the Victorian and Edwardian Public School* (Cambridge: Cambridge University Press, 1981; new second edition, London and Portland, OR: Frank Cass, forthcoming), Chapter Seven. See also J.A. Mangan 'Moralists, Metaphysicians and Moralists: The "signifiers" of a Victorian and Edwardian sub-culture', in S. Bandy (ed.), *Coreobus*

Triumphs: The Alliance of Sports and the Arts (San Diego, 1988), pp.141–62. and J.A. Mangan, 'Gamesfield and Battlefield: A Romantic Alliance in Verse and Creation of Militaristic Masculinity', in J. Nauright and T.J.L. Chandler (eds.), *Making Men* (London, 1988), pp.141–57.

4. K. Gregson and M. Huggins, 'Sport , Music-hall Culture and Popular Song in Nineteenth-Century England', *Culture, Sport, Society*, 2, 2 (Summer 1999), 82–102.

5. J. Hill, 'Cocks, Cats, Caps and Cups: A Seminotic Approach to Sport and National Identity', *Culture Sport, Society*, 2, 2 (Summer 1999), 1–21.

6. See the forthcoming article by Sebastiao Votre in *Culture, Sport, Society* (2000).

7. See J.A. Mangan, 'Prologue: Britain's Chief Spiritual Export: Imperial Sport as Moral Metaphor, Political Symbol and Cultural Bond', in J.A. Mangan (ed.), *The Cultural Bond: Sport, Empire, Society* (London and Portland, OR: Frank Cass, 1992), pp.7–9.

8. For a discussion of this term, see Eduardo P. Archetti, *Masculinities: Football, Polo and the Tango in Argentina* (Oxford, 1999), pp.xv–xvii.

9. See J.A.Mangan, 'Aggression and Androgyny in and beyond Sport in the Post Millennium', *Revue Française de civilisation britannique* (forthcoming, 2000).

Local Contests and Global Visions: Sporting Difference and International Change

GERRY P.T. FINN and
RICHARD GIULIANOTTI

The collection opens with three articles that explore forms of ethnic or 'racial' exclusion in three different settings in which, paradoxically, soccer is also appropriated in different ways to give representations of national unity. The first piece, by John Hughson, examines the shifting contours of fan support in Australian domestic soccer. Hughson draws upon earlier work to underline the association of the Australian game with ethnic 'community networks'.[1] The most dominant national sports in Australia have been the predominantly British colonial ones, such as rugby league, rugby union and cricket. These sports reflected a sometimes ambivalent, but usually affectionate, connection with Britain, whereas the indigenous football code of 'Australian Rules' provided a sense of Australian camaraderie and departure for a new life.[2] Domestic soccer failed to take off in popularity until the large immigration of Southern Europeans to Australia in the early post-war period, giving rise to the racial typification of the game as 'wogball'.[3]

Latterly, the attempt by the Australian soccer federation to 'Aussify' soccer in Australia has had real consequences. The game has been given the appearance of being more national in its organization, notably through the foundation of the 'A-League'. The ethnic ties of the original clubs still remain in terms of their cultural history and symbolism, though their names have been changed. Ironically this change is a throwback to the previously dominant governmental assimilationist policy, rather than the 'multicultural' perspective now being evolved. Perhaps most significantly, Australian domestic soccer has been boosted by the creation of clubs that make evident 'British' modes of support among fans, notably expatriates from England and Scotland. Hughson draws particular attention to Perth Glory; another illustration would be the Northern Spirit side from north Sydney. For the 1999 season, both clubs had home gate averages of over 14,000, around double that of their rivals. Hughson explains this fandom according to Michel Maffesoli's concept of the urban neo-tribes, which tend to be relatively affective and fluid in terms of cultural identification. It remains to be seen for how long these clubs can continue to hold the passion and attendance of their 'neo-tribal' supporters.

The case of soccer in the United States has some historical parallels with Australia, but more important differences. In the USA, colonial ties have been long gone. In North America, sport generated more a sense of separate cultural and historical identity, as the white settlers in America adapted European sports and called them their own. Baseball and American football were followed by basketball and, to a lesser extent, ice hockey, as sports that functioned to establish a dominant North American identity. Soccer remained a marginal cultural practice; popular and with a long historical background in the old immigrant urban centres, and with a new significance among some sections of the growing Hispanic-American community. This sense of soccer, as old European or new South or Central American, meant that it was seen to denote an ambivalence towards identification with the USA. Attempts to found a glitzy, all-star American soccer league in the 1960s and 1970s failed. The game lacked a grassroots basis; the emphasis on its 'late modern', glamour aspects represented a doomed shadowing of the corporate strategies adopted by far more successful and established sports, especially the NBA.

However, soccer has become established as a huge participatory sport in the United States, with up to 18 million registered players, notably among suburban, middle-class families. As Andrews explains, the game's social meaning has inevitably become entangled in the class and racial stratification of American society. Drawing upon ethnographic research in southern United States, Andrews argues that local soccer clubs now constitute a network of lifestyle enclaves for these privileged social groups. But the game remains a marker of ethnic marginality, because it has now evolved into a cultural resource controlled by the powerful and social elite of the dominant ethnic majority communities of the United States.

Both Australia and the USA show how soccer provides internal markers of differentiation within national contours. That complexity is also evident in Scotland. Use of football as a form of ethnic differentiation and exclusion has been habitually camouflaged by the use of the rubric 'religious sectarianism'. 'Sectarianism' refers to, but avoids any detailed description of, the history of ethnic divisions between Protestant Scots and Catholic Irish in Scottish football and society generally. The main institutional embodiments of this cleavage in football are the Glasgow clubs, Rangers and Celtic, collectively known as the Old Firm, which dominate domestic league and cup tournaments. The essay by Gerry Finn provides a critical analysis of media and academic accounts of the 'Old Firm' and illustrates how 'sectarianism' obscures a deeper understanding of racialization and ethnic division in Scotland;[4] it has an especially pernicious influence on contemporary views of other ethnic minority communities in Scotland. The rhetoric surrounding the use of 'sectarianism' also undermines the scope for exploring international parallels. Finn is particularly critical of the work of B. Murray and H. Moorhouse for providing 'realist' and self-contradictory analyses of 'sectarianism' in Scottish football and society.[5]

The next four pieces look at football and its relationship to the construction and reproduction of national identity. In Africa football is considered to be 'culture-neutral', so that African players are believed to be only minimally influenced by Westernized values and practices.[6] Instead, the game has become a crucial medium in the project to found national identities. In the war-torn states of Liberia, Sierra Leone and Rwanda, football might serve to promote some forms of reconciliation between conflicting ethnic communities, while offering some help to rehabilitate the traumatized and dispossessed.[7] Unfortunately, the examples described in the previous three essays imply a more pessimistic interpretation of the likely outcome. Other African societies have been less recently scarred by contemporary violent ethnic conflict and the wider consequences of imperialism. Perhaps in these African states football does represent one cultural medium through which senses of nationhood may be generated and the case for global equality and standing may be advanced. Cameroon has proved to be one of the most successful of African football nations, bursting onto the international stage in the opening game of the 1990 World Cup finals when they defeated the holders, Argentina. In her essay on Cameroonian football, Vidacs argues that the national team known as the 'Indomitable Lions' can certainly help to sustain the 'imagined community' of national identity, perhaps even engendering a pan-African consciousness.[8]

However, local Cameroonian teams help to confirm identities with strong local ties that can cross-cut or conflict with national associations.

South American nations, like the African states, may be seen to be relatively peripheral by the Eurocentric élite of the self-perceived Western core,[9] but nations like Argentina and Uruguay do have long and illustrious football histories. Pablo Alabarces and Marìa Graciela Rodrìguez argue that football provided a strong medium for the expression of nationality, with Buenos Aires very much at the centre. The national game has fallen under the influence of two authoritarian governments: Peronism in the 1940s, and the military junta of the 1970s. Latterly, football has been forced to carry an ideological burden for the political neoconservatism of Menem. Alabarces and Rodrìguez note that the high point in the relationship between nationalism and football came through the ongoing Maradona saga, a player of unparalleled technical excellence who embodied a range of contradictory moral and cultural meanings.[10] At the dawn of the new millennium, Argentinian football (as with the wider Argentinian society) occupies a peripheral role within the global sports environment. The club championship is increasingly dominated by the dictates of television, while the players leave for Europe at a younger age than ever before. Argentinian clubs have come under greater pressure to reform their corporate structure, and to switch from a communitarian membership set-up to one that mirrors the purer business model of European clubs, with chief executives, directors and shareholders.[11]

In Uruguay, we find an even more problematic case of structural decline in terms of football and general national status. As Richard Giulianotti explains, the game of football had an exceptionally strong impact in cementing senses of Uruguayan national identity in the early part of the twentieth century. While Uruguay had several charismatic, foundationary figures in military and political terms (notably Artigas and Batlle), it was through football that a sense of national identity was established at popular cultural levels. Uruguay's political and economic pragmatism mirrored its exploitation of two football styles (English and Scottish). That footballing pragmatism resulted in extraordinary success during the Olympics in 1924 and 1928, and at the 1930 and 1950 World Cup finals. The latter tournament served to project this geographically peripheral and small nation on to the world stage, and gave rise to a new mythology about the national Uruguayan character. However, Uruguay's political economy has become increasingly dependent upon overseas commodity prices, while its football players are also now groomed for cheap export, to try to balance the domestic (football) finances. Meanwhile, the declining status of the national team can be seen as a crucial cultural referent for the sense of cultural and national pessimism that has permeated Uruguay throughout the 1990s. To assuage this sense of decline and decay and to stir the national side out of torpor and encourage better results, the national sports media has employed an aesthetically regressive, militaristic discourse on the 'warrior' status of its players.

The construction of media narratives on national football sides is examined more fully by Nicolà Porro and Pippo Russo in their essay on Italy versus Germany football matches. Specifically, Porro and Russo discuss the media narratives surrounding three momentous matches between these nations: the 1970 World Cup semi-final, the 1982 World Cup final, and the preliminary round clash at the 1996 European Championships. They illustrate how football matches are laden with political and cultural symbolism. More significantly, the authors also highlight the benefits of a diachronic approach to examining the media/sports relationship, by teasing out the continuities and differences in the meanings through which these matches were interpreted by the media. Football is seen here as possessing its own symbolic universe that is mediated, appropriately enough by the mass media, in a symbiotic relationship with political, cultural and economic realms. Hence, the meaning of each game builds upon previous fixtures while also referencing the wider discourses between nations, in this instance particularly Germany and Italy. Future research in this area may also explore the continuities and differences between media constructions of club and national fixtures, particularly given the greater frequency of, and prestige attached to, European club competitions.

While the media play a critical role in framing the meanings of football fixtures, at a more grassroots level the supporters themselves generate complex, discursive understandings of the game. The study by Gary Armstrong and Malcolm Young examines one category of fan practices and discourses that has been generally overlooked by academics, namely the songs and chants that surround football matches. As part of football's carnivalesque atmosphere, fan chants are filled with ironic humour and graphic corporeal imagery.[12] Consequently, they are at odds with the continuing and ever intensifying pressure within the football industry to sanitize spectating conditions for new 'customers'.[13]

Most recently, as Armstrong and Young identify, this trend has been lent greater legal-juridical muscle through legislation. The authors note that the policing of football crowds has tended to confuse expressive fans (including the most vocal, singing spectators) and hooligan groups, when no such a priori relationship exists. Ironically, this has led to the effective outlawing of expressive fandom, at a time when the marketing of football trades on the 'passion' and 'atmosphere' of games as part of an overall 'entertainment' package. Armstrong and Young note how the targets and imagery of fan chants and songs have changed over the decades, and recognize the often haphazard nexus of these fan airs to popular forms of music, both mainstream and obscure.

More fundamental shifts in youth and popular culture have been associated with the recent rise of soccer in Japan, which is the subject of John Horne's essay. Football crowds at the new J. League are more accommodating towards women, who tend to be in the avant-garde of Japanese cultural changes; the marketing behind the J. League has also sought to encourage a 'festival' atmosphere among fans, which draws heavily on the visual imagery of club matches in Spain, Italy and England.[14] The new J. League began in May 1993, and quickly expanded from 10 to 20 teams. Franchises are granted to clubs with a 'farm team', youth organization and a stadium holding at least 15,000; more importantly, they need strong financial support from a major Japanese company.

The league promised to be more successful than its predecessor, the JSL, a 'corporate-amateur'[15] league that began in 1965 and saw average crowds slump to under 2,000 by 1977. The J. League's initial success was helped by grassroots interest (with over 7,000 children's teams, twice that of Japanese baseball) and good television audiences. As Horne points out, Japanese football has also established a strong international presence, in terms of the global division of football labour, institutional power and financial standing. Along with the USA, the J. League is a financially appealing setting for fading European and South American stars to play out the final years of their professional careers. At the same time, some clubs in Europe and South America have recruited Japanese players to play professionally; an attractive inducement for these signings is the potential sale of club merchandise within the Japanese market. FIFA's drive to penetrate new and more lucrative markets has helped Japan to win the rights (with South Korea) to co-host the World Cup Finals in 2002. That faith has been reciprocated through powerful financial deals and sponsorship arrangements between J. League teams and major Japanese industries and advertising agencies.[16]

The Japanese dream is to realize the successes of their predecessors as World Cup hosts: most recently illustrated by the case of France. In the closing article, Patrick Mignon assesses the condition of French football following the home nation's victory at the 1998 World Cup finals. The French case provides a sobering refutation of the notion that glory at club and national level go hand-in-hand in the contemporary global game. There can be no doubt that the French national team has benefited immensely from the youth training systems that have been established through a unique and far-sighted partnership between the state, local authorities, football clubs and the French football association. By contrast, we may note the general failure of the British Home Nations in international competition as a possible reflection of the free market system that generally pervades player recruitment, coaching and enskilling. Yet, the efficacy of the French player coaching serves to undermine the European standing of an already fragile club system. In short, French clubs cannot resist the financial and legal pressures that entail an annual exodus of élite players to Germany, Spain, Italy and England. The *Bosman* ruling allows foreign clubs to acquire out-of-contract players for nothing; even the introduction of Pay-TV has not sufficiently enriched French clubs to match the wealth of their continental rivals. The French national team may continue to play 'champagne football', but in the immediately foreseeable future the pick of the local vintage will be purchased for foreign collections, and taken abroad to be developed and matured: some special purchases will be returned for a few French national displays, but most will be consumed elsewhere.

Our collection concludes with an epilogue from the editors which develops some of the themes indicated by Mignon and the other contributors. Specifically, we examine the state of nations relative to the increasingly global and commodified nature of football. We discuss the problems that confront the national football associations and their representative teams in co-existing with the burgeoning financial and political power of the largest football clubs in the world. These clubs are becoming 'transnational corporations' that can operate with greater disregard for national boundaries, whether in legal, cultural or financial terms. It might seem that these large-scale commercial developments would eradicate the communal role historically played by football clubs, leaving local identities behind them. That is possible. Some would hope that could mean an end to racism and social division. Yet the paradox is that no matter how football clubs do change, they must always represent some sort of difference in relation to social identity. The evolution of football clubs will not lead to conformity, let alone uniformity. Without some framing of difference in association with football clubs, there can be no contest: without some social difference there would be no social significance to this match between two opposed teams. The issue is not social difference as such: the issue is how we conceptualize social difference,[17] how it evolves, and then how we sport social identities when we come together to compare how we match up.

NOTES

This collection and the two co-authored essays have been jointly produced by Finn and Giulianotti. To underline this collaborative effort the order of presentation of names has been reversed for the final essay, while the collection itself retains the usual alphabetical order.

1. J. Hughson, 'Australian Soccer: "Ethnic" or "Aussie" – The Search for an Image', *Current Affairs Bulletin*, 68, 10, (1992), 12–17.
2. See, for example, R. Pascoe, *The Winter Game: The Complete History of Australian Football* (Melbourne, 1995).
3. W. Vamplew, '"Wogball": Ethnicity and Violence in Australian Soccer', in R. Giulianotti and J. Williams (eds.), *Game Without Frontiers: Football, Identity and Modernity*, (Aldershot, 1994).
4. P. Dimeo and G.P.T. Finn 'Scottish Racism, Scottish Identities: The Case of Partick Thistle', in A. Brown (ed.), *Fanatics! Power, Identity and Fandom in Football* (London, 1998), pp.124–38 and P. Dimeo and G.P.T. Finn, 'Racism, National Identity and Scottish Football', in B. Carrington and I. McDonald (eds.), *Racism in British Sport* (London, 1999).
5. See G.P.T. Finn '"Sectarianism" and Scottish Education', in T.G.K. Bryce and W. Humes (eds.), *Scottish Education* (Edinburgh, 1999) for a wide-ranging discussion of 'sectarianism'.
6. A. Mazrui, 'Reflections on the Gender Gap', in W.J. Baker and J.A. Mangan (eds.), *Sport in Africa* (London, 1987), p.219.
7. P. Richards, 'Soccer and Violence in War-Torn Africa: Soccer and Social Rehabilitation in Sierra Leone', in G. Armstrong and R. Giulianotti (eds.), *Entering the Field* (Oxford, 1997).
8. See also B. Vidacs, 'Football and Anti-Colonial Sentiment in Cameroon', *Mots Pluriels* (electronic journal), 6 (1998).
9. See, for example, A. Tomlinson and J. Sugden, 'Global Power Struggles in World Football: FIFA and UEFA, 1954–74, and their Legacy', *International Journal of the History of Sport*, 14 (1997), 1–25.
10. E. Archetti, '"And Give Joy to My Heart": Ideology and Emotions in the Argentinian cult of Maradona', in G. Armstrong and R. Giulianotti (eds.), *Entering the Field: New Perspectives in World Football* (Oxford, 1997).
11. R. Giulianotti, 'Playing An Aerial Game: The New Political Economy of Soccer', in J. Nauright and K. Schimmel (eds.), *The Political Economy of Sport* (Minnesota, forthcoming).
12. On the carnivalesque, see R. Giulianotti, 'Scotland's Tartan Army Abroad: The Case for the Carnivalesque', *Sociological Review*, 39, 3 (1991), 503–27. On the carnivalesque and flow experiences in relationship to social identities, see G.P.T. Finn, 'Football Violence: A Societal Psychological Perspective', in R. Giulianotti, N. Bonney and M. Hepworth (eds.), *Football Violence and Social Identity* (London, 1994), pp.91–127.
13. On the notion of fan as 'customer', see I. Taylor, 'Soccer Consciousness and Soccer

Hooliganism', in S. Cohen (ed.), *Images of Deviance* (Harmondsworth, 1971); and C. Critcher, 'Football since the War', in J. Clarke, C. Critcher and R. Johnson (eds.), *Working Class Culture: Studies in History and Theory* (London, 1979).

14. H. Nogawa and H. Maeda, 'The Japanese Dream: Soccer Culture Towards the New Millennium', in G. Armstrong and R. Giulianotti (eds.), *Football Cultures and Identities* (Basingstoke, 1999), pp.228–9.

15. Ibid., p.224.

16. T. Jun and S. Kazue, 'Scoring Big with Soccer', *Japan Quarterly*, 40, 4 (1993) 418–25.

17. See G.P.T. Finn, '"Sectarianism" and Scottish Education', in T.G.K. Bryce and W.M. Humes (eds.), *Scottish Education* (Edinburgh, 1999) and Finn in this collection for further discussion of these issues.

1

A Tale of Two Tribes:
Expressive Fandom in Australian Soccer's A-League

JOHN HUGHSON

SOCCER AND POST-TRIBES

The term *post-tribes* has been recently used by Gary Armstrong to describe parochial football fans. Drawing on his ethnographic study of the Blades, a group of hooligan supporters who follow English club team Sheffield United, Armstrong notes that life in the 'post-tribe' is 'fluid, unstable and transient' in character. Commitment to the tribe is dependent on the ongoing attraction of tribal-related activities.[1] According to Armstrong, 'when the attraction wanes, members leave and such tribes can die'. This is a refreshing take on football hooliganism, differing from previous accounts which bear similarity to early functionalist studies of youth deviance as a full-time career. It prepares for a fruitful analysis of parochial fandom in the contemporary football stadium in relation to the shifting supporter allegiances accompanying the changes in premier and lower league competitions at a time of upheaval in the 'world game' across the globe. Armstrong's reference to football post-tribes draws on the notion of neo-tribalism, developed in the work of M. Maffesoli. For Maffesoli, neo-tribalism is a postmodern form of sociality in which collective forms of identity are based on sentiment rather than rationality.[2]

The notion of neo-tribe, or postmodern tribe, connects with the current interest in sociology and cultural studies in explaining identity formation and construction in contemporary social contexts.[3] Importantly, the categorization of neo-tribes shifts the analytical focus away from Weberian understandings of identity in individualistic expression, to the 'collective processes' which give life to group identities.[4] A related mode of enquiry is reflected in contemporary studies of football fandom, the 1994 volume *Football, Violence and Social*

Identity, edited by Richard Giulianotti and associates at the University of Aberdeen, candidly declaring such an interest in its title. A number of subsequent works, including the recent anthology edited by Adam Brown, *Fanatics! Power, Identity and Fandom in Football*, have kept the analytical spotlight of football academe on collective identity/ies.[5] The focus on identities has opened the field of football scholarship to a variety of international contexts and settings which were previously excluded, albeit unintentionally, from a domain of academic activity that exhibited an anglo-centric fixation on class. Accordingly, Australian soccer-supporting groups which have a primary identification in ethnicity rather than class, have now moved on to the international stage – at least in terms of academic research.[6]

MAFFESOLI AND NEO-TRIBES

Maffesoli's work on neo-tribes promotes a discussion of expressive rather than rational forms of collective identity. This emphasis is particularly relevant to the consideration of parochial football supporters and is influential to the idea of expressive fandom developed in this essay. The expressive nature rather than rational foundation of the neo-tribe in Maffesoli's work has been recently highlighted in an excellent study by K. Hetherington:

> ... the important thing to recognise is that this concept of a neo-tribe, and the groupings and identifications it is used to describe, is associated not with rationality and its modes of identification and organisation but with sentiment, feeling and shared experience – with affectual forms of sociation.[7]

This is not to suggest that the neo-tribe and its actual examples, such as groups of football fans or anti-nuclear protesters, are a rabble. Neo-tribes will be ordered to certain extents and in different ways. They are, indeed, organizations, but not rationalistic organizations in the Weberian sense. Indeed, the term neo-tribe is contrived by Maffesoli to rescue Weber's 'emotional community' from the marginalized place it inhabits in the great theorist's schema. The emotional community may be 'changeable in composition', 'ill-defined in nature' and 'lacking in organisation' but, for Maffesoli, unlike Weber, it is a form of human association which *exists in its own right*.[8] The neo-tribe is regarded by Maffesoli as a postmodern form of sociality in which association with others derives from free choice based on affectual commitment and instinct. Although an obvious admirer, Hetherington suggests that Maffesoli goes a little too far in his ascription of choice to neo-tribes. In particular, Hetherington is concerned with Maffesoli's tendency to unbind class, gender and ethnicity from the complexity of relations which are tangled within the formation of neo-tribes. One does not have to be a structuralist in the strictest functionalist sense to accept that these familiar structural factors have a great bearing on micro-group affiliation in contemporary society. As Hetherington suggests, although neo-tribes are formed by free choosing social actors, this does not mean that life is rosy within the neo-tribe (not that Maffesoli actually suggests this is so). Neo-tribes evince a 'troubled politics of identity in which people try to renegotiate their identities'.[9] In the case of parochial football supporting subcultures in different national urban locations, these identities appear to be very much connected to familial and social background. As will become apparent in the discussion of supporter groups associated with the Australian A-League, ethnic background can be an important aspect of identification within neo-tribal gatherings.

Maffesoli's wont to downplay the significance of structural factors in neo-tribal formations has much to do with his interest in the everyday activity of neo-tribal behaviour. From his perspective, to concentrate on structural factors risks detracting from the free agency provided to individuals through engagement with the neo-tribe. For Maffesoli, identities are formed through the practices arising from the elective and affective ties of members of the neo-tribe, rather than from ideological positions linked to social structure.[10] From this basis, Maffesoli is interested in the particular forms of style and symbolism favoured by neo-tribes to parade their group identities. There is, of course, nothing new about an academic fascination with group style and related public performance. In relation to youth subcultures, various publications associated with the Centre for Contemporary Cultural Studies (CCCS) at the University of Birmingham in the 1970s remain exemplary.[11] These studies not only focused on the style of youth subcultures but sought to examine the development of subcultures in relation to the influence of 'parent' cultures. These older cultural studies, therefore, made an allowance for the lingering influence of structure in a way Maffesoli, perhaps hastily, bypasses.

The importance of Maffesoli's work is in the theoretical insight it provides for a contemporary understanding of micro-group formation whether in regard to groups assembled in order to pursue alternative lifestyles, youth subcultural groups (including football supporters) or mid-age subcultural groups such as country music fans. Although not intending to do so, previous cultural studies work, that of the CCCS for example, tended to present a static image of youth subcultures being formed in response to an overarching form of social power. Dominant power and its countervailing forms are characterized in works such as *Resistance through Rituals*, with reference to Gramsci's notion of hegemony.[12] Youth subcultures such as mods and skinheads are seen to construct an oppositional ideology which delivers them, to some extent, from the dominant ideology of the prevailing capitalist order. Maffesoli's account of subcultural, or neo-tribal, resistance is much more attuned to the times – assuming we live in something approximating a postmodern society. For Maffesoli, collective identities are not only fragmented but the resistance they effect is not aimed at a singular force. Resistance resides within the spaces occupied by neo-tribes and will 'burst forth'[13] as the members of neo-tribes seek to overcome repressive forces which circulate within these relevant spatial fields – the football stadium, the factory, the shopping mall or whatever the particular site may be. Maffesoli associates the micro-resistance of neo-tribes with *puissance* (the 'will to live') – a vitalism derived from the pursuit of everyday pleasure. Maffesoli shares a modest view of social life, now familiar to postmodern social theory – i.e. a view of social life divorced from teleology.[14] However, unlike other key theorists usually placed under the postmodernist rubric (Baudrillard, for example), Maffesoli remains very optimistic about the richness of human experience emanating from everyday social activity. This is because Maffesoli refuses to acknowledge the death of the social. Society is retained in his theory via the medium of the notion of *sociality*, drawn from the inspiration of Simmel. Sociality is the basic social experience of people participating together in everyday life, the life of the neighbourhood according to Maffesoli.[15] Maffesoli's optimism for the positive sociality that stems from human engagement can be read in his very description of routine daily practices: 'the street scene of the megalopolises: the amateurs of jogging, punk or retro fashions, preppies and street performers invite us on a travelling road show'.[16]

NEO-TRIBES AND SPACE

This reference to the mobility of sociality indicates Maffesoli's recognition of the nomadic character of contemporary social life. It is not to suggest that people have become narcissistic or hyper-individualistic, as some contemporary communitarian theorists would have it, but that the affiliations which people strike are 'fluid', 'occasional' and, prone to 'dispersal'. Maffesoli thus distinguishes between class tribalism and neo-tribalism. An implication from these characterizations is that neo-tribalism may be a superior form of social bond as it is based on affective rather than ascriptive grounds of affiliation. We are reminded here of a similar characterization drawn by the urban studies theorist G. Suttles in his distinction between communal and community forms of association.[17]

Although Maffesoli sees the contemporary social actor as something of a nomad, he remains very much concerned with the spaces occupied by people during their social wandering. Indeed, the formation of neo-tribes results from the collective human occupation of spaces. An awareness of the social and cultural geography of relevant spaces is, therefore, crucial to the study of neo-tribes. Maffesoli thus refers to the 'proxemics' or 'proximity' of neo-tribes. Hetherington has developed a related discussion of proximity around the term *social centrality*.[18] Social centrality captures the idea of a particular place being the focal point of neo-tribal gathering and related activity. Such central places are where the 'expressive' and 'alternative' identities of the neo-tribe are eked out. Neo-tribes tend to exist on the margins, both of society and in the public arenas they gravitate towards as their point of assembly. Hetherington thus notes the paradox involved in at once discussing the centrality and marginality of place.[19] The places chosen by neo-tribes as the point of gathering will, of course, depend on the particular neo-tribal formation. Some places, particularly those associated with neo-tribal youth, are general sites of social centrality, for example, the shopping mall. The football stadium is a more specialized central place in which neo-tribal identities are displayed by groups of fans not only with supporter affiliations to opposing teams, but with different types of supporter affiliations to the same team. All central places are used by neo-tribes as a performance site where the collective identity is publicly paraded.[20] The more marginalized the particular neo-tribe within the social arena where the performance occurs, the more likely the performance is to incur the wrath of social control agents in that arena. Accordingly, the activities of parochial football supporters have been responded to with a variety of control measures to circumscribe their behaviour, or performance, in the football stadium.

In keeping with Maffesoli, the notion of social centrality needs to be understood in terms of space as well as place. While neo-tribes occupy places physically, they occupy spaces metaphorically. As neo-tribes tend to be marginalized within the physical spaces they occupy, it is through the claiming of space that they are able to express their distinctive identities. Spaces are occupied through a shared imagining and a collective sense of feeling and being. Elsewhere, I have taken the term *thirdspace* from the postmodern geographer Edward Soja to discuss this metaphorical understanding of space in relation to football supporting subcultures.[21] Unlike conventional notions of space, the thirdspace is not bounded, but remains open ended. It is a representational space and those who occupy it enjoy a 'critical spatial awareness' which they use to create identities of their own choosing. This is not to suggest that neo-tribes have discovered some kind of magic formula whereby they can conjure identities at will. The spaces they are able to claim are the gaps which inevitably appear within any form of micro-social system. Neo-tribes operate on an opportunistic basis that involves making the most of the room made available to them. This is very much the case for parochial football fans who engage in practices which contravene the rules of football officialdom and perhaps the law. These supporters push the margins as best they can in an effort to enjoy a football fandom of their own choosing rather than one sanctioned by sporting officialdom. In so doing they affect a collective *expression* of identity – the hallmark of the neo-tribe.

MARSH AND THE NAKED APES

The discussion of groups of parochial football fans as tribes is, unsurprisingly, not new. In common parlance the term tribe has probably enjoyed currency since football hooliganism became recognized as a social problem in the late 1960s. However, in the small but growing field of academic research into football-related violence, the term tribe has been viewed with caution. Indeed, it is almost exclusively associated with the 1970s work of Peter Marsh and his colleagues at the University of Oxford. Football violence is only one aspect of Marsh's investigation into the collective or group enactment of violent behaviour. His study of terrace culture at the home ground of Oxford United is compared in published work with collective violence in a number of contexts in both contemporary western and hunter gatherer societies.[22] The basic thesis for Marsh is that football hooliganism, so-called, is a form of ritualistic aggression common to tribal groupings of men across history and various geographical locations. The emphasis on violence as a form of ritual downplays the seriousness of football hooliganism indicative in its popular conceptualization as a social problem. Indeed, Marsh argues very persuasively that football hooliganism is not fundamentally about violence, but an *illusion of violence*. This is not to deny that actual violence has occurred over the years on football terraces. Actual violence inevitably occurs, from time to time, as a result of the physical proximity of hostile groups of young men within and outwith the football stadium. However, for Marsh, the violence associated with football hooliganism is more an affectation of violence, a ritualistic display of bravado common to tribal gatherings of men. Contrary to the popular image of the football crowd as a rabble – the dangerous mass perceived by Le Bon and subsequent alarmist social critics of crowds – Marsh emphasizes the rule-bound nature of life on the terrace. In *The Rules of Disorder* Marsh and colleagues argue that the enactment of ritualistic violence by football hooligan tribal groupings is framed within an informal organizational context.[23] While not arguing for a rational basis of football hooliganism, this view suggests that football hooliganism is an assortment of ritualistic practices which are intentional and therefore not irrational. This dispels the public perception of football hooliganism as mindless violence. This is a view expressed in most of the subsequent academic discussions of football hooliganism.

Marsh's depiction of the ritualistic practices of football hooligans was an important interruption to the debate and it maintains relevance for theoretical interpretations of football-supporting subcultures in terms of Maffesoli's neo-tribes. There is, however, an important difference between Marsh's interpretation of tribes and Mafessoli's of neo-tribes. Identifying this difference gives indication of why Marsh's work has been largely dismissed by subsequent academic researchers into football hooliganism. Marsh explains violence with reference to the ideas of unfashionable (at least in academic circles) evolutionary psychologist Desmond Morris. Via Morris, Marsh argues that ritualized aggression is 'part and parcel' of the symbolic communication systems of the male species. Accordingly, Marsh is able to liken young men confronting each other on the terraces to chimps fighting in the jungle. His acknowledgement that 'chimps lack … the power of language to aid their ceremonial patterns of aggression management' goes little way to placating a sociological concern with his anthropomorphological assumption about male species aggression.[24] Marsh remains optimistic that natural male aggression will not manifest into actual violence because humans have the capacity to expend their aggression through non-violent means of conduct. Quite simply, he provides a catharsis or safety valve explanation of football hooliganism. For most males aggression will be released in an unproblematic way through sport or other activities that afford the release of pent-up tensions. Limited or controlled violence is positively sanctioned in some of these activities, boxing and rugby football for example. In the case of football hooliganism the situation is clearly problematic as the release of aggression can occasion unacceptable violence. However, Marsh suggests that the football terrace provides a relatively safe social arena where young males can ritualistically act out their aggressive impulses (usually not involving actual violence) without coming to too much harm or causing harm to others. As the idea goes, it is better for young men to beat their chests in front of each other under the watchful eye of social control agents such as the police rather than confront each other in totally unsupervised social environments.

How Marsh would respond to the current reality of most football hooligan activity being pushed outside of the confines of the football stadium by the strict forms of surveillance imposed within would be interesting to know, but is beyond the scope of this study. The importance of Marsh to the current discussion is his recognition of the tribal aspects and associated rituals of football hooligan subcultures. Divested of its postulates about natural male aggression his work goes some way to explaining how young men establish affective bonds with others through the formation and living out of tribal identities on the football terrace. When considering contemporary groups of parochial male football supporters as neo-tribes, Marsh's emphasis on aggressive masculinity remains important, even if male aggression needs to be reconsidered as socially derived rather than naturally given. However, a lingering problem with Marsh's approach is the implication that his essentialist view of male aggression has for interpretations of male conduct. From his perspective it is a causal necessity for men to act out their aggression sometimes in tribal contexts such as football hooliganism. Tribal formations of football hooligans are, thus, something of an inevitability and their hooligan behaviour (so interpreted) predictable. This is at odds with Maffesoli's idea that neo-tribe membership is fluid and based on choice. It also suggests that the affectual commitment afforded to the neo-tribe by its members arises from human nature rather than social circumstance. Football hooliganism undoubtedly does allow young men to release tensions and anxieties, but the basis of such masculine tensions and anxieties is social rather than innate.

MATZA AND SUBTERRANEAN VALUES

A way of furthering the discussion and providing a link between the tribal theory of Marsh and the neo-tribal theory of Maffesoli is through recourse to the work of American deviance theorist David Matza (and his associate Gresham M. Sykes). Although largely overlooked within contemporary sociology, Matza's work has much to offer to contemporary studies of youth and leisure, as may be indicated by the example of football hooliganism. Of particular interest is Matza's term *subterranean values*.[25] Matza proposed the term as a means of countering the predominant trend within post-war functionalist sociology to define deviant behaviour in a very fixed way. For example, Matza rejected Albert Cohen's idea that youth subcultures operated according to a set of subcultural values that were deliberately framed in opposition to the cultural norms of adult society. The so-called delinquency of youth was, according to Matza, better explained by the divergent positions held by youth and adults in relation to an indeterminate system of subterranean values. Subterranean values exist below, but not apart from, the surface value system (discussed by Matza in terms of middle-class values) and are not the exclusive province of social deviants. Indeed, subterranean values, which involve 'the search for adventure, excitement and thrills' are common to all members of society.[26] While avoiding the essentialist overtones of a catharsis explanation, Matza suggests that subterranean values involve the pursuit of hedonistic yearnings that are suppressed in the routine of daily life associated with work. Subterranean values are, therefore, mostly satisfied in the social realm of leisure and for most people in a non-deviant way or through 'concealed' deviance that does not produce a public response.

Writing in 1961, Matza and Sykes foresee the emergence of a leisure-based society in which the division between work and leisure will become increasingly blurred. It will be of no surprise to him today that the rationalist constraints of the workplace have been extended into arenas of leisure associated with capitalist enterprise. Accompanying this trend is a restriction on the ability of people to enjoy the pursuit of subterranean values in certain leisure contexts without infracting the rules of acceptable conduct that are arbitrarily imposed on the domains where leisure occurs. The football stadium may be seen in such a light. Boisterous forms of behaviour which once may have been permitted on the terrace are now disallowed. The rationalization of the football stadium has, hence, circumscribed the pursuit of subterranean values by football crowds. Those members of the crowd who behave in a manner contrary to the rules of conduct within the stadium are likely to be defined as deviants, namely football hooligans, and prone to punishment. However, the continuation of football hooliganism in its various guises and degrees of belligerence, indicates that the contemporary football stadium is a contested leisure site in which some supporters continue to pursue subterranean values. This is to suggest that the pursuit of subterranean values through the attendance of professional soccer matches, in a variety of international locations including Australia, can only occur in a deviant way. The rationalist agenda of soccer administrators has been foisted on to supporters to the extent that it determines and governs acceptable conduct within the stadium. The football stadium may be a promoted as a 'theatre of dreams' in late modernity, but it is no longer a place where 'adventure and thrills' can be actively pursued. Conformity rather than self-expression is the name of the game.

Matza's term subterranean values bears interesting comparison to Maffesoli's notion of puissance. The pursuit of subterranean values exhibits a highly expressive commitment to pleasure seeking as a relief from the routine of work and other areas of life concerned with rational commitment to the pursuit of instrumental goals and obligations. Again, for Matza, subterranean values do not exist in opposition but in symbiotic relation to surface values. For Matza, people cannot be neatly classified into a Mertonian-type schema in accordance with their acceptance or otherwise of institutionalized goals and means of attainment. Rather, most people will accept surface values (in terms of accepting both that social life needs to be underpinned by altruistic principles and that there will be a generally accepted means of going about the business of life) while harbouring and pursuing subterranean values. However, as society has become increasingly rationalized, not only in the work arena but also in the area of leisure, subterranean values become more difficult to pursue without tags of deviance being applied. This trend, to some extent, explains the emergence of neo-tribes as people band together to pursue their subterranean values in a variety of imaginative ways and contexts. It is those neo-tribes which operate in arenas exhibiting a high degree of rationalization which are most likely to earn the wrath of moral entrepreneurs and be labelled as deviant. As indicated above, the soccer stadium is a highly pertinent example in this regard. Supporters are now asked to follow their teams in a manner deemed suitable by the authorities who run the game. Birmingham theorist John Clarke's prediction that football was headed down a path toward 'disinfected commitment' and 'contained partisanship' has proven prescient.[27] However, it is the argument of this study that the football stadium continues to be used for the pursuit of subterranean values. Supporters who band together in the pursuit of such values through following a football team form an affective bond indicative of a neo-tribe. Most importantly, not all of the followers of a particular team can be regarded as members of the neo-tribe so considered. It is those members who evince a collective *expression of identity* who can be considered as a neo-tribe. These are the fans who pursue subterranean values through football support and who can be distinguished from the majority of fans who submit to the formulaic type of support decreed by soccer officialdom. Accordingly, it is useful to distinguish between *expressive fans* and *submissive fans* of football. This distinction prompts the question of whether or not expressive football fandom is tantamount to football hooliganism. This need not be the case. Expressive fandom can certainly be enjoyed without the violence or aggression customarily associated with football hooliganism. However, given that expressive fandom will involve the contravention of rules of conduct set out for football fans, it is likely to be interpreted by those in control of the sport as hooliganism all the same.

NEO-TRIBALISM IN AUSTRALIAN SOCCER: MARK I

The final sections of the essay consider the formation of neo-tribes and the pursuit of subterranean values in association with Australian soccer and its premier competition, the A-League. Two different forms of neo-tribal affiliation are considered in relation to two distinctive forms of supporter groups currently noticeable at A-League matches. The first are the youth supporter groups that follow long-established clubs with a link to particular ethnic communities from non-English speaking Southern European backgrounds (NESB). The second are groups that follow newer clubs in the A-League which do not have an identifiable linkage to ethnic communities. It is noted, however, that some of these teams provide a vehicle for an emergent form of British ethnic identity attractive to young male expatriates and tourists gathered in Australian cities. These two types of group are the latest supporter manifestations associated with Australian premier league soccer. As discussed elsewhere, football hooligan groups as youth subcultures did not emerge in Australia until the 1990s.[28] The first youth subcultural groups to emerge were those supporting teams with traditional affiliations to NESB communities. In Sydney, for example, groups emerged in support of Sydney United (Croatian), Sydney Olympic (Greek) and Marconi (Italian).

Stylistically, these groups, known respectively as the *Bad Blue Boys* (BBB), the *Hellas Hooligans* and the *Stallions*, present an amalgam of dress ensembles associated with football hooligan subcultures familiar in both Britain and Europe. They share with the predominant *casual* hooligan style in Europe an interest in fashionable menswear and, particularly, expensive accessories such as sunglasses and jewellery. However, in acknowledged defiance of the casual mode of dress, these groups follow the tradition of wearing team colours with some members wearing the team shirts and others carrying team scarves. Some members of these groups, particularly the BBB, affect a paramilitary look that is slightly reminiscent of skinhead hooligan style. While members of these Australian groups are aware that the wearing of colours and an overt stylistic declaration of their hooligan persona is out of step with hooligan supporters of teams in higher profile leagues abroad, their retention of colours strikes an affective bond with their parent culture. Such a bond is a crucial dimension to the soccer-supporting experience of these groups. It can be argued that these groups are engaged in a strategy of identity construction, whereby they deliberately build a subcultural identity which adapts a received tradition from the ethnic parent culture into a relevant and contemporary form of youth representation. This has been discussed elsewhere in detail with reference to the BBB supporters' group.[29] This borrowing or poaching of symbols from the Croatian parent culture by the BBB should not be read as a token gesture. The BBB live a form of 'practised culture' to be distinguished from the 'symbolic ethnicity' that Herbert Gans associates with NESB yuppies in the United States. Symbolic ethnicity involves dipping into an ethnic background at will while simultaneously maintaining a diversity of social contacts through work and other sources.[30] In contrast, a practised culture involves the maintenance of close ties with the ethnic community in leisure and, in some cases, work. However, although maintaining tight relations of ethnicity, the relationship is not static. Indeed, the identity that arises from the association struck by groups such as the BBB with their parent culture remains fluid and open to possibility, particularly to members on an individual basis.

A related contemporary example which indicates a drift between 'practised culture' and 'symbolic ethnicity' is that of the young Lebanese males in western Sydney, studied by Noble and colleagues.[31] Participants in this study were seen to move between positions of 'strategic essentialism' and 'strategic hybridity'. From the essentialist position ethnicity is unproblematic – the boys see themselves as Lebanese first and foremost. From the hybrid position the picture is more complex – the boys see themselves as an indistinguishable mix of cultural influences. Strategy is the key term for Noble and colleagues because the boys will represent themselves in essential or hybrid guise, depending on context and circumstance. When comparing themselves to the rest of the boys at school, they opt for an essentialist characterization of 'being Lebanese'. Such a strategy appears to provide a collective means to cope with the mark of difference applied in the school yard. At home the boys are more likely to recognize their hybridity as a means of establishing (or unmarking) their cultural difference from that of their parents. The strategy involves seeking room for manoeuvre. If an 'Australian' cultural identity can be established, then the boys are hopeful that their parents might relax the normal rules of the Lebanese household and, *inter alia*, allow them to go out in the evening with friends. This example is not to trivialize the issue but to recognize that strategies of ethnicity are very much connected with routine daily practices. Similarly, the shifting of positions between essentialism and hybridity, although contradictory, is not indicative of 'confused and inarticulate adolescents grappling with complex experiences'. The fluidity of positions highlights the strategic nature of the social manoeuvring of such youth in the quest for spaces that provide optimal opportunity for the expression of relevant individual and collective identities.

As indicated earlier, the collective quest for space becomes most apparent in public forums where youth gather. Some forums provide a place where youth are especially able to engage in activities of 'expressive identity' which are most relevant to them. The soccer stadium has offered such opportunities to NESB youth which have been taken advantage of by groups like the BBB. Attempts by soccer authority to marginalize the space within the soccer stadium for the expression of ethnic identity has resulted in the BBB becoming more reliant on strategies of hybridity rather than strategies of essentialism. As the discretionary bans on the display of ethnic and national emblems within A-League stadiums are more tightly enforced, the symbolic display of ethnicity has to be more subtly coded. For the BBB this becomes the *necessary work* of *symbolic creativity* to which Willis refers.[32] To keep their expressive identity alive, these young men have to rethink the means of its representation. More secret visual codings and chants become the order of the day. If the police and security officers within the stadium do not know what is going on, then they are disempowered from enforcing their authority. Therefore, the stronger the social sanction against an essentialist display of identity, the more appropriate a strategy of hybridity becomes. While social identities are generally discussed in contemporary social theory as being hybrid (or fragmented, fractured, multiple, contingent, dispersed), rather than essential, it is the ability of groups of individuals to engage appropriate strategies of collective identification (be these essentialist or hybrid) that is indicative of the post-tribe in action. The BBB and similar formations of NESB youth may thus be regarded as post-tribes within Australian soccer support.

NEO-TRIBALISM IN AUSTRALIAN SOCCER: MARK II

Recent developments within the Australian A-League have provided for the emergence of new, and different, forms of support that are not formed on the basis of NESB ethnic identity. As the league has expanded to become more of a national competition with new teams being the sole representatives of cities and regions and their clubs having no link with ethnic communities, the possibility of new brands of support arise. It is early in the piece to be decisive about the supporter trends in respect of these newer team entities but two emergent forms of support can be broadly identified. First, a non-parochial form of fandom, associated most noticeably with the Brisbane Strikers team, that fits very comfortably with the future of soccer support in the A-League imagined by the leadership of Soccer Australia. This type of support involves fans (often families) who attend the match dressed in the official team kit and who are equipped with licensed Soccer Australia merchandise such as flags and baseball style caps. These are orderly fans who comply with the behavioural codes imposed by Soccer Australia and who use the soccer stadium as nothing more than a forum to root for the team. These supporters are *submissive* fans as defined earlier. They, undoubtedly, enjoy their soccer-supporting experience, but they do so in a way that totally accepts the rules laid out in the micro-societal context of the soccer stadium. For this reason, they are not *expressive* fans in the manner of groups such as the BBB. Submissive fans might be seriously committed to supporting their team but they do not have an *affective* commitment to supporting it in terms of their choosing and in a manner that demonstrates an expressive identity. If anything, submissive fans indicate a collective identity which is ascribed on the basis of their willingness to fulfil the ideal image of the supporter desired by soccer officialdom.

As well as this mode of submissive fandom, a particular mode of expressive fandom has emerged in Australian soccer in connection with the rationalization of the A-League and the associated trend towards 'one team city' clubs. When the Perth Glory entered the A-League in 1996 it immediately drew a home crowd following that more than rivalled the numbers managed by the established teams. A considerable portion of the crowd that gathered behind one of the goal ends soon became known as the 'Boys from the Shed'. The young men assembled in this section of the crowd appear to be almost exclusively of British background and their soccer support signifies a very public display of British (mainly English) identity in a manner unfamiliar to Australian society. That this phenomenon should occur first in the city of Perth is not surprising. As a nearest port of entry Perth has traditionally had a disproportionately high share of British migrants in comparison to other Australian cities. However, the identity of British migrants in Perth, and other Australian cities, has generally remained unexamined within Australian sociology.[33] A view that the colonization of Australia by the British has created a cultural dominance that renders the study of British identity (particularly Englishness) in Australia unnecessary still pervades the academy. Accordingly, the English migrant experience has not held an interest in studies of ethnicity and multiculturalism. Indeed, the Australian multicultural agenda excludes the English as an ethnic group.

Without entering a debate about whether English ethnicity should have had a place within Australian ethnic studies in the past, it is becoming apparent that new forms of English identity, pertinent to migration and settler trends within Australian cities, are emerging. A recent study by Viviani on population trends in Australia finds that migrants groups still tend to cluster within certain areas of Australian cities.[34] Interestingly, she finds that clustering does not only apply to assumedly less 'integrated' groups such as the Vietnamese and other South-East Asian groups, but to some more established migrant groups namely the Italians and the English. The study indicates a new type of English migrant who is attracted to the sun and the surf of Australian beach suburbs. In some areas such as Manly in Sydney, the British make up the largest proportion of the migrant population. The numbers of British people in such places could indeed be greater than official statistics indicate. Statistics do not account for the 'illegal' immigration emanating from the large perennial intake of young British backpackers, some of whom outstay their tourist status by taking up temporary residence and also 'black' employment in hospitality areas such as bartending and waitering.

As difficult as it might be to define an overall trend, it appears that a new pattern of English migrancy in Australia has emerged in recent years. Whereas the traditional image of post-war migration from England is a family resettling in an outpost of the Commonwealth in search of a better life, the new image is of a young single itinerant person (male or female) who may stay in Australia for an extended period if a job opportunity arises and if visa requirements can be met or avoided. This new type of transient migration fosters its own form of communal gathering for English people. A number of pubs in Australian cities have become 'central places' in this regard. Some pubs cater specifically to a young English clientele by showing Premier League football matches on satellite television. While such broadcasts might internally divide English people into respective supporter camps and serve as a reminder of North–South England rivalries, the public viewing of the England matches in the 1998 World Cup in pubs most clearly showed a new face of English identity in Australia. It is in a related context that the 'Boys from the Shed' can be considered.[35] The major apparent difference from the mixed gender grouping of English supporters gathered to watch the World Cup in pubs is that the 'Boys from the Shed' are, as their name suggests, an exclusively male subculture. This is, of course, a significant difference, and an important issue to consider in the construction of a contemporary collective English identity in Australia. To what extent do the 'Boys from the Shed' invoke an Englishness steeped in a nationalism that excludes women? This question has been raised as a concern by Tara Brabazon in a recent paper on the 'Boys from the Shed'.[36] Brabazon fears that the chants of Englishness which may be heard from the group conjure the lost British Empire and all of the chauvinistic trappings that go with it.

Brabazon's concern warrants investigation as does her related criticism of Soccer Australia's facile acceptance of the 'Boys from the Shed' as Australian soccer's 'loudest and most famous' crowd. This acceptance sits uncomfortably against the rejection of NESB supporter groups such as the BBB. It implies either that some ethnic supporter allegiances rather than others are acceptable within the A-League, or that that the 'Boys from the Shed' are not recognized by Soccer Australia as an ethnically based supporter group. The Englishness of the 'Boys from the Shed' is, admittedly, paraded differently from the 'Croatianness' of the BBB. The team they support, the Perth Glory, does not have a traditional ethnic affiliation, and the 'Boys from the Shed' do not explicitly use the soccer terrace as a forum for parading English nationalism in the way the BBB do Croatian nationalism. However, if predictions about the emergence of a new English nationalism in the wake of the decline of Britain as a political entity are correct, then the football stadium is an obvious forum for the display of this inchoate nationalism.[37] Should the George Cross begin to appear on 'the Hill' where the 'Boys from the Shed' gather, as it does on the terraces when England fans assemble for an international game, then Soccer Australia will surely have to face up to an unintended consequence of its NESB de-ethnicizing agenda.

LISTENING TO THE 'NEW LADS'

However, from the perspective of related scholarship, it is only through ethnographic research that further insight into the particular form of

English identity constructed by groups such as the 'Boys from the Shed' will be gained. The only related work to date is David Moore's pioneering ethnography of English skinhead subculture in the suburbs of Perth. Importantly, Moore's study revealed that the location of English migrants in Australian society cannot be taken for granted. The young men studied by Moore carried a strong sense of otherness which found a subcultural expression through an identification with 1970s English skinhead style, argot and social practice.[38] The 'Boys from the Shed' do not appear to affect an extreme version of hard masculine English identity and, therefore, are not readily identifiable with skinheads or football hooligans. Again though, the presence or otherwise of such elements within their ranks will only be revealed through ethnographic investigation.

The apparent 'new laddishness' rather than hard masculinity of the 'Boys from the Shed' nevertheless indicates an attachment to Englishness which is indicative of a neo-tribal identity. Attachment to the group appears to be highly emotive but likely to be transient, in keeping with the new form of British migrancy discussed above. In the soccer-supporting context, the 'Boys from the Shed' are expressive fans who have constructed a supporter style in their own terms which allow for the pursuit of subterranean values. This much they have in common with NESB ethnic supporter groups such as the BBB. To this point in time their novelty has been welcomed by soccer authority and media commentators alike. However, seemingly in fear of an outbreak of English style football hooliganism, the administration of the Perth Glory club have pre-empted such activity by installing surveillance cameras on 'the Hill' and by employing security staff to police that section of the stadium on match days.[39] The expressive nature of fandom exhibited by the 'Boys from the Shed' has them precariously positioned within the Australian soccer stadium. Their image as the fans that 'Australian soccer needs'[40] could shift to one of reviled football 'yobs', even hooligans, in the wake of any negative media reportage. Given the track record of commercial television and the tabloid press on the reportage of Australian soccer 'riots',[41] a moral panic about the 'British disease' coming to Australia is not difficult to envisage. Such an outcome would certainly complicate life for the 'Boys from the Shed' and possibly see their rather essentialist strategy of ethnic identity take on a hybrid form.

Such potential shifts in the strategies of identity by the 'Boys from the Shed', or other emergent subcultures of English soccer support in

Australia, should be of major interest to academics studying the social and cultural relations of football. However, such studies must proceed on the principle of wanting to know about these groups in their own terms. While it is certainly appropriate that sexist aspects of these supporter cultures are criticized, criticism should not foreclose a sociological study of collective expressions of social identity.[42] With regard to a group such as the 'Boys from the Shed', sociology and cultural studies should want to know what 'being English' means to these people rather than just forecasting the negative implications of young men 'being English' in Australian society. If Maffesoli is correct in declaring the present day as the 'time of the tribes' then we need to know how the tribes are constituted and what makes them tick. This will only be revealed by suspending judgement and getting up close. Some tribes will be easier to get close to than others, depending on a variety of factors to do with both the tribe and the researcher. The recent British-based studies by Armstrong and Giulianotti reveal the fruits of ethnographic work on neo-tribes of football supporters.[43] For example, rather than taking precepts about class into their studies, class emerges as an issue out of the focus on the identity of the groups. Ethnographic studies on the identity of neo-tribes in Australian soccer can be as revealing as these British examples. This is particularly so with regard to issues of ethnicity and multiculturalism. Rather than taking for granted what 'being Croatian' or 'being English' means to people in Australian society, it is useful to study group contexts where related affective identities are collectively formed and displayed. The terraces of the A-League are a 'central place' for such gatherings and a key research site within the Australian metropolis for examining the 'spaces' in which ethnic identities are most tellingly expressed.

NOTES

1. G. Armstrong, *Football Hooligans: Knowing the Score* (hereafter *Football Hooligans*) (Oxford, 1998), p.306.
2. M. Maffesoli, *The Time of the Tribes: The Decline of Individualism in Mass Society* (hereafter *The Time of the Tribes*) (London, 1996).
3. For a discussion of postmodern tribes see Z. Bauman, *Intimations of Postmodernity* (London, 1992), pp.198–9.
4. K. Hetherington, *Expressions of Identity: Space, Performance, Politics* (hereafter *Expressions of Identity*) (London, 1998), pp.48–9.
5. R. Giulianotti, N. Bonney and M. Hepworth (eds.), *Football, Violence and Social Identity* (London, 1994); A. Brown (ed.), *Fanatics! Power, Identity and Fandom in Football* (London, 1998).

6. J. Hughson, 'The Bad Blue Boys and the "Magical Recovery" of John Clarke' (hereafter 'The Bad Blue Boys'), in G. Armstrong and R. Giulianotti (eds.), *Entering the Field: New Perspectives on World Football* (Oxford, 1997), pp.239–59.
7. *Expressions of Identity*, p.52.
8. *The Time of the Tribes*, p.12.
9. *Expressions of Identity*, p.53.
10. Ibid., p.56.
11. S. Hall and T. Jefferson (eds.), *Resistance through Rituals: Youth Subcultures in Post-war Britain* (hereafter *Resistance through Rituals*) (London, 1976); P. Willis, *Profane Culture* (London, 1978); D. Hebdige, *Subculture: The Meaning of Style* (London, 1979).
12. *Resistance through Rituals*, pp.11–12.
13. *Expressions of Identity*, p.64.
14. *The Time of the Tribes*, p.53.
15. Ibid., p.119.
16. Ibid., p.76.
17. G. Suttles, *The Social Construction of Communities* (Chicago, 1972).
18. *Expressions of Identity*, p.106.
19. Ibid., p.107.
20. Ibid., p.105.
21. J. Hughson, 'Soccer Support and Social Identity: Finding the "Thirdspace"', *International Review for the Sociology of Sport*, 33, 4 (1998), 403–9.
22. P. Marsh, *Aggro: The Illusion of Violence* (London, 1978).
23. P. Marsh, E. Rosser and R. Harre, *The Rules of Disorder* (London, 1978).
24. *Aggro: The Illusion of Violence*, p.42.
25. D. Matza and G.M. Sykes, 'Juvenile Delinquency and Subterranean Values', *American Sociological Review*, 26, 5 (1961), 712–19.
26. Ibid., 716.
27. J. Clarke, 'Football and Working-Class Fans: Tradition and Change', in R. Ingham (ed.), *Football Hooligans in Wider Context* (London, 1978), pp.37–60.
28. J. Hughson, 'Is the Carnival Over? Soccer Support and Hooliganism in Australia', in D. Rowe and G. Lawrence (eds.), *Tourism, Leisure, Sport: Critical Perspectives* (Sydney, 1998), p.171.
29. 'The Bad Blue Boys ', p.256.
30. H. Gans, 'Symbolic Ethnicity: the Future of Ethnic Groups and Cultures in America', *Ethnic and Racial Studies*, 2, 2 (1979), 1–20.
31. G. Noble, S. Poynting and P. Tabar, 'Youth, Ethnicity and the Negotiation of Identities', paper presented at The Australian Sociological Association Annual Conference (Hobart, 1996).
32. P. Willis, *Common Culture: Symbolic Work at Play in the Everyday Cultures of the Young* (Milton Keynes, 1990).
33. A notable exception is the study of English skinhead subculture in Perth by D. Moore, *The Lads in Action: Social Process in an Urban Youth Subculture* (hereafter *The Lads in Action*) (Aldershot, 1993).
34. *The Australian*, 24 September 1997.
35. Future studies should also give recognition to other groups of 'English' supporters associated with new national league teams such as the Sydney based Northern Spirit.
36. T. Brabazon 'What's the Story Morning Glory? Perth Glory and the Imagining of Englishness', *Sporting Traditions*, 14, 2 (1998), 53–66.
37. *The Scotsman*, 30 January 1999.
38. *The Lads in Action*, pp.12–14.
39. S. Mullin, 'Glory Be!: The Success of Perth Glory off the Field', *Studs Up* (Fanzine), 24 (1997), 12–13.
40. Australian sport commentator Bruce McAvaney speaking on Channel Seven's *Sportsworld* programme, 26 January 1997.
41. J. Hughson, 'The Wogs are at it Again: Media Reportage of Australian Soccer "Riots"', paper presented at the No Longer Black and White Conference on the Media, Ethnic and Racial Conflict (Melbourne, 1996).
42. Given the masculinist nature of football supporting subcultures it is very likely that sexism will

characterize the social practises of such groups. For a discussion of this in relation to the 'Bad Blue Boys' see J. Hughson, 'The Boys are Back in Town: Football Support and the Social Reproduction of Masculinity', *Journal of Sport and Social Issues* (forthcoming). Matza himself recognized that young men are likely to engage in excessive masculinist behaviour in their pursuit of subterranean values. Thus, warning must be given against a false impression of subterranean values as being necessarily humanistic. Their self-expressive nature cannot ensure such a relationship. In the context of expressive football fandom it is a very real concern that neo-tribes will continue to exclude women. However, it is only by studying these groups that such exclusion and related sexist practices can be revealed.

43. *Football Hooligans*; R. Giulianotti, 'A Sociology of Scottish Football Fan Culture' (unpublished PhD thesis, University of Aberdeen, 1996).

2

Contextualizing Suburban Soccer: Consumer Culture, Lifestyle Differentiation and Suburban America

DAVID L. ANDREWS

> The biggest trend I see in the market is that soccer is transitioning from a sort of sub category to a core sport at a much broader level than it had been before.[1]

According to A. Markovits and S. Hellerman, the popularity of recreational soccer in the United States has not translated into mass audiences for televised soccer, hence they conclude, 'Still no soccer in the United States, at least on any meaningful scale.'[2] One wonders what compelled the authors to make such an assertion. Even in purely economic terms, soccer is a meaningful entity within contemporary America: Nike/IMG's $500 million investment in the US Soccer Federation over the next decade, and the estimated $245 million in soccer equipment sales during 1998, both attest to that fact.[3] Moreover, soccer's most profound incursion into American existence can be discerned from its centrality for millions of suburban American families. No longer a 'mini-passion of suburban America',[4] youth soccer participation has emerged as a defining practice at the core of American life. Indeed, such has been youth soccer's material and symbolic penetration of the suburban landscape, that the game presently enunciates the dominant rhythms and regimes of suburban existence every bit as naturally as the single family home, ballet classes, sport utility vehicles, lawn sprinkler systems, *The Gap*, and the imperious Martha Stewart.

Rather than evolving from a specific research study or location, this discussion draws from over ten years of ethnographic work on suburban soccer cultures in a number of metropolitan areas across the Mid-South and Mid-West regions of the United States. Adopting the cultural studies method of 'articulation', the data is used as a resource for the 'practice of drawing lines, of mapping connections',[5] between broad societal forces and the practices of everyday life, from which it is possible to begin to interpret the suburban American soccer phenomenon. In short, and in the tradition of cultural studies within which 'context is everything and everything is context',[6] I seek to contextualize, and thus render *meaningful*, the suburban soccer practice. Following a genealogy of soccer in the United States, the discussion forges an understanding of this peculiarly American soccer scenario, by making connections (or articulations) between soccer and the broader social forces within post-war suburban locations. I argue that soccer has been appropriated as part of the innately competitive, socially differentiating, and highly stylized lifestyles, through which individuals attempt to seek membership of the valorized suburban middle class.

FROM IVY LEAGUE TO SUB-DIVISION

> What has happened is that soccer was viewed by the general populous [*sic*] as ethnic, urban and very blue collar. What we find, however, is that while there is still a base of ethnic and urban supporters, the reality is that soccer today is mom and dad, two kids, two lawn chairs, Saturday afternoon with the family dog, watching the kids play, $40,000 income, mini van.[7]

Despite the current ascendancy of American football, baseball, basketball and, to a lesser extent, ice hockey, at intercollegiate and professional levels, it should not be overlooked that soccer has had a presence on the American continent for over three centuries. As Sugden noted, 'In terms of longevity and international competition soccer is the elder statesman of American sport.'[8] Soccer's American lineage (in its 'folk football' form) can be traced back at least to the early part of the seventeenth century, as witnessed by Henry Spelman's observations of Virginia colonists in 1613. A game similar to the pre-modern versions of soccer was also played at Yale in 1765. These early American games originated in Britain, since the North Atlantic connection proved influential in the evolution of modern American sport. Within the first half of the nineteenth century the ethos of muscular Christianity, and the attendant fledgling kicking and handling football games, fermented within the English public school system. These innovations were subsequently exported to North America, primarily via the migration of staff and pupils. By the advent of the 1860s, football – particularly its kicking version – had secured a discernible presence within many East Coast preparatory schools and universities. Northeastern universities such as Columbia, Princeton, Rutgers and Yale even used the 1863 English Football Association as a guide for creating the uniformity necessary for intercollegiate competition. Indeed, the first intercollegiate football game was played between Rutgers and Princeton in 1869 using soccer rules 10. Subsequently, the first unofficial international soccer match involving a representative US team occurred in East Newark, New Jersey, in November 1885 with a 1–0 victory over Canada.[9]

Soccer's initial elite social standing in the Eastern United States was terminally disrupted by the spectre of working-class participation and rampant professionalism, with which the game became associated as a result of its popular evolution in England and other parts of Europe during the last quarter of the nineteenth century.[10] Following their English counterparts, America's gentlemen and elite institutions – ever aspiring to uphold the obligatory amateur ethos – rejected soccer in favour of the more socially desirable, but more vaguely understood, pursuit of rugby. Interestingly, it has been asserted that the relative ignorance of rugby's rules and favoured practices was a significant factor in allowing the game to be easily appropriated by the American power elite housed within institutions of higher learning. The game was thus redefined as American football according to the conjunctural social, cultural, economic, and political contingencies of turn of the century America.[11] Indeed, such was the grip that universities had over the development of the game, that by 1898 Caspar Whitney declared, 'The history of American University football is the history of American football.'[12] Despite this conspicuous social exclusivity, by the turn of the twentieth century football had joined baseball, its more proletarian spring/summer counterpart, as a solidifying cornerstone of America's popular sporting imaginary.[13] Concurrently, and conversely, soccer was displaced to the margins of popular culture, reflecting the latter's material and symbolic dynamism.

While Stuart Hall correctly identified that oppositional practices can be co-opted and neutered by dominant ideologies,[14] so an emergent practice such as soccer in mid/late nineteenth century America, can – within a relatively short space of time – be conclusively distanced from the mainstream of national popular culture. This process was accentuated with the mass influx of poor migrants from Europe, which swelled the urban American population in the first few decades of the twentieth century. Soccer had become a part of many of these immigrants' everyday experiences due to its rapid spread via British commercial expansion, from which it was diffused among the industrial working classes throughout the world. With America's urban industrial centres being sustained by workers of (amongst others) Polish, Irish, Russian, German and British extraction, significant segments of this diasporic working class brought with them a clearly defined understanding of, and predilection for, soccer. This was evidenced by the foundation of teams with explicit ethnic affiliations, such as Fleisher Yarn FC (Philadelphia, PA), First German Americans SC (Philadelphia, PA), Hakoah All-Stars (New York, NY), Stix, Baer and Fuller FC (St. Louis, MO), and Shamrock SC (Cleveland, OH). Despite the ethnically diverse background of soccer participants, early American representative teams retained a distinctly Anglo/Celtic demeanour. Of the 16-man squad representing the United States at the first World Cup tournament in Uruguay in 1930, five were born in Scotland, one in England, and of the remaining ten who were born in the US, most had surnames (Oliver, Brown, Douglas, Tracy, Vaughn) which would seem to indicate they were of British or Irish origin. By the time of the next World Cup in Italy in 1934, the US side had changed its ethnic complexion, with the inclusion of numerous players with obviously non-Anglo ethnic backgrounds. These included Edward Czerkiewicz, Joseph Martinelli, Werner Nilsen, Aldo Donelli, Julius Hjulian, and Thomas Amrhein. Moreover, the Philadelphia German-Americans, unrepresented four years earlier, now fielded five members of the 18-man squad.[15] With the increased presence of non-Anglo ethnic players, at both the grassroots and representative levels, soccer became conclusively identified as an urban pastime that was alien, multi-accentual ethnic, and hence definitively non-American.[16]

Despite the evident ethnic constitution of American soccer, it would be a mistake to overstate the rates of soccer participation amongst the European immigrant population as a whole. Taking into account American football's prevailing association with the preparatory schools and universities of the East Coast aristocracy, 'baseball won the allegiance of immigrants who wished to cast their lot with their new homeland' as the game became 'unquestionably a vehicle for Americanisation' in the first few decades of the twentieth century.[17] Without wishing to dismiss Guttmann's assertion outright, he appears to insinuate that adopting *American* sport practices was tantamount to a wholesale rejection of ethnic identities. Clearly, this is a gross oversimplification of the relationship between sport and the American immigrant experience. In his socio-historical analysis of an Italian immigrant community in St. Louis, Mormino points toward the complexities and tensions that perhaps more insightfully characterized sport's role in the formation of urban-ethnic values in the first half of this century: 'On the one hand, athletics fostered acculturation to American ways of life by mixing nationalities in team play ... On the other hand, organized recreation promoted ethno-religious identity through competition and the preservation of parish-colony teams.'[18]

Certainly, many immigrants left soccer, and other popular practices, along with their surnames at Ellis Island in a conscious attempt to assimilate into the New World. Many immigrants did not. Continued devotion to this non-American practice illustrated the complex social processes which fashioned modern American subjectivities, and indeed the modern American nation itself. Soccer – like aspects of diet, religion, customs, and folklore – played a more obvious function in assuaging new immigrant anomie, than either baseball, basketball, or football. This was achieved because, even though its tenure as an aspect of popular European culture had been remarkably brief, soccer was widely associated with ethnic Otherness. Thus, in both a material and symbolic sense, soccer was able to connect *new* – and potentially dislocated – Americans to a perceived and therefore reassuring fragment of their cultural heritage. Over time, soccer became a part of a simulated cultural heritage for subsequent generations 'hyphenated Americans',[19] whose participation celebrated an invented tradition which often had little or no relevance to the actual experience of their forebears.[20]

During the 1920s and 1930s the expanding print and radio networks of the American mass media manufactured a *golden era* in American sports. National interest in baseball and football was stimulated through the shrewd articulation of figures such as Babe Ruth, Lou Gehrig, Harold 'Red' Grange, and Knut Rockne, as quintessential American heroes.[21] In boosting newspaper circulation and radio audiences, this strategy resulted in both baseball and football becoming ever more firmly located at the core of the national psyche. In contrast, soccer's pronounced multi-accentual ethnic identity stunted its national appeal, thus restricting its ability to attain the status of American pastime in terms of mass participation or consumption. Added to this, an intensifying climate of xenophobic paranoia engulfed the immediate post-Second World War era, and by the early 1950s resulted in the American public becoming 'suspicious of all things which were not stamped "made in America"'.[22] Within this context of overt American 'nativism', it was hardly surprising that the United States pyrrhic 1–0 victory against England in the 1950 World Cup Finals should have been met with such perfunctory press coverage as appeared in the *New York Times*, where Larry Gaetjens' winning goal was even wrongly attributed to Ed Souza. J. Sugden[23] has asserted that the American public's pronounced lack of interest in this victory was largely attributable to the fact that Gaetjens was born in Haiti. Perhaps more accurately stated, American press and public apathy is explained by the perception of soccer as an essentially foreign game, played by immigrants who seemingly preferred to cling to their non–American roots: a distinctly unAmerican activity in the early 1950s.

Since the end of the Second World War, there have been numerous attempts at setting up professional soccer leagues, each targeted at taking advantage of the increased discretionary income being earned by the American populace. Thus, at various times and within varyingly expansive markets, the International Soccer League (ISL), the National Professional Soccer League (NPSL), the North American Soccer League (NASL), and the United Soccer Association (USA), all competed for customers.[24] The overcrowded nature of the soccer marketplace, coupled with the undersized soccer market, provided a very poor prognosis for these leagues, only one of which (the NASL) made any significant, if fleeting, impact upon American sporting culture. Founded in 1968, the NASL rose to prominence through the signing, and innovative marketing, of a host of foreign soccer mercenaries. The popularity and economic viability of the league peaked in the mid-1970s, from whence steadily declining attendance figures, coupled with a flawed economic and managerial plan, sent the league into a terminal decline. In 1985 the NASL finally folded. It had been, up to that point, the most concerted effort at popularizing soccer to a mass American audience.[25]

Although an ephemeral aspect of the American professional sporting scene, the NASL did have a 'significant American legacy'[26] in terms of its impact upon youth soccer participation. From the early 1970s NASL teams such as the Tampa Bay Rowdies, the Seattle Sounders, and the Chicago Sting, implemented grassroots youth soccer programs designed to stimulate interest in NASL among the nation's expanding suburban hoards. By the 1980s, 'All that NASL missionary work, all those clinics',[27] in conjunction with Title IX of the 1972 Education Amendments Act (a piece of legislation designed to address issues of gender equity within publicly funded education), heightened soccer's visibility and increased opportunities for organized involvement in the game. As a consequence, between 1981 and 1991 participation in high school soccer increased 83.78 per cent, from 190,495 to 350,102, the number of private and community-based teams expanded, as did the quantity of soccer programmes offered at collegiate level.[28] The expansion in youth soccer participation has continued during the 1990s. By 1997 soccer (8,646,000 participants) was firmly established as the second ranked sporting activity for 6–11 year olds: sandwiched between basketball (11,014,000) and baseball (4,400,000). Soccer (4,981,000 participants) was also the third ranked sporting activity for 12–17 year olds, behind basketball (12,409,000 participants) and volleyball (7,493,000 participants).[29] Hank Steinbrecher, executive director and general secretary of the United States Soccer Federation, has even identified a soccer involved sub-population of some 45 million 'Soccer Americans'. This comprises 18 million (70 per cent of whom are under the age of 18) direct participants, and 27 million 'involved family members'.[30] Moreover, with approaching 20 million registered soccer players, and 50 million described as 'soccer literate', there is compelling evidence to suggest that the evolution of soccer in the post-war era has been 'America's silent sporting revolution'.[31]

Spawned as part of the political process that brought the 1994 World Cup to the United States, Major League Soccer (MLS) debuted in 1996, and represented the latest attempt to establish a truly national and economically viable professional soccer league: this time by harnessing *America's silent soccer revolutionaries*. The 'quirky demographics'[32] of MLS's stated core constituencies of consumers are the numerous ethnic minority populations (primarily those of South and Central American descent), many of whom inhabit America's impoverished inner urban and economically transitionary suburban locales, and the legions of predominantly European American 'Soccer Americans' residing in the affluent suburban sub-divisions that punctuate the peripheries of America's 67 Metropolitan Statistical Areas (MSAs).[33] As Zwick and Andrews noted:

> Rather than expressing a common affinity toward the game, America's starkly contrasting soccer cultures express the structural

inequalities that continue to blight the American social formation. While in many impoverished urban Hispanic American communities soccer is often fervently upheld as a symbol of hope, pride, and identity, within the predominantly European American spaces of suburban affluence, the game has been conclusively appropriated into everyday regimes of privilege.[34]

MLS's marketing strategy is at least partially based on an intuitive understanding of the multi-accentual relationship between soccer participation/interest, place of habitation, socio-economic status, and ethnicity. The suburban nature of this correlation has been concretely confirmed by D. Andrews *et al.*'s examination of soccer within metropolitan Memphis.[35] In this empirical study, registered youth soccer players were found to be disproportionately represented in areas where spatial location and per capita income designated them as affluent American suburbs. These elite suburbs accounted for 89.89 per cent of metropolitan youth soccer players, yet only 37.01 per cent of the metropolitan under 18 population. Within Memphis's conglomeration of affluent suburban neighbourhoods, there existed a distinct ethnic homogeneity, with European Americans comprising 84.90 per cent of the total population. Given these sporting, socio-economic, and ethnic spatial distributions, it was no surprise that the ethnographic phase of this study concluded that soccer in suburban Memphis was an almost exclusively European American practice: 'of the hundreds of players observed during the course of the interviewing process, only two were black'.[36]

Whilst it would be imprudent to extrapolate the Memphis suburban soccer scenario to the rest of the United States, there is considerable anecdotal evidence from other metropolitan locales that corroborates our model.[37] Notwithstanding its multi-ethnic manifestations, as the *American century* draws to a close, soccer in the United States can be considered 'a white, middle-class, suburban sport, just the opposite of the game's demographics in most of the world'.[38] Following Grossberg's understanding of cultural dialectics, a popular practice – such as suburban soccer – can only be understood as being 'always constituted with and constitutive of a larger context of relationships'.[39] For that reason, the following discussion will locate the historical, political, economic and cultural arrangements responsible for shaping the contemporary suburban context, out of which this peculiarly American soccer phenomenon emerged.

SUBURBAN CULTURES OF CONSUMPTION

> Suburbanization necessitated a more expensive way of life than
> people had known in modest urban apartments; television told
> people what they needed to buy; and in the empty leisure left by
> equally empty work, buying itself became a way of life.[40]

Although this discussion is focused on soccer's relation to the suburban
American experience at the end of the twentieth century, it should not
be overlooked that contemporary manifestations of suburban existence
represent the latest (and by no means the last) phase in the continuing
reformation of metropolitan spaces and populations around the central
logic of commodity consumption.[41] Within the post-war context, the
'decentralisation of population from the cities'[42] to suburban peripheries
was markedly different from previous migrations, particularly in terms
of scale and scope. The suburban American nation was born, and
subsequently grew from 41 million in 1950 (27 per cent of total US
population) to 76 million in 1970 (37 per cent of total US population),
by which time suburban dwellers outnumbered either their urban or
rural counterparts.[43] Continuing this trend, the 1990s has witnessed the
ascension of American suburban dwellers to the absolute majority of the
national population.[44] The spatial relocation of millions of
predominantly young, and yet hugely expectant, Americans during this
era represented an unparalleled movement from urban cores to suburban
peripheries, of a sizeable – if relatively homogeneous – proportion of the
nation's populace. This mass in-migration spawned an imposing, home-
owning suburban middle class, located both spatially and symbolically
between city and country. These suburban American spaces and their
populations constituted, in S. Zukin's terms, the suburban American
landscape[45] within the post-war national popular imaginary.[46]

Despite their cultural, economic and political presence, American
suburbs are by no means homogeneous bastions of upper-middle-class
affluence, for, 'Within contemporary America, the adjective suburban
could legitimately encompass anything from zones of underclass
poverty, to sectors of middle/upper class affluence, and a multitude of
variations in-between.'[47] This became particularly relevant among
America's maturing post-war suburbs, where populations began to
differentiate along the lines of economic capital. Subsequent phases of
outward residential development advanced this suburban fragmentation,

through the construction of evermore spacious and opulent homes, and the occupation of older housing stock by less affluent, often ethnic minority, inhabitants. By the 1980s the post-war American suburb represented an ever distending patchwork quilt, patterned by variously sized consumption communities (ranging from collections of houses to vast sub-divisions) whose common lifestyles exhibit contrasting degrees of affluence. Nevertheless, despite its inherent variability and fluidity, the vision of the American suburb that pervades the popular imagination continues to be that of the European American post-war bourgeois utopia. These suburbs are dominated by an aesthetic and consumer-oriented possessive individualism, underpinning a more self-righteously advanced adherence to notions of achievement, morality and privilege.

The process of post-Second World War suburbanization was inextricably tied to the need to re-activate America's burgeoning mass consumer culture which – having sprouted in the early decades of the century – was temporarily derailed by the Depression, and diverted by the forces of military Keynesianism. With apologies for oversimplifying the complexities of Keynes' economic theory, stimulating widespread home ownership (through massive suburban in-migration) was an important mechanism for successfully regulating the balance between the productive and consumptive forces within the Fordist economy. Certainly, the calculated post-war activation of American home ownership addressed a number of intermeshing social and economic problems. First, it alleviated the chronic housing shortage created by, amongst other things: the depression and wartime economies; the millions of returning GIs; and, the rapidly expanding post-war populace. Second, it regenerated the American building industry – a key economic impetus and indicator – that had lain relatively dormant during the depression and war years. Third, it greatly stimulated the post-war economy by providing privatized settings (homes) to revitalize consumer culture. Without wishing to understate the importance of the first two factors, this discussion reflects on the third, since the relationship between home ownership policies and post-war mass consumer culture was crucial in moulding today's suburban landscapes of consumption.

The American government's championing of home ownership as a catalyst for economic growth was initiated in 1934 with the passing of the National Housing Act. This legislation established the Federal Housing Administration (FHA) as an agency for prompting the growth of moderately priced private housing. The subsequent 1944 Serviceman's Readjustment Act (part of the GI Bill of Rights) and the 1949 Housing Act, made house mortgages – thereby home ownership – even more accessible to the general public, and large-scale residential building ever more profitable for private investors. Consequently, single-family housing starts escalated from 114,000 in 1944 to a record high 1,692,000 in 1950,[48] as huge tracts of America's metropolitan peripheries were rapidly transformed into the types of mass residential suburban communities (epitomized by the prototypical Levittown, Long Island, New York) so famously dissected by William H. Whyte, and Herbert J. Gans.[49] The multiplier effect of mass homeownership led to increases in mass consumption: consumption, stimulated by the purchase of consumer durables to furnish and upkeep one's pristine *dream home*. This post-war repositioning of the suburban home as a 'temple to consumer society'[50] escalated the demand for consumer goods, which assured relatively high levels of mass employment, and subsequently created a stable and affluent workforce ready and able to partake of the new consumerist ethos. Thus, as J. Lears noted, the term '"consumer culture" had unprecedented validity as a description of the sprawling suburban society developing in the wake of war-built prosperity'.[51]

In at least two senses, the first generation of post-war suburban Americans was a homogeneous group: first, owing to overtly segregationist public and private housing initiatives, suburbanites were almost exclusively of European American descent;[52] second, they were of sufficient financial wherewithal to be able to afford to partake in this internal diaspora.[53] Nevertheless, the mask of whiteness and relative prosperity belied the inherent diversity of these new suburbanites. Many of those relocating from America's inner urban cores had lived in close proximity to others from the same ethnic grouping. The preponderance of urban neighbourhoods dominated by Italian Americans, Polish Americans, or Slovak Americans, had ensured that cultural and ethnic 'difference was preserved in districts and quarters in the abrasive display of the juxtapositions of street culture'. Wrenched from culturally and ethnically distinct social milieux, many post-war suburbanites found themselves ensconced in homogenizing suburban spaces, where differences were relegated to the 'ghostly images of family albums'.[54] Within this 'present-tense culture',[55] commodity consumption became the primary *lingua franca* through which an unfolding suburban identity and existence was realized to self and others.

Although many of the structural foundations were being put in place (i.e. mass employment, mass home ownership, and mass transport), it would be remiss to assume there existed a seamless transition between America's military and suburban-based consumer economies. Late 1940s America was wracked by an internal contradiction between the values of a fledgling economic system that demanded accelerating rates of commodity consumption, and the purchasing reticence expressed by a financially shell-shocked populace mindful of depression and war-time insecurities. Thus, many Americans in the immediate post-war era understandably adhered to those residues of the Protestant work ethic prefigured on an ascetic discipline of 'thrift, hard work and sobriety'.[56] For America's consumer economy to become a viable proposition, the notion of the freely consuming subject had to be substantiated and legitimated in the minds of the American public.

As with many cultural changes within modern America, the post-war shift from a 'puritan orientation' to a 'hedonistic ethos of spending and credit'[57] was engineered by the advertising industry which, at this time, entered a new realm of creativity and influence with the rampant spread of network television. During the course of the 1950s television soared from a position of relative exclusivity to being a popular institution at the core of American life: in 1950 only 9 per cent of American households owned a television, this figure escalated to 86 per cent in 1959, when the average American watched more than five hours of programming per day.[58] As an advertiser-supported mass medium, virtually from inception, American network television was a *selling machine* that infiltrated the American psyche by concocting commercial narratives that assuaged the guilt felt by many post-war Americans with regard to unfettered spending. As a well-known contemporary commercial byline exclaimed, 'You deserve the right to drive a Cadillac.' Network television championed utopian visions of suburban existence centred on commodity acquisition.[59] Thus, through mainstreaming narratives such as the television situation comedies *Leave it to Beaver* and *My Three Sons*, the populist American dream discourse (historically associated with the American middle class) was thus relocated to the *new* consumer middle class, living in America's *new* suburbs.[60]

During the 1950s membership of the new suburban class was exhibited through the consumption of particular domestic commodities, the acquisition of which set suburban individuals apart from the urban hoards. By being 'defined and asserted through difference', the post-war suburban landscape became a key site of class-based power, prestige and privilege.[61] In an era not far removed from the deprivations of the Great Depression, America's new found 'godly materialism'[62] saw the fearless frontiersman usurped by the unbounded suburban consumer within the national popular imaginary. In other words, the democratic mythos of the freedom-seeking American citizen was replaced by that of the commodity-seeking national citizen-consumer.[63] An epidemic of peer-referenced spending ensued:

> By the fifties, the Smiths had to have the Joneses' fully automatic washing machine, vacuum cleaner, and, most of all, the shiny new Chevrolet parked in the driveway. The story of this period was that people looked to their own neighborhoods for their spending cues, and the neighbors grew more and more alike in what they had. Like compared with like and strove to become even more alike.[64]

Many social commentators decried the unimaginative, bland and monotone culture of normalized suburban consumerism. 'In their very inoffensiveness and desire to fit in, suburban Americans seemed to critics to embody our own national version of the "self-policing state" – the society that had sailed into a calm, dead-level ocean of conformity.'[65] Such criticisms, however perceptive, failed to recognize the stultifying suburban homogeneity of the early-mid 1950s as merely a phase in the relentless commodification of American existence.

Toward the end of the 1950s the maturating economies of scale within America's Fordist economy reduced production costs for mass consumer goods. Previously restricted commodities such as automobiles, refrigerators and televisions became accessible to a broader spectrum of the population. The new affluence and social status of the American working class created anxiety among a suburban populace now challenged to differentiate itself from lower status groupings. Rejecting their earlier conformism towards consumption, many suburbanites sought to (re)affirm an elevated social standing by engaging in escalating cycles of competitive consumption.[66] In simplistic terms, the doctrine of 'Keeping up with the Joneses' was rejected in favour of an obsessive desire to keep at least one step ahead of them. Rather than allaying middle-class insecurities, if anything, they were heightened by the advancement of a culture of unremitting competitive upscaling. For, through 'fear of falling'[67] down the American class ladder, suburban consumers were compelled to continually aspiring to *bigger and better* *thing*s, and were thus consigned to what C. Lasch characterized as feelings of perpetual dissatisfaction and status anxiety: the 'new forms of discontent peculiar to the modern age'.[68] Out of this fundamentally competitive cultural context, the American suburban soccer phenomenon was to emerge.

COMPETITIVE LIFESTYLING AND SUBURBAN YOUTH SOCCER

> Parents say they want their kids to have the absolute best opportunity – whether it's a camp, a private school or an elite soccer team ... The emphasis shifts from fitting children into a community as peers of others to giving them an edge or an advantage. To explain why would be a sociological question. It's just something our generation has been guilty of.[69]

During the mid-1980s the aggressively individualizing neo-liberal economics of the Reagan administration encouraged an epidemic of consumer spending which further blurred traditional socio-economic boundaries.[70] America's maturing commodity democracy meant the process of suburban differentiation could no longer be effectively realized through the acquisition of commercial goods, regardless of their economic worth.[71] As a result, the suburban middle class turned to a more sophisticated mechanism for securing social distinction: broadly characterized by a turn to the aesthetic.[72] As the novelist, Stephen King, noted sardonically, 'My generation ... traded God for Martha Stewart. She's this priestess of etiquette who says that when you shovel snow from your drive, you oughta leave an inch or two at the sides, because it looks so nice.'[73]

Conjoining financial (economic capital) and educational resources (cultural capital), the suburban middle class presently derives its superior sense of self (social capital) from the assemblage of 'goods, clothes, practices, experiences, appearance and bodily dispositions they design together into a lifestyle'.[74] This focus on the aesthetic rendered suburban existence an effect of consumer taste, rather than being in any way linked to the possession of the economic capital necessary for its realization. Prompted by the overt individualism and cultural moralizing of the Reagan revolution, lifestyles thus became viewed as an effect of individual choice and sophistication. They were not necessarily overdetermined by 'the choice of destiny' which for those less fortunate are 'produced by conditions of existence which rule out all alternatives as mere daydreams and leave no choice but the taste for the necessary'. Being steeped in spurious notions of freedom and individuality, the notion of suburban lifestyles as 'tastes of luxury' conveniently obscured the privileged social and economic conditions of which they are a product.[75]

By exuding a persuasive sense of consumer sovereignty,[76] the practice of competitive lifestyling also concealed the collective regulation that continues to frame suburban existence. Assembling a particular lifestyle is evidently an active process, but one simultaneously enabled and constrained by the distinguishing influence of the class habitus. As an 'internalized form of class condition and of the conditionings it entails', the habitus acts below the level of consciousness, and in concert with the possession of various forms of power (capitals), to shape subjective experiences (practices) within objective structures (fields).[77] Suburban lifestyle projects are less a search for true individualism, and more a stylized expression of class-based cultural associations. As P. Bourdieu noted, taste is an 'acquired disposition to "differentiate" and "appreciate" ... to establish and mark differences by a process of distinction'.[78] In this sense, the habitus is a learned, yet wholly internalized, system of dispositions, preferences and tastes. It informs an individual's capacity to act in the social world in a way that embodies his or her class position.[79] Hence, suburban lifestyles can be viewed as aesthetically oriented 'classified and classifying practices' that betray collective belonging as they seemingly celebrate consumer individuality.[80]

The late twentieth-century American suburb represents a complex social space, comprising multiple interrelated fields and sub-fields (housing, decor, diet, employment, education, dress, leisure, sport). Within this setting, individual agents compete for various types of capital (economic, cultural, intellectual, physical), which underpin their lifestyle practices and are regulated by the codes of suburban taste cultures. Acts of consumption coalesce to constitute the lifestyle projects through which suburban subjects become actualized to selves and others. The ontological well-being of the suburban populace is always in the process of being realized (if never actually achieved) through the implicit challenging of fellow consumer adversaries in the competitive marketplace. The ritualized public forums of suburban display –

excessive malls, extravagant country clubs, and indeed, exclusionary soccer fields – have become civic promenades for the performance of individuals' carefully managed, commodity-based lifestyles.

Over the past two decades youth soccer has become embroiled in the suburban context to the extent that it contributes to the very constitution of this competitive 'universe of practices and consumptions'.[81] Soccer's socio-spatial distribution is at least partly attributable to its position as 'an elective luxury', only afforded by the not inconsiderable wealth of parents.[82] As an illustration, participation in *competitive* youth soccer has been estimated to cost between $3,500 and $4,000 per year: a figure that includes the direct (annual membership fees, uniforms, boots and soccer balls for practice sessions) and indirect (entrance fees, travelling, accommodation, meals and entertainment expenses incurred during regular trips to weekend tournaments) costs of participation.[83] Without question, the economics of competitive soccer instantiate a degree of social exclusivity, from which the game derives a 'distinctive rarity'.[84] This at least partly explains the division within many youth soccer communities: between low status, relatively inexpensive and relaxed *recreation* teams, and their high status antithesis, the costly and competitive travelling teams with which suburban soccer is synonymous. Predictably, the competitive ethos of suburban culture has normalized the travelling team, as the *de rigueur* form of soccer involvement. Such is the degree to which recreational participation is socially frowned upon, in many areas, recreational leagues simply do not exist for anything but the younger age groups.

Access to the considerable amounts of spare time demanded by soccer involvement (identified by Bourdieu as a transformed form of economic capital)[85] is also a telling determinant in the class distribution of suburban soccer participants. Quite simply, the lives of affluent youthful suburbanites incorporate an 'absence of necessity'; there is no financial compulsion to enrol in the part-time workforce.[86] Evidently, only those from sufficiently affluent backgrounds are afforded the luxury of being able to participate in soccer games/practice sessions, four days a week during the closed season, and five days a week during the season, as is required by many coaching regimes.[87]

Although steeped in the economics of suburban privilege, youth soccer represents an important cultural field[88] upon which the aesthetic logics of the suburban habitus are practised and displayed. This observation would be of little surprise to any card-carrying historical materialist, for as Marx famously noted, 'even the most abstract categories ... are by the very definiteness of the abstraction a product of historical conditions as well, and are fully applicable only to and under those conditions'.[89]

Having been raised within a climate of competitive aestheticism, the offspring of the suburban middle class are fully attuned to the nuances of converting economic capital to cultural capital, through the ever evolving process of consumer stylization of the self.[90] The search for distinction through the aestheticization of existence is an important part of the soccer experience, especially for children in the older age categories. The increasingly convoluted taste cultures of middle class youth are evidenced within the soccer setting: there is even evidence to suggest that 'soccer style' has informed wider aesthetic trends.[91] Thus, merely responding to the fleeting ascendancy of particular fashion statements (be they Adidas, Nike, Umbro, or alternative 'other'; single coloured or multi-coloured; round-necked or v-necked; cotton or nylon; 'grunge', 'retro', or 'urban') requires considerable financial investment on the part of parents. Clearly, youth soccer cultures represent an adolescent arena for the playing out of the suburban middle-class habitus. In order to ensure a sense of cultural belonging, it is vital that individuals are attuned to ever changing codes of aesthetic propriety, 'Wearing a passé t-shirt, sporting an unsuitable haircut, or having a bad hair day, would be immediately criticized for being an indication of lack of care of the "self"'.[92] Moreover, given the *visible* nature of soccer involvement, parents are equally important as a forum for the aesthetic projection of the self. This is evident in the near parodic uniformity of cosmetic appearance, dress, and choice of luxury vehicle, exhibited by parents at games, practices, and meetings: vividly illustrating the normative regulation underpinning consumer individuality. Thus, although manifest in very different cultural products and expressions, both players and parents use the soccer field as a context for the expression of the middle class habitus, through which they exude membership of the suburban élite.

> Suburban youth soccer is also a particularly interesting site of lifestyle differentiation. It can be viewed as a sub-field within the larger field of child-rearing, among the most outwardly visible, and hence obsessively nurtured, sites of suburban lifestyle.[93]

As embodied signifiers of parental lifestyle, and thereby class position, every aspect of children's lives has been exposed to the suburban regime of competitive lifestyle consumption. The constitution of a child's education, apparel, footwear, toys, bodies, teeth, and even soccer boots, are points of social distinction and comparison that compel parents to conform to ever escalating norms of stylized existence. This phenomenon is readily apparent within the realm of children's leisure practices, hence what J. Schor[94] characterized as the escalating standard for children's birthday parties: manifest in the current predilection for outsourcing the 'entire event to Chuck E. Cheese's, the Discovery Zone, the Mining Company, or some other business that stages a memorable event for the kids'.[95]

Suburban soccer culture evidences the extent to which the more mundane aspects of children's leisure time have been engulfed by the normalizing competitive lifestyle ethos: this 'generation of parents ... keeps starting children off younger and younger, pushing them harder and harder, not just in soccer but in music, competitive-admissions pre-schools, ballet, foreign languages'.[96] No longer seemingly allowed to engage in unstructured or unsupervised play, many young suburbanites are press-ganged by their parents into gruelling after-school schedules of commercially organized 'extended education', despite the financial, logistical, and/or emotional problems frequently posed to children and parents alike.[97] Exhibiting the kernel of the suburban habitus, the motivation for such prompting appears to be the conspicuous manufacture of healthy, cooperative, goal-oriented and competitive children. Suburban parents routinely regale soccer as an appropriate activity that: encourages the right type of corporeal aesthetic for boys and girls alike (i.e. it is cast as a healthy alternative to the abnormalizing and aggressive masculinity of American football);[98] instils a teamwork ethic and achievement orientation which can be transferred to other realms of existence; provides a competitive environment within which their offspring are challenged to excel; and, even (somewhat laughably) represents a structured activity that 'keeps kids off the streets'.[99] These sentiments betray the extent to which suburban soccer has become a 'wholly owned subsidiary of competitive adults',[100] in that they betray and seek to assuage parental anxieties about their own lives. Moreover, for many suburban parents, not providing one's offspring with the requisite experiences derived from competitive soccer participation is both an expression of suburban failure, and tantamount to an admission of child neglect.

Fully and enthusiastically incorporated as part of the suburban aesthetic, youth soccer participation has become the sporting version of 'Tuscan extra virgin olive oil': a manifest expression of suburbanites desirous lifestyle *sophistication*.[101] This observation has been noted and nurtured by the denizens of Madison Avenue (the hub of America's advertising culture) who – within a multitude of advertising campaigns for products as diverse as Lender's bagels, Dutch Boy paints, Cellular One mobile phones, and McDonald's fast food – have used positioned soccer referents to substantiate their objects of production (archetypes of the utopian suburban lifestyle) and interpellate their preferred subjects of consumption (consumers identifying with, or aspiring to, the utopian suburban lifestyle). This ubiquitous representational strategy is ably illustrated within a recent television commercial for the Buick Regal automobile:

> *[An affluent suburban sub-division]*. Some families get more done in a day than others do in a week.
> *[The family is introduced, smiling in front of their spacious single family dwelling. They jump into the car, hasten to a soccer game, and return rapidly]* They're the first to do anything, including to say:
> *[One of the daughters greets the audience]*: 'Hey, how's it going?' Now there's a car that does as much as your supercharged family.
> *[The family embarks on another journey]*. Introducing the new supercharged Regal GS. No other sports sedan squeezes in so much supercharged 'fun', power, and standard safety features into your daily routine.
> *[Having returned home, the family sets out for a children's party. The son is wearing a banana costume]*. Regal GS by Buick.
> *[Their bassett hound howls. The car returns to pick-up the dog]*: 'Hey, life's a blur'.
> *[The dog is put in the back of the car, and once again the family is on its way]*. The all new Regal GS, the official car of the supercharged family.

Within this commercial, suburban soccer is used as a benchmark constituent of the *supercharged* suburban aesthetic. As such, the game acts as a principal 'source, as well as an indicator of social differentiation' for the innately competitive suburban middle class.[102] However, as with many other suburban practices, participation in youth soccer is commonly viewed as a lifestyle choice, thereby obscuring the very real economic barriers which preclude many from involvement. In so doing, the uncomfortable notion of socio-economic classes is erased, and the suburban middle class allowed to bolster its overactive sense of self-righteous achievement and privilege.[103] Thus, and somewhat refining Zukin,[104] although a central feature of the suburban topography, youth soccer represents an effective sublimation of the very real social class relations (and indeed gender and race relations only implied herein), through which a suburban landscape of the powerful (white middle class) is both structured and experienced.

NOTES

1. Nike representative Sandy Bodecker, quoted in Soccer Industry Council of America, *Soccer in the U.S.A.: An Overview of the American Soccer Market* (N. Palm Beach, 1997), p.6.
2. A.S. Markovits and S.L. Hellerman, 'Soccer in America: A Story of Marginalization', *Entertainment and Sports Law Review*, 13, 1/2 (1995), 255.
3. See Sporting Goods Manufacturers Association, *1998 State of the Industry Report*; and L.E. Sunderland, 'Deal could mean Bonanza of $500M to U.S. Soccer: Venture with IMG, Nike seen Shoring Foundations', *Baltimore Sun*, 22 April, 1998, 3E.
4. T. Post, 'Feet of the Future', *Newsweek Special Issue* (1994), 60–5.
5. L. Grossberg, *Bringing It All Back Home: Essays on Cultural Studies* (hereafter *Bringing It All Back Home*) (Durham, NC, 1997), pp.260, 261.
6. L. Grossberg, 'Cultural Studies, Modern Logics, and Theories of Globalisation', *Back to Reality? Social Experience and Cultural Studies* (Manchester, 1997), p.7.
7. Hank Steinbrecher, executive director and general secretary of the United States Soccer Federation, quoted in G. Pesky, 'On the Attack: The Growth of Soccer in the United States', *Sporting Goods Business* (1993), 31.
8. J. Sugden, 'USA and the World Cup: American Nativism and the Rejection of the People's Game' (hereafter 'USA and the World Cup'), in J. Sugden and A. Tomlinson (eds.), *Hosts and Champions: Soccer Cultures, National Identities and the USA World Cup* (Aldershot, 1994) p.219.
9. J.A. Lucas and R.A. Smith, *Saga of American Sport* (Philadelphia, 1978), p.5; J. Holliman, *American Sports (1785–1835)* (Durham, NC, 1931); E. Dunning and K. Sheard, *Barbarians, Gentlemen and Players: A Sociological Study of the Development of Rugby Football* (New York, 1979); D. Reisman and R. Denny, 'Football in America: A Study in Culture Diffusion' (hereafter 'Football in America'), *American Quarterly*, 3 (1951); Sugden, 'USA and the World Cup'; C. Jose, *The United States and World Cup Soccer Competition: An Encyclopedic History of the United States in International Competition* (hereafter *The United States and World Cup*) (Metuchen, NJ, 1994), p.183.
10. S. Wagg, 'The Business of America: Reflections on World Cup '94' (hereafter 'The Business of America', *Giving the Game Away: Football, Politics and Culture on Five Continents* (Leicester, 1995), pp.179–200.
11. M. Oriard, *Reading Football: How the Popular Press Created an American Spectacle* (hereafter *Reading Football*) (Chapel Hill, NC, 1993); 'Football in America'.
12. C. Whitney, 'American Football', *The Encyclopaedia of Sport* (London, 1898) p.424.
13. See M.S. Kimmel, 'Baseball and the Reconstitution of American Masculinity, 1880–1920', *Sport, Men, and the Gender Order: Critical Feminist Perspectives* (Champaign, IL, 1990); Oriard, *Reading Football*.
14. S. Hall, 'Notes on Deconstructing "The Popular"', *People's History and Socialist Theory* (London, 1981).

15. Jose, *The United States and World Cup*.
16. S.A. Riess, *City Games: The Evolution of American Urban Society and the Rise of Sports* (Urbana, IL, 1991).
17. A. Guttmann, *A Whole New Ball Game: An Interpretation of American Sports* (Chapel Hill, NC, 1988), p.56.
18. G.R. Mormino, 'The Playing Fields of St. Louis: Italian Immigrants and Sport, 1925–1941', *Journal of Sport History*, 9 (1982), 15, 16.
19. Anon., 'Soccer's last frontier', *The Economist* (1993), 100.
20. See E. Hobsbawm and T. Ranger, *The Invention of Tradition* (Cambridge, 1983).
21. See B.G. Rader, 'Compensatory sport heroes: Ruth, Grange and Dempsey', *Journal of Popular Culture*, 16, 4 (1983); W.I. Susman, *Culture as History: The Transformation of American Society in the Twentieth Century* (New York, 1984).
22. Sugden, 'USA and the World Cup', p.240.
23. Ibid.
24. See P. Gardner, *The Simplest Game: The Intelligent Fan's Guide to the World of Soccer* (hereafter *The Simplest Game*) (New York, 1996), pp.242–59.
25. T. Toch, 'Football? In short pants? No helmets?', *Science and Society*, 116, 23 (1994).
26. P. Hersh, 'Soccer in U.S. at Crossroads: World Cup seen as Last Resort to Stir Fan Sport' (hereafter 'Soccer in U.S. at Crossroads'), *Chicago Tribune*, 3 June 1990.
27. Gardner, *The Simplest Game*, p.225.
28. See G. Pesky, 'The Changing Face of the Game', *Sporting Goods Business* (March 1993), 32; 'On the Attack: The Growth of Soccer in the United States', *Sporting Goods Business* (April 1993), 31; J.M. Schrof, 'American Women: Getting their Kicks', *Science and Society*, 19 June 1995.
29. Soccer Industry Council of America, *1998 National Soccer Participation Survey* (North Palm Beach, FL, 1998).
30. H. Steinbrecher, 'Getting in on Soccer: The Hottest Sport to reach International Markets', *Marketing with Sports Entities* (Atlanta, GA, 1996).
31. Anon., 'Major League Soccer: Growing Stars', *The Economist* (1996), 27.
32. Ibid.
33. See F. Delgado, 'Major League Soccer: The Return of the Foreign Sport', *Journal of Sport and Social Issues*, 21, 3 (1997); J. Langdon, 'MLS Ad Campaign to Target Hispanics', *USA Today*, 23 January, 1998; D.E. Hayes-Bautista and G. Rodriguez, 'L.A. Story: Los Angeles, CA, Soccer and Society', *The New Republic* (1994); M. Malone, 'Soccer's Greatest Goal: Cultural Harmony through Sports', *Americas* (1994).
34. D. Zwick and D.L. Andrews, 'The Suburban Soccer Field: Sport and the Culture of Privilege in Contemporary America' (hereafter 'The Suburban Soccer Field'), in G. Armstrong and R. Giulianotti (eds.), *Football Cultures and Identities* (Basingstoke, 1999), pp.211–22.
35. D.L. Andrews, R. Pitter, D. Zwick and D. Ambrose, 'Soccer's Racial Frontier: Sport and the Segregated Suburbanization of Contemporary America', in G. Armstrong and R. Giulianotti (eds.), *Entering the Field: New Perspectives on World Football* (Oxford, 1997).
36. Ibid.
37. See Anon., 'Soccer's Last Frontier'; S. Coughlin, 'Soccer: America's New, Big Kick the World's Sport Comes of Age in the United States', *Asheville Citizen-Times*, 25 July 1997; Gardner, *The Simplest Game*; M. Harpe, 'Soccer Dollar Limits Blacks', *News and Record* (Greensboro, NC), 28 May 1995; D. Russakof, 'Okay, Soccer Moms and Dads: Time Out! Leagues Try to Rein in Competitive Parents' (hereafter 'Okay, Soccer Moms and Dads), *Washington Post*, 25 August 1998; 'USA and the World Cup'; S. Walker, 'Defending the Sabbath from Soccer', *The Christian Science Monitor* (1997); C.P. Winner, 'U.S. soccer needs infusion of heart', *USA Today*, 15 June 1998.
38. Hersh, 'Soccer in U.S. at Crossroads', 1.
39. Grossberg, *Bringing It All Back Home*, p.257.
40. B. Ehrenreich, *Fear of Falling: The Inner Life of the Middle Class* (hereafter *Fear of Falling*) (New York, 1989), p.35.
41. See H.C. Binford, *The First Suburbs: Residential Communities on the Boston Periphery 1815–1860* (Chicago, 1985); R. Fishman, *Bourgeois Utopias: The Rise and Fall of Suburbia*

(New York, 1987); K.T. Jackson, *Crabgrass Frontier: The Suburbanization of the United States* (hereafter *Crabgrass Frontier*) (New York, 1985).

42. M. Savage and A. Warde, *Urban Sociology, Capitalism and Modernity* (Basingstoke, 1993), p.76.
43. D.B. Holleb, 'The Direction of Urban Change', *Agenda for the New Urban Era* (Chicago, 1975).
44. B. Kleinberg, *Urban America in Transformation: Perspectives on Urban Policy and Development* (Thousand Oaks, CA: Sage, 1995); N. Lemann, 'The New American Consensus: Government Of, By and For the Comfortable – The Smallness of Centrism', *The New York Times Magazine* (1998); G.S. Thomas, *The United States of Suburbia: How the Suburbs took control of America and What They Plan to do with It* (New York: Prometheus Books, 1998).
45. See S. Zukin, *Landscapes of Power: From Detroit to Disney World* (hereafter *Landscapes of Power*) (Berkeley: University of California Press, 1991).
46. See R. Silverstone, 'Introduction', *Visions of Suburbia* (London and New York: Routledge, 1997).
47. 'The Suburban Soccer Field'.
48. Jackson, *Crabgrass Frontier*.
49. W.H. Whyte, *The Organization Man* (New York, 1956); H.J. Gans, 'The Levittowners' (New York, 1967).
50. B. Fine and E. Leopold, *The World of Consumption* (London, 1993), p.68.
51. J. Lears, *Fables of Abundance: A Cultural History of Advertising in America* (hereafter *Fables of Abundance*) (New York, 1994), p.247.
52. See Jackson, *Crabgrass Frontier*; G. Wright, *Building the Dream: A Social History of Housing in America* (Cambridge, MA, 1983).
53. Zukin, *Landscapes of Power*.
54. Silverstone, 'Introduction', *Visions of Suburbia*, p.8.
55. C. Hitchens, 'Goodbye to All That: Why Americans are not Taught History', *Harper's* (November 1998), 37.
56. M. Featherstone, 'The Body in Consumer Culture', *Theory, Culture and Society*, 1, 2 (1982), 19.
57. D. Slater, *Consumer Culture and Modernity* (Cambridge, 1997), p.29.
58. S.D. Stark, *Glued to the Set: The 60 Television Shows and Events that Made Us Who We Are Today* (New York, 1997).
59. S. Ewen, *Captains of Consciousness: Advertising and the Social Roots of the Consumer Culture* (New York, 1976); C. Lasch, *The Culture of Narcissism: American Life in an Age of Diminishing Expectations* (hereafter *The Culture of Narcissism*) (New York, 1979); Lears, *Fables of Abundance*.
60. J. Clarke, *New Times and Old Enemies: Essays on Cultural Studies and America* (London, 1991).
61. P. Bourdieu, *Distinction: A Social Critique of the Judgement of Taste* (hereafter *Distinction*) (Cambridge, 1984), p.172.
62. A. Schlesinger, *The Politics of Hope* (Boston, 1963), p.84.
63. Slater, *Consumer Culture and Modernity*.
64. J.B. Schor, *The Overspent American: Upscaling, Downshifting and the New Consumer* (hereafter *The Overspent American*) (New York, 1998), p.8.
65. Lears, *Fables of Abundance*, p.252.
66. Schor, *The Overspent American*.
67. Ehrenreich, *Fear of Falling*.
68. Lasch, *The Culture of Narcissism*, p.72.
69. Joe Provey, editor of *Soccer Jr.* magazine, quoted in Russakov, 'Okay, Soccer Moms and Dads', A1.
70. See Clarke, *New Times and Old Enemies*; L. Grossberg, *We Gotta Get Out of this Place: Popular Conservatism and Postmodern Culture* (London, 1992).
71. *The World of Consumption*.
72. See Clarke, *New Times and Old Enemies*; N.G. Duncan and J.S. Duncan, 'Deep Suburban Irony: The Perils of Democracy in Westchester County, New York', *Visions of Suburbia* (London, 1997); Ehrenreich, *Fear of Falling*; Schor, *The Overspent American*.

73. Stephen King, quoted in P. Conrad, 'Everybody's nightmare', *The Observer Review*, 9 August 1998, 1.
74. M. Featherstone, *Consumer Culture and Postmodernism* (London, 1991), p.86.
75. Bourdieu, *Distinction*, p.178.
76. Slater, *Consumer Culture*.
77. Bourdieu, *Distinction*, p.101.
78. Ibid., p.171.
79. C. Lury, *Consumer Culture* (Cambridge, 1996).
80. Bourdieu, *Distinction*, p.171.
81. P. Bourdieu, 'Programme for a Sociology of Sport', *In Other Words: Essays Toward a Reflexive Sociology* (Stanford, 1990), p.159.
82. Bourdieu, *Distinction*, p.178.
83. Zwick and Andrews, 'The Suburban Soccer Field'.
84. P. Bourdieu, 'Sport and Social Class', *Social Science Information*, 17, 6 (1978), 835.
85. Ibid., 834.
86. See Bourdieu, *Distinction*; and 'The Forms of Capital', *Handbook of Theory and Research for the Sociology of Education* (Westport, 1986).
87. Zwick and Andrews, 'The Suburban Soccer Field'.
88. P. Bourdieu, *The Field of Cultural Production* (New York, 1993).
89. D. McLellan, *Karl Marx: Selected Writings* (Oxford, 1977), p.355.
90. Slater, *Consumer Culture*.
91. See K. Grish, '7 on Soccer: On the Road to Strong Sales, Soccer Manufacturers Navigate Fashion Avenue', *Sporting Goods Business*, 31, 7 (1998); A. Perez, 'Soccer Looks: Soccer Fashion', *Sporting Goods Business*, 30, 5 (1997).
92. Zwick and Andrews, 'The Suburban Soccer Field'.
93. Schor, *The Overspent American*, p.85.
94. Ibid.
95. J.H. Gilmore, 'Welcome to the Experience Economy', *Harvard Business Review* (1998), 97.
96. Russakov, 'Okay, Soccer Moms and Dads', A1.
97. Ehrenreich, *Fear of Falling*, p.82.
98. M.N. Hornung, '3 billion people can't be wrong', *Chicago Sun-Times*, 17 June 1994; Wagg, 'The Business of America'.
99. John Talley, Vice-President of Outback Sports (Soccer Division), personal communication.
100. Russakov, 'Okay, Soccer Moms and Dads', A1.
101. 'USA and the World Cup', 247.
102. Schor, *The Overspent American*, p.30.
103. N.G. Duncan and J.S. Duncan, 'Deep Suburban Irony: The Perils of Democracy in Westchester County, New York'.
104. Zukin, *Landscapes of Power*, in R. Silverstone (ed.), *Visions of Suburbia* (London, 1997), pp.161–79.

3

Scottish Myopia and Global Prejudices

GERRY P.T. FINN

'SECTARIANISM' AND RACISM

Examination of the relationship of Celtic and Rangers to Scottish society offers one route to explore so-called 'sectarianism' in Scottish society.[1] The relationship between football and the wider society is a complex one. Even the relationship between on-field and off-field events within the ground is more complex than lay accounts usually assume.[2] Abuse between supporters within football stadiums can indeed have a risible and playful element to it, but although that does mean that malice is not inevitably present, neither does it mean it must be absent.[3] On occasion supporters appear able to draw on an overflowing drain of effluent as the source of their invective against those (players or fans) they have allocated to minority group status.[4] More often than not, racism is much more banal, and less striking. Racist comments simply assemble and reassemble common societal beliefs. That is the case with racist abuse, in all of its manifestations; even extreme forms depend upon some symbiosis with less virulent types. Unfortunately that recognition has tended to be hindered by the false association of football's racism with hooliganism, resulting in the more subtle expressions of racism being ignored.[5]

Investigation of Celtic and Rangers demands awareness of these complexities in the relationship between extreme and moderate expressions of prejudice. That awareness recognizes the mistake, a common mistake, of focusing on the extreme behaviour of supporters to the neglect of the clubs, and their everyday interrelationships with each other and Scottish society.[6] Yet it is here that the expression of prejudice as taken-for-granted beliefs, passed off as eternal verities, is common, and often overlooked. At issue is the way that these two clubs have become enmeshed historically in the expression of social identities of two social communities in Scotland: crudely, these identities can be presented as Irish-Scottish or Catholic for Celtic and Scottish-British and Protestant, but more correctly anti-Catholic, in the case of Rangers. These two recurring identity themes still allow many variations to be played out. Supporters do play their part: they act as an operatic chorus in which variants of social identities are proclaimed and claimed, projected and rejected. Seldom, if ever, is this rich repertoire of identification other than the dramatic use of commonly held Scottish socio-historical beliefs about the two clubs and Scottish society. These supporting performances, however, do illustrate that study of Celtic and Rangers can allow majority–minority relations in Scotland to be investigated, and that supporters can display the full range of these stock beliefs. However, serious study is necessary to evaluate and disentangle the true social significance of Celtic and Rangers in Scottish society from claim and counter-claim. That aim demands that popular myths and populist histories be closely scrutinized, for the narration of these commonly believed accounts are an important means by which prejudice is expressed, represented, upheld and sustained.[7]

B. Murray[8] and H. Moorhouse[9] provided respectively the first serious historical and sociological descriptions of the Glasgow clubs in relation to Scottish society. So it is important to recognize that both rely almost uncritically on the traditional account that presents the ethno-political nature of Rangers to be a response to Celtic's origins in the predominantly Catholic, Irish-Scots community. Indeed so dominant is this account that it has even appeared in an official Rangers history.[10] Rather than scrutinize these popular myths and populist histories, in a striking demonstration of the validity of T. van Dijk's analysis of the role of élites in the perpetuation of racism,[11] these two academics offer a spurious legitimacy to this dominant and self-serving account of the social majority. One effect, though for Moorhouse clearly unintended, and sometimes directly contradicted, is to allow a belief in a mythological Scotland to be retained. Scotland can remain imagined to be egalitarian and largely free of prejudice: a myth at the core of Murray's beliefs. Something labelled 'sectarianism' may be acknowledged, especially in the field of football,[12] but it is the Irish-Scots that are held responsible for the emergence of this aberration amidst supposedly otherwise excellent intergroup relationships in Scotland. 'Sectarianism' as a usage disguises the reality of the nature of this societal prejudice, which is more correctly identified as the continuation in a more acceptable form of anti-Irish racism.[13] Unfortunately the dominant account of 'sectarianism' in Scottish sport is proving sufficiently adaptable to be used to dismiss efforts at participation by other Scottish minority communities too.[14]

D. McCrone considers the equation of being Scottish with egalitarianism to be a 'mystical' belief, and further comments: 'It is as if Scots are judged to be egalitarian by dint of racial characteristics, of deep social values. Man (or at least Scotsman) is judged to be primordially equal: inequality is man-made, created by the social structure he (for the myth is essentially male-centred) erects, or which are erected by others around him.'[15] Acceptance of this illusion of an egalitarian Scottish society is very evident in Murray's account. Although Moorhouse is not influenced by this myth, another illusion he shares with Murray distorts both their views. Both Murray and Moorhouse rely on 'realist' notions of prejudice:[16] it is the actions of the minority community that lead to its subsequent treatment. Murray accepts that 'sectarianism' exists, but he argues that 'sectarianism' was introduced by the Catholic Irish-Scots: 'In fact the real origin of sectarianism in Scottish football lay in the very formation of Celtic Football Club and their unprecedented success. The success of Celtic at the time coincided with a resurgence of catholic militancy both in local affairs and Irish national affairs.'[17] Murray accepts that prejudice, though sometimes he prefers 'social snobbery' as a more apt description,[18] has been directed against this minority. However, if the minority complains about this treatment, then he castigates the community for the failure to realize that it brought this prejudice on itself.[19] He judges that 'Celtic supporters, like the catholic community in general, have generally been unable to recognise their own part in generating the prejudice that they undoubtedly have had to face. By a far too easy cry of "Foul!" they have enveloped themselves in a persecution complex instead of seeking explanations for the antagonism they aroused.'[20] Elsewhere, and often, much too often, he summarizes minority protest at the prejudice it faces as paranoia.[21]

There is a psychiatric clinical term *paranoiac* or *paranoid* type,[22] but Murray is confident enough in his own psychiatric expertise to lay claim to some striking advances in this specialist field of study. Those who criticize him, or those who follow (or whom Murray *believes* follow) a line of argument that is critical of him, are diagnosed to be paranoid too. (He even detects little groups of paranoid academics acting in concert against him.)[23] Allegations of paranoia are actually deployed by Murray as discursive techniques to dismiss, rather than debate, analyses that identify racism in Scottish society. Denials of racism are common across diverse societies that remain racist.[24] In this specific form of denial, Murray extends everyday lay use of paranoia. Academic criticism of Murray leads him to defend himself by accusing other academics of paranoia because they have criticized him. What might appear the ultimate academic defence is transparently an obstacle to serious academic debate.[25]

A useful study of the experiences of the Irish or, more often, people of Irish descent in Britain has been carried out on behalf of the Commission for Racial Equality (CRE).[26] It confirms that their experiences often merit being described as racist. Yet, because many operate within a racist framework that assumes the colour-coding of 'races', this description of anti-Irish prejudice proves difficult for some to accept. The report is also informative on the extent to which this form of racist prejudice is simply denied: even raising it as an issue produces 'hostility'. The report concluded that, in Scotland, anti-Irish racism and anti-Catholic prejudices were interwoven with the Catholic religion serving as an index of probable Irish ethnicity. Both Murray and Moorhouse, in quite different ways, take stances in direct opposition to the conclusions of the CRE report. However, the substance of their accounts and analyses offers evidence that confirms many of the findings in the report. That Murray and Moorhouse fail to recognize the extent to which their own writings are contaminated in this way merely underlines the value and validity of the adoption of an anti-racist perspective to what is passed off as 'sectarianism' in Scottish football.

THE BLAME GAME: ASSERTION AND SPECULATION

Murray did pioneer academic research into Celtic and Rangers, collectively known as 'The Old Firm'.[27] Murray's research, however, is badly flawed.[28] One crucial failure was that he failed to examine the socio-political evolution of Rangers. Obliquely, Murray now admits to this glaring omission. In a recent work[29] he comments on research reported by G. Finn[30] that outlined some results of the examination of important political and social affiliations of leading figures in the history of Rangers, and he concludes that: 'Further work on the associations of high-ranking Rangers with such associations would be most interesting.'[31] Yet, without this essential knowledge about the socio-political complexion of Rangers and its membership, there can be no informed evaluation of the dynamic evolution of the complex of interrelationships between Celtic, Rangers and Scottish society. There cannot even be any valid assessment of Rangers alone. Nevertheless, here is reiterated the same dominant account as if it was supported by research. Celtic is blamed for the introduction of ethnicity, politics and religion into Scottish football, leading Rangers eventually to respond in kind; a response that somehow became the refusal of Rangers to play Catholics.[32]

When Murray had simply failed to carry out the required research himself, this presentation of judgements without evidence could be interpreted as a sign of his overly enthusiastic advocacy of an unsupported position. Now he accepts evidence of strong political influences on Rangers and, much less important by itself, of the club's early powerful associations with Freemasonry.[33] Rangers can be identified with support for Ulster Unionism and the Protestant cause before the establishment of Celtic as a force in Scottish football. Yet Murray's persistence with his past thesis now leads him to advocate an insupportable position. Evidence to the contrary is disregarded as he insists on claims that not only cannot be substantiated, but no longer fit the available evidence as he continues to assert that 'there was nothing religious in the origins of Rangers, and they were Protestant only in the sense that the vast majority of clubs in Scotland were made up of Protestants' and 'that they had no particular religious connections'. He then goes on to state that:

> Being Protestant at this time did not necessarily mean being anti-Catholic, but it frequently was the case, and when this was linked to opposition to Irish Home Rule, then the two could come together in a potent mix. Rangers were no more anti-Catholic than most clubs in Scotland in their early days, although some of their most prominent directors were freemasons and Unionists.[34]

Now this really is an intriguing quotation, and worth some further examination as it is typical of the style of argument and analysis offered by Murray.[35]

Murray correctly states that anti-Catholic attitudes and being Protestant were not one and the same. But, he is also right to observe that this precise association was very common in the nineteenth century. Unionism, the political expression of opposition to Irish Home Rule, was highly significant in its impact on attitudes to Irish Catholics and their descendants. In the case of Rangers, he now acknowledges that 'some of their most prominent directors were freemasons and

Unionists'. Yet, like the effect of this new evidence on Murray, the Unionism of these 'prominent' directors has somehow failed to have had any real impact. Elsewhere opposition to Irish Home Rule could contribute to a potent mix, but not apparently at Rangers.[36] And, although the issue of masonic membership can be neutral, in Scotland it has for too many[37] freemasons been closely aligned with anti-Catholic attitudes. Consequently, in the case of Rangers, links with freemasons offer further pointers to the club's core values.

Although Murray accepts opposition to Irish Home Rule to be an influence on Rangers in its early days, he avoids recognition of the probable impact of those beliefs on the club.[38] In 1988 he accepted that over a century earlier, Rangers' new club patron, John Ure Primrose, had previously left the Liberal Party over Irish Home Rule, but he explained that away too. Then he speculated on Primrose's motivation, suggested that his liberalism did not extend to Irish Home Rule, and judged that this was 'not particularly unusual'. By that he implied that most clubs had their own straying Primroses to display. Again, this account was not rooted in any evidence. In a flowery summary, Murray conjectured that Primrose's opposition to Irish Home Rule was because: 'Many men of liberal disposition were genuinely appalled at the absence of such virtues in the Catholic Church and believed it their duty to save others, even Catholics, from such evils.'[39] It is interesting to learn that such strong attitudes as these are not to be interpreted as being anti-Catholic: instead they are to be seen as a sign of liberal thinking. It is very instructive to learn that Murray so strongly equates Irish Home Rule with Rome Rule.[40] Clearly, anti-Catholicism mixed with Unionism, it appears from his argument, could even be a potent force for good: Protestants and 'even Catholics' were to be saved from 'such evils' as being Catholic. Consequently, the question of what Murray would perceive as anti-Catholic attitudes is more than a little perplexing.[41]

Murray's repetitive claim that Rangers differed little from most other Scottish clubs is speculation in the guise of an assertion. Much research remains to be done on the socio-political backgrounds of Scottish clubs. However, there is already reason to argue that Scottish football clubs represented a range of various political associations. Certainly Rangers was not the most extreme example of associations with the anti-Catholic and anti-Irish political right. The club was not a direct expression of the extreme imperialist, militarist, anti-Catholic and anti-Irish prejudices that led John Hope, a very prominent Edinburgh Conservative and legal figure, to establish the Third Edinburgh Rifles Volunteers (3rd ERV). Then, based on his regiment, Hope approved the setting up of the very first Edinburgh association football team.[42] Nonetheless, the sporting relationship of the 3rd ERV with Edinburgh Hibernian teaches another lesson. Football clubs had to co-operate to create football competition. Co-operation between Rangers and Celtic has been a much misunderstood factor in analysing the relations and political significance attached to the various clubs.[43] Claims of good sporting relationships between the clubs do not mean that Rangers had then no special or specific political associations.

From its earliest days Rangers sought the assistance and patronage of Conservative politicians. One event illustrates some of these relationships. In its very first years, Rangers received considerable support from Alexander Bannatyne Stewart, of Stewart and Macdonald in Glasgow.[44] A.B. Stewart, originally hailed from Bute, where he was Convenor of the County. For business reasons he spent much time in Glasgow. He had a large residence near Glasgow, and he retained a substantial house in Rothesay. Stewart, a prominent Conservative and Freemason, was 'a staunch adherent of the Church of Scotland'.[45] When Rangers' members elected his son to be the new club president, A.B. Stewart arranged that a charity match be played in Rothesay to honour his son's elevation. After the match, Stewart hosted a formal reception, which was attended by Charles Dalrymple, the local Conservative MP, as one of the guests of honour. In thanking the players for their efforts on behalf of the charity fund, Dalrymple joked that, in his view, no political meaning could be attached to football. Stewart's reply to the toast adopted a different position, with a markedly anti-Irish stance:

> He thought their worthy Member was wrong in saying that no political meaning could be got out of football. If he (Mr Stewart) was sitting in Parliament he would have been inclined to have played football with the heads of the Irish Obstructionists - (great laughter, during which Mr Dalrymple was seen to whisper to Mr Stewart.) Mr Stewart remarked that Mr Dalrymple had just informed him it would not have been Parliamentary to have said so. The O'Gorman might have fallen upon him - (loud laughter.)[46]

Stewart's robust sense of 'humour' on how to treat Irish nationalists in the House of Commons demonstrates the strength of his political attitude to the Irish question. Stewart was also a significant figure in the cross-class alliance entitled the Glasgow Conservative Working Men's Association.[47] This Conservative organization married politics to Protestantism and received considerable support from the Orange Order. Stewart's son replaced an exceptionally prominent figure in Protestant Conservative circles as Rangers president. He was the recently deceased Alexander Whitelaw, who had been a central figure in the Association. The Association was particularly exercised by the perceived threat to the privileged position of Presbyterianism in the overwhelming majority of Scotland's schools. As was common across Europe, the State was in the process of taking responsibility for schooling from the churches. In an attempt to surmount internal divisions within Presbyterianism on the relationship between the State and religion, the proposed 1872 Education Act fudged the position of religious instruction within State-funded schools. Religious instruction was neither prescribed nor proscribed. The insertion of a conscience clause in the act that allowed withdrawal from religious instruction, nonetheless, gave a clear signal of what was expected. And the Act's creation of School Boards which would be elected along religious lines guaranteed the continuation of Presbyterian dominance on the new schools.[48]

For the Glasgow Working Men's Conservative Association this was not good enough: it agitated to have the position of Presbyterianism in State-funded schools strengthened. The Association mobilized strenuous political protest against what it portrayed as 'secular education' and in the defence of 'The Bible in the School'. The campaign by the Scottish Conservatives and their Orange allies was a nation-wide one, and it was successful. An amendment was made to the preamble of the Act which, though differently phrased, became known as the 'use and wont' clause. It allowed the maintenance of religious instruction in new State-funded schools for as long as the local community wished it. The effect was to confirm this supposedly national system of education to be non-denominational Presbyterian.

The campaign had a particular impact in Glasgow. In 1873 Whitelaw, representing the 'use and wont' cause, was elected to the Glasgow School Board, and became its first chairman. The following year, in 1874, on the back of the same campaigning theme, Whitelaw became the first Tory MP to be elected in Glasgow since 1832. Whitelaw represented a Conservative Party that had very strong Orange associations. Given the interrelationships between Conservatism and the

Orange Order in Scotland, it was inevitable that Whitelaw attended some Orange social functions. Whitelaw himself never joined the Order, but his son, later also a Conservative MP, did and became an Orange Lodge Grand Master.[49] The associations between Rangers and political Protestantism and anti-Catholic and anti-Irish sentiments in the 1870s, long before the appearance of Celtic in 1888, are made very clear in the club's selection of its presidents.[50]

The associations between political Protestantism, education and Rangers are particularly significant, because Murray demonstrates little understanding of the interrelationships between schooling, community and religion in Scotland. Unsurprisingly, given his other beliefs and criticisms, he believes the relationship between religion, ethnicity and education in Scotland to have been the work of the Irish-Scottish Catholics. So strong is his acceptance of traditional mythology that again he feels no need to put his trenchant views to any empirical test. There is no presentation of any historical evidence, no engagement with historical sources. Instead, he berates Celtic and the Catholic Irish-Scottish community for the existence of Catholic schools. In his vehement comments about State support for Catholic schools, he insistently reiterates traditional majority prejudices directed against the Catholic Irish-Scots minority.[51] He presents a partial and historically ill-informed account of the subsequent 1918 Education (Scotland) Act and its consequences.

Yet this was the Act that placed both Catholic and Episcopalian schools, and Catholic and Episcopalian teacher-training colleges, on the same financial footing as their nondenominational but *de facto* Presbyterian counterparts. The Act produced the first truly national system of education in Scotland.[52] Murray is clearly unaware of the existence of the Episcopalian sector in Scottish education. Control of schooling was not a Protestant or Catholic issue. Episcopalians could be as exercised as Catholics by Presbyterian dominance of Scottish education. Episcopalian concerns over the role of Presbyterianism in State schools tells its own tale, and confirms Catholic Irish-Scots' anxieties too. The Episcopal Church was not just another Protestant Church: the Episcopal Church in Scotland was, and remains, in union with the established Church of England, the church to which British monarchs must still pledge allegiance on their accession to the throne.[53] As Catholicism was judged to be an 'alien' religion,[54] and as the Irish were seen to be an inferior 'race', there can be no doubt that the fears of the Catholic Irish-Scots about respect for their beliefs in Presbyterian dominated nondenominational schools were legitimate.

Nonetheless, Murray uses the establishment of Catholic State schools as another reason to attack the Irish-Scots and Catholicism. He is unaware that the 1918 Education (Scotland) Act set up the first *inclusive* national State education system in Scotland. He even writes that, as long as Catholics persist in retaining Catholic schooling, they 'then … must expect that other Scots will harbour certain suspicions about them'.[55] His neglect of the historical development of Scottish schooling means that he is unaware of the extent to which his comments echo the racist criticisms of the inter-war years. State support for Catholic schools was used by both extreme and moderate right-wing politicians to illustrate a perceived racial threat by the 'Irish' to Scotland. Then there was no doubt about the precise nature of the suspicion deliberately aroused by this political use of State-support for Catholic schools, and applied to Catholics or Irish-Scots. Nor can there be any doubt about the way that these various factors became thoroughly intertwined within a complex of beliefs that can only be described as racism.[56] Murray appears oblivious to the social reality of this historical past: it is obvious that he has no understanding of the complexity of Scottish racism.

RACISM AND MULTICULTURALISM

Scottish society is spellbound by the myth of its own egalitarianism. Murray is enchanted by this notion too. When he first tried to dismiss any suggestion of racism in Scotland, he wrote: 'however much we may dislike it, anti-catholicism is part of Scotland's history and can be understood in those terms. Racism is odious and foreign to all that Scotland stands for.'[57] Ironically, Murray's resounding declaration of his faith in the sheer contradiction between Scottishness and racism is a near perfect illustration of McCrone's analysis that the 'mystical belief' in Scottish egalitarianism depends on a 'primordial' sense of being Scottish, believed to be bestowed 'by dint of racial characteristics, of deep social values'.[58] Murray places great trust in this myth of a Scotland free of racism, the persistent belief of the majority community, despite contradictory objective evidence and testimony to the contrary from the lived experience of many of Scotland's minority communities. His own use of 'foreign' unhappily provides a self-generated contradiction to his denial of any possibility of xenophobia or racism in Scotland. Instead he projects racism to be the property of other (foreign) peoples. He had earlier spoken of racism 'fouling English grounds', so it was clear which 'foreign' country he had most in mind. But this attribution of racism to England is no more than the usual device by which attention to racism in Scotland is deflected.[59]

Presumably in response to earlier criticisms, there is now the appearance of a shift in Murray's position on racism: sadly his misunderstanding of racism as a social force ensures that no substantial change has occurred.[60] No longer though, or so it at first seems, is Scottishness an antidote to racism. He now appears to recognize that the power of the image of religious division can obscure the existence of racism: 'religious bigotry often being regarded in Scotland as stronger than racial prejudice. However that may be, Scotland is no more immune to racial prejudice than other countries ...' Murray still fails to recognize the connection between religious bigotry and anti-Irish racism, but he does distance himself from his earlier unfair comparison of Scotland and England. Now he suggests that, in relation to the racist barracking of black players in England in the 1970s and 1980s, 'there is little ground to believe that the situation in Scotland would have been any different'.[61] Although he now offers a more accurate assessment, the problem remains: it is his beliefs, not an engagement with evidence, that directs his interpretations. In 1988 he chose to ignore evidence of racism in Scotland, and instead merely asserted his erroneous beliefs on the matter: in 1998 this new account remains driven more by belief than evidence.[62] To confuse the evaluation of the extent of his conversion some more, there is no admission of his earlier, now self-contradicted proclamations.[63]

This failure to understand racism is underlined by a denial of the link between racism and 'sectarianism'. Murray argues that 'Scotland and Ireland have common Celtic roots and if it wasn't for religion would have very little to divide them – certainly not racism.'[64] Here he confirms that he has himself fallen prey to the effects of everyday racism. He implies that for racism to be evident there must be 'real' racial difference. Yet 'race' is always a social construct erected on the basis of relatively meaningless, and ultimately irrelevant, minor differences within the one human race. Indeed, one of the benefits of studying anti-Irish racism is to contradict the supposed objectivity of 'race' and expose the sheer nonsense of racism in its most dominant contemporary form, that which assumes that 'races' are colour-coded for their easy recognition.[65] Murray must learn that social divisions among the peoples of the world are never some form of 'racial' absolute: they are always human social constructions. Nor is it uncommon for religion to be inextricably interlinked with racism. The appalling history of anti-Semitism in Nazi Germany should alert us all to that sad reality.[66] In Britain, Protestantism provided the unifying bond, and Catholicism was associated with alien beliefs and peoples.[67] In Scotland, the Catholicism of the Irish was for some both the confirmation of their racial degeneracy and the means by which their racial encroachment into Scottish life could be detected.[68]

Just as Murray fails to realize that anti-Irish racism is obscured by the use of 'sectarianism', for which he blames the Irish-Scots, so he still woefully misrepresents the nature of racism in Scotland. Indeed, the legitimization of these common confusions, when added to the blanket denial of racism in Scotland, make progress in the development of anti-racism in Scottish football and society especially problematic.[69] He confirms the scale of these problems when he extends his analysis to comments on Asian-Scots in relation to football. He identifies a concern in Britain about the absence of British Asians from football,[70] and he recognizes a similarity with the experience of the Irish-Scottish community that leads him to offer the same form of analysis:

> The assumption was that it was prejudice against the Asians that had kept them out, under the excuse that gave the title to two Asian researchers' project: 'Asians Can't Play Football'. Much of this has echoes of the accusations of prejudice by Catholics of a few decades ago; but not all the blame rests with the host community.[71]

Murray's deployment of 'assumption' and 'accusations of prejudice' are as telling as his use of the notion 'host community'. Presumably it is his declaration that prejudice was assumed that has influenced his failure to engage with the evidence of prejudice presented by Bains and Patel,[72] the authors whom he fails to name, but casually refers to as 'the two Asian researchers'.[73] Instead Murray opts to discuss the 'host community', and he outlines efforts in Scotland to remedy this exclusion. In particular he identifies Celtic's involvement with the Scottish Asian Sports Association and the 'Fair Play for Asians' campaign mounted by the broadsheet *Scotland on Sunday*. However, he concludes:

> *Scotland on Sunday* claimed that Asians were forced out onto the

margins of Scottish football by 'abuse, discrimination and ignorance', and no doubt there is much truth in this: there are some communities, however, that prefer to keep to themselves. The absence of Asians from football is not necessarily an indication of prejudice against them.[74]

Again Murray's unease with the newspaper findings, its 'claims' as he prefers to label them, is obvious, and he commences the retreat to his own cherished beliefs about how minority communities must be held responsible for the predicament in which they find themselves. Despite reporting the concern of the Asian-Scottish community at being excluded from Scottish football, and a little of this community's own efforts to remedy the matter, he proceeds to neglect this evidence of interest and determination to participate in football, and quickly reverts back to the dominant majority viewpoint.

He believes that the absence of Asian-Scots from football is to do with Asian cultural difference and, at present, a lack of football ability and commitment.[75] Moreover, just as he attacks a caricature of Catholicism, he demonstrates his fair-mindedness by giving Islam the same treatment. The potential for racism in criticism of Islam is recognized by him, but then juxtaposed with his denial that racism need be evident at all. Then, to add to this uncertainty, he accepts the existence of 'race' and recognizes the potential for confusion in discussions of 'culture, religion and race' but comments that 'this can never condone open bigotry and racism'. He writes, in his usual juxtaposed style:

> However, many who are uncomfortable with Muslim practices today need not be racist, although many are, just as Protestants who were once suspicious of Catholicism were not necessarily bigots, although many were. There are distinctions between culture, religion and race that can be easily confused, but this can never condone the open bigotry and racism that have too often scarred the face of football. On the other hand, if racism is to be measured by the exclusion of Asians from football, this must also have something to say about the countless numbers of blacks who are playing in football teams all over Britain today.[76]

Murray's final sentence confirms his inability to handle the complexity of the different forms that racism can take or to develop the subtlety of analysis required to identify its presence. His opposition to the condoning of '*open* bigotry and racism' (emphasis added) deserves little praise. The problem is that these overt forms are in a symbiotic relationship with the more covert manifestations, which must too be condemned and, more pertinently, avoided by scholars too.[77]

Murray's uncertainty is even more apparent when he makes what he conceives to be a gesture in the direction of multiculturalism. Unfortunately, he has a distorted notion of what this term means: 'Multiculturalism is the acceptance of people of various ethnic backgrounds into the host culture, a celebration of difference and diversity.'[78] He endorses a model of society in which power remains with the majority community and, despite comments to the contrary, he remains committed to an assimilationist strategy towards minorities. Not only is there a dominant 'host culture', a phrase usually taken to attribute inferior 'guest' status to minority groups, but it is this 'host culture' that '*accepts*' others '*into it*' (emphases added). His inability to understand, even accept multiculturalism, is fully exposed by the caricature he creates in his attack on Maley who had been anxious about proclamations of Scotland as a Protestant country.[79] As Murray now tries to claim that his own criticisms of the Catholic Irish-Scots are an expression of 'secular views' based on the '(Catholic) Church's interference in personal and political matters',[80] it might be expected that he would condemn the suggestion that any one religious tradition should be equated with the notion of the country or the nation: not so.

He defends the very notion itself:

> Maley ... takes a swipe at Graham Walker for daring to suggest that 'Scotland is a Protestant country'. He makes the assumption that this statement leaves no room for those who are not Protestant. Here we have one of the ironies of multiculturalism, when the host country is turned on by those who it had hoped to integrate and finds itself forced to justify itself before the more recent immigrants: Christians defending Christmas and Easter before Muslims: Protestants in Scotland having to apologise for having been there for a few hundred years and feeling that somehow the country of their forebears has something to do with them. Even the supporters of Glasgow Rangers, no blushing violets in defending their own position, have been assailed to such an extent that they now exhibit on occasion a paranoia more usually associated with their rivals on the other side of the city.[81]

Here are deployed the passions that lurk beneath his contradictory statements. Is it that he fears multiculturalism and proposes a model of society in which social power resides with those citizens who can make some prior ancestral claim: others cannot expect the same civil and democratic rights? To Murray, 'immigrants' too readily become unwelcome guests who simply do not know their place, and not only make absurd demands, but 'turn on' the 'host country'.[82] And, in some way only known to Murray, the treatment of supporters of Glasgow Rangers is another example of the unfairness associated with 'multiculturalism'. He then sums up his Scotland in another example of his expertise in juxtaposing contrary sentiments: 'Scotland is many things. It is Protestant, but far from exclusively so.'[83]

The problem is that, despite semantic obscurantism, his Scottish society must be accepted to be predominantly Protestant. Within that dominant value-system, there will be 'room' for some others, but only if they pose no awkward questions to that society. This model of society is one in which some societal change is accepted, but only when on the terms dictated by the majority community. Throughout Murray's accounts he relies implicitly on a mystical model of some form of Scottish essentialism. That appears in his views on egalitarianism, racism and in his orientation to minorities. These communities feature in caricature merely to demonstrate either the suitability of celebrating the supposed lack of Scottish prejudice or are cast as potential problems; often they feature as both. For Murray, Scotland remains a Protestant country, one that generously accepts other ethnic communities, but really only on the expectation that they will conform. So the insistence of Catholic Irish-Scots or Islamic Asian-Scots on retaining a sense of different faith and values is objectionable to the majority, a judgement with which Murray agrees: that is why he can comment that the determination of the former community to retain Catholic schools is sufficient justification to 'harbour suspicions about them'.[84] That judgement is the same one passed on the establishment of Celtic Football Club. Given this analytic framework, in which any disharmony *must* be the fault of the minority, and in which the majority need not reflect on its own assumptions and prejudices, perhaps it should be no surprise that his writing suggests that Scotland has celebrated multiculturalism since the turn of the century. In Murray's imagined Scotland, Italians, Poles, Lithuanians and Chinese have all found a society that truly is like no other in the world.[85]

As Murray restates support for the myth of Scottish egalitarianism, so he begins to revert to his 1988 position at the end of his 1998 book. In doing so, he reiterates his consistently confused belief that it is minority communities that cause racism or prejudice. It is this part of his confusion, his consistent and insistent confounding of cause and effect, that is particularly worrying. It is true that racism makes its most public appearances in response to the presence of a minority community. Yet, the availability of a target community against which racism can be vented does not sustain the argument that the minority community caused the racism. The minority presence presents an excuse for the 'cause' in which racism is expressed, but that is very different from the minority community having caused racism. Unfortunately, this model of prejudice is one constant feature in the expression of Murray's beliefs. As Irish-Scots caused so-called 'sectarianism', so other minority communities cause racism. Only by blaming minorities for any prejudice observed in Scottish society, can he retain his belief in the myth of Scottish egalitarianism.

Murray's account of racism, however, takes an even more disturbing turn. Once he has adopted the model that holds minorities necessarily responsible for their own prejudicial treatment, it is only a small step to move onto an even more offensive version. Murray appears to attribute the cause and power of racism to the size of the target community. For some decades now this belief has been criticized as the 'numbers game'. Many years ago, R. Moore noted that this approach not only identifies the minority to be the problem, but defines the 'problem' to be proportionate to the size of the minority population. Acceptance of this framework not only ensured no principled opposition to racism, but: 'The argument about numbers is unwinnable because however many you decide upon there will always be someone who campaigns for less and others for whom one is too many.'[86]

Yet Murray still pronounces that, 'In Scotland Jews have not had to suffer the overt anti-Semitism that has been their lot in too many other countries.' His belief is: 'That the Jewish population of Scotland was never more than 15,000 can account in some measure for the absence of widespread anti-Semitism.'[87] Murray then also retreats to something close to his earlier position on the absence of racism in Scotland when he claims that: 'This has perhaps also been the case with regard to racism against the small numbers of Scots of Afro-Caribbean or Asian background.' But then he makes a further qualification, and a grudging admission: 'There has been prejudice, and there has been violence[88] against Scots from such backgrounds ... but historically Scotland's ethnic animosities have been directed mainly against Scots of Irish-Catholic origin. Even the English, Scotland's largest immigrant group, have had little to fear so long as they kept their accents under control.'[89]

Again the Irish-Scots appear to distract from charges of more general Scottish prejudice. Again Murray's peculiar juxtaposition of opposed thoughts rather than an integrative synthesis of them into a coherent analysis is on display. Murray, despite desperately trying to have it all ways, simply cannot disguise the overwhelming power of his mystical belief in Scottish egalitarianism: that leads him to assume minority communities in Scotland usually experience little in the way of intergroup prejudice. In his last sentence he cannot disguise his distrust of any social difference, and his sheer inability to comprehend how difference can be accepted as a positive aspect of social diversity. His comment may be intended to be a joke[90] but if so, it is a revealing one, and one that does emphasize his assimilationist model of society, and of Scottish society in particular. If Scotland's 'host culture' is to 'accept' its English 'guests' into it, then they have to be quiet. For Murray, the English should disguise their accents, and by implication their Englishness.[91] That offers no solution, and no remedy for tackling prejudice. Instead it buttresses prejudicial beliefs. For more visible rather than audible minorities, 'passing' oneself off as a member of the majority is not even an option. His quiet insistence on the second-class status of some citizens courts dangers, especially for those whom the 'host culture' has problems 'accepting'.

MISUNDERSTANDING PREJUDICE AND DISCRIMINATION – AND OTHER ERRORS

When Moorhouse first explored the 'Old Firm',[92] he drew on Murray, and very similar sources to Murray. Therefore, he agrees that Rangers' anti-Catholic policy emerged in the inter-war period. Neither Murray nor Moorhouse provides any evidence to prove this to have been the case. Instead they merely present speculative variations on the traditional belief system, which is wrong and, consequently, so are they.[93] However, it is understandable why this time-frame has been selected as the probable period for the policy. From soon after the end of the Great

War until the Second World War there was a marked escalation in prejudice and an intensification of overt discrimination against the minority community in Scotland. Expression of the prejudice commonly took the form of anti-Irish racism,[94] though Murray and Moorhouse misunderstand its nature. C. Brown has identified this period to be when the opposition to the Catholic Irish-Scots was at its peak.[95] One lesson does not appear to have been learned from this historical development and that is that the assumption of an inevitable progression towards better intergroup relations simply can not be sustained. In intergroup relations there is a need for vigilance: complacency and denial aid the maintenance of prejudice. As long as prejudice remains, discrimination remains a possibility. That points to another, less obvious, lesson. As psychologists have recognized for a long time, prejudice and discrimination are not one and the same.[96] Substantial decreases in discriminatory practices can not be assumed to identify a similarly marked decrease in prejudicial beliefs.

Moorhouse is confused about the nature of prejudice altogether. He argued that 'football is now one of the main vehicles of the ethnic antagonism it is supposed to represent' but then concluded that 'ethnicity has by no means disappeared in Glasgow' and that 'there still is a sensitivity to ethnic background'. Nonetheless, he still proceeded to claim that 'The Old Firm clash now largely *is* the hostility, a tradition, a Scottish tradition, an echo not a reflection of what *is*. Their matches are important for sectarianism to be shown to be a lively social issue and as a plank in Scottish identity' (original emphases).[97]

Now there is a conceptual problem here. Moorhouse touches on the complexity of the relationship between football and society, and representation and reality, but then falls into a semantic trap of his own making, and an error that he repeats in later work too.[98] A representation must also be a vehicle[99] for ethnic antagonism; language itself provides a clearer example of this necessity. Through language prejudice is represented, carried and also enacted. Moorhouse must be confusing prejudice and discrimination, the most common failing of analysts of Scottish intergroup relations. It is true that football has long been one of the most dramatic representations of this conflict, and that Rangers has been an especially potent symbol of discrimination in Scotland: it is also true that discrimination against Catholics and Irish-Scots is commonly accepted to be much decreased.[100] However, that acceptance is not the same as stating that prejudice against this community has been eliminated. The confusion between discrimination and prejudice is evident in these accounts. Moreover, prejudicial talk commonly appears most in relation to those areas in which a minority community is visible: the two most common areas of visibility for Catholic Irish-Scots are Celtic and Catholic schools. Murray and Moorhouse provide sustenance to the common prejudices directed against the minority in both of these areas of Scottish life.

Without knowing it, Moorhouse had provided an early warning of his own inexpertise in analysing prejudice, discrimination and social identity. In 1986 Moorhouse judged that the economic power of Rangers should enable it to compete with English clubs and sign English players. Moorhouse scoured the history of Rangers to see if the club had signed English players, and concluded:

> They do not but this can hardly be a matter of money, but must be a matter of policy. Rangers are a Protestant club who will not sign Catholics ..., but it would seem that they operate other restrictions as well ... Thus while Rangers' policy of not playing Catholics is often attacked (and, presumably applauded) in Scotland, to the sociologist it is just as odd that they have *never* signed a top-class Englishman. Up to 1980 the club had had 112 Scottish internationalists among their players but not *one* English internationalist.[101] (original emphases)

So Moorhouse announced the discovery of another discriminatory practice by Rangers. Moorhouse is correct. That policy would be odd. Then, again, his discovery is untrue. As a result, Moorhouse does not demonstrate the determination of Rangers' efforts to ease 'identification' with the nation or that Rangers 'is unwilling to translate its great financial power so as to break out of the role of being clearly seen to represent the nation – of being the more or less unsullied champion of (protestant) Scotland'.[102] Nor was it necessary to advocate that Scottish football, in the case of Rangers, 'broke free from its pure Scottish identity'.[103] Only Catholics were unacceptable at Ibrox: by its signing policy Rangers showed that it was an anti-Catholic club, not simply a Protestant one. Rangers throughout the century had played a small number of players from a variety of countries.[104] English players were not discriminated against. In official club publications Rangers boasted of past successful English players.[105]

That pride is most obviously expressed in an official history actually cited by Moorhouse in a previous article:[106]

> The year 1909 brought three new gallants to the colours, men of brawn and sensitivity who quickly assimilated the 'feeling' of being a Ranger, something that cannot be bought, something intangible, yet is there within you strong and uplifting and, at times, almost overpowering. They were Willie Reid, the centre-forward with the dynamite in his boots, Herbert Lock, the daring Southampton goalkeeper, and William Hogg, the doughty forward. Hogg cost us just £100, yet he was one of the finest forwards in England and had represented his country against Scotland, Wales and Ireland in 1902. He played for us in various positions in the forward line before settling down at outside right. He gave the impression of a big boy bubbling over with animal spirit. Lock was a signed player for us three weeks before Hogg, and he was, therefore, the first Englishman to be brought from England to wear the colours. Tom Murray, who had already worn Light Blue, was English-born, but he joined us from Aberdeen. Lock played ten seasons for us and helped in the winning of five League Championships.[107]

So Rangers not only signed Englishmen, and at least *one* English international in Hogg, but these players were readily accepted into Rangers and quickly seen to be representative of Rangers. That they were English would not conflict with the Unionist and anti-Catholic prejudices manifest in Rangers, a club that represented a form of being Scottish-British. Instead, these English players were perfectly acceptable and very well able to represent the identity and ethos projected by Rangers.

However, drawing in part on his 'discovery' of Rangers' anti-English policy, Moorhouse was later to judge 'anti-Englishness [to be] the essence which defines Scottishness'.[108] Now there is a worrying trend towards anti-Englishness in relation to Scottish football and society, and one that Murray, as we have seen, slips into on occasion too. Yet in neither Scottish football nor Scottish society has this been some historically continuous force.[109] In the past Scottish football has often represented a sense of a common Britishness, in union with England.[110] Despite Moorhouse's own claims, Rangers represented one expression of this British social identity. More often, and in harmony with the expression of this specific Scottish-British identity, it was opposition to Catholics and to the Irish (or more properly their descendants) that acted as one of the most important markers of Scottishness.[111] Nonetheless, indirectly Moorhouse was correct: anti-English sentiment has been on the rise in Scottish society. That should act as another warning that Scots are not immune to xenophobic prejudice and provide another antidote to the complacent, smug and self-congratulatory acceptance by too many Scots of their self-awarded prize of inherent egalitarianism. Nonetheless, that potential message is obscured. Instead, Moorhouse plays down, and sometimes claims the near eradication, of the only form of societal prejudice, albeit disguised by use of 'sectarianism', that is commonly accepted to be present in Scotland.

Paradoxically though, Moorhouse does not totally relinquish his own use of various interpretations of 'sectarianism',[112] as is apparent when Moorhouse explores how changes in European football impact on Scottish football. It is in this context that he discusses the 1989 signing by Rangers of Maurice Johnston, the first clear breach in the club's no-Catholics policy.[113] Moorhouse still cannot deny the role of ethnicity in Scottish football, as he tries to explore these processes of change; after all, ethnicity remains identified by him as the second important factor that structures Scottish football.[114] So, although Moorhouse does his best to play down its effect, he continues to vacillate in his assessment of its influence on events around Scottish football. The contradictions in his position become ever more apparent when he turns his attention to Edinburgh and tries to explore the relationship between the capital city of Scotland and Heart of Midlothian and Hibernian. Moorhouse's confusion over the social reality of the ethnic divisions in Scotland is evident as he struggles to come to terms with the symbolism of Hearts and Hibs, while trying to make his way through the tale of the projected take-over of Hibernian by Wallace Mercer, the chairman of the rival Hearts.

Moorhouse immediately has to recognize that these 'two of Scotland's "big clubs"' were also 'linked into the ethnic divide though never in ways as pronounced as the Glasgow clubs'.[115] In describing the intensely negative response from those associated with both clubs, Moorhouse states that 'This is not at all to say that Mercer was hit by a 'wave of violence' or 'sectarian hatred' but he did appear to be unprepared for the reaction provoked', which Mercer denounced as 'tribalism'. Moorhouse presents Mercer as claiming to have won the 'business argument', but conceding publicly that he had lost the 'social argument'. In private, Mercer observed that the 'existence of 'Protestant/Unionist Hearts' and 'Roman Catholic/Republican Hibs' was another factor he had failed to contend with.' Mercer claimed never to have experienced 'sectarianism' before. As Moorhouse notes: 'Which is an attempt to suggest that the middle class areas of the cities may not exhibit ethnic division in the same ways as working class areas. Still, the middle class of this most middle class of cities certainly did get involved ...' And Moorhouse then quotes top Edinburgh legal figures in favour of Edinburgh football's 'tribalism'.

None of this quite fits Moorhouse's overall argument, nor does his subsequent identification of the role of Catholic entrepreneurs, who were not really interested in football, in saving Hibs.[116] However, he does manage to detect one sign of modernization in inter-ethnic relations, but one that others had failed to hail:

> In the end some Catholic entrepreneurs stepped in to buy just enough shares to protect Hibs' independence while declaring they were not really concerned with football but thought Edinburgh should have two clubs, 'in the interests of the city's community' (*Glasgow Herald*, 13 June 1990). For whatever reason, and again to no big fanfare, Mercer recently appointed the first Catholic football manager Hearts have ever had. The remaining unresolved matter is the future and what it holds for clubs even as big on the Scottish scene as Hearts and Hibs if Rangers do pursue Euro-ambitions.[117]

There was a very good reason for the absence of a fanfare[118] for this appointment: it would have sounded off-key. Moorhouse's assertion deserves the red card. The first Catholic manager of Hearts was a former player with city rivals Hibernian, James McGhee, who was appointed to the post in 1908.[119] Now, to lose one set of historical figures, as Moorhouse does with Rangers' English players is carelessness, but to lose yet another, this time the first Catholic manager of Hibs, is to establish a pattern: Moorhouse's research and analyses are simply unreliable.[120] False claims and grand tales are relayed on the back of Moorhouse's strong beliefs. McGhee is of importance not just for being the first Catholic manager: his appointment by Hearts in 1908 is another cautionary reminder of the dangers in assuming continuous (and continuing) historical progress in intergroup relations. The installation of McGhee as manager shows an openness on the part of the Hearts board near the beginning of the twentieth century that was not to be matched until close to its end. Sadly McGhee's reign was a very brief one. In the eyes of too many his ethnic background and his religion were hindrances to him.[121] He only lasted to mid-season 1909–10, and was dismissed after problems with the playing-staff, especially the club's local hero, Bobby Walker.[122] It was some 80 years before Hearts risked the appointment of another Catholic as club manager.

Moorhouse believes that the ethnic symbolism around Scottish football is not to be taken too seriously.[123] Perhaps that is why he can pursue his research in a less than rigorous manner. Nonetheless, he is correct to identify examples of overstatement about the extent of this Scottish ethnic divide; there can also be forms of supposed humour. Unfortunately, these are not signs that prejudice is absent: 'humour' and overstatement are no strangers to societal prejudices. The underlying problem is once again the genuine misunderstanding of prejudice, its different forms of expression, and its complexity. The problem is that there is a very serious side to prejudice, and a very serious side to the ethnic dimension in Scottish football. This neglect of rigour leads him into especially dangerous territory.

From themes like these: the endorsement of traditions of anti-Irish racism and racist identities

Moorhouse examined two fanzines: *Not the View* (*NTV*) was first produced by Celtic fans in 1987; *Follow, Follow* (*FF*) was established by Rangers fans in 1988. Moorhouse ambitiously tried to explore a number of different themes. One result was that his study loses focus in places, but there is a consistent concentration on the relationship of these fanzines to 'sectarianism'. He comments that *FF* persistently applies 'derogatory' and 'relentlessly humourless and, deprecating references' to Celtic and the Celtic support, that 'very often ... take on a sharp political edge'. According to *FF*, Celtic is not to be viewed as a football club but as 'a pseudo-religious, paramilitary organisation'. Despite this demonstration of prejudice against Celtic and its support, like Murray, *FF* accuses all associated with Celtic to suffer from 'paranoia'. Indeed, the fanzine believes that the club is treated too favourably and its 'support'[124] for the IRA[125] neglected by the media. *FF* provides 'connections' between Celtic & 'IRA sympathisers', of which according to Moorhouse the 'most spectacular' was when the then editor of the *Celtic View*, the club's official newspaper, was taped 'condoning IRA bombings'. At a social event set up by another magazine, to which both he and the editor of the *Celtic View* had been invited to explore 'sectarianism' in Scotland, the editor of *FF* taped the editor of the *Celtic View*. A very drunken *Celtic View* editor reportedly tried to defend the totally indefensible: he argued that the IRA bomb on Remembrance Day in Enniskillen in 1988 was justified.[126] Celtic strenuously made its opposition to his comments clear, and his editorship of *Celtic View* was ended.

There is a very mixed message from *FF* on the issue of violence, and an even more perplexing position on bigotry. Moorhouse quotes *FF*: 'We have not, and will not, encourage bigotry or violent attacks on other fans.'[127] Nonetheless, the fanzine has defended fan violence. It defended Rangers fans who had fought with police determined to remove a Union flag the fans had displayed. *FF* denied that this was hooliganism, but was instead a form of patriotism to be equated with 'the same devotion to our country's flag ... exemplified at the Boyne, the Somme, Passchendale, Tobruk, El Alamein and Monte Cassino'.[128] Now, although there can be a problem in interpreting the meaning behind the display of United Kingdom Union and Irish tricolour flags in association with Celtic and Rangers, for *FF* interpretation of the Irish tricolour, the emblem of the Irish State, is easy: it is simply the '"fascist tricolour" of the IRA'.[129] Despite this identification of Irishness with the IRA, one of the most common manifestations of modern anti-Irish racism,[130] *FF* claims to be opposed to racism. Moorhouse explains that *FF* claims not to attack Irishness or religion, but racism, bigotry and support for 'IRA sectarian gangs' and that 'many Celtic supporters and the club fall into these categories'![131]

Nonetheless, *FF* very firmly defends the singing of loyalist paramilitary[132] and Orange songs. On behalf of *FF*, Moorhouse summarizes the *FF* argument that 'No-one could find them offensive unless they were social workers, IRA sympathisers, anti–Protestant bigots or some combination of these.'[133] Presumably it is in this context that the fanzine argues that 'Glasgow isn't and never was Belfast. The songs and chants in support of the UVF or IRA are all pretty Mickey Mouse.'[134] *FF* here makes two points worth some elaboration. That Glasgow is not Belfast should be such a truism as not to require statement. Yet, *FF* is correct: sadly this point not only deserves consistent repetition, but some care in interpretation too. That Glasgow is not Belfast ought to help put the ethnic divide in Scotland into proper perspective, but that proper perspective cannot be obtained by denying that this ethnic division remains to be remedied. There can also be little doubt that for the vast majority of those supporters, of either club, who participate in these songs and chants, that this activity marks the limit of their association with militant loyalism or republicanism. However, that does not mean these gestures are acceptable. It is even more intriguing then, that *FF* argues participation in republican songs and chants is offensive, but opposition to loyalist songs and chants is the sign of a bigoted IRA sympathizer.[135] In addition, *FF* strongly supports Protestantism and argues that Rangers can remain proud of this religious association, because Protestantism was 'historically associated with pluralism and liberalism'.[136]

Moorhouse is unable to see the contradictions in the *FF* positions. He takes at face value its denial that it is bigoted and proceeds towards his adoption of the *FF* view of 'sectarianism' in Scotland. As a result, he simultaneously accepts some of the charges *FF* makes against Celtic supporters. He wonders:

> What are 'sectarianism' and 'religious bigotry' exactly? How significant are they in modern Scotland? Do Scottish authorities condone the songs, flags and slogans of the Celtic support which do, often, seem to express support for organisations committed to the breaking up of the 'United' Kingdom and which conduct bombing campaigns in English cities?[137]

Moorhouse then uses this stance, directly derived from the perspective of *FF*, to interrogate the content of *NTV*. He judges that '*Not The View* is virtually silent about what *Follow Follow* charges Celtic and its supporters with – support for the IRA and its tactics. In short, the Celtic fanzine adopts a routine, unreflective easy portrayal of the significance of "sectarianism" in Scotland ...'[138] It is not yet clear exactly what these comments on the *NTV* stance on 'sectarianism' mean. There is no good reason either why he should believe that the agenda for *NTV* should be determined by the line promoted by *FF*. Nor is it clear why he neglects his own extracts from *NTV* as evidence against this bizarre *FF* accusation that Celtic is 'a pseudo-religious, paramilitary organisation'. *NTV* supported the Celtic board's campaign against the singing of any religious or political songs by fans. Moreover, *NTV* makes its position clear that it will refuse to become involved in the politics of 'the highly emotive subject of Ireland: a subject which we will continue to avoid in the pages of *NTV* since we agree that Celtic Football Club is not the context within which to address such issues'.[139] Moorhouse comments that *NTV* makes frequent attacks on the 'sectarianism' of Rangers. He expands on this supposedly 'unreflective' *NTV* view of 'sectarianism': '*Not the View* promotes the ideology that there is widespread discrimination, systematic discrimination, in Scottish society against Catholics and Celtic football club though its writers sometimes wonder if this is just their own "paranoia".'[140]

Moorhouse's own evidence then is that *NTV* argues that there is widespread 'sectarianism' in Scottish society. *FF* disputes this account, denies the *NTV* view of 'sectarianism', but instead promotes the belief that Celtic, its support, and the IRA are, in effect, interchangeable.[141] Both fanzines clearly stake out identity positions based on this ethnic division in Scotland. Given his own evidence, Moorhouse's final summary of his study is puzzling, and becomes ever more so, the further he develops it. He undertakes a meandering account of his own, academically uninformed,[142] view of the significance of social identities, which he then relates to this ethnic division in Scotland, before concluding that these social identities no longer exist in any meaningful way. Moreover, he claims that the circumstances that these social identities depend upon 'are highly unlikely to occur in Modern Scotland'. He argues that his 'case study of the two major fanzines reveals that they can hardly be judged as agencies for promoting any profound "sectarian" *activity* in Scotland. Both fanzines preach against sectarianism and have little to say to their readers about religion in any form' (original emphasis). Moorhouse's summary again flies in the face of his own evidence. He states that both 'preach against' 'sectarianism', but what he has shown is that both are preaching against the 'other side', which is further evidence of the relevance of social identities.

Moorhouse then claims that '*talk* of ethnic antagonism is rather more prevalent than evidence of meaningful ethnic division. Analysts slide too easily between was and what is, there is a sleight of hand from rhetoric to reality.' It is Moorhouse here who is bamboozled by his own semantic legerdemain. Here he denies the very social significance of the expression of prejudice, which is what happens in talk, and why this *activity* is important. The power of the prejudicial word has been widely recognized, which is why there is now State legislation against prejudicial talk.[143] Moorhouse, in his study of the fanzines, has produced considerable evidence of exactly this form of talk, especially from *FF*, which he now simply ignores.[144]

He then challenges Finn's attempt to present these persistent prejudices against Celtic and the Irish-Scots community as a deep-rooted psychological response dependent on traditional Scottish societal beliefs about this minority community. Moorhouse charges:

> Nor will it do to claim that, 'anti-Irish and anti-Catholic sentiments are dredged up from the murky depths of those as yet inadequately analysed but commonly shared collective myths' or that, 'Ireland and things Irish still induce a strong, almost visceral anti-Irish sentiment in many Scots and a desire that Irish associations be "eliminated"', when what *Follow Follow* argues, with more evidence than diviners of contemporary 'sectarianism' usually provide, is that Celtic and their fans seem to show support for groups who advocate the use of, and use, weapons against civilian targets in many parts of the United Kingdom. Talking about 'dual identities', the validity of 'honouring' Irish roots, 'conspiracy theories', and asserting that the failure of Scottish society to recognise the validity of different Scottish social identities has been well captured in the treatment of the Irish Scots soccer clubs (Finn, 1991, p. 383) scarcely gets to the roots of this criticism of a continuing 'Irish connection'...[145]

Now, in fact, *FF*'s persistent reliance on social identities is clear in Moorhouse's extracts. Indeed, *FF* provides a textbook case of the ascription of a derogatory and dangerous social identity onto a minority community. As a result, ethnic identities cannot be dismissed as insignificant in Scotland. Moorhouse's own account underlines the power of the *FF* belief that 'Celtic and their fans' are involved with the IRA. He provides one of the clearest examples of the way that Irish-Scots are denied a 'dual identity' and are forbidden to '"honour" Irish roots'. It is this very effort to do so, the very effort to declare that duality, that makes the minority such objects of, in Murray's terms, 'suspicion'. Now this is the realist model of prejudice being applied with a vengeance. For *FF* that Irish connection is no less than direct association with the activities of the IRA, who have been engaged, literally, in an armed conspiracy against the British State. The consistent thundering of this viewpoint by *FF* provides direct support for Finn's argument.

Moorhouse should have critically engaged with the absurdities emanating from *FF*, a process that should have inevitably led him to revise his views of the nature of intergroup relations associated with Rangers and Celtic in Scotland. Instead, he took the only other option if he was to escape from his own self-imposed contradiction. He disregards his own evidence of the extreme anti-Irish and anti-Catholic prejudices propagated by *FF*, and instead endorses the *FF* case. Moorhouse agrees that *FF* presents sound criticism of Celtic and its fans: he accepts *FF*'s criticism to be a valid one based on a valid arguments.[146] Although the case-study of *FF* presents sufficient evidence to justify *NTV*'s complaints, Moorhouse dismissed the *NTV* account of 'sectarianism' as an 'unreflective easy portrayal of the significance of "sectarianism" in Scotland'. Now it is he who urges that the use of 'sectarianism' be halted. His own account shows precisely why a much clearer description of exactly what does constitutes 'sectarianism' is so essential.

It is then almost a relief to turn to Murray, and find, if somewhat belatedly, that he is very critical of what he now describes as the 'open bigotry and racism' of *FF*.[147] Looking at some more recent issues of the fanzine, Murray reports even more comments consistent with those treated with such generosity by Moorhouse. *FF* describes Celtic as a club 'steeped in bigotry and support for terrorism', and claims that it was 'founded by bigots, for bigots, with the purpose of bigotry its main aim'. Murray condemns *FF* for 'equating every Celtic fan with gun-happy terrorists' and advises that *FF* 'give up the ludicrous notion that the club is in thrall to the IRA'.[148] Unfortunately, the relief offered by Murray is short-lived. Although he condemns *FF*, his own analysis has too many points of overlap with that of *FF*. He very wrongly claims that Rangers fans have ceased anti-Irish and anti-Catholic songs and chants. But what is one to make of Murray's campaign for the retention of some of those songs so loyally defended by *FF*? Murray wishes the Rangers support to roar out 'The Sash', the anthem of the Orange Order. Presumably he wishes the crowd to give voice to its usual version, with its obscene comments about the Pope?

That would certainly tie in with Murray's strong support for the anti-Catholic ditty 'No Pope of Rome'. It is sung to the tune of 'Home on the Range' and takes the form:

No, no Pope of Rome!
No chapels to sadden my eyes!

No nuns and no priests
And no rosary beads,
And every day is the Twelfth of July.[149]

Previously Murray merely acclaimed this anti-Catholic song to be one that 'stands out as being of some worth'.[150] Now, he gives full-throated support to this anti-Catholic anthem. He determines that it is inoffensive and should be sung because, according to Murray, it has 'little to do with present-day realities and as such can be seen to be more humorous than provocative'.[151] Yet this ditty celebrates the 'ideal' of a land, guided by Orange Order principles, and free of anything to do with Catholicism.[152] That Murray proclaims the song to be inoffensive is revealing, but consistent with his stance on the status of minority groups in Scottish society. Minorities are to be denied any voice in the matter: instead, they will be told what is deemed acceptable. His support for this song says much about his lack of judgement in the assessment of intergroup relations in Scotland, and elsewhere too.

Moreover, Murray, despite his protestations against *FF*, has in the past articulated a related position on Celtic and the IRA. Although the first Irish tricolour was a gift from the Irish State to honour Celtic's Irish connection, he has repeatedly attacked the flying of the Irish tricolour at Celtic Park. Most recently, however, he has quietly reversed his position on this matter.[153] Murray was, though, in the past also guilty of adding to, rather than exposing, the confusion of Irishness with the IRA, which has been the repeated complaint of members of the Irish and Irish-descended community in Britain. He commented that 'The tricolour is the flag of the Irish Republic and to many a symbol of IRA terrorism.'[154] Now that argument should have led to demands that the Union flag that also flies over Celtic Park be lowered too. After all, it is equally as true, and just as illogical (and as preposterous) to write that 'The Union flag is the flag of the United Kingdom and to many a symbol of both loyalist terrorism and fascist parties.' The appropriation of national flags by paramilitary groups cannot make the national flags illegitimate. Indeed, as both republican and loyalist paramilitary groups are outlawed by the Irish and UK governments, this is simply an unacceptable position.

Murray did recognize that the attacks on Celtic for displaying the Irish tricolour in 1952 were no more than evidence of bigotry against the minority community. It was sad that he failed to recognize the sheer illogicality, bigotry, and even more dangerous nature of the argument that to continue to fly the Irish tricolour can somehow be seen as support for republican paramilitaries.[155] It is even more important that this contemporary version of anti-Irish bigotry be resisted. Yet he stated:

> In the period after 1969 and the civil war in Ulster the flying of the Irish tricolour took on a new significance, and the club's refusal to take it down could be seen, despite its strenuous denials, as giving some support for the terrorist atrocities being committed in the name of that flag. In Ulster that is certainly how Celtic are seen, just as Rangers are seen as the champions of the Protestant cause.

Fortunately, such a crude view, in which Rangers champion Protestantism, while Celtic support republican 'terrorist atrocities', does not dominate everybody's thinking in Northern Ireland.[156]

Prejudice, Discrimination and Extermination

Prejudice is a very complex social phenomenon, and capable of expression in quite different ways. In his classic study, G. Allport identified different levels of intensity: talk (anti-locution), avoidance, discrimination, physical attack and extermination. Allport noted how 'polite prejudice' can be seen to be harmless when restricted to 'idle chatter', but that there was a progression, and each level of activity is made easier by the actions taking place at the level below.[157] More recent research has identified the significant role of the talk of political, media and academic elites in the reproduction of ethnic dominance and racism.[158] Sadly Murray and Moorhouse do reproduce dominant, traditional accounts, that have been common in the media. Murray flirted repeatedly with accounts that skirted around categorizing Irish-Scots associated with Celtic to be associates of the IRA. His reversal on this position is to be welcomed. It is more than unfortunate that Moorhouse appears to endorse the *FF* account that asserts this to be a general truth.

The failure of media and academic accounts to analyse this culture of prejudice, but instead to participate in its reproduction is not only regrettable, but unacceptable. Spurious legitimization is provided for a realist theory of prejudice in which the minority is held primarily responsible for the way that it is treated. That adds to the culture of prejudice. This whole circular process is exemplified by Murray's judgement that suspicion is an inevitable result of the minority community's own actions. Now the existence of that culture of prejudice does not diminish the responsibility of individuals for their own actions. That is true whether their contributions take the form of writing, producing fanzines, or more serious activities. Nonetheless, this culture of prejudice does help explain why individuals do see the minority so negatively. And, as a result, all forms of prejudice identified by Allport are potential outcomes.

That is why it is so unacceptable when Murray treats intergroup murder as something apart; something that cannot fit into this culture of prejudice, rather than as an extreme example of the intensity to which this prejudice can be taken. He comments that 'every society has its pathological criminals, and in Scotland this can occasionally be given a sectarian label'.[159] He then briefly examines the murder of Celtic fan Mark Scott by Jason Campbell in 1995. Scott was merely making his way back to the city centre from Celtic Park. The direct route goes through the Bridgeton area of Glasgow, still an area with a strong loyalist presence. There, in an unprovoked assault, he had his throat cut from behind him by Campbell. Murray notes that Campbell was 'well-known for his hatred of Catholics' and that his father and uncle were imprisoned 'for serious crimes associated with the UVF'.

Murray's apparent wish now to avoid the use of 'sectarian' for this crime again identifies the need for much greater clarity in determining precisely what is being discussed. This culture of prejudice in Scotland, complete with the rhetoric that justifies treating Irish-Scots with suspicion, and for some includes excusing allegations that Celtic and its fans are to be identified with the IRA, provides enough of a framework of beliefs that will lead to some people advancing to this extreme level of intense prejudice. Now this act is an extreme, and atypical, example of this prejudice.[160] Nonetheless, this extreme end of the spectrum of prejudice is as much one form of its expression as is the banal and much more common form of prejudicial talk. Moorhouse's dismissal of one extreme, the banal, everyday expression of prejudice, and Murray's dismissal of the other extreme, the atypical and horrific expression of prejudice through murder, reveals the different, but equally limited, understanding that each has of the nature of prejudice.

Jason Campbell's family connections in the UVF included some highly significant figures. His uncle 'Big Bill' Campbell was very well known in Belfast, and when he died, following an illness, one of the murals just off the Shankill was dedicated to his memory in the summer of 1997.[161] Jason Campbell's family associations with the UVF returned him to the media spotlight in October. One of the earliest consequences of the Northern Irish peace process was that prisoners held in prison in Britain were returned to Northern Ireland to serve their time. Few loyalist paramilitaries were held in prisons in Britain, as most offences committed had taken place in Northern Ireland. The UVF suspected that the United Kingdom government was more impressed by the IRA ceasefire. To test out the sincerity of the British government, the Progressive Unionist Party (PUP), the political wing of the UVF, short of suitable UVF prisoners, included Campbell in what it termed its 'shopping list', and requested that he be allowed to serve out his time in Belfast.

Once the story broke, it led to an uproar.[162] One of the most significant features in this dispute was the outrage expressed by loyalist paramilitaries, who see themselves as soldiers fighting on behalf of the United Kingdom.[163] To them, Campbell was nothing but a simple murderer. A senior UVF member in Glasgow denounced the request. He even added that the UVF was so disgusted by Campbell's actions that he would be killed by the organization. He claimed that the PUP had been advised not to make this proposal. He countered: 'Jason Campbell is scum. He is not one of us. He is a Rangers fan who made up his mind to cut the throat of a young Celtic fan. The UVF doesn't kill Celtic fans. We kill the IRA but we don't kill football fans.'[164] It is a salutary lesson to learn that members of the UVF are much more able to recognize that Celtic and its fans have no association with the IRA than are some fanzines or academic commentators.

David Ervine, one of the PUP leaders in Northern Ireland, apologized for the upset caused, especially to Mark Scott's family, and he admitted that it had been a poor suggestion. Nonetheless, Ervine did offer an intriguing justification for the proposed move of Campbell, and one that showed that he also had a much better grasp of the complexity of prejudice than many others too. He argued that Campbell's family wished him to be moved to Northern Ireland and placed among UVF prisoners who would then help to rehabilitate him. Ervine said:

> In Scotland there isn't any hope of Jason Campbell being anything other than the sectarian person who made that attack. But UVF prisoners who have trickled out of the Maze are productive members of the community. They are changed people. Jason

> Campbell is a victim of our creation. His family have had sustained amounts of grief but a transfer will perhaps save them from further grief. They want him where there will be an influence and control and where he can see a different view of the world.

Ervine did by then have to make the best of what was a very poor situation, and one which had presented the newly emerging PUP in a catastrophic light. Nonetheless, there can be no doubt that Campbell was very much a product of his social environment. Confirmation of the power of that value-system followed very soon afterwards. In November 1977 there was a very similar attack on another Celtic fan making his way home. Sean O'Connor had his throat cut in a similar manner to that of Mark Scott. He was lucky to survive. The assailant was Campbell's friend Thomas Longstaff.[165] Ironically in Northern Ireland, Ervine is right: many prisoners and former prisoners are working very hard to overcome their own prejudices. Certainly those who have been close to the former UVF leader, Gusty Spence, such as David Ervine himself, attest to how their time in prison with Spence did lead them away from violence and to attempt to understand the nature of Northern Irish society and its problems. One very significant witness of the most recent actions of these men has called them 'missionaries for peace' and that, by observing them, he has 'come to believe more deeply than ever before in the power of human redemption'. That man is Senator George Mitchell, who has been such a significant influence on, and close observer of, the peace process in Northern Ireland.[166] Ervine was wrong to apply to have Campbell transferred. However, he was correct to identify the need to create the circumstances in which prejudice can be combated: he was correct that Scotland has still yet much to do.

CONCLUSION: TRADITION AND COMBATING PREJUDICE IN SCOTTISH SOCIETY

There is a serious problem with a society that is so determined not to face up to the range and extent of the societal prejudices contained within it. Scottish myths befog much of the social terrain. A wind of change is needed to blow them away. Beliefs in some Scottish essentialism that leads to an immunity from racism and other global forms of prejudice is truly a nasty case of myopia. Academics need critically to dissect, not reproduce, traditional self-serving justifications about the nature of Scottish society. Accurate accounts of the history of Scottish football and critical analysis of the dominant tales that surround the contemporary sport offer one important way forward.

Education should become a means by which societal prejudices can be tackled, rather than a topic around which further false narratives of minority responsibility for social problems can be spun. Lessons can be learned from educational programmes developed in Northern Ireland. A similar programme to Education for Mutual Understanding is long overdue, and in Scotland it must be linked into anti-racist and anti-discriminatory programmes.[167] In part that is because of the way that 'sectarianism' can be readily transferred to provide negative accounts of other minority communities too.[168] That adds to the need to dispense with the unhelpful label of 'sectarianism', which obscures the reality of anti-Irish racism, and the way that form of racism is interwoven with anti-Catholic prejudice too. Anti-Protestant prejudices in Scotland must also be tackled. The development of an educational programme of this nature could disabuse learners of their acceptance that races do exist.

In the context of Scottish football a sustained attack on racism in all its forms is long overdue.[169] Moreover, it will become ever more urgent to explain the Irishness of Celtic more sympathetically. One of the surprising consequences of the modernization of Scottish football is that it appears to be leading Celtic to place much greater emphasis on its Irish ancestry than it has for some decades.[170] There is an obvious reason for this rediscovery of its diasporic identity. Not only does that rediscovery provide greater marketing opportunities for the club throughout Ireland,[171] but a much clearer focus on Celtic as a *joint* Irish and Scottish club *may* allow it to grow into a genuinely global soccer presence. As the influence of television, particularly the impact of television income, becomes ever more important, then clubs from countries with smaller television audiences risk being disregarded by the emergence of super-clubs with genuine global appeal. Celtic is limited by its location in a small country with a population of some 5 million people. However, if Celtic could become the global footballing representative of the *Celtic*, Irish *and* Scottish, diaspora, that would allow the club to enter a different ball-game.

Rangers, one of the richest clubs in world football, is also restricted by the very small pond of Scottish football, but it is assumed to have the potential to become a team with a global purpose. Walker pondered whether the signing of Maurice Johnston in 1989 would halt or interrupt the traditions of Rangers.[172] The problem is that the signing of the first Catholic by Rangers was not a gesture of reconciliation, but instead, as both Murray and Moorhouse recognize, presented as a means of putting one over on Celtic. Rangers sign Catholics but they now retain more than an image problem: they now have a serious identity problem. Since 1994 other Catholics have been signed, but they have been forbidden to bless themselves on the field by the club.[173] Meanwhile, despite this Catholic presence in the ranks of Rangers, other players play around with loyalist symbolism. Paul Gascoigne pretended to play an Orange Order flute on three different occasions, which reveals much about the seriousness with which it was treated in the club. Other English players adopted other Orange poses too.[174] There have been persistent reports of after-match celebrations at which loyalist and Orange standards have been sung.

The most revealing celebration took place on the night that Rangers celebrated winning the 'treble' of the main Scottish trophies in 1999. An official supporters' event at the Rangers ground was visited by the players, who took a break from the club's own official celebrations, which were being held elsewhere in the stadium complex. The players took the Scottish Cup with them, won that day in the final against Celtic. The party included the deputy chairman of Rangers, Donald Findlay, QC, who is also a prominent Scottish Conservative, a leading Scottish legal figure, and was the rector of St Andrews University, Scotland's oldest university.

At the Rangers celebration, Findlay joked about how the club had no longer to be seen to be 'sectarian', prompting laughter from those gathered there. Then he added that: 'You have to be very careful or you end up on the front page of *The Daily Record*.' He did,[175] and he was to appear on many other front pages and television news bulletins too. Someone had taken a video of his performance as Findlay then launched into what seemed to be the full Rangers repertoire of loyalist and Orange songs. He was joined in this singing by some of the players. In one of the songs they sang of being up to their 'knees in Fenian blood' and uttered the challenge, 'Surrender or you'll die'.[176] This song honours the Billy Boys from Bridgeton, an early loyalist and also fascist gang. Fenian is a pejorative term for Irish or Catholics.[177] Findlay's performance came only a few hours after one young Celtic fan had been murdered and another was seriously injured when he was wounded by a shot fired from a crossbow.

Once the story broke, Findlay met his friend the Rangers chairman, David Murray, and he offered his resignation, which was then accepted. Although Findlay's performance continues to resonate, its real significance is still to be fully grasped in Scottish society or, for that matter, by Findlay himself. His opposition to the banning of either racist or 'sectarian' chanting was already a matter of public record. Moreover, he was also spell-bound by Scottish myths: neither of these prejudices was a problem in Scotland; for example, the exclusion of Asian-Scots was simply because they were not good enough yet to play in Scottish football. Findlay summed up his views:

> In short, I don't think Scottish football has a 'racism' or 'sectarian' problem, although that doesn't mean we should be complacent about it. But to ban chanting on the basis that it is sectarian is not only impossible to implement, it would ruin the game as we know it ... the regular songs are part of a tradition and no-one has the right to tell someone else that their beliefs are wrong.[178]

Findlay should have known much better by 1999. As one school friend of the murdered Mark Scott pointed out, Findlay had been defence counsel for Campbell, and should have learned much more about the grip of this prejudice on Scotland, and its consequences too.[179] As Findlay had also been the defence lawyer for Longstaff, he had been given another opportunity to realize the significance of supposedly banal societal prejudices on the actions on others.

In what was to prove his valedictory address as a club official, Findlay criticized the 'anti-Rangers brigade'. He wrote:

> Rangers is the greatest Club in the world, not the greatest team, but we will continue to pursue that goal. Our greatness comes from the fact we stand together and we believe in what we stand for ... It's the club that matters. Not individuals. We will always do what we believe is right for Rangers where success and tradition go hand in hand. And to those who do not like us – frankly we do not care.[180]

The question has to be exactly what do Rangers now 'stand for' and what is the club's 'tradition', previously identified by Findlay, in part, as being the very songs that he had to resign over. This is another tradition to be faced up to, and analysed, if prejudice in Scottish society is to be challenged and, for this, Rangers does need to care. Critical engagement with Rangers will be necessary to move that club, and a substantial section of Scottish society, truly forward. Although Rangers has signed Catholics in the last decade, the club seems stuck, facing two ways. It takes pride in an unexplained past, which is closely identified with the practice of discrimination: signing Catholics players can be presented as little more than the need to select from as wide a pool as possible to ensure that the team is successful, while the club somehow remains the same, as Findlay implies.[181] The problem for Scottish society is that Rangers needs to be seen to have embraced change for principled reasons. It needs to be more open about the past, and explain why that policy operated. It should display a genuine openness to Catholics and the practices and symbols of their religion within the club. It needs to own up to the past injustice of its former discriminatory policy, offer an apology and a promise of future justice for all minorities in Scotland. In that way Rangers can make a massive step forward, and be identified with, and represent, interethnic reconciliation in Scotland. That would be a worthwhile identity to project onto the global football stage.

NOTES

1. 'Sectarianism' is an especially unhelpful term. For further discussions of its inadequacy, see G.P.T. Finn, '"Sectarianism" and Scottish Education', in T.G.K. Bryce and W.M. Humes (eds.), *Scottish Education* (Edinburgh, 1999); G.P.T. Finn, 'Prejudice in the History of Irish Catholics in Scotland', invited paper in symposium 'Sectarianism in the West of Scotland', Annual Conference of the History Workshop Journal, Glasgow (1990a); G.P.T. Finn, 'Racism, Religion and Social Prejudice: Irish Catholic Clubs, Soccer and Scottish Society: I The Historical Roots of Prejudice', *International Journal of the History of Sport* (hereafter *IJHS*), 8 (1991a), 70–93; G.P.T. Finn, 'Racism, Religion and Social Prejudice: Irish Catholic Clubs, Soccer and Scottish Society: II Social Identities and Conspiracy Theories', *IJHS*, 8 (1991b), 370–97. P. Dimeo and G.P.T. Finn, 'Scottish Racism, Scottish Identities: the case of Partick Thistle', in A. Brown (ed.), *Fanatics! Power, Identity and Fandom in Football* (London, 1998); P. Dimeo and G.P.T. Finn, 'Racism, National Identity and Scottish Football', in B. Carrington, and I. McDonald (eds.), *Racism in British Sport* (London, 2000).
2. See, for example, G.P.T. Finn, 'Football Violence: A Societal Psychological Perspective', in R. Giulianotti, N. Bonney and M. Hepworth (eds.), *Football, Violence and Social Identity* (London, 1994a).
3. See Armstrong and Young, in this collection, for examples from the range of fan exchanges.
4. Paradoxically, when racist abuse is obviously offensive, it may be presented as a form of hooliganism rather than racism, see L. Back, T. Crabbe and J. Solomos, 'Racism in Football: Patterns of Continuity and Change', in Brown (ed.), *Fanatics!*; Dimeo and Finn, 'Racism, National Identity and Scottish Football'.
5. See L. Back *et al.*, 'Racism in Football'; Dimeo and Finn, 'Scottish Racism, Scottish Identities'; Dimeo and Finn, 'Racism, National Identity and Scottish Football'.
6. G.P.T. Finn, 'Sporting Symbols, Sporting Identities: Soccer and Intergroup Conflict in Scotland and Northern Ireland', in I.S. Wood (ed.), *Scotland and Ulster* (Edinburgh, 1994b).
7. For variations on this approach: M. Billig, *Ideology and Opinions: Studies in Rhetorical Psychology* (London, 1991). M. Wetherell and J. Potter, *Mapping the Language of Racism: Discourse and the Legitimation of Exploitation* (London, 1992); T.A. van Dijk, *Communicating Racism: Ethnic Prejudice in Thought and Talk* (Newbury Park, CA, 1987); T.A. van Dijk, *Elite*

Discourse and Racism (Newbury Park, CA, 1993).

8. See B. Murray, *The Old Firm: Sectarianism, Sport and Society in Scotland* (Edinburgh, 1984) (hereafter *The Old Firm*); B. Murray, *Glasgow's Giants: 100 Years of the Old Firm* (Edinburgh, 1988) (hereafter *Glasgow's Giants*); B. Murray, *The Old Firm in the New Age: Celtic and Rangers since the Souness Revolution* (Edinburgh, 1998) (hereafter *The Old Firm in the New Age*).

9. See especially H.F. Moorhouse, 'Professional Football and Working-Class Culture': English Theories and Scottish Evidence', *Sociological Review*, 32 (1984), 285–315.

10. J. Fairgrieve, *The Rangers! Scotland's Greatest Football Team* (London, 1964). These views have not been uncommon in the media. The Rev. James Currie, unofficial chaplain to Rangers, repeated this account in various interviews. It could be presented as a defence of Rangers and, in addition, be accompanied by a denial that the club pursued an anti-Catholic policy. That left any accusations of prejudice firmly with the club's supporters, which was presented as a response to the supposedly provocatively 'sectarian' nature of Celtic.

11. van Dijk, *Elite Discourse and Racism*.

12. Moorhouse is erratic on this point, but usually interpreted as disputing its existence: see below. Moorhouse is intent on emphasizing an anti-English dimension to Scottish life. That does exist but, like all forms of prejudice, is complex, and much more complicated than Moorhouse's ahistorical caricature: see below. As a result, Moorhouse is seen to dismiss prejudice from Scotland. See Murray, *The Old Firm in the New Age*, pp.192–3.

13. For example, see R. Miles, *Racism and Migrant Labour* (London, 1982); R. Miles and A. Dunlop, 'Racism in Britain: The Scottish Dimension', in P. Jackson (ed.), *Race and Racism: Essays in Social Geography* (London, 1987). G.P.T. Finn, 'Multicultural Antiracism and Scottish Education', *Scottish Educational Review*, 19 (1987), 39–49; see also Finn, 1991a, b, 1999.

14. See Dimeo and Finn, 'Scottish Racism, Scottish Identities' and 'Racism, National Identity and Scottish Football'.

15. David McCrone, *Understanding Scotland. The Sociology of a Stateless Nation* (Routledge, 1992). McCrone believes that Scottish myths can be adapted for positive purposes; cf. Dimeo and Finn, 'Scottish Racism, Scottish Identities' and 'Racism, National Identity and Scottish Football'.

16. See Finn, 1999 for a fuller account of 'realist' theories of prejudice employed to defend majority groups. See also G.P.T. Finn, 'Thinking Uncomfortable Thoughts about Prejudice: is educational intervention prejudiced by a prejudice against prejudice?', *Psychology of Education Review* (2000, in press) for an attempt to relate how common notions about prejudice, and the reliance on overly simplistic models of prejudice, hinder efforts at prejudice reduction.

17. Murray, *Glasgow's Giants*, p.87.

18. See Murray, *The Old Firm*, p.100. He writes: '... the Scoto-Irish were faced by a social snobbery that verged at times on racial arrogance, caricatured on occasions as the Apes so beloved of some (mainly English) Victorian cartoonists. Far from being assimilated, which they would not have wanted in any case...' Murray manages to avoid specifying racism which slides into 'racial arrogance' but which is really no more than 'social snobbery'. Moreover, he sees this 'racial arrogance' to be more properly a phenomenon exhibited by those who were English. He also presents 'assimilation' to be the ideal strategy for majority-minority relations: see later, and Finn, 1987.

19. This use of 'paranoia' by Murray along with his seeming recognition of prejudice creates the illusion of balance and at first appears an advance on the common use of paranoia, which is to deny that there is prejudice. However, this 'balance' disappears in the face of any serious examination. The minority community is still held primarily to be at fault, and prejudice and paranoia become interchangeable.

20. Murray, *The Old Firm*, p.105.

21. 'Paranoia/bigotry, bias against' constitutes one of the biggest entries in the *Index* to Murray's 1984 book. The compiler of this index is correct. For Murray these concepts are interchangeable. See Murray, *The Old Firm*, p.287. Note that Murray's semantic gymnastics are in evidence in the section 'Prejudice or Paranoia', *The Old Firm*, pp.104–16. Here Murray concludes that paranoia grossly exaggerates the existence of any prejudice.

22. See, for example, *Diagnostic and Statistical Manual of Mental Disorders* (Washington, DC,

1994).

23. Murray, *The Old Firm in the New Age*, p.200: Murray attributes to me considerable power to influence others. However, the positions of myself, Bradley and Maley are not indistinguishable. My 'powers' of influence do not extend to Murray. He misinterprets or misrepresents my criticisms of his work. I have not criticized him for his 'secular' views (Murray, *The Old Firm in the New Age*, p.202).

24. van Dijk, *Elite Discourse and Racism*. The use of paranoia to define minority Irish-Scots and their actions deserves further study.

25. Murray only offers one specific rjeoinder to my earlier criticisms, and that is in a footnote, see Murray, *The Old Firm in the New Age*, pp.214–15. Murray identified some of the ludicrous consequences of 'Old Firm' rivalry (*The Old Firm*, p.13). One was opposition to a chair in Celtic Studies in Australia, because the average Scot was supposed to have an aversion to the word 'Celtic'. Murray made no comment on this ahistorical and inaccurate claim. I concluded that he 'apparently agrees' with the sentiment expressed (Finn, 1991a, 90). This still appears the likeliest interpretation. If I am wrong, I am sorry but content that this is the biggest error Murray could locate. The interpretation was made in the context of Murray's general refusal to see the establishment of Celtic as a positive intention of the Irish-Scots to participate in Scottish society. If he does now accept that Celtic was a name that represented common Irish and Scottish roots, then that contradicts his persistent rejection of the establishment of Celtic as a token of the Irish-Scottish community's intention to contribute as Irish-Scots to Scottish life: see, for example, Murray, *The Old Firm in the New Age*, p.142. Also see note 64 below.

26. M.J. Hickman and B. Walters, *Discrimination and the Irish Community in Britain. A report of research undertaken for the Commission for Racial Equality* (London, 1997). The report notes that there has been a dearth of research into this area and, as a result, it has in some places come to conclusions that require additional research and further scrutiny. Nonetheless, this report is a welcome addition to this debate.

27. This term was used to refer to their income generation, especially when playing one another, and to their dominant economic power within Scottish football.

28. See Finn, 1990b, 1991a, b, 1994b; Dimeo and Finn, 'Scottish Racism, Scottish Identities', and 'Racism, National Identity and Scottish Football'. And also G.P.T. Finn, 'Faith, Hope and Bigotry: Case-Studies in Anti-Catholic Prejudice in Scottish Soccer and Society', in G. Walker and G. Jarvie (eds.), *Sport, Leisure and Scottish Culture* (Leicester, 1994c).

29. Murray, *The Old Firm in the New Age*.

30. Finn, 1991a and 1994b, or so it appears: see note 31.

31. This acknowledgement is only displayed in a footnote. See Murray, *The Old Firm in the New Age*, p.211. Murray neglects to cite the Finn publications. Murray draws here on Finn (1994b), but also Finn (1991a), and elsewhere on Finn (1991b), but given his acerbic comments on these two *IJHS* articles (see Murray, *The Old Firm in the New Age*, pp.214–15), it is clear that to cite them would be a self-contradiction. So he does contradict himself, but just does not own up to doing so. He does cite Finn 1994c, which he now describes as 'excellent' (Murray, *The Old Firm in the New Age*, p.214). Murray's review of this collection (see *IJHS*, 12 (1995), 197–9) was very critical of this article. He has managed to reuse almost all of the comment from that earlier review that Finn is 'obsessed with the anti-Catholic sectarianism which he sees oozing out of every pore of the Scottish body politic' but now deploys it against Finn (1991 a, b) instead. It is informative to discover that this judgement can be made regardless of the particular content and substance of the article to which it is applied. It is a revelation to discover that Murray can replace his early scathing judgement with the later one of 'excellent'.

32. Neither Murray nor Moorhouse offers an explanation, though both provide various speculations.

33. For one of the few contemporary accounts of Scottish Freemasonry in its historical context, see: G.P.T. Finn, 'In the Grip?: A Psychological and Historical Exploration of the Social Significance of Freemasonry in Scotland', in T. Gallagher and G. Walker (eds.), *Sermons and Battle Hymns. Protestant Popular Culture in Modern Scotland* (Edinburgh, 1990b).

34. All quotes are from Murray, *The Old Firm in the New Age*, p.34.

35. Juxtapositions of contradictory evaluations abound in the Murray canon. However, this

specific one illustrates Murray's evasion of contradictory evidence.

36. Perhaps Murray's position is that all Scottish clubs with a Protestant membership were equally anti-Catholic, rather than 'only' Protestant in membership. If so, then this political opposition to Irish Home Rule, added to anti-Catholic views, should still have made Rangers a more potent footballing force for the expression of these views.

37. This phrasing is deliberately ambiguous. This powerful trend in Scottish Freemasonry has been subject to strong criticism by some senior Scottish masons: see Finn, 1990b. Some senior masons were also very critical of the misuse of freemasonry in association with Rangers.

38. These influences were ignored by Murray in 1984. I informed Murray in the period between his two publications about the role of Primrose. See Finn, 1991a, 83–7.

39. Murray, *Glasgow's Giants*, p.186.

40. The division over Irish Home Rule was one of the main faultlines between Liberals (and other radicals) and Conservatives in British politics in the late nineteenth century. There were politicians who did not fit easily into these opposed categories. However, some complexity does not legitimise the translation of rhetorical objections to Irish Home Rule voiced by the political right into some supposedly cosy compatibility with a 'liberal disposition'.

41. Here it is worth noting Murray's strong support that Rangers fans continue to sing the anti-Catholic anthems 'No Pope of Rome' and 'The Sash': Murray, *The Old Firm in the New Age*, p.153. For further discussion, see below.

42. Finn, 1994c.

43. Finn, 1991a, 1994b.

44. Histories of Rangers wrongly attribute support for the club from Stewart and Macdonald to the latter name. See W. Allison, *Rangers: The New Era, 1873–1966* (Glasgow, n.d.), p.187.

45. See *Rothesay Chronicle*, 29 May 1880.

46. *Rothesay Chronicle*, 30 August 1879. The reference to 'the O'Gorman' is to Major Purcell O'Gorman, an Irish Nationalist MP, who was famous for 'his wit and humour and no less his corpulence'.

47. I am grateful to the Scottish Conservative and Unionist Association for granting me access to the archival collection held in the National Library of Scotland. Stewart's son was also a Conservative.

48. R.D. Anderson. *Education and the Scottish People*, 1750–1018 (Oxford, 1995).

49. See E. MacFarland, *Protestants First. Orangeism in 19th Century Scotland* (Edinburgh, 1990); W.S. Marshall, *The Billy Boys: A Concise History of the Orange Order in Scotland* (Edinburgh, 1996).

50. More on the early Rangers will still appear in *The International Journal for the History of Sport*, cf. Murray, *The Old Firm in the New Age*, p.214.

51. Moorhouse makes some similar comments, but only in passing: Murray does so in passion.

52. For a summary see Finn, 1999.

53. It is seldom recognized that institutional discrimination against Catholics is built into the very essence of the United Kingdom State. One astonishingly belated discovery was that by Michael Forsyth, former Conservative Secretary of State of Scotland, who only touched on one aspect of this discrimination, when he complained about the ban on members of the Royal family marrying Catholics. He described it as 'Britain's grubby little secret'. His discovery of this 'secret' only came once he and his party were out of government, once he had lost his own parliamentary seat, and after 18 years of Tory rule. His comment was presented in the context of an attack on the Labour government, elected in 1997. He put it forward as an important 'sin of omission', in an attack on the government for its determination to bring about other forms of constitutional change! Reported on both STV Teletext and BBC (Scotland) Ceefax, 26/7 January 1999.

54. See Murray, *Glasgow's Giants*, p.95. He reports that, as the Irish influence on Catholicism in Scotland became increasingly strong, 'Catholicism in Scotland was thus confirmed as an alien creed. It was the religion of Rome or the religion of Ireland: in neither case was it Scottish.' It is surprising that Murray now wishes to deny that religion and racialized ethnicity became intertwined. And for the sake of historical accuracy it should be noted that, rather than being 'alien', Catholicism was the religion of Scotland prior to the Reformation.

55. Murray, *The Old Firm*, p.275. Murray's comments on the provision of Catholic schools in

Scotland are becoming increasingly extreme, see Murray, *The Old Firm in the New Age*. Unfortunately, he has little understanding of the history or psychology of this complex issue.

56. S.J. Brown, 'Outside the Covenant': The Scottish Presbyterian Churches and Irish Immigration, *Innes Review*, 42 (1991), 19–45; R.J. Finlay, 'Nationalism, Race, Religion and the Irish Question in Interwar Scotland', *Innes Review*, 42 (1991), 46–67; Finn (1999).

57. Murray, *Glasgow's Giants*, p.175.

58. McCrone, *Understanding Scotland*, chapter 4. McCrone acknowledges that academic commentators have helped sustain this belief.

59. Miles and Dunlop, 'Racism in Britain: The Scottish Dimension', p.119. Also see R. Miles and L. Muirhead, 'Racism in Scotland: A Matter for further Investigation?', in D. McCrone (ed.), *Scottish Political Yearbook 1996* (Edinburgh, 1986). Miles and Muirhead also identify the role of academic commentators in generating support for belief in that special Scottish egalitarianism.

60. Murray could have clarified his position by locating his views in the context of the literature on racism and football, especially Scottish football: see J.Horne, 'Racism, Sectarianism and Football in Scotland', *Scottish Affairs*, 12 (1995), 27–51; Finn 1991a, b; Dimeo and Finn, 'Scottish Racism, Scottish Identities' (and since Murray, *The Old Firm in the New Age*, Dimeo and Finn, 'Racism, National Identity and Scottish Football').

61. Murray, *The Old Firm in the New Age*, p.43, for both quotes.

62. Murray (*The Old Firm in the New Age*, pp.43–4) provides some limited anecdotal evidence of abuse of black players in games in Scotland. Ironically, some similar evidence of racism was provided by Murray (*The Old Firm in the New Age*, pp.176–7), but then ignored by him in his determination to declare racism to be 'foreign' to Scotland. The real confusion lies with Murray's limited conceptualization of racism.

63. Presumably Murray's own confusion explains his failure to acknowledge his earlier directly opposed claim.

64. Murray, *The Old Firm in the New Age*, p.206. Recognition that Celtic is a common reference point for both Scots and Irish is at odds with his persistent denial that the emergence of *Celtic* Football Club should be seen as the minority community participating with the majority community in the sporting life of Scotland. See note 25 above.

65. See Finn, 1987. See also Dimeo and Finn, 'Racism, National Identity and Scottish Football'.

66. For the complexity of anti-Semitism in German society during the Nazi regime, see I. Kershaw, *The 'Hitler Myth'. Image and Reality in the Third Reich* (Oxford, 1989).

67. L. Colley, *Britons: Forging the Nation, 1707–1803* (New Haven, CT, 1992); C.G. Brown, *Religion and Society in Scotland since 1707* (Edinburgh, 1997).

68. See Finn, 1999 for some examples. See also Dimeo and Finn, 'Racism, National Identity and Scottish Football'.

69. Finn, 1987, 1991a, b; Horne, 'Racism, Sectarianism and Football in Scotland'; Dimeo and Finn, 'Scottish Racism, Scottish Identities'; 'Racism, National Identity and Scottish Football'. The section interrelating 'sectarianism' and racism in contemporary Scotland was edited out without the author's agreement from Finn, 1994c. That reveals the depth of the misunderstanding of this issue. In his *IJHS* review Murray advocated that even more radical editorial surgery should have been undertaken.

70. The correct nomenclature for the various communities that constitute the 'Asian' community in Britain is still an issue. See Dimeo and Finn, 'Scottish Racism, Scottish Identities', p.137. The focus in this article is on diasporic communities from India, Pakistan and Bengal. For the sake of consistency with the usage Irish-Scots, Asian-Scots will be used here, but it is an unsatisfactory and clumsy title.

71. Murray, *The Old Firm in the New Age*, p.206.

72. See J. Bains with R. Patel, *Asians Can't Play Football* (Solihull, 1996). See also J. Bains and S. Johal, *Corner Shops and Corner Flags: The Asian Football Experience* (London, 1998).

73. Murray's refusal to engage with this research and his identification of Bains and Patel as 'Asian researchers' has a resonance with his identification of the 'sympathies' of Finn, Bradley and Maley and his general treatment of their arguments too.

74. Murray, *The Old Firm in the New Age*, p.207.

75. Part of Murray's 'evidence' here is to compare the world status of footballers produced by Africa and Asia. The relevance of this simplification of a complex comparison is less than

obvious in the context of Asian-Scots, especially amidst Murray's stereotypical discussion of Asian-Scots and business.

76. Murray, *The Old Firm in the New Age*, p.208. Murray's apparent identification of Asian-Scots as Muslims is incorrect, though Islam is the dominant faith for these Scots. He also assumes homogeneity among Muslims, which is incorrect. He also neglects the different religious traditions within Islam.

77. See, for example, R. Brown, *Prejudice - Its Social Psychology* (Oxford, 1995); Billig, *Ideology and Opinions*; Finn, 1999, 2000.

78. Murray, *The Old Firm in the New Age*, p.192.

79. Murray criticizes Maley for failing to distinguish between assimilation and integration. However, it is clear that Murray himself cannot do so. Indeed, he provides proof that the two terms can refer to remarkably similar assumptions about the place of minority communities in society: see, for example, Finn, 1987.

80. Murray, *The Old Firm in the New Age*, p.200. Murray's self-justification touches on a very wide debate about rights and values in pluralist societies, but it is evident that his vision is very restricted here too.

81. Murray, *The Old Firm in the New Age*, p.203. Murray's ever sensitive 'paranoia' detectors are yet again deployed. Perhaps this quote from Murray should have been scanned too.

82. Ibid. Murray intriguingly equates Catholic Irish-Scots and Islamic Asian-Scots again. Both are identified as potential 'enemies within'.

83. Ibid. It could appear that this is a statement of wistful regret. The rest of this section is strange, with in places a depiction of a rosy, romantic past. Yet does seem to communicate acceptance of a changed Scotland, but one in which Protestantism should remain in a privileged position.

84. See note 55 and textual discussion.

85. Murray, *The Old Firm in the New Age*, p.192. In support of this account, Murray decides that for Lithuanians, Poles and Italians 'their religion was no problem', which is a sudden ditching of his commitment to the acceptance of anti-Catholic prejudice in Scotland, but this isolation of the Irish-Scots would render them even more culpable! However, a number of studies disprove Murray's rosy picture. See, as an introductory list, the Billy Kay edited *Odyssey Collections* (both Edinburgh, 1980 and 1982), but see too J. Millar, *The Lithuanians in Scotland. A Personal View* (Colonsay, Argyll, 1998). The complexity of the Italian Experience in Scotland deserves further research, but see T. Colpi, *The Italian Factor* and *Italians Forward* (Edinburgh, 1991). Murray's inexpertise is such that he even uses the word 'Tallies', which most Italians judge to be a term of abuse, in the midst of his claim that the Italian community did not experience prejudice in Scotland! It should also be noted that some in these communities were Jewish: see note 87 below and the textual commentary, too.

86. See R. Moore, *Racism and Black Resistance in Britain* (London, 1975). For a good introduction, and as further evidence of how long this has been recognized as a racist framework, see P. Dickinson, 'Facts and Figures: Some Myths', in J. Tierney (ed.), *Race, Migration and Schooling* (London, 1982).

87. He relies on a partial reading of K. Collins, *Second City Jewry: The Jews of Glasgow in the Age of Expansion* (Glasgow, 1990): see also K. Collins, *Aspects of Scottish Jewry* (Glasgow 1987); H. Maitles, Fascism in the 1930s: The West of Scotland in the British context, *Scottish Labour History Society Journal*, 27, 7–22 (1992). Finally, Ralph Glaser's trilogy on his experiences growing up in the Gorbals gives the lie to Murray's suggestion that anti-Semitism was absent. See R. Glaser, *Growing Up in the Gorbals*; *Gorbals Boy at Oxford*; *Gorbals Voices, Siren Songs* (London, 1986, 1988, 1990).

88. Violence against minority members is incorrectly represented by Murray to be the result of individual psycho-pathology, not societal prejudice. See Murray, *The Old Firm in the New Age*, pp.195–6, and see textual commentary below.

89. See Murray, *The Old Firm in the New Age*, p.192 for the various quotes.

90. If so, it is in poor taste, but this interpretation is preferable to accepting it as a serious statement.

91. Murray reveals an anti-English prejudice that ranges from mild to unpleasant, as in this example. For this phenomenon on a wider scale, see, for example, G.P.T. Finn and R. Giulianotti, 'Scottish fans, not English hooligans! Scots, Scottishness and Scottish football',

in Brown, *Fanatics!*.

92. Moorhouse, 'Professional Football and Working-Class Culture'.
93. Both are wrong, as will be explained by Finn in *IJHS*.
94. For example, S.J. Brown, 'Outside the Covenant'; Finlay, 'Nationalism, Race, Religion and the Irish Question in Interwar Scotland'; Finn, 1999.
95. See C.G. Brown, *The Social History of Religion in Modern Scotland since 1730* (London, 1987); C.G. Brown, *Religion and Society in Scotland since 1707* (Edinburgh, 1997).
96. This mismatch was well demonstrated many years ago: R.T. LaPiere, 'Attitudes versus Actions', *Social Forces*, 13 (1934), 230–7.
97. All quotes, Moorhouse, 'Professional Football and Working-Class Culture', p.311. He suggests a few areas in which he believes ethnicity can be seen, and he also inaccurately refers to 'segregated schools'. Murray frequently also uses this value-laden term. Although this reference is common usage in Scotland, and a sign of the prejudice aroused by denominational schools, it is simply wrong. The 1918 Education Act ensured that the provision of denominational schooling does not constitute segregation.
98. See below, the section on Moorhouse's analysis of Celtic and Rangers fanzines.
99. Presumably Moorhouse means vehicle in the sense of a mechanism to carry or to transport?
100. Evidence to *measure* satisfactorily the extent of this decrease is too limited. To an extent, it remains an assumption, but one I share.
101. H.F. Moorhouse, 'Repressed Nationalism and Professional Football': Scotland versus England', in J.A. Mangan and R.B. Small (eds.), *Sport, Culture, Society: International Historical and Sociological Perspectives* (London, 1986), pp.57–8. Moorhouse repeats this claim in some subsequent articles. For example, H.F. Moorhouse, 'On the Periphery: Scotland, Scottish Football and the New Europe', in J. Williams and S. Wagg (eds.), *British Football and Social Change: Getting into Europe* (Leicester, 1991), p.203. The argument appears almost word for word in H.F. Moorhouse, 'It's Goals that Count? Football Finance and Football Subculture', *Sociology of Sport Journal*, 3 (1987), 245–60.
102. Moorhouse, 'Repressed Nationalism and Professional Football', p.58.
103. Ibid., p.59. Rangers had by then a long history of signing players from a number of different countries. Since 1986, and especially 1988, and changes in ownership, Rangers has trawled the world in its determined search for top-class players.
104. In the 1935 Rangers gave Mohammed Latif, an Egyptian Muslim, who was a Physical Education student at Jordanhill College, one game in the first team. *Govan Press*, 20 September 1935.
105. In the *Rangers Handbook 1957–58*, under the heading 'A brilliant keeper' is an obituary of Herbert Lock which describes him as follows: 'An Englishman from Southampton, Lock quickly won the hearts of Rangers supporters when he arrived at Ibrox in 1908 ...' and 'Lock ... was such a brilliant player in his day that he was reserve English goalkeeper to the brilliant Sam Hardy.'
106. See Moorhouse, 'Professional Football and Working-Class Culture', p.313.
107. W. Allison, *Rangers The New Era* (Glasgow, 1966), p.231.
108. Moorhouse, 'On the Periphery: Scotland, Scottish Football and the New Europe', p.203.
109. Moorhouse criticizes my own alleged failure to explore anti-Irish and anti-Catholic prejudices outside of football. See H.F. Moorhouse, 'From zines like these? Fanzines, Tradition and Identity in Scottish Football', in G. Jarvie and G. Walker (eds.) *Scottish Sport in the Making of the Nation: Ninety Minute Patriots?* (Leicester, 1994), p.192. He presents a research programme probably beyond the scope of any single researcher. However, even Moorhouse himself has never examined anti-English prejudice, this supposedly defining factor of Scottishness, other than in relation to the football field. Murray, unlike Moorhouse, criticizes me for taking such a widespread focus that, so Murray alleges, I find anti-Irish and anti-Catholic prejudices everywhere, especially in 'the sectarianism that oozes out of every pore of the Scottish body politic'. Murray, *The Old Firm in the New Age*, p.185; *IJHS*, 12 (1995), 197–9 also. Although my exploration of societal prejudices in society is not restricted to football, only a few areas of Scottish life have been tentatively explored. However the research is neither restricted to Scottish society nor to a concern about anti-Irish and anti-Catholic forms of prejudice. This research is part of ongoing study into societal prejudices in association with equality work in general. A starting point can be found in Finn, 1987. Much does remain to be researched.

110. Finn, 1994b; Finn and Giulianotti, 'Scottish fans, not English hooligans!'; Dimeo and Finn, 'Racism, National Identity and Scottish Football'. Scottishness and Englishness in relation to football merits proper historical and social examination to which so far it has not been subjected.
111. Again the inter-war years demonstrate some of the depths that the expression of this particular variant of societal prejudice could reach in the twentieth century.
112. See note 1, and Dimeo and Finn, 'Racism, National Identity and Scottish Football', for fuller discussion of Moorhouse and 'sectarianism'.
113. See Finn, 1994b on some of the complexities surrounding the interpretation of this signing.
114. Moorhouse, 'On the Periphery: Scotland, Scottish Football and the New Europe', p.202.
115. All quotes from Moorhouse, 'On the Periphery', pp.212–13.
116. This is an incomplete account of the purchase of Hibernian, and one that neglects the history of ethnic complexity around Hibernian: see Finn, 1991b, pp.385 and 397. Moreover, the main Catholic entrepreneur has turned out to be (now Sir) Tom Farmer, the founder of the Kwik-Fit business, a moderately active Conservative, and a descendant of a prominent figure in the early days of Hibs, which he claimed was a motivating factor in his becoming involved. Soon after Farmer was to invest in Prince Edward's film company. There is a paradox in Moorhouse's modernizing thesis: he overstates the undoubted progress in *inter*-ethnic complexity but tends to understate minority *intra*-ethnic complexity – an analysis confirmed by Moorhouse ('From zines like these?'), see below.
117. Moorhouse, pp.212–13. Indented quote from p.213.
118. For Moorhouse this is the second missing fanfare. He claimed, 'A second Catholic has now played in the Rangers team to no fanfare' (p.206). Not until Boli signed in summer 1994 was another acknowledged Catholic signed by Rangers. Lots of rumours wrongly 'identified' various players during that period. It may be that Moorhouse's unspecified Catholic was John Spencer. Spencer, however, had disclaimed any religious beliefs, though one of his separated parents was Catholic and he had attended a Catholic school. It is a frequent surprise to many including, as one can surmise from their accounts of the State provision of Catholic schools, Murray and Moorhouse, to learn that there is *no* requirement that pupils at Catholic schools be themselves Catholic.
119. A. Mackie, *The Hearts. The Story of Heart of Midlothian F.C.* (London, 1959), p.114; D. Speed, B. Smith and G. Blackwood, *The Heart of Midlothian Football Club: A Pictorial History 1874–1984* (Edinburgh, n.d.), p.43.
120. With apologies to Oscar Wilde, but academic standards should be demanding.
121. D. Lamming, *A Scottish Soccer Internationalists' Who's Who, 1872–1986* (Beverley, North Humberside, 1987), p.137; Speed *et al.*, *The Heart of Midlothian Football Club*, p.44.
122. Bobby Walker was an especially popular player at Hearts, and in other circles too. When he died, aged 51, in 1930, there was a very impressive turn-out at the masonic funeral given by Lodge the Heart of Midlothian 832. Speed *et al.*, *The Heart of Midlothian Football Club*, p.76.
123. Indeed, for Moorhouse '… it is properly understood as a burlesque of what now exists.' H.F. Moorhouse, 'From zines like these?', p.191.
124. All quotes in this paragraph, Moorhouse, 'From zines like these?', p.178. On this occasion, by his use of inverted commas Moorhouse does appear to wish to distance himself from the claim.
125. The IRA is the Irish Republican Army. The IRA has been the dominant republican paramilitary organization and has until very recently used violence to pursue its goal of a united Ireland. The IRA is an illegal organization in both the Irish Republic and the United Kingdom.
126. Apparently, he made use of that indefinable, ever-elastic notion of 'legitimate' targets: for many within Republicanism, this argument was simply unacceptable as an excuse for Enniskillen. These so-called 'mistakes' intensified the ideological dilemmas posed for the republican movement by the IRA's political violence, and that led to the inevitable move away from violence: see G.P.T. Finn, 'Qualitative Analysis of Murals in Northern Ireland: Paramilitary Justifications for Political Violence', in N. Hayes (ed.), *Doing Qualitative Analysis in Psychology* (Hove, 1997a); G.P.T. Finn, 'Visual Images as Social Representations of the Northern Irish Conflict', paper presented at the XXVI International Congress of Psychology (Montreal, 1996).
127. Moorhouse, 'From zines like these?', p.180.
128. Ibid, p.179.

129. Ibid.

130. Hickman and Walters, *Discrimination and the Irish Community in Britain.*

131. Moorhouse, 'From zines like these?', p.179.

132. The most important loyalist paramilitary groups which used violence to pursue the goal that Northern Ireland should remain part of the UK are the Ulster Volunteer Force (UVF) and the Ulster Defence Association (UDA). For loyalist justifications of paramilitary violence see Finn, 1997a.

133. Moorhouse, 'From zines like these?', p.179.

134. Ibid., p.180.

135. These contradictions, following the use of the 'Mickey Mouse' disclaimer', are common in prejudicial frameworks: see Billig, *Ideology and Opinions.*

136. Moorhouse, 'From zines like these?', p.180.

137. Ibid., p.183.

138. Ibid., p.189.

139. Ibid., p.186.

140. Ibid., p.189. *NTV*'s self-addressed comments on 'paranoia' reflect the frequency of its use in Scottish society.

141. As is common in most expressions of prejudice, *FF* does sometimes moderate this stance and argues that not all Celtic supporters can be categorized in this way. That complexity, however, is then negated by the consistent identification of Celtic itself with the IRA. That in turn means that *all* Celtic supporters must be guilty of supporting the IRA.

142. Moorhouse makes no attempt to engage with the rich literature on identities. Instead, he simply asserts his own beliefs, followed by his own judgement of its insignificance!

143. Ibid., p.191. See van Dijk, *Communicating Racism, Elite Discourse and Racism.*

144. In his desperation to claim that 'sectarianism' is no loner evident in Scotland, he attempts to enlist McCrone, *Undersdtanding Scotland*, which he claims has little on 'sectarianism'. In fact McCrone does cover topics that some would include under this meaningless label. Strangely, McCrone scarcely mentions football: does that mean that Moorhouse would wish to argue that football plays no role in modern Scotland? Ironically McCrone's most notable reference to football is when he discusses Scottish *identities*, in particular one which he now judges largely to be in decline, that forged between Protestantism and Unionism. However, McCrone comments: 'This identity consisted of a complex of inter-related elements of Protestantism and Unionism welded together by a strong sense of national and imperial identity, and symbolised by the Union Jack (still an emblem of Glasgow Rangers Football Club).' McCrone, *Understanding Scotland*, p.158.

145. Moorhouse, 'From zines like these?', pp.191–2.

146. Versions of these criticisms of *FF* and Moorhouse's analysis were first presented in two papers: G.P.T. Finn, 'Intergroup Prejudice: Football, Religion, History and Scottish Society', paper presented to the Scottish Graduate Centre in Sport, Leisure and Physical Education Research Seminars (Moray House Institute, Heriot-Watt University, Edinburgh, January, 1997b); G.P.T. Finn, 'Scotland, Soccer, Society: Global Perspectives, Parochial Myopia', paper presented to the North American Society for Sports Sociology Annual Conference: Crossing Boundaries (Toronto, September, 1997c).

147. Murray made no criticism of *FF*, nor of Moorhouse's comments, when he reviewed the Walker and Jarvie collection of essays. Murray, *IJHS*, 12 (1995).

148. Murray, *The Old Firm in the New Age*, p.184.

149. 12 July is the date when Orange Order marches are held to commemorate the victory of King William of Orange at the Battle of the Boyne in 1690.

150. Murray, *Glasgow's Giants*, p.153.

151. Murray, *The Old Firm in the New Age*, p.180.

152. This song title was even chosen as the title for a book on militant Protestantism in Scotland: S. Bruce, *No Pope of Rome Anti-Catholicism in Modern Scotland* (Edinburgh, 1985).

153. Murray now simply contradicts his past statements on this issue: see Finn, 1991b, pp.390–1 and 394. Murray states: 'The Irish tricolour flying above the stadium is no longer the irritation it once was, and there is little the club can do about away supporters who add IRA messages to the tricolour banners they wave in support of Celtic.' Murray, *The Old Firm in the New Age*, p.146.

154. Murray, *Glasgow's Giants*, p.210.
155. There are *some* Celtic supporters who do sing and chant in support of the IRA. Most of this is indeed offensive to many Scots, including many other Celtic fans. The Celtic board has a long history of actions and rebukes directed against this behaviour, and that history goes back to at least the 1960s.
156. Murray, *The Old Firm in the New Age*, p.71. Murray's phrasing is not helpful here. Both clubs do represent variants of community identities in Northern Ireland: see Finn, 1994b. That is very different from the clubs being seen as proxies for paramiltary organizations.
157. G.W. Allport, *The Nature of Prejudice (25th Anniversary Edition)* (Reading, MA, 1979), pp.14–15.
158. See, for example, van Dijk, *Elite Discourse and Racism*.
159. Murray, *The Old Firm in the New Age*, p.195. Murray's misuse of psychiatric categories is even less acceptable here.
160. As there is no official monitoring of these crimes, no precise evaluation can be made of their occurrence.
161. See *Combat* (July 1997). *Combat* is officially a magazine for the expression of all loyalist opinions, but the magazine is recognized to be the unofficial publication of the illegal UVF.
162. See for example, *Daily Record*, 19 October 1997. The suggestion caused similar expressions of outrage in Northern Ireland too, see *Newsletter*, and *Irish News* in this period too.
163. See Finn, 1997a.
164. *Daily Record*, 10 October 1997.
165. See newspaper reports on Longstaff during the trial at the end of November 1998. He received a sentence of ten years for attempted murder.
166. See G. Mitchell, *Making Peace* (London, 1999), pp.185–6.
167. See Finn, 1987, 1999, 2000 for more discussion of these issues and the potential role of education.
168. See Dimeo and Finn, 'Scottish Racism, Scottish Identities', and 'Racism, National Identity and Scottish Football'.
169. See Dimeo and Finn, 'Racism, National Identity and Scottish Football'.
170. For example, see *Celtic View*, 28 April 1999 and 5 May 99.
171. An official Celtic store opened in Dublin in late 1998.
172. G. Walker, '"There's not a team like the Glasgow Rangers": Football and Religious Identity in Scotland', in Gallagher and Walker (eds.), *Sermons and Battle Hymns*. Also see Finn, 1994b.
173. Ludicrous as this ban is, its sheer stupidity was highlighted by the arrival of Seb Rozental, who said he would stop blessing himself now that he was with Rangers. Rozental was from Chile, where it was such a common practice that Rozental had adopted it, too, although he was in fact Jewish.
174. Finn and Giulianotti, 'Scottish fans, not English hooligans!', p.193.
175. *Daily Record*, 30 May 1999.
176. Murray, *The Old Firm in the New Age*, p.180, comments: 'Songs about being up to one's knees in Fenian blood challenge decency, although it is a great song – witness the way that it has been taken up by many supporters elsewhere. While sectarian killings in Ireland and England continue, however, songs and chants in praise of the killers are somewhat sick.' Which is scarcely a strong condemnation. And do 'sectarian' killings in Scotland not matter, or is that old belief in the Scottish immunity to prejudice leading to selective blindness rather than myopia this time?
177. The Fenians were Catholics *and* Protestants opposed to British rule of Ireland.
178. *Glaswegian*, 28 September 1995.
179. See letter from Cara Henderson, 'Singing a history of hatred', *Herald*, 4 June 1999.
180. Donald Findlay, 'View From the Vice Chair', *The Rangers Monthly* (June 1999). From its contents, this column must have been written after Findlay's singing session, but it may have been completed before the consequences became apparent.
181. Most commentators (e.g. Moorhouse 'On the Periphery'; Murray, *The Old Firm in the New Age*) interpret the signing of Catholics by Rangers to be pragmatism on the part of the club.

4

Football in Cameroon:
A Vehicle for the Expansion and
Contraction of Identity

BEA VIDACS

INTRODUCTION: A DAY AT THE STADIUM

We are at the Ahmadou Ahidjo Stadium of Yaoundé, Cameroon on 22 June 1997 immediately following Cameroon's disappointing tie against Gabon as part of the qualifying rounds for the African Nations' Cup Finals. Cameroon has done rather badly in the match. After trailing by 2–0 and then 2–1, at the last minute Gabon managed to score an equalizing goal, leaving Cameroon's qualification for Ouagadougou in doubt.

As a dispirited Cameroonian team and a jubilant Gabonese team are leaving the stadium, a corpulent older man comes up to me and my companion, a Cameroonian coach, in great agitation. He starts by saying that he is very angry. He then pointedly remarks that he is angry at the Second Vice President of the FECAFOOT, the football federation, because the latter had prohibited a man, wearing a bishop's hat, a bishop's staff and a white robe sporting the green-red-yellow of the Cameroonian flag, from encircling the stadium during half-time. In fact the 'bishop' is a familiar figure at all international matches at the Yaoundé stadium. In excited tones our friend exclaims, 'It's the Bamileke, always the Bamileke!' ('Ce sont les Bamilekes, toujours les Bamilekes'). He goes on to explain that, had he been allowed to proceed, the bishop would have protected the national team, and that he (our speaker) had been told that the result was going to be 2–0, and would stay that way. 'It's impossible that every time there is an international match the Bamileke betray us. Because the bishop would have protected us, but Colonel Tchatchou didn't let him.'

CAMEROON'S ETHNIC MAKE-UP: THE BAMILEKE–BETI QUARREL

In order to understand the deeper meaning of these accusations, I should explain first of all that Cameroon is a multiethnic nation where there are upwards of 200 ethnic groups and the Bamileke are one of the largest of these. The FECAFOOT official in question is a Bamileke whereas the speaker himself is a Beti, which is a collective name for people of the south, and from whose ranks Paul Biya, the president of Cameroon, hails.

Cameroon's triple colonial heritage is unique. The country was first colonized by the Germans (1884–1916). Following the First World War, the former German colony became a League of Nations trusteeship administered by the British and the French, dividing the territory into British and French Cameroon. The West province referred to in the present essay as the 'homeland' of the Bamileke belonged to the French administered territory. The people of the southern half of former British Cameroon voted to rejoin French Cameroon (East) just before independence, whereas the northern half voted to join Nigeria. As a result of the British colonial legacy, an English-speaking minority (about 20–25 per cent of Cameroon's population) came into being which has developed a separate 'ethnic' identity as 'Anglophones'. They mostly live in the present North-West and South-West provinces. This identification as 'Anglophone' overrides other ethnic divisions among them and, in many instances, sets them apart from the French-speaking majority of the country. Other major divisions within Cameroon are between the Muslim north and the Christian south.

The Bamileke originate in the West Province, but have also migrated and settled widely all over Cameroon. They are seen by many as controlling the economy of the country. Indeed, because of their economic dynamism, they are resented by many people in Cameroon, and the phrase 'the Jews of Cameroon' has been used about them in debates. Although the phrase obviously compounds stereotypes, it does indicate the nature of the structural position of the Bamileke in Cameroon, and the kinds of prejudices they face. In addition, the Bamileke are in political opposition to the current political regime. They are not the only ones. Cameroon's Anglophone minority was in the forefront of initiating multipartyism. In fact, Cameroon's most important opposition leader, Ni John Fru Ndi, is an Anglophone. There are prominent opposition figures among the Beti as well, but certainly the Bamileke are perceived by Cameroonians as being among the most staunch critics of the current regime.

Like many other ethnic groups in Africa, the Bamileke have been constructed as a group as a result of colonization.[1] The term Bamileke unites a number of groups from Cameroon's Grassfields who live in highly hierarchical societies. However, these are fairly independent units which do not really constitute a centralized whole.

The Beti as a group are of even more recent origin, consisting of ethnic groups which, until recently, were seen as separate entities (Ewondo, Boulou, Eton, and so on) and the word Beti was originally a linguistic term describing the interrelated languages of these various groups. Their emergence under the collective name Beti dates to the 1982 rise to power of Paul Biya, who is a Boulou. Traditionally, these societies of the southern forest region of Cameroon were small, autonomous acephalous societies, with very little sense of commonality.

In recent years, Biya's regime has increasingly tried to put more and more administrative power into Beti hands, and in the ethnic charges and countercharges that are now rife in Cameroon both groups accuse each other of ruining the country. The Bamileke see the Beti as being lazy and using their closeness to power to enrich themselves at the expense of the country, while the Beti accuse the Bamileke of likewise enriching themselves and disregarding the needs of the country. The relationship of the two groups has become increasingly bitterly antagonistic over the past couple of years since the beginning of multipartyism in Cameroon in the early 1990s, and P. Geschiere,[2] following J. Lonsdale,[3] has characterized it as an example of 'political tribalism'.

THE PLACE OF FOOTBALL IN CAMEROONIAN SPORT

Football is the most important sport in Cameroon. People refer to it as 'sport roi' (literally the 'king sport', meaning the most important sport) and it animates their feelings in many ways. As most men have played it in childhood, and often in their teens and early manhood, it is a game everybody claims to understand, and thus have an interest in. Also, given the proliferation of teams of various levels, a very large number of people have taken an active part in football, both as players and as managers or officials of some sort. Everywhere in Yaoundé, where there is a team playing there will be spectators as well, no matter how impromptu the team is. People even stop to watch children play, and often comment that they like to see children play because they play a more original and interesting kind of football.

Thus, it is not surprising that sport news is dominated by football. For example, the popular *Sport Matin* programme on the radio, which broadcasts every morning, is almost entirely composed of football-related news and announcements, and other sports will be mentioned only rarely, usually on account of a good home performance in an international competition. The same can be said about the sports pages of newspapers appearing in Cameroon. They too are dominated by football news. For example, a quick overview of the first 21 issues of the weekly paper *Génération*[4] shows the following coverage during an approximately five-month period: in the sports section there were 36 longer features dealing with sport, of which 28 dealt with football; there were also 27 shorter articles, usually less than ten lines long, and of these 15 covered football; while 12 dealt with other sports. In addition, there were 11 further articles about football outside the sports section, six of these in one issue of the paper,[5] where the investigative central theme was the much debated collection for the Indomitable Lions for the 1994 World Cup.[6] No other sport merits mention outside the sports section. *Génération* is a paper of the Cameroonian intelligentsia opposed to the current political regime, and is the most intellectual of all the Cameroonian newspapers. It combines investigative journalism and serious social analysis with bourgeois general interest articles. *Challenge Sport*, a weekly paper devoted entirely to sport, also shows an overwhelming interest in football. The issue of 28 March 1995, for example, devotes approximately nine pages out of 12 to the sport.[7]

We can see that the coverage of football in Cameroon is extensive, becoming almost exclusive during an event such as the World Cup. The national radio (CRTV) devoted five and a half hours daily to the 1994 World Cup, besides covering the matches and providing football-related news coverage under the regular news. This is without counting the special football-related programming of provincial stations. During the 1994 World Cup, as part of this coverage, CRTV ran a call-in radio programme, *Bonjour l'Amérique*, and its English-language counterpart, *Hi America*, which was supposed to rally Cameroonians to support their team. In the event of Cameroon's early elimination from the World Cup, it also served as a safety valve to allow Cameroonians to express their bitterness and frustration at their poor performance.[8]

BRIEF HISTORY, AND THE OFFICIAL AND UNOFFICIAL
ORGANIZATION OF FOOTBALL IN CAMEROON

Football, according to S. Tsanga,[9] was introduced in Douala in the 1920s
by African migrants, and quickly spread to Cameroonians. As elsewhere
in Africa, and in the colonial world in general, the colonizers attempted
to exclude the 'natives' from playing against them, and thus several early
clubs had a European and an 'indigenous' team.[10]

The first Cameroonian teams evolved in Douala and Yaoundé,
respectively, the economic and political capitals of the country, and until
recently these two towns remained the centres of the sport. This,
however, seems to be changing, as some Western Cameroonian and other
provincial teams gain more and more prominence. At first these teams
were recruited on a strictly ethnic basis, and as Clignet and Stark[11]
demonstrate, this went to the point that transfers of players to ethnically
different teams were regarded as betrayal. These days this is less
important, as players and coaches are fairly mobile, but the supporter
base and the managers and officials of most teams remain ethnically
determined, although, especially in the case of the more prestigious
teams such as Tonnerre, Canon and Union de Douala, they draw on a
wider set of supporters than the merely ethnic.

In the English-speaking Western part of the country (North-West
and South-West Provinces) which was under British colonial rule until
1961, football had a somewhat different history, because there the most
important teams became those sponsored by various 'corporations and
governmental agencies'.[12] Even today, PWD Bamenda (Public Works
Department Bamenda) is the foremost team of the Anglophone
Northwest Province.

The formation of the Cameroonian football federation
(FECAFOOT) followed in 1959, just before independence, and it joined
FIFA in 1962. Cameroon has been participating in international football
ever since, won the African Nations Cup twice (1984, 1988), and has
participated in four World Cups (1982, 1990, 1994, 1998). In 1990, the
Indomitable Lions, the national team, created a sensation in the World
Cup by reaching the quarterfinals, and defeating Argentina, the holders
of the title, on the way.[13]

The structure of official Cameroonian football is as follows. There is
a first division where 16 teams compete from all over the national
territory. Each of Cameroon's ten provinces organizes second division

championships, the champions of which vie for the three places that become vacant in the first division through the '*Interpoules*' competition, which traditionally has been held in Yaoundé and Douala, although in recent years there have been some attempts to move Interpoules to other parts of the country. For example, in 1994 they were held in the regional towns of Bamenda and Bafoussam; and although in 1995 they were back in Douala and Yaoundé, they have been alternating among various provincial towns, so that in 1998 they were held in Ebolowa and Buea. In addition, there is also the third division or '*la ligue*', where teams compete at the departmental or district level. In theory there is also a '*championnat de corpos et veterans*' (championship of corporations and veterans) organized by the FECAFOOT, but these tend not to function very well, even though both corporations and veterans do play all over Yaoundé, and presumably elsewhere too.

There is also the Cup of Cameroon for which all teams of all three divisions compete. The final of the Cup of Cameroon is a much awaited festive event where the President of Cameroon always appears to provide further pomp to the proceedings by his presence. The fact that he never fails to attend the Cup final is a reminder that the state in general, and the President in particular, take football very seriously. The President is the one who hands over the Cup and he personally congratulates the players. There is also a championship in women's football, as well as the women's version of the Cup of Cameroon, but most female teams are located in Yaoundé and Douala, and the female version of the sport is not yet practised very widely.[14]

In addition to these official forms of football, there are many other ways in which football structures Cameroonians' spare time and interests. There are the '*championnats de vacances*', organized in school holidays, sometimes referred to as '*les interquartiers*', where various neighbourhoods of Yaoundé hold mini-championships. In addition, there are the '2–0', the 'old boys' teams', and village championships, which will be discussed later.

ETHNICITY AND FOOTBALL

As mentioned above, the ethnic component has not disappeared in Cameroonian football, and in fact on lower levels of the competition and especially outside the official system of national championships, there are many instances of ethnicity being *the* driving principle of football.

Village championships, organized by migrants bringing together members of the village in town, are an important addition or alternative to traditional village meetings. The expressed goals are to 'animate' and allow the town-born young members of the village to get acquainted with each other. I observed the village championship of the Bamendjoun, a Bamileke chiefdom, over a six-month period in 1995. The Bamendjoun grouping (*groupement*) consists of six villages and are united under the leadership of a chief. The six villages organized a football championship and a cup competition in Yaoundé. The most important criterion for playing in one of the six teams was that the players had to be a descendant of the village, either paternally or maternally. Some of the players were also actively playing in 'official' teams (sometimes in the second, but usually in the third division) and therefore teams that fielded more 'professionals' had an intrinsic advantage. As a result, it became important to scrutinize the origins of the players. I have witnessed debates about the legality of a certain player on a team, including calling for elderly witnesses. Because the witnesses then explain how the player can be considered a member of the village, such disputes also lead to revisions and relearning of traditional ways of reckoning kinship.

The organization of the championship was along official lines, so much so that the various forms and administrative details followed closely those of official football. The referees, too, were active referees of the second and third division. The organizers of the championship volunteered their time and, apart from the president and treasurer, consisted mostly of the players themselves. The matches I observed were a community event, 100–300 people attended them and, unlike at the official championships, the number of women present almost equalled the number of men. This is a clear indication of the community nature of these events. Unfortunately, this village championship has stopped functioning because of controversies over the handling of money that came in at the post-cup gala. One of the organizers remarked to me that it was a pity because the championship had become like a post office for the village: everyone knew where to go to find everybody.

Village championships also take place locally, when youngsters who regularly arrive 'home' for the summer holidays are organized to participate in impromptu championships all over Cameroon. This is so widespread that many 'official' teams have difficulty holding on to their players during the summer holidays as youngsters disappear into the villages.

Despite the continued importance of ethnicity in football and thus its role in maintaining ethnic distinctions and boundaries, it is also undoubtedly leading to a crossing of boundaries on the level of the everyday practice of the sport. Not only does football create non-traditional standards of behaviour, such as a new notion of time, or a turning upside down of patterns of respect (e.g. age v. youth), but also, and most importantly, it creates linkages among people who would not otherwise be linked.[15] In the course of a sporting career, football players come into contact with a great many people from all walks of life. As players, they often play on multi-ethnic teams and, even when they play on a team that is ethnic, that is to say its supporters and leadership are identified with a single ethnic group, the players themselves will come from a variety of ethnic groups. This is because, despite ethnicity, teams and especially coaches, who do much of the recruiting, are often willing to find the best players regardless of ethnic origin. The average football player will have played in at least three or four teams and the ethnic mix he will have been exposed to is far larger than would be the case were he not playing football. In addition, teams, especially in the first division, but even at lower levels of competition, often play official and unofficial matches outside their regular milieu and inevitably will make contact with coaches and players from other teams and other ethnic groups. In Yaoundé, players often recruit each other and, interestingly, in many cases they will not be of the same ethnic group.

RELATIONSHIPS BEYOND FOOTBALL

Football creates relationships which endure beyond an active career. Much of the human structure of Cameroonian football is made up of former players, so much so that the innumerable more or less volunteer coaches, the officials of the federation and the referees for the most part have played football in their youth, and all seem to know each other as former team mates, coaches and players. This leads to a complicated set of alliances, which do not necessarily conform to the rules of ethnic exclusivity.

Then there is the '2–0', which is an institution in itself, uniting former players in recreational football. These matches consist of the old boys' teams, which play on weekends. The name '2–0' originates in the practice (dictated by having too many would-be players), of having two teams play until one of them leads by two goals, at which point the losing team will yield its place to those still waiting to play.

The '2–0' team, of which I was an honorary member, contained the representatives of at least six ethnic groups and the friendships that developed were very far from being ethnically determined. The team, AMIAF, constituted what could be seen as a voluntary association, but instead of the ethnic homogeneity characteristic of many urban African voluntary associations it consisted of a variety of ethnic groups. Among the noticeable interethnic friendships was that between a Bamileke and a Bassa; the two were practically inseparable. If you saw one of them you could be sure that the other was not far away. The former had been the coach of the latter. Another, for some time inseparable, pair was a Bamileke and a Douala. The former had his own young team and the latter for a while was its only supporter. Supporter here means turning up for training sessions, providing advice and financial support.

Another man on the team, a former second division player who is Bamileke, started his career in a team in Douala and played not in a Bamileke team in Yaoundé but in a Beti team of Sangmelima, a nearby town. He describes his experience with football as something that helped him establish himself in his career as a carpenter because, instead of money, he asked the leadership of his Sangmelima team to provide him with contacts for job orders. At present he does most of his work for a government company which sells goods to government employees on credit. This ensures that he has a steady source of income, which in the current economic climate of Cameroon is especially important. His access to the company's store is through a Bassa member of the old boys' team, and he faced great difficulties getting paid for his delivery when his team member was on summer leave. Incidentally, this carpenter was also instrumental in organizing the village championship mentioned above. Thus, being ethnic and co-operating across ethnic lines are not necessarily contradictory.

THE NATIONAL TEAM

While football is an important vehicle for the maintenance and continuation of ethnic identities and differences, it is just as important in the creation of national identities and national distinctiveness. Cameroonians support the national team even when, fearing that the government is going to take advantage of victories, they resent football. The government in fact does try to do this whenever possible. For example, the victorious performance of the national team in Italy in 1990 went a long way to calm Cameroon's turbulent political climate in the wake of the country's transition to multiparty politics. Paul Biya has done everything to appropriate the image of the Lions in order to claim their victories for himself. Among other forms this appropriation has taken are election campaign posters, a postage stamp showing him with a football and the image of a lion, and having a popular football player endorse him in election advertisements. These attempts were only partly successful, however, because, even though Biya managed to maintain his hold on power, his attempts to usurp the success of the Lions has earned him the ridicule of a large part of the population and, after the national team's 1994 World Cup fiasco the government, despite all efforts to deflect the censure for the defeat, got blamed by most people.[16] Interestingly, the government handled the 1998 World Cup much better, and when Cameroon was eliminated, to a large extent as a result of questionable refereeing, the government managed to turn the event to its advantage, by making it look like a victory, 'stolen' by the Hungarian referee. Even though in the latter case the Cameroonian people found themselves on the same side as their government, some opposition papers were quick to point out that this incident should show everyone (including and especially the government) how bad it felt to have a clear victory snatched away, making a clear reference to the 1992 presidential elections where, according to the opposition, John Fru Ndi's victory was 'stolen' by Biya.[17] In any case, in the heat of the moment, when actually watching an international match where Cameroon is playing, people root for the national team, and derive great pride from the exploits of the Lions.

Cameroonians themselves recognize that the national team brings unity and holds them together. As one caller to *Bonjour l'Amérique* expressed it during the 1994 World Cup 'football is the only thing that unites practically all Cameroonians'.[18] This sentiment was often echoed both in *Bonjour l'Amérique* and my interviews.

A *Bonjour l'Amérique* listener, who had gone to the studio in person, said the following just before Cameroon played Russia, its last remaining match in the first round of the 1994 World Cup:

> I myself would say that no matter who plays, that the people know, that the people who are in the United States know, that the Cameroonians have done all … have done all, didn't they … to show, that they love their national team. Well, no matter who plays, that he should play thinking … that he should play Wednesday

thinking of the fact that we ... that we count on this team, we count
on it because it is a question of national pride, we count on it that
the remainder of the competition should go very well and if later
on we leave [the competition] that we leave it honourably.[19]

His comments were in part addressing the ever-present question of
bonuses, and the effort Cameroonians made through the Coup de Cœur,
the nationwide collection set up to help the Lions before the World Cup.
In part he was reacting to the news of dissent among the team members
regarding who would play. But what is really significant is his sentiment
that the team should uphold the honour of the nation.

Another caller, this time an Anglophone man, was also keeping the
honour of the nation in mind:

Yes, I think I am a football fan and I have been trying to watch all
the matches that are ... that are played and really football brings
honour to a nation. If you look inside Africa you'll find that
Cameroon is being honoured by most African countries and why
not Europe, European countries, because of the performance in
1990.[20]

In fact, what people lamented most about Cameroon's first round
elimination was that Cameroon's prestigious image, gained in 1990, had
been lost. When listening to these statements it is hard not to realize that
the national team elicits nationalist sentiments in Cameroonians.

NATIONALISM AND SPORT: THE SIMULTANEOUS MOMENT AND THE IMAGINED COMMUNITY

Sport is the vehicle *par excellence* for national sentiments. Given the way
international competitions are organized, it is nations, however defined,
that are pitted against each other, and such structures have a way of
imposing themselves on the popular imagination. With the advance of
mass media into quite remote areas, the simultaneous moment, about
which Benedict Anderson is so eloquent, regarding the relationship
between the novel and the rise of nationalism in Europe and elsewhere,
is particularly evident when the majority of the population of an entire
country is able to watch a football match at the same time.[21] Add to this
that in Cameroon, and in Africa in general, the majority of these
spectators are literally watching the match together because in

Cameroon, for example, most people watch international matches not in their living rooms with their immediate, nuclear families, but in public spaces: bars, for the most part, where for the price of a few beers people unrelated to each other gather to watch matches. In fact, even if they are watching at home, chances are that there will be neighbours, relatives, servants or friends availing themselves of the opportunity to watch the match, thus once again the event is more public than one would expect. There are also giant screens set up in large cities where hundreds of people can and do gather together to watch a match. There are simultaneous radio broadcasts of international matches as well, so even people in remote areas can follow the competition, again usually in public rather than in private, as not everyone owns a radio. So the imagined community is rejoicing and seething, literally all at once, and of course it is both real (in the immediate sense) and imagined in the Andersonian sense, because people in their immediate communities know that there are other immediate communities of the same kind experiencing what they are experiencing. They know this for no other reason than because, the day after the match, the radio will broadcast man-on-the-street reactions to the match from all ten provinces of Cameroon. D. Spitulnik,[22] analysing radio in Zambia, also sees the broadcast of international football matches as one of the main instances where Zambian national identity is articulated, with football serving as an effective rallying cry for national unity.

To extend Anderson's thesis on the rise of nationalism, football is a major force in imagining the nation. This is not only so in the above outlined scenario of imagining the nation through the communal experience of watching and rooting for the national team; it is also evident in the very structure of the national championship and the Cup of Cameroon which helps make the abstraction of Cameroon as an idea, as a unit, real in the minds of the people. Although this structure is not so different from the rest of the world's, its significance in terms of the imagined community of the nation is not to be ignored.

THE INTERPLAY BETWEEN ETHNICITY AND NATIONALISM IN AFRICAN SPORT

What is really striking about our stadium friend's explanation of the Indomitable Lions' disappointing performance is that it highlights an often neglected aspect of the influence football plays on the relationship between ethnicity and nationalism in Cameroon, and I suspect elsewhere in Africa too. And that is that sport, and especially football, incites the loyalties of people on different levels so that they can act to promote national as well as ethnic sentiments.

Much of the rather sparse literature on sport in Africa seems to deny that it has national integrative functions, although such functions have been amply illustrated elsewhere, especially in Europe.[23] Rather, the emphasis has been on the divisive aspect of sport, which brings out the 'ethnic' in Africans.[24]

Similarly, in the anthropological literature of the past 30 years, ethnicity is seen as the most important dividing line in Africa. There has been an almost rigid division, more often than not unacknowledged, where Africans are seen as ethnics, and Westerners as nationalists. Yet ethnicity and nationalism are not the mutually exclusive categories being presented. In analysing ethnicity, anthropologists have come to describe ethnicity as situational and flexible.[25] Ronald Cohen defines ethnicity 'as a series of nesting dichotomizations of inclusiveness and exclusiveness ...' where '... the cultural identifiers used to assign persons to groupings ... expand or contract in inverse relation to the scale of inclusiveness and exclusiveness of the membership'.[26]

There is an argument for adding nationalism as one more of these flexible and situational identities, an alternative that can be chosen at certain times from among other identities. The various alternatives need not be consonant with each other. This makes sense also because of the segmentary nature of sports competition. When lower level teams are opposed to each other the identities that come to the fore are local identities, when higher level teams are opposed to each other the inclusiveness and scope of the identities evoked match the level of the competition, and this allows for, or even invites, these 'nested' identities.

Thus, at issue is not so much whether sport is promoting unity or divisiveness. It clearly does both. In Africa it even goes beyond nationalism in promoting even more overarching, pan-African identifications. For example, after Cameroon's stellar showing in the 1990 World Cup, *Jeune Afrique*[27] in a band headline cutting diagonally across the lower right corner on its title page said 'Africa among the great', referring to Cameroon's and Egypt's showing at the World Cup. A few weeks later, upon the conclusion of the competition, which of course had been won by Germany, the *Jeune Afrique*[28] headline declared

'It is Cameroon that Won!' – in handwritten block letters superimposed over the photograph of a stadium covering the entire front page.

Certainly in 1994, after Cameroon was eliminated from the competition, Cameroonians were quick to shift their allegiance to Nigeria, the only remaining African side in the competition. Many bought the Nigerian flags being sold in Yaoundé on the night of Nigeria's match against Italy. When Nigeria lost the match a Francophone Cameroonian friend told me the next morning that he had been so upset that he almost cried. This is despite the fact that Cameroon has had a continuing border dispute with Nigeria over the Bakassi peninsula. The dispute is closer to the hearts of the government than the people at large. Nevertheless Cameroonians on the whole are convinced that they can beat Nigeria in football any time.

How easily this identification is made, and how one African country is made to stand for the whole of Africa, is shown by the following statement by a woman caller to the English version of the call-in radio programme, the day of the Nigeria–Italy match: 'Well, to start off the Nigerian side showed up a good game and I am sure they defended the *... the African nation* as a whole and all I can wish them that they should keep on and try to, at least fly *the flag of Ni .... Africa.* ... I hope [they] will attend may be even the semi-finals.'[29] The ease with which she treats Nigeria and Africa as interchangeable terms shows that she sees the good performance of Nigeria as holding up the honour of Africa as a whole. Given that by this time Cameroon had already been eliminated, she like many others is now rooting for Nigeria as the African team, hoping that they will go far in the competition. One could object that Europeans do not automatically support the next European team when their own has lost, but shifting of loyalties in such a case is a question of power relationships, where such switches are facilitated by Africans' perception of a commonality of fate *vis-à-vis* Europe, which is of course the product of their colonial history, of being dominated and exploited by Europe and the continuing structurally weak position that African countries share in relation to Europe and the United States today.

This line of argument follows to some extent what J. Lever[30] has to say about the interplay of the unifying and divisive functions of football in Brazil. I agree with her that football is capable of both uniting and dividing people, however, while she sees this as paradoxical, I regard it as an outcome of the segmentary nature of the game's organization. At the same time I include nationalist and pan-Africanist (as well as ethnic) sentiments in the framework of co-existing and available identity choices, where the scope of inclusiveness will be triggered, and to a great extent determined, in relation to situation.

To what extent it will be 'determined' seems to depend on the level at which we find ourselves. That is to say, Cameroonians followed this system of increasingly widening nesting identifications throughout the 1994 World Cup to the point where, in the final, the majority supported Brazil against Italy, on the grounds that 'Brazil is a third world country, like Cameroon' and possibly also because there are blacks on the Brazilian team.[31] However, at this level of inclusiveness the identification was much less binding, and a minority felt perfectly at ease supporting Italy, whereas it is unlikely that it would have been possible to support Italy against Nigeria openly.

J. Arbena[32] objects to Lever's analysis on the grounds that conceivably watching international football, a 'global game', could work to wash away not only ethnic, but also nationalist divisions, as he puts it, 'in favour of a greater sense of transnational community, if only through a sense of shared experiences and the consequences of operating within similar institutions and regulations'.[33] Arbena's argument that football in and of itself does not uphold governments, and that the gains in popularity of regimes and leaders is only momentary, is well taken, but my point here is on a different level. In this proposed framework of nested identities, pan-Africanism today does not make nationalist or ethnic sentiment impossible tomorrow or even the next minute, as can be seen from the contribution of the woman caller quoted above. Nor does nationalist sentiment exclude ethnic sentiment (and vice versa) as evidenced by our friend's statement at the stadium.

Put somewhat differently, in all the debates about ethnicity and nationalism, little attention has been paid to nationalism in areas, especially Africa, where we are not expecting to see it. In a 1996 volume on African ethnicity, Fardon,[34] for example, devotes only one paragraph to nationalism in his conclusion to a highly imaginative analysis of the constraints imposed on 'ethnic narratives' by their respective interethnic contexts. As an aside (actually, in brackets) he mentions that nationalism should be evident in Africa, if at all, on the level of organized sports.[35]

NATIONALISM AND ETHNICITY: TWO SIDES OF THE SAME COIN

To return to our stadium interlocutor, he is being ethnic and nationalist at the same time. His very presence at the stadium is an indication that his interest in football goes beyond the purely ethnic. Presumably someone with an ethnic interest in football would go to the stadium only when his ethnic team plays. I happen to know this man and know that he is present at every match played at the stadium, but there are many other people who only turn out for the matches played by their own team, and that often happens to be an ethnic team. His fervent need to find an explanation for the result is also proof of his national sentiments. Yet the exegesis he chooses to present, apart from its magical undertones, is purely ethnic. He singles out an individual, who, even if the story of his constraining the bishop is true (about which I have no information), was only doing his duty, presiding over the peaceful unfolding of the match. And, in addition to blaming the Colonel for the result, he jumps from him (an individual) to his ethnic group and generalizes that the *entire* group is *always* trying to sabotage Cameroonian success in *all* international matches. The point is that in one breath our man is being both a nationalist and an ethnic chauvinist, questioning the patriotism of groups other than his own in a way that also involves questioning who exactly constitutes the nation.

Many of the contributions to the radio programme, *Bonjour l'Amérique*, bear witness to the fact that indeed football on the international level elicits from Cameroonians the same kind of nationalist fervour as we are used to elsewhere. In many of my interviews, the majority of interviewees predictably supported their own ethnic teams, but at the same time they also supported the national team. Often what we find is that people go to matches only when their team plays and when the national team plays. This is no different from any European fan who will support his own team (chosen on whatever basis) and the national team, and no one sees any contradiction in this. Cameroonians act in exactly the same way and we are surprised because we supposed them to be ethnic to the exclusion of all else.

What they debate is the definition of the nation, who is a true patriot, who is betraying us. And this is where nationalism, the 'unifying force', becomes divisive, in denying other people's intentions to uphold the honour of the nation.[36] This essay has demonstrated that football is a two-edged sword and, while it can be both ethnic and nationalist, even when it is nationalist it can be divisive.

CONCLUSION

In conclusion, football in Cameroon both reinforces ethnic ties and cuts across them. Whether it does one or the other will vary contextually: people do support their local 'ethnic' teams, but in the same breath also support the national team. What they contest is whether everyone supports the national team to the same extent and, by implication, whether everybody deserves to be part of the nation. At the same time, through the experience of football as a practice, people gain a wider social network which cuts across ethnic links and binds them together in novel ways.

NOTES

The fieldwork for the research on which this study is based was supported by the Wenner-Gren Foundation for Anthropological Research. An earlier version of this essay was presented at the 1997 Annual Meeting of the North American Society for the Sociology of Sports.

1. See P. Geschiere, 'Kinship, Witchcraft and the Moral Economy of Ethnicity: Contrasts from Southern and Western Cameroon', in L. de la Gorgendière, K. King and S. Vaughan (eds.), *Ethnicity in Africa: Roots, Meanings and Implications* (Edinburgh, 1996), for a discussion of the constructed nature of the two groups and the differences in the way in which they cope with new inequalities in their midst.
2. Ibid.
3. J. Lonsdale, 'The Moral Economy of Mau-Mau', in Bruce Berman and John Lonsdale (eds.), *Unhappy Valley, Conflict in Kenya and Africa* (London, 1992).
4. *Génération*, Yaoundé (August 1994 to early January 1995), that is to say at the tail end of the 1994 World Cup.
5. Ibid., I, 17, 12 December 1994.
6. For more detail on the Coup de Cœur see P. N. Nkwi and B. Vidacs, 'Football: Politics and Power in Cameroon' (hereafter 'Football'), in G. Armstrong and R. Giulianotti (eds.), *Entering the Field: New Perspectives in World Football* (Oxford, 1997).
7. *Challenge Sport* (Yaoundé) II, 61.
8. For a more detailed analysis of the programme and changes in its tenor see 'Football'.
9. S. Tsanga, *Le Football camerounais des origines à l'indépendance* (Yaoundé, 1969) (hereafter *Le Football*).
10. See W. J. Baker and J. A. Mangan, *Sport in Africa, Essays in Social History* (London, 1987); Laura Fair, 'Kickin it: Leisure, Politics and Football in Colonial Zanzibar, 1900s–1950s', *Africa*, 67 (1997); P. Martin, 'Colonialism, Youth and Football in French Equatorial Africa', *International Journal of the History of Sport*, 8 (1991); B. Stoddart, 'Sport, Cultural Imperialism, and Colonial Response in the British Empire', *Comparative Studies in Society and History* 30 (1988); *Le Football* (Yaoundé, 1969).
11. R. Clignet and M. Stark, 'Modernisation and Football in Cameroun', *Journal of Modern African Studies*, 12 (1974).
12. H. M. Mokeba, 'The Politics and Diplomacy of Cameroon Sports: A Study in the Quest for

Nation-building and International Prestige' (unpublished PhD thesis, University of South Carolina, 1989); see also 'Modernisation and Football in Cameroun'.

13. J.-C. Kodo-Ela and A. M. Masika, *Il était une fois ... les Lions Indomptables du Cameroun* (Yaoundé, nd) Collection Hommes et Evénements.

14. . Kuper, *Football against the Enemy* (London, 1994).

15. 'Modernisation and Football in Cameroun'.

16. See 'Football' for further details of how the government is trying to take advantage of football victories.

17. *La Nouvelle Expression*, 381, 26 June 1998, 6

18. *Bonjour l'Amérique*, 27 June 1994, 7

19. *Bonjour l'Amérique*, 28 June 1994, 1

20. *Hi America*, 2 July 1994, 7

21. B. Anderson, *Imagined Communities* (London, 1983).

22. D. A. Spitulnik, 'Radio Culture in Zambia: Audiences, Public Words, and the Nation State (I and II)' (unpublished doctoral dissertation, The University of Chicago, 1994).

23. J. Hargreaves, *Sport, Power and Culture: A Social and Historical Analysis of Popular Sports in Britain* (New York, 1986); J.A. Mangan (ed.), *Tribal Identities: Nationalism, Europe, Sport* (London, 1996) (hereafter *Tribal Identities*); J.A. Mangan, Richard Holt and Pierre Lanfranchi (eds.), *European Heroes: Myth, Identity, Sport* (London, 1996).

24. T. Monnington, 'The Politics of Black African Sport', in Lincoln Allison (ed.), *The Politics of Sport* (Manchester, 1986); T. B. Stevenson, 'Sports Clubs and Political Integration in the Yemen Arab Republic', *International Review for the Sociology of Sport*, 24 (1989).

25. J. Vincent, 'The Structuring of Ethnicity', *Human Organization*, 33 (1974); R. Cohen, 'Ethnicity: Problem and Focus in Anthropology', *Annual Review of Anthropology*, 7 (1978).

26. Ibid., 387, emphasis in the original.

27. *Jeune Afrique* 1538, 20–26 June1990.

28. *Jeune Afrique* 1541, 11–17 July 1990.

29. *Hi America*, 2 July 1994, 7, emphasis added.

30. J. Lever, *Soccer Madness* (Chicago, 1983). As she puts it 'Sport's paradoxical ability to reinforce societal cleavages while transcending them makes soccer ... the perfect means of achieving a more perfect union between multiple groups', ibid., p.7. In the case of Cameroon it is impossible to share this optimism; the processes I am talking about are much more indeterminate.

31. I have not heard the latter explicitly stated in the case of the World Cup final, but judging by the commentary and keen interest with which Cameroonians scrutinized the racial composition of foreign teams, it is more than likely that this factor played a part in the ready identification of many Cameroonians with Brazil. To give an example of this kind of scrutiny, there were many jocular comments on why Saudi Arabia was considered an Asian team in the World Cup, when clearly many of their players were black.

32. J. L. Arbena, 'Nationalism and Sport in Latin America, 1850–1990: The Paradox of Promoting and Performing "European" Sports', in J.A. Mangan (ed.), *Tribal Identities*.

33. Ibid. p.225.

34. R. Fardon, '"Crossed Destinies": the entangled histories of West African ethnic and national identities', in L. de la Gorgendière *et al.* (eds.), *Ethnicity in Africa: Roots, Meanings and Implications*.

35. Ibid., p.142.

36. B. F. Williams, 'A Class Act: Anthropology and the Race to Nation Across Ethnic Terrain', *Annual Review of Anthropology*, 18 (1989).

5

Football and Fatherland:
The Crisis of National Representation
in Argentinian Soccer

PABLO ALABARCES AND
MARÌA GRACIELA RODRÍGUEZ

From its early days soccer in Argentina has provided a strong forum for the representation of nationality. A series of international successes, and a catalogue of 'heroes', germinated an epic narrative, in which soccer contributed, in an important way, to the 'invention of a nation'. Starting from the populist experience of early Peronism in the 1940s, the relationship between soccer (sport) and nationality intensified, with a visible climax in the 1980s and 1990s, through the 'Maradona saga'. Today, the globalization of the soccer stage coincides with a crisis or fracture in the representation of nationality through the Argentinian game. Yet, at the same time, there has been in the daily agenda of the Argentinian public an infinite expansion of soccer that crosses gender and classes. Soccer therefore appears to be the only medium capable of developing epic nationalism in times of conservative neopopulism; yet soccer seems unable to produce it. Our analysis centres on this tension within the Argentinian game.

If the relationship between sport and nationalism has been abundantly explored,[1] the texts of Eduardo Archetti provide an excellent analysis of the origins of this relationship for the particular case of Argentinian soccer.[2] Taking that as the starting point, this essay tries to examine historically the representation of nationality through soccer, identifying the different ways in which that relationship was built up, and clarifying what we understand as a crisis in soccer's capacity to invest the nation with meaning. Contemporary stages of globalization and mediation demonstrate a split in the representation of the Argentinian nation through sport; according to our hypothesis, Argentinian soccer is unable to solve this problem by building a new national sports epic.

THE MYTHOLOGICAL FOUNDATION

Like the rest of the American continent, Argentina is an invented country; in the fiction of its 'discovery', in the violence of its conquest and annexation, and in its imaginary depiction as a land of plenty (the 'Silver Land' that scarcely fits the reality of its origins). Moreover, in its difficult construction as a modern state during the nineteenth century, Argentina was reinvented on several occasions. The civilian wars that characterized its history from 1810 to 1880 were also furious and opposing discursive battles where hegemony was itself contested. What the wars resolved, ultimately, was the capacity of one social sector to impose a definitive meaning of the 'nation'. Argentinian history is indeed a strongly contested game of discourses, and not merely a story about the establishment of a State, a geographical space or a legal corpus.

The end of the century and the beginning of the new one threatened to jeopardize this difficult construction of the shared sense of the state. Argentina became an immigrant country, and the entry of European migrants fractured not only the economic and social model, but also the past narrative of the nation. Until that moment the hegemonic model had talked about the victory of civilization over barbarism, and of European culture over American savagery. Yet the rapid modernization of Argentinian society required the use of new discourses that could dissolve the dangers within the new working classes, most notably their attraction to socialist and anarchist appeals. New, dominant discourses were needed to maintain the construction of national unity in the face of these fragmenting, heterogeneous identities. The dominant class, itself revealing differences and contradictions, replied by creating an elite nationalism, which posited, especially from 1910, the most important myths of unification. This official narrative prevailed over all others. It featured a pantheon of national heroes; the *melting pot* image appeared to inspire the assimilation of immigrants, along with the subsequent myth of ethnic unity; and a story of national origin began which instituted the *gaucho* as an epic figure and the hero of Argentina.

As Rosana Guber states, 'although not without conflicts, the Argentinian State was extremely effective in making assimilation compulsory'.[3] Its efficacy rested on two mechanisms. One was the public school, which was employed as a fundamental tool of the State for identity construction among the working classes. The other was an early culture industry which, aided by technological modernization and rapid urbanization, built a mass audience that included a working-class constituency that had experienced a rapid rise in literacy during the first few years of the twentieth century. The new narrative of national identity was thus granted wide and effective exposure within mass culture. Initially this was communicated by telegraph and print, then, from 1920 onwards, via radio and cinema. In spite of its private character (the State did not introduce its own media policy until the 1940s), the mass culture actively engaged in the reproduction of these hegemonic stories, especially in the form of *gaucho* mythology.

However some variations appeared in this process. The new professional class employed in the mass media in the main backed the narrative of elite nationalism, but they had been raised within the sympathetic modern urban middle classes. However, their massive and heterogeneous audience presented another set of expectations rooted in their own engagement with everyday life. Beside the gauchos of Leopoldo Lugones and Ricardo Rojas[4] or the *compadritos* of Jorge Luis Borges, the true heroes of the working classes appeared, and they were the sportsmen. As Archetti points out, in their discussion of national identity, sport journalists constituted a kind of doubly peripheral intellectual group. Sports journalists could not create a legitimate construction of national identity, because it was 'true' literature or the arts that was granted this legitimacy, but their journalistic efforts did impregnate the language of their audience. From the 1920s onwards, soccer became, through the sport magazine *El Gráfico*, one important hegemonic support for the creation of national identity: the magazine thus became 'a cultural text, in a narrative that is used to think about national and male issues'.[5]

The process described by Archetti took a variety of paths. It needed rites of passage: if national identity was to be built on soccer, it was necessary to explain the transition from English invention of the sport to its creolization. It needed a differential practice: the couplet of we (the nation) and they (the others) found its imaginary expression in a differentiated playing style, better narrated than lived in any football reality, but still an expression that yielded a great capacity for the production of social meanings. It needed a sporting success that would effectively represent national identity. And national success was claimed for the Boca Juniors European tour in 1925, the silver medal in the 1928 Amsterdam Olympics, and second place at the first World Cup of 1930 in Uruguay.[6] To support this epic construction of the nation, heroes like

Tesorieri, Monti, Orsi, Seoane, to name but a few, were found. And, if the nation was built primarily from the middle classes, and not from the dominant elites, then other deviations also appeared. Instead of the pastoral idea of the nation (rooted in the *gaucho* myth and in primary rural production), the nation that was built in soccer was able to assume an urban form, with an urban sense of time and space. Instead of an idea of the nation anchored in the heroic pantheon of patrician families and Hispanic tradition, soccer introduced a national identity which was represented by the working classes. Instead of the *gaucho* archetype, the national heroes proposed by soccer's own organic intellectuals were members of the existing, recently urbanized, working classes, themselves newly literate and pressing for cultural and political influence through the first wave of Argentinian populism (the Radical Party of Yrigoyen).

Renato Ortiz has stated that the construction of national identity was a consistent preoccupation throughout Latin America: 'The concern was to build a State and a modern nation and it was tradition which would finally provide the main symbols for the nation to end up identifying with.'[7] In the Brazilian case, these symbols became the samba, carnival and soccer. Ortiz adds: 'I have no doubt that this choice among diverse symbols took place mainly because of the State's performance .... The need of the State to present itself as a popular one implied the re-evaluation of those practices which increasingly began to possess mass characteristics. The formation of the nation then crossed through the first moment: the construction of its "people"'.[8]

This shift from a 'collective memory' – a live and everyday one – to the 'national memory' – a virtual and ideological one – is made by the State.[9] More precisely, it is the State's intellectuals and mediators who build the discourse of national identity. In Argentina, the early modernity of the national education system, its cultural industry and its massive audiences, enabled a group of professional, media intellectuals to emerge, and to elaborate a discourse of nationality that was in many ways different from that produced by the official intellectuals of the State. We propose that this popular, national discourse was based upon soccer, and that it spread among the working classes from the 1920s onwards. It then attained a hegemonic status two decades later.

FATHERLAND, SPORT AND POPULISM

The 1945–55 decade is an interesting period, highlighting the inter-relationships between sport, the working classes and the political-cultural operations of a State then attempting to build a new economic framework. To secure working class consent for the project of industrialization, the State needed to introduce cultural mechanisms that could elaborate a new communitarian meaning for the nation. This period can therefore be defined as being centred upon an 'official nationalism' in which the 'cultural system of a particular class' used State mechanisms to generate a particular sense of 'community'.[10] The State introduced compulsory education, State propaganda, an official interpretation of history (to recreate the 'foundation of the fatherland'), militarism, and other strategies that favoured this production of national identity.

Populism in Argentina can be seen as an attempt to re-invent the fatherland through the inclusion, within urban culture, of the huge working classes, who were supposed to be the beneficiaries of wealth redistribution. The political participation of these masses was no longer to be seen as illegitimate. Instead, politics was apparently widened to include their claims, which were also now presented in the media.

This period is important for investigating the relationship of sport and nationalism for three reasons. First, the spread of sport (among the élite and lower orders); second, the sudden expansion and consolidation of the cultural industry, with its strong interventionist features; and third, the bursting on to the political stage of the working classes. They now appeared as 'the people', which not only determined the time frame of this populist process, but focused attention on sport as a device for the construction of new, national symbols and referents.

Sporting spectacles became a new national ritual, with a deeply symbolic repertoire that had until then been practically unimaginable within the political realm.[11] In this way, sport operated via the articulation of a civil and political consensus in which it generated a set of emotions, needs and subjectivities related to the narrative of patriotic feeling. For the first time, the sports spectacle validated participation in the repertoire of nationalism, and the legitimacy of both was supported by the link with populism.

In this sense sport became a suitable stage for the exhibition of this new populist symbolism, and for the interventionism of the State.[12] Within media discourses, one can find the negotiation of a new collective between the State, working classes and the media, where citizenship and 'the people' seem to be rendered as equivalent terms. Official press discourses at this time also included a youthful dimension, so that the old meaning of being Argentinian was more easily displaced by a notion of the future, which helped the past to be forgotten.[13]

This national imagery was not unrelated to the actions of the State. Some of the strength of this new imagery rested in the actual re-distribution of gross domestic product (GDP) which did re-assign resources to general welfare.[14] Sport policy, which reflected this departure, was framed to represent an image of democratic participation, and aimed at producing community involvement and improving elite performances.[15] A new legal framework was created to achieve these aims. This mixing of community participation and international competition is fundamental to an understanding of the relationship between the media representation of successful Argentinian sport and the experiences of the citizenry (as participants and audiences). In this period the working classes also became increasingly acquisitive en route to their reincarnation as cultural consumers.[16]

This decade was a period marked by a great number of sporting successes and outstanding performances on both local and foreign stages.[17] These victories became a key mechanism for re-asserting a nationalistic epic. One of the most efficient devices was *Sucesos Argentinos*, movie newsreels which showed sport performances in communitarian settings (such as tournaments for children) and the extensive provision of public works (the inauguration of multi-sport buildings, and so on), and which also broadcast the honour of Argentinian athletic achievement. On the other hand, fictional movies also allow us to decipher the relationship of Peronism to the cultural industries and their key agents. Cinema became one of the most important mechanisms for the illustration of nationalistic epics, and the nationalist message was enhanced by references to cultural production, to economic growth and to the State support that the successful athletes received.

Thirty per cent of all Argentinian films dealing with sport were produced during this populist period of only ten years of national cinema history. Such a proportion indicates the burden placed on sport by consumer expectation. And, during Peronism, sport films were not mere documentaries; instead they made explicit, even boastful, references to the State system. As a re-interpretation of nationalism, some of these fictional products evoke a deep analysis.

Towards the end of *Pelota de trapo* (1948), perhaps the most important film because of its quality, and powerful populist effect, there is an intriguing scene. The main character, Comeuñas (Armando Bó), a star soccer player who must retire due to heart disease, is requested by fans to play for Argentina in a South American cup final against Brazil. In the dressing-room, his friend and manager refuses to let him play. But, entranced by the Argentinian flag which flutters over the stadium, Bó's character insists to his friend: 'There are many ways to give your own life for the country. And this is one of them.' Faced by such heartfelt pleading, his friend accepts and Comeuñas enters the field. Unsurprisingly, he scores the crucial goals, but although he has chest pains, he resists his seemingly inevitable fate and does not die. Has the fatherland recognized his brave effort, and decided against his ultimate sacrifice? Beyond the melodrama, this piece refers (for the first time in Argentinian sport movies) to an interpellation that explicitly links sporting performances with the populist national cause. This new association of representatives of the mass of the people with the glory of the nation allowed members of the working class, who had previously occupied unstable and illegitimate roles, to share in this construction of nationality.

Escuela de campeones (1950) narrates the story of the Alumni club, the first Argentinian team, and its founder Alexander Watson Hutton, the Scottish teacher who is considered to be the founding father of soccer in Argentina. The film was part of the portfolio of the Artistas Argentinos Asociados, whose scriptwriter was Homero Manzi, well known as an intellectual proponent of Peronism and as the author of a pedagogic history for mass consumption.[18] Again, we can see that soccer was considered to be an important component in the narrative of nationality, as was, for instance, the biography of the eminent Domingo Sarmiento, which was filmed as *Su mejor alumno*.

These films represented the hopes of a social class for whom sport (especially soccer, already by then a professional sport) had become a possible mechanism for social and cultural mobility. Sports heroes are icons of the republican concept of egalitarianism that is suited to modern societies; they appeal to the citizens through their simple mortality; heroes are rooted in the meritocratic principle which presupposes the formal equality of both opportunities and resources.[19] In other words, the 'popular heroes' are not different from us: they just have deservedly gained more money.[20] And the mass media is an ideal tool for transmitting the epics of sport heroes and, in this way, reasserting the belief in equality. A good example of the glorification of sport in this period centres on the almost mythical sporting prowess of the boxer José María Gatica, the 'Monkey'. In this sense, Argentina relies on a historical image of 'global sporting heroes', which locates these talented, mediated athletes as a kind of national reference point. This heroic imagery rests upon the retention of a strong connection with the sportsman's own community, although each performance must also be located within a specific historical stage of the development of the global media. And this lineage of Argentinian sports heroes attains its crowning moment with Diego Maradona.

DIEGO MARADONA: (THE FIRST? THE LAST?) ARGENTINIAN SPORTING GLOBAL HERO

The heroic narrative is articulated around the individual who stands out from the rest by his or her own merits, and who therefore serves to reaffirm that personal success is not an impossibility. C. Bromberger states, however, that skill is not enough, that other features, like luck or deception, also determine a triumphant outcome, and in 1986 Diego Maradona demonstrated not only his own football merits but also the role of these external forces.[21] Against England he displayed something of his power over these external influences when he conjured up the first goal with the assistance of the 'hand of God', before he then proceeded to wave a spell over the English defence to score the second goal, one of the most enchanting ever seen.

However, this double excess of Maradona contains its own obstacle to the building of a new patriotic reference around soccer. Archetti correctly points out that Maradona's performance does not seem to be associated with a sense of 'national style': instead Maradona is considered to be unique. Archetti explains: 'The problem, from the Argentinian point of view is not only the fact that heroes are universalized in a context where soccer belongs to a kind of "world global culture", but that they are perceived as "historical accidents", as "products of an arbitrary nature".'[22] Maradona also understood his personal significance in a similar way, declaring: 'God plays with me'. From this viewpoint, the narrative of an Argentinian soccer style seems to be no more than a myth: individualism is the true story.

However, it is Maradona's global status, allied to his outstanding skill, that makes him a key reference point. He not only spent the major part of his career abroad; he also displayed his exceptional skill and prowess in the Argentinian shirt on many occasions. Maradona's dual symbolism spins in two directions: concentrically, towards the nation, he is the reference point; eccentrically, towards the world, Maradona seems to be Argentina's best and most emblematic ambassador. And Maradona is not a 'simulacrum' of the post-industrial society, as J. Baudrillard would propose, because his image does not precede the reality of his performance: instead the two coincide.[23]

During its global phase, the image of Diego Maradona contained the three elements of myth identified by B. Baczko: an affective context; a real phenomenon that can be converted into a set of discourses; and actors who give a meaning to this process.[24] The global sporting role, and the international economic value, of Maradona allowed Argentina to see itself, not as a major producer or purchaser in international financial markets, but as a potential stakeholder none the less. Maradona also added a much needed legitimizing value to Argentinian soccer itself. In 1978, Argentina had won the World Cup, but the result of the Argentina–Peru match had aroused considerable suspicion, and the perverse, militarized environment in which the tournament took place had not created the desired image for Argentinian soccer or society. But this dubious success in 1978 was instead replaced by the image of Argentina as the undisputed, and legitimate victors of 1986 and by the 'near' triumph as runners-up in 1990.[25]

Maradona's talent on the pitch has also allowed, with considerably less anguish, further elaboration on the theme of national identity. The 'hand of God' against the English team can even be read as a piece of creole knavery ('picardía criolla') against old enemies. After all, the matter was even significant enough in England to be raised within the portals of the University of Oxford: the goal played an important part in the updating of old national conflicts, in which the Falklands/Malvinas defeat remains an important issue.[26]

What Maradona as sporting hero sets out is the meaning of the fatherland. The apotheosis of Maradona in Argentina puts him at the centre of a hermeneutic struggle among different societal sectors, who seek to appropriate his meaning for their cause. In this sense it becomes possible to ask if it is soccer that now represents the fatherland? And, if so, then can soccer displace politics in Argentina?

The 1994 World Cup saw the climax to this struggle over meaning.

The global image of a truculent, disgraced Diego Maradona, accused of drug-taking, triggered contradictory themes and interpretations: was he the hero of the fatherland or an anti-hero, and an emoting opponent of the calm intellectual? Was his a positive energy that sparked emotion throughout an entire nation, or was his a negative energy that distorted the image of Argentina? Subsequently each new drama involving Maradona has established a tension between how the events are to be encoded and how their meaning is to be interpreted. It is not that these debates have replaced discussions on the national issue, but they have occurred in tandem with this wider discussion, albeit in a somewhat haphazard fashion.

At the centre of that tension, one now finds the media's vacillation on whether to include Diego Maradona in the pantheon of those to be characterized as a 'genius'. There are those who believe that the facts of Maradona's early career brook no argument;[27] others ponder whether he can now be expelled from the immortality to which he had earlier been so popularly elected. Some insist that he should now be simply excluded from any collection of 'enlightened men', as a result of his lack of academic, and especially moral, education. The real Maradona proves to be a complex backdrop to the struggle over his meaning. He does not appear in the context of previous events, but as a set of emotions, perceived necessities and subjectivities which are related to patriotic feelings rather than to factual truths. The dominant classes' preference for a legitimate, upright national model for Argentina, has collided with Maradona's erratic actions and statements, not only on the sports field but also in the turbulent public display of his private life. Moreover, Maradona's life refused any simple packaging. These contradictions and inconsistencies made it very difficult for strong ideas to be produced around Maradona in some, essentialist sense of national identity. At the same time, efforts to address the collective inspirations of Maradona's contradictory human condition simply swung, like his own political comments, from the political left to the political right like a ceaseless pendulum.

If, for some in the media, Maradona was to be equated with great wealth, for others he could also be presented as a lost, wandering soul: that image resonated with a sense of a society in which the most elementary political references can simply collapse. Maradona had appeared to offer the chance (perhaps the last chance) of providing the Argentinian fatherland with an anchored centre, located in the very image of Maradona. Yet this apparent prospect had always been an impossibility. First, there were Maradona's increasingly ambiguous position in the soccer universe and his uneven professional performances. Second, there were his rapidly changing friendships and his own erratic political opinions which made him an 'object' whose possession was to be coveted by very different Argentine figures at different times. But also (and perhaps this is the most intriguing element) it was his erratic condition that allowed for the updating of values that were essential to national identity and culture.

THE FRACTURE: TRIBAL SOCCER IN GLOBAL TIMES

In a recent work, Archetti states that part of Maradona's epic is its continuity with the mythological tradition. Archetti explains: 'in a global scene where the production of local territories and identities is supposed to be difficult because the lived-worlds of local subjects tend to become deterritorialized, diasporic and transnational ones',[28] it is the continuity of the myth of the Argentinian style embodied by Maradona that allows this identity to survive. However, with the exit of Maradona from this scene, the local–global mediation of the national hero is put in crisis. His expulsion from the 1994 World Cup coincided with the second round elimination of the Argentinian team, suggesting a cause-effect relationship. Maradona, kicked out of the World Cup, drags the whole nation down with him. From there, Argentina's global stock depreciates, and the nation declines into its traditional and scarcely relevant position of food producer and weak exporter of cheap commodities: no image of Argentina as a global stakeholder remains. The mythology of Argentinian soccer, a mixture of successes and heroes, of original styles and careful play, is also seen, unexpectedly, to lack any real referent.

The following years illustrate this picture. Maradona became an ineffective and non-systematic player; in his erratic political behaviour, progressive politics were abandoned and he seemed to find a niche near to populist neoconservatism. Maradona's personal stature declined so that he no longer represents a sense of nationality.[29] Argentinian soccer players, although they continue to be exported massively to Europe, are seldom exceptional figures, and hardly any play in the very best teams. The explosion in access to cable television services, and with it the international sport scene, has allowed Argentinian audiences to confirm that their domestic game is excluded from these new global arenas.

Argentinian soccer, then, is in a crisis situation similar to the one which followed the Swedish World Cup in 1958, when the six goal defeat by Czechoslovakia fractured all earlier senses of national composure.

However, this crisis is not only a football one. It is not only the failure of a tactical system that is confirmed, but also the collapse of the mythological coupling of soccer and nation in which, during the Populist periods, the State claimed to be Argentina's greatest hero. This collapse has occurred in conjunction with the full globalization of Western capitalism. Argentina cannot by itself respond appropriately to the question of how it is to deal with the development of this global dimension. So how does Argentina mark itself out within the flow of transnational discourses now? Renato Ortiz points out that the globalization process deflects discourses and products from the national popular and towards the international popular. In this new discursive frame, the traditional symbols of the Brazilian nation-state – samba, carnival, soccer – are replaced by new global products: publicity, and Formula 1.[30] What is interesting is that in this new system of goods and commodities, sport and the heroic reappear: Ayrton Senna, three times World champion, martyr of global motoring, hero of the Brazilian nation. Brazilian culture seems to have discovered its own particular global form, by penetrating global markets with symbolically luxury goods for the privileged. Even if Ronaldo and Denhilson are not the best soccer players in the world, they are the most expensive.

Alternatively, a collision of discourses takes place in Argentina. A hegemonic political and economical neoconservatism which proclaims Argentina's entry to the First World, coexists daily with the negative experiences of the middle and working classes: the acute deterioration of living conditions, increasing poverty and the negative rather than positive effects of the global market place (the declining value of domestic goods, and increasing unemployment and drug trafficking). To make matters worse, traditional Argentine goods like soccer – as a profitable export and as symbolic capital – have also disappeared from the market.

Argentinian soccer seems unable to produce new global heroes. An epic story is not possible without heroes to support it. The post-Maradona void is too great. In consequence, what prevails are small and domestic Latin American epics. The exacerbation of a mild jingoism has released hints of anti-imperialism that were prevalent, for example, in the traditional football confrontation with England. The resulting chauvinism and racism shelter in the myth of ethnic unity, between the reality of Latin American multi-ethnicity and massmedia paranoia, which explains all Argentinian defeats via some kind of global conspiracy theory. The industrial explosion of global telecommunications and the scale of sports programme audiences finds Argentina in too weak a situation to impose itself 'naturally' on this new order. Hence, media discourses manufacture and replace the strictly sporting strategies with marketing ones. Here the soccer player Ariel Ortega is paradigmatic. Ortega is acclaimed as a new Maradona. He is given the number 10 shirt for the national team. His sale to Spain (to a second rate team, Valencia) is promoted as a continuation of the Maradona story. The rough treatment which he receives from rival defences (the test of every hero) is especially noted in the attempt to validate the tale. And his class extraction is emphasized: arising from the poor classes of Argentina's interior, Ortega (called Orteguita, a *pibe*, like Maradona, a new boy who transgresses the mature and hyperprofessionalized soccer world with his brio and enthusiasm) is shown to be one of the last Argentinian players with this traditional background. But, without players who possess these humble origins, there can be no epic myths that illustrate the supposed opportunity for sudden social mobility in Argentina. Yet nowadays the Argentinian working classes, subjected to deplorable conditions of malnutrition and illiteracy in childhood, are excluded from the hyperprofessionalism of global sport and its elite practice.

But while professional soccer excludes these classes, football is still embraced by all those it touches. No discourse in Argentinian society is a stranger to football: daily life suffers from *futbolitis*;[31] domestic soccer minutiae flood on to the front pages not only of the popular press, but also the quality media; intellectual discourses also surrender to the attraction of the moving ball. The traditional over-representation of the working classes in football has been displaced by an apparently classless appeal. And, in that expansion, soccer still practices a gender imperialism too, despite the accelerated incorporation of women, both on television and at stadiums, and via the appearance of many women who work as sport journalists.

Despite this invasion of new soccer territories, the lack of unifying myths within sport cannot supplant the weakness of the traditional national stories. After Peronism, the deterioration of modern Argentinian institutions – the State, the education system, the Trade

Unions – makes it hard to find, short term, new discourses and symbols that might represent national identity. Meanwhile, soccer is submerged in a state of exacerbated *tribalization*, where local oppositions – clashes between traditional rivals, the capital-province opposition, the neighbourhood rivalries in a city – are stretched out to the point where they shape primary identities.[32] Moreover, the national team is now overpowered by these processes, and is accused of being merely a faction owing allegiance to clubs rather than the nation. Once an emblem of unity, the team is now seen to be determined by tribal logic. The prior discourse of nationality is absent, in the same way in which the neo-conservative State is absent from everyday life.

Contemporaneously, the emblem of national unity is delivered by the cultural industry. The multimedia company America TV, in triumphalist style, broadcast several games from the Latin American World Cup qualifiers from 1996–98. It made a giant flag (approximately 150 metres wide and costing $40,000) which was 'donated' to an 'Argentinian supporter' to be used at the home match against Ecuador. The flag was in Argentinian colours, with the logo of the channel printed in its lower half, along with a legend saying 'Argentina is passion' (the motto of the television channel is 'America is passion'). It was shown at the beginning of the game and during the *intermezzo*, filling a whole terrace of the stadium, thus allowing the television camera opposite to capture this advertisement. Meanwhile, sheltered from view beneath the flag, spectators were threatened by dozens of pickpockets who demanded that they hand over their belongings. Thus, between the sponsorship of patriotism and delinquency, our national story continues.

NOTES

1. See among others J. MacClancy (ed.), *Sport, Identity and Ethnicity* (Oxford, 1996); J.A. Mangan (ed.), *Tribal Identities: Nationalism, Europe, Sport* (London, 1996); P. Lanfranchi (ed.), *Il calcio e il suo pubblico* (Napoli, 1992); R. Giulianotti and J. Williams (eds), *Game Without Frontiers: Football, Identity and Modernity* (Aldershot, 1994); A. Brown (ed.), *Fanatics! Power, Identity and Fandom in Football* (London, 1998).

2. See E. Archetti, 'Argentina and the World Cup' (hereafter 'Argentina'), in J. Sugden and A. Tomlinson (eds.), *Hosts and Champions: Soccer Cultures, National Identities and the USA World Cup* (Aldershot, 1994); 'Nationalism, Football and Polo', paper presented at the workshop, *Locating Cultural Creativity*, University of Copenhagen (October 1994); 'Estilo y virtudes masculinas en *El Gráfico*: la creación del imaginario del fútbol argentino', *Desarrollo Económico*, Revistas del Ciencias Sociales, 35, 139 (1995); 'The Potrero and the Pibe: Territory and Belonging in the Mythical Account of Argentinian Football', unpublished paper; '"And Give

Joy to My Heart": Ideology and Emotions in the Argentinian Cult of Maradona', in G. Armstrong and R. Giulianotti (eds.), *Entering the Field: New Perspectives on World Football* (Oxford, 1997).

3. R. Guber, 'Reflexiones sobre algunos usos nacionales de la Nación', in *Causas y Azares*, 5, 61.
4. Lugones and Rojas were the main intellectual figures behind Argentinian nationalism of the 1920s.
5. Archetti, 'Estilo y virtudes masculinas en *El Gráfico*', 440.
6. The idea of a creole style, which merges different tactical elements with individual practices, is related to the foundation of certain mythical places like the *potrero* (urban wasteground), and of popular figures like the *pibe* (carefree boy) (see Archetti, 'The Potrero and the Pibe'). But certain evidence points out that this imaginary construction worked widely within the new urban society: already in 1919, the first edition of the children's magazine *Billiken* showed on its cover 'The champion of the season', the image of a dishevelled boy clothed in soccer gear and bearing the marks of a tough game. This was exactly the opposite image to the 'official' one, that of a neat, obedient and scholarly boy, which was then hegemonic. Images that were contrary to the discourses of the leading classes circulated through the media, even in a contradictory way: the publishing company of *Billiken*, which also publishes *El Gráfico* belongs to the most conservative and Catholic sectors of Argentinian society. See M. Varela, *Los hombres ilustres del Billiken* (Buenos Aires, 1994).
7. R. Ortiz, 'Lo actual y la modernidad', *Nueva Sociedad* (Nov.–Dec. 1991), 96.
8. Ibid.
9. These categories are employed in R. Ortiz, *Cultura brasileira and identidade nacional* (São Paulo, 1985).
10. B. Anderson, *Comunidades Imaginadas* (Méjico, 1993), p.21.
11. See N. García Canclini, *Culturas híbridas: estrategias para entrar y salir de la modernidad* (Méjico, 1991).
12. The Peronist government intervened right across the whole media system. Radio and television and some graphic media were nationalized. Peronism also established a state-private industry partnership in some areas of the graphic media, but this was under the control of men of straw. See G. Mastrini and M. Abregú, 'Orígenes de la televisión privada argentina' (mimeo, 1990); R. Noguer, *La radiodifusión en la Argentina* (Buenos Aires, 1985); M. Plotkin, *Mañana es San Perón* (Buenos Aires, 1993).
13. Are we at the point, noted by E. Renan, where forgetfulness plays a role in the formation of the Nation? This collective amnesia, for this author, is indispensable to the formation of a collective imagining of the nation. See E. Gellner, *Cultura, identidad y política* (Barcelona, 1993).
14. The State policies of this period were part of a broad welfare programme embracing health, education, women's promotion, social welfare, distribution of cultural goods, etc.
15. We refer here to the organization of the 'Campeonatos Infantiles Evita' (children's championships), and the 'Torneos Juveniles Juan Perón' (youth tournaments). These competitions reached the whole nation and were complemented by the involvement of the Unión de Estudiantes Secundarios (secondary students' union) and the university and technical associations. See S. Senén González, 'Perón y el deporte', *Todo es Historia*, 345 (April 1996).
16. The soccer case is peculiar because during this period the number of direct spectators rose considerably: 'On the 1946–1950 quinquennial an average of 12,755 tickets were sold at each match; meanwhile the 1951–1955 one registered an average of 12,685 tickets. If we take annual values, 1954, with 15,056 spectators by match, has established the top record of a decade in which the attendance average has never been less than 10,000'. See A. Scher and H. Palomino, *Fútbol: pasión de multitudes y de elites* (Buenos Aires, 1988), p.79 (our translation).
17. During the 1945–55 decade, Argentina lived through an era that can be termed a 'sports party'. At the first Panamerican Games, in 1951, hosted in Buenos Aires, Argentina won 153 medals: 66 gold, 50 silver and 37 bronze. In more global terms, we can point to: the first victory against England in 1953; the 1950 triumph of Argentina in the World Basketball Championship; the South American Football Championships in 1946 and 1947; the gold medal won by Delfo Cabrera in the London Olympics in 1948; the victory of Domingo Marimón in the same year in the motoring competition Buenos Aires-Caracas, otherwise known as 'América del Sur'; the

outstanding performance of Juan Manuel Fangio in Europe, who in 1951 and 1954 won the World Motoring Championship; the triumphs of the boxer José María Gatica; the respective boxing Championship titles obtained by Pascual Pérez and Rafael Iglesias at their own weights; the World Junior Chess Championship won by Oscar Panno, etc.

18. Argentinian history is narrated through the films *La guerra gaucha*, *Su mejor alumno*, *El último payador*.
19. See A. Ehrenberg, 'Estadios sin dioses', *Revista de Occidente*, 134–5, (July–August, 1992).
20. This is an essential difference observed by Vittorio Dini between the mythological heroes and the modern sporting ones: 'The lower the original social and cultural condition, the higher is his/her capacity of being represented as a hero.' See V. Dini (ed.), *Te Diegum, genio, sregolatezza e baccettoni* (Milano, 1991), p.46 (our translation).
21. C. Bromberger, 'The Passion for Football and the World Cup', in J. Sugden & A. Tomlinson (eds.), *Hosts and Champions*.
22. 'Argentina', p.56.
23. J. Baudrillard, 'La precesión de lo real', in *Cultura y Simulacro* (Barcelona, 1987).
24. B. Baczko, *Los imaginarios sociales. Memorias y esperanzas colectivas* (Buenos Aires, 1991).
25. During the 1976–1983 military dictatorship, Diego Maradona played in two World Championships: the Youth Championship of Japan in 1979 and the World Cup of Spain in 1982. The first one was screened in Argentina with a black line across the screen to cover up opposition banners against the government. The second one, coinciding with a very poor performance by the national team, happened in the context of acute political crisis: defeat in the Falklands War and the fall of the military junta.
26. Receiving the 'Master Inspirer of Dreams' award from a group of students at the University of Oxford, Diego Maradona admitted, somewhat elliptically, to the famous 'Hand of God'.
27. Varela, *Los hombres*, p.57.
28. Archetti, 'The Potrero and the Pibe', p.15.
29. P. Alabarces & M. Rodríguez, *Cuestión de Pelotas* (Buenos Aires, 1996).
30. Ortiz, 'Lo actual y la modernidad'.
31. The word comes from the name of a theatre play which opened recently in Buenos Aires, where soccer is presented as a psychological pathology that affects every citizen. The main character is a traditional member of the urban middle classes. The piece has important repercussions for the critic and the audience.
32. M. Maffesoli, *El tiempo de las tribus* (Barcelona, 1990).

6

Built by the Two Varelas:
The Rise and Fall of Football Culture and
National Identity in Uruguay

RICHARD GIULIANOTTI

The sky-blue shirt was proof of the existence of the nation: Uruguay was not a mistake. Football pulled this little country out of the shadows of universal anonymity.[1]

Other countries have their history, Uruguay has its football.[2]

If a society has been notably successful in practising a cultural discipline, then it is to be expected that Western sociologists and anthropologists will soon arrive to investigate. In the case of football cultures, we find much evidence that the leading nations have been researched and written on at some length. Argentina, Brazil, Holland, Italy, England, Germany, Sweden and Scotland (*sic*) have each been examined by academics in papers for Western audiences, with later attention turning to the prospective football powers in Africa and the Far East. To date, a serious deficiency in this scholarly project is the minuscule coverage given to one of the world's most important football cultures in South America. Whereas the more voguish football cultures of Argentina and Brazil have been well documented by historians and social analysts, the remarkable case of Uruguay has been largely ignored by Western investigators, save for the odd conference paper or short historical reference.[3]

In its infancy, South American football was dominated by Uruguay. Historians have unearthed a wealth of primary source documents and personal effects, such as letters and diaries, which testify to the Uruguayans' fanaticism in watching or discussing football, and their technical excellence in playing the game.[4] International results from the first half of the century testify to this dominance. The team known as *los celestos* (skyblues) for their national colours, won the gold medal in football at the 1924 and 1928 Olympics; momentous achievements given greater lustre by the fact that both tournaments were held in Europe

(Paris and Amsterdam) when football teams playing in different continents tended to find the going much more difficult than today.[5] Uruguay then hosted and won the inaugural World Cup finals in 1930, still captained by the great Nasazzi, the 'first *caudillo* of Uruguayan football'.[6] This home victory was followed 20 years later by the Uruguayans' greatest success at the finals in Brazil. The records further demonstrate that Uruguay have won the South American championship on 17 occasions, and the equivalent club tournament, the Copa Libertadores, eight times (five times by Peñarol, three times by Nacional).

Uruguay's illustrious football history is miraculous when viewed solely in social demographic terms. The national population did not reach one million until the first few years of the twentieth century, rising by about 25 per cent per decade until the early 1930s, when the figure passed 1,750,000.[7] The population has risen slowly since then, relative to other South American nations, and is around the 3,250,000 mark as the century ends. The majority are the descendants of late nineteenth- and twentieth-century migrants from Spain and Italy, the original indigenous population having been all but wiped out during early European colonization. Current estimates put the ethnic composition at 88 per cent white, 8 per cent mestizo and 4 per cent black, with most of the latter descended from Brazilian migrants. Mediterrranean influence is reflected in the identity of some of Uruguay's greatest players: Nasazzi, Gestido, Scarone from the 1930 team; Maspoli, Gambetta, Ghiggia, Schiaffoni from the 1950 side. Montevideo was the obvious beneficiary of this European influx, swollen further by the migration of rural labourers from Uruguay's interior. The capital claimed 30 per cent of the national population at the turn of the century, rising to approximately 45 per cent today.[8] Its power is reflected in the failure of Uruguay's provincial teams to survive in a First Division dominated by Montevideo clubs.

FOOTBALL AND THE NATION: INTERCHANGEABLE HISTORICAL METAPHORS

Uruguay's football history might be said to provide a metaphor for the nation's turbulent genealogy. Established officially as the Oriental Republic of Uruguay in 1828, Uruguay became a buffer state on the La Plata river between Brazil and Argentina. The first two decades of independence were riven with civil war; the Blanco Party that controlled the interior laid siege to Montevideo, which was then under the aegis of the opposition Colorado Party. Though the battle ended in 1851, the two parties have since dominated Uruguayan political life. As the Colorados retained greater powers, so the Blancos responded with two failed revolutionary uprisings in 1897 and 1904. At their conclusion, the Colorado leader, Batlle, set in motion a string of social reforms which pulled Uruguay out of feudalism and on to the brink of liberal modernity. The *batllismo* policies saw education expand, the state was secularized and greater economic interventionism promoted infrastructure developments.

Football took root in Montevideo at this time. Like other South American nations, football's social genesis in Uruguay derived from British influence in the maritime industries, the construction of railways and the education system.[9] The first predominantly soccer club, Albion FC, was founded in June 1861 in Montevideo; two decades later there were reports of football being played in physical education classes in the British high school.[10] While the British game was being cultivated, so too were European economic relationships and social values that were central to rapid modernization.[11] Nevertheless, in line with the game's working-class predominance in the United Kingdom, the activities of British railway workers had a more lasting success. In 1891, 118 British and Uruguayan employees of the British-owned Central Uruguayan Railway founded the Central Uruguayan Railway Cricket Club; Englishman Frank Hudson became the first president. By the start of the First World War, the local members' penchant for football rather than cricket had come to determine its activities, as the club was renamed Peñarol, after the locale where the railway works were situated.[12] The club colours, of black and gold stripes, were borrowed from those used by the railroad as distress signals, while *los carboneros* ('the coal-shovellers') remains a popular club nickname.[13]

The great pre-war Peñarol team was assisted mostly by two exceptional players, John Harley and José Miguel Piendibene Ferrari. Harley was born in Glasgow in 1886, and, following a sojourn across Argentina, arrived in Uruguay in 1909. He captained the Peñarol side for eight years, playing at centre-half while teaching those around him the passing game, before retiring in 1920. At five years Harley's junior, Piendibene made his Peñarol debut at the age of 17 in 1908, going on to play for a full two decades as the club's most prolific goal-scorer, showcasing throughout the technical skills that local *criollos* could bring to the game's highest level.[14]

In order to 'snatch sports from the hands of foreigners', and to challenge the British football hegemony, the Club Nacional was founded by Hispanic students at the University of Montevideo in 1899.[15] In priding themselves on being the definitively 'Uruguayan' side, Nacional were also the more middle-class entity, and retained a ban on black players for over 20 years. The wider British influence was gradually expunged in the official culture of Uruguayan football; its working language was transferred into Spanish and the national football association became the Asociación Uruguaya de Fútbol, affiliating to FIFA in 1923. Today, the British parenting of Uruguayan football continues primarily through what Raymond Williams would term its 'residual' aspects, such as the names of smaller clubs: Liverpool, River Plate, Rampla Juniors, Racing and Wanderers.[16] The latter had been founded in 1902 after splitting from Nacional, and became a footballing refuge for the upper middle-classes including the old British élite. Wanderers remained determinedly amateur, thereby authenticating its class and cultural distinctions from more working-class and Latin clubs.

As football became established in the southern cone, largely under British patronage and wherever the railroads sprang up, so Argentinian and Uruguayan teams developed in symbiosis. The donation of a trophy by Sir Thomas Lipton in 1902, to be competed for by clubs from Montevideo and Buenos Aires, helped to germinate the style of *fútbol rioplatense* (football from the Rio de la Plata).[17] Matches between Argentina and Uruguay took place on a regular basis, acquiring a derby atmosphere. In 1916, prior to one fixture, the authorities printed too many tickets for the game which was soon sold out, entailing its postponement. Enraged fans responded by setting fire to the stadium in a blaze that left only the central pavilion standing. Jingoistic sentiments became more pervasive as the two nations competed on the world stage. Following Uruguay's success in the 1924 Olympics, the Argentinians challenged the new champions to a two-legged friendly to assuage their pride. After drawing 1–1 in Montevideo, the second match in Buenos Aires descended into farce, the game being abandoned due to crowd encroachments and the visitors' fear for their safety. At the rescheduled game, Argentina were leading 2–1 when the crowd started throwing stones at the Uruguayan players, who responded by returning the barrage. One player was arrested for police assault and the game was abandoned with five minutes remaining as the Uruguayans trudged off for their own safety. Six years later, the violent rivalry was rekindled as Argentina lost to Uruguay in the Montevideo World Cup final. After the match, fans rioted in Buenos Aires; Uruguayan institutions were attacked, one woman was stoned and two people shot dead.[18]

The British role behind Uruguay's successes should not be underestimated. Crucially, the Uruguayans had been exposed to more than one British playing style. While other football nations in South America and Europe had tended to learn and settle on a single aesthetic, the early Uruguayan players had been tutored in two distinctive playing traditions: the 'kick and rush', physical game of England, and the more refined, methodical, passing game from Scotland.[19] Uruguayan teams were able to switch between either model of play, according to the demands of the particular game. At the 1924 Olympics in Paris, the Uruguayans were the 'revelation' of the tournament, thrashing the hosts 5–1 with a 'style that has been variously described as combining artistry, entertainment, virtuosity, and professionalism'.[20] Uruguay were particularly adept at employing counter-attacking manoeuvres, giving rise to the popular refrain, 'Argentina attack, Uruguay score!'

Domestically, Uruguay's early footballing successes had also been facilitated by the nation's economic growth and strong modernization of its civil infrastructure. Parks and football grounds were built into urban development for the workers to exercise their leisure time. The number of public playing areas in Montevideo alone went from two in 1913 to 118 in 1929, effectively securing the next generation of talented players.[21] Black players were soon entering the national team on merit, to the chagrin of South American opponents and the delight of many European audiences: the midfielder Andrade, the 'Black Marvel', was the fullest illustration of this trend.[22] However, Uruguay's first World Cup success in 1930 also marked the end of its formative, economic good times. The Great Depression struck and Uruguay's large ranching economy, with its emphasis on meat, wool and dried-beef exports, began to contract. Batlle's death in 1929 left a huge political void. Yet, economic recession failed to dampen the cultivation of national identification. Uruguay was gradually transformed from a curious melange of disparate ethnic groups to a nation that housed common cultural practices and symbols, most notably its victorious football team. In 1932, the year after professional football was introduced, a decade-long political dictatorship began that produced a conservative response to Uruguay's problems, and intensified internal migration from countryside to Montevideo. The competitive development of Uruguayan football during the 1930s and 1940s was handicapped similarly by severe financial problems.[23] Only Peñarol and Nacional could offer reasonable remuneration; players with smaller teams would look to join them or, more profitably, transfer to teams in Argentina or southern Europe. Disputes over professionalism were partly to blame for Uruguay's failure to attend the 1934 World Cup finals in Italy, in defence of their title, or the 1938 finals in France.[24] Like Argentina, Uruguay was also threatened by the theft of its best players by Italy, who 'naturalized' them as Italian citizens. Of these *oriundi*, the most illustrious was Andreolo, who filled the vital centre-half position as Italy retained the World Cup in 1938. As in football, so in the economy: Uruguay was at the weak end of her financial relationships with the Old World.

Soon after, however, external demand for Uruguay's farming products picked up, and brought the nation its most profitable times, as democratic government returned. The Second World War and the Korean War were major economic fillips, and helped give Uruguay the highest income per capita in Latin America. And during this time, the Uruguayans experienced their greatest footballing successes.

1950: THE COMING OF THE SECOND VARELA

It is in this context that César Aguiar forwards the argument that Uruguay is a nation built by the 'two Varelas'. The first, President Jose Pedro Varela, had contributed particularly to the foundation of general education in the late nineteenth century, preparing the new citizens for higher occupational positions.[25] A comparative deficit appeared within the cultural and symbolic spheres which would otherwise cement the nation into a sense of shared identification and popular consensus. The victory of the Uruguayan team in 1930 had helped to repair this shortfall. But, Uruguay needed a heroic figure and epic moment, which could encapsulate its prosperity and self-belief at home, and its significance on the international stage. The emergence of the second Varela, Obdulio, filled this lacuna, in his position as captain of the Uruguayan national team at the 1950 World Cup finals in Brazil. He performed the central role in the epic of the *Maracanazo*.[26]

As the tournament drew to its conclusion, through its final round of games between the last four teams, Brazil needed only a draw from its last match against the Uruguayans in Rio's Maracanã stadium. The partisan home crowd of 200,000 had viewed victory as a formality and had already prepared its carnivalesque celebrations. Famously, Jules Rimet, the President of FIFA, had penned a congratulatory speech for the Brazilians, and clasped it in his hands during the game. In defiance, the Uruguayans displayed a deep sense of national pride during the warm-up, striding around the Maracanã to show the home supporters their emblematic shirts. Constant Brazilian pressure was rewarded three minutes after half-time when the home side took the lead. Before play could restart, Varela took the ball under his arm and approached the English referee to complain, in Spanish, that the goal had been offside. He refused to return the ball until he had made himself understood; the lack of a common language saw an interpreter called before the match restarted. The delay disorientated Brazil. The Uruguayans equalized through Schiaffino and then Ghiggia scored the winner. Throughout the match, Varela had shown immense leadership, most notably in breaking up the waves of Brazilian attacks.

The match had a profound impact on the cultural psyche of the two nations. The Brazilian fans' immediate response was silent incomprehension, marred by several isolated cases of suicide. Later, in a resurgence of racial stereotyping, the black players in Brazil's defence were targeted as scapegoats.[27] Black goalkeepers are still regarded as footballing oxymorons in Brazil.[28] (Ironically, in Uruguay, the lionized Varela is known simply as *El Negro Jefe*, the 'Black Chief'.) The subsequent four World Cup triumphs (1958, 1962, 1970, 1994) may even be regarded as acts of penance by these national squads for the public capitulation of their forebears in the one tournament hosted by Brazil.[29] The match had a stronger symbolic impact upon Uruguayan identity. Not only had the football team triumphed over giant odds, but Varela's valorous performance had personified a profound sense of national belief and self-determination. The argument with the referee became an almost mythical moment, a metonym for the new Uruguay, and a pivotal image in the formulation of a collective memory within this modernizing nation. Before the tournament, Uruguayans may still have been interpreted as an ensemble of different ethnic groups, with a relatively amorphous sense of common identity. This underdeveloped 'we-image' was suddenly translated through the intensely charismatic persona of Varela into a strong 'we-ideal', the competitive and victorious insistence of the captain and his team.[30] Moreover, through the looking glass of this historical juncture, it could be imagined that globally, Uruguay would be seen as a serious national entity.

In retrospect, one might argue that Uruguay's two World Cup triumphs were assisted by European absence. Only Yugoslavia, France and Romania entered in 1930, the greater European superpowers (particularly the British ones) believing that the tournament lacked credibility. Though European interest had been cemented by 1950, the post-war reconstruction had barely begun by the time of Uruguay's second victory. More seriously, by that stage, it was apparent that social demographics had started to determine the parameters of the national side's technical virtuosity *vis-à-vis* their opponents. Victory may have been secured against Brazil, but the hosts had shown greater finesse and artistry, only to be overcome by the Uruguayans' heart and self-belief. Increasingly, the qualities of endeavour, teamwork and dedication came to distinguish the national side from its more populous South American rivals.

Although the match is recorded as a classic, defeat to Hungary in the Switzerland World Cup finals of 1954 is interpreted generally as Uruguay's first ever loss in serious international competition, marking a watershed in the nation's football fortunes.[31] Soon after, top players like Ghiggia and Schiaffino were lost to the Italian national team as new *oriundi*.[32] The national decline had been assuaged by victories at club level, most notably *los años de Peñarol* (the 1960s), during which they won the World club championship twice.[33] But since the mid-1950s the players have resorted increasingly to a nervous, physical style of play. According to Rafael Bayce, this decline is hastened by the twin processes of unrealistic public expectation and hostility towards its football exports.[34] The Uruguayan media voice the populist assumption that Uruguay should be one of the three or four South American qualifiers for all World Cup finals, alongside Brazil, Argentina and (presumably in the fourth qualifying spot) either Peru, Paraguay or Colombia. Yet, since being outclassed in the 1970 Mexico finals in the semi-final against Brazil, Uruguay's record at the highest level has not consummated such deep expectation. Failures to qualify in 1978 and 1982, and most recently in 1994 and 1998, must be coupled with poor performances in the finals of 1974, 1986 and 1990, in which Uruguay were eliminated before the quarter-finals. As the public routinely demand a return to the old values and methods, so the enervated internationalists of more recent times have taken the field in fear of their predecessors' shadows.

Early mistakes entail a loss in confidence, and the resort to a safer, more aggressive and physical style that reflects the media and public thinking on football as war by proxy. Particular pressure is put on those stars returning from more lucrative exile abroad; supporters criticize their efforts as corrupted by the lazy, rich, unpatriotic lifestyle that is allegedly enjoyed in foreign climes.[35]

ENTERING DECLINE: ECONOMIC AND PSYCHOLOGICAL INDICES

During the 1950s the plight of the national team was mirrored in the political and economic realms as Uruguay went into steady decline. The voters deserted the Colorados to elect the Blancos to power for the first time since 1865. Their failure to arrest Uruguay's decline, followed by the Colorado's ineffective administration from 1966–72, saw greater public protests and increasingly violent government crackdowns on students and trade unionists. The urban guerrilla group, the Tupamaros, became active, seeking to spark a socialist revolution through terrorist incidents. The government's inability to eliminate this threat strengthened the military's hand. The subsequent coup of 1972 was a desperate measure by rightist forces aimed at preventing the rise of a popular 'Broad Left'.[36] Initially, the new regime propped up the economy; wage restraints were imposed, high interest rates attracted lenders and the nation's infrastructure was rebuilt. However, the human cost of this 'stability' was appalling. Uruguay acquired the world's highest per capita rate for political prisoners; torture, disappearances and killings were routine instruments of social control, in tandem with press censorship and the dissolution of oppositional associations. A constitutional plebiscite was rejected by voters in 1980; the economy went into free fall, the currency collapsed and hundreds of businesses folded.

During military rule, the differentiation of football and formal politics regressed as democratic channels of public association were curtailed. The future Uruguayan President, Julio Maria Sanguinetti of the Colorados, was at this time the president of Peñarol, one of the few public positions that did not attract dangerous scrutiny. Other politicians of the same generation boast a past in football politics. The leader of the leftist Encuentro Progresista, Tabare Vazquez, was the president of the Progresso club, a small outfit from one of Montevideo's working-class *barrios*; and the future Vice-President of Uruguay and leader of the New

Sector coalition, Hugo Batalla, was once the president of the national football association (AUF).

While other politicos were driven to expending their energies within football, it would be an exaggeration to claim that more exploitative motivations were behind such participation. In South America, political interference is less common than actual involvement in the politics of football, that is in using the game as a 'trampoline' for energizing one's public image and springing into mainstream electioneering.[37] The military were also aware of football's populist potential. Peñarol were twice saved from financial collapse by the military rulers, who also organized a couple of international tournaments in 1980–81 for former World Cup winners.[38] Neither strategy comes close to the activities of Argentina's junta in staging the 1978 World Cup finals. Yet for some intellectuals on Uruguay's broad left, the game's public centrality was open to question; it reified social inequalities and deflected political energies from the fight to restore a less totalitarian state. These reservations were neatly encapsulated, in metaphorical language, by the popular Uruguayan group Rumbo, in a song entitled *Orsei* (Offside). The lyrics tell the story of a garage worker, who stops himself acclaiming a goal by his football hero, after reflecting on the huge salary differences between them.[39] In another song, Rumbo draws a further football-political analogy by noting the referee's rising powers and tendency to 'exile' players, a clear reference to the stream of dissenting Uruguayans who were then leaving the country.

The return to free elections was negotiated in 1984, re-establishing Uruguay's international status as the 'Switzerland of South America', its only true democracy.[40] The Colorados' leader, Sanguinetti, was elected president and full democracy and human rights were restored. But Uruguay's huge foreign debt could not be repaid so easily, leading to his replacement by the Blancos' Lacalle in 1990.[41] The presidency was swapped again in 1995, as Uruguay's economy began to stabilize and economic indicators fell inside more positive parameters. The economy has been further assisted by the growing integration of the southern cone nations through the Mercosur free trading agreement, involving Uruguay, Brazil, Argentina and Paraguay.[42]

The political culture has, however, been more successful in shrugging off violent methods than has the national football culture, which has shifted between two ideal types of play: the cerebral and the markedly physical. Archetti has written of how modern Argentinian football has been shaped by the dialectical interplay of two opposing tactical philosophies, as expressed by two World Cup-winning coaches. On one hand, there is the coach of 1978, César Menotti, and his technically orientated, aesthetic perspective; on the other is the coach of 1986, Carlos Bilardo, and his methodical, instrumental approach towards winning the game.[43] A similar binary may be interpreted as operating in Uruguay, with the recent influences of two coaches. On the one hand there is Oscar Washington Tabárez, a reflective almost aesthetic figure, known as a cosmopolitan teacher within the game, and committed to a technical style of play. On the other hand, there is Omar Borrás, a fitness expert and former national team manager, whose stock plummeted as early successes atrophied and the team resorted to a more physical, indeed brutal style of play.[44] Borrás's popularity had always been affected by his support for the military regime, though his attitudes epitomized wider views of what Uruguayan football required. In his penchant for physical play, at least, there is a genuine homology with the social control tactics employed by the military.

Paradoxically, while the objective picture of Uruguayan society has improved, and as the economy finds stability, the mood of its populace in the late 1990s has never been more pessimistic. Psychosocially, there is a collective perception that Uruguay is a decaying nation, where no discussion of the future may begin without strong valediction of a remarkably successful past. Social surveys and media perorations confirm that Uruguayans feel the most insecure of all Latin American nations. And yet comparatively, Uruguay is a long way along the 'civilizing process': there is no civil war or conflict zones on its borders; the constitution and its political custodians are relatively unchallenged; incidents of public violence are relatively rare; unemployment and general crime have not risen markedly in recent years.[45] It may be that football, upon which Uruguay was so reliant during its modern formative years, is playing a crucial role here. The public sense of entropy finds a ready referent in the obvious decline of the national team. The collapse of the domestic game affords more regular evidence of that decline, and it is to that development that I now turn.

FOOTBALL CULTURE: *MANYAS Y TRICOLORES*

History records that, at club level, the pre-eminence of Peñarol and Nacional has gone virtually unchallenged. Since 1933, the two sides have monopolized the championship, with Peñarol winning 33 times and Nacional 24 times.[46] The top two's popularity means they can enjoy privileges, such as to train 'in old, colonial-style home grounds and play their games in the huge Estadio Centenario, an open, concrete, multi-tiered bowl'.[47] Their duopoly is more than just mirrored within the political arena by the Colorados and Blancos, there being a nexus of football and politics here that is almost symmetrical. Peñarol's early association with the immigrant Italian community has not hindered its notorious connection with the Colorados, for whom Garibaldi was an inspirational figure. In the way of binary oppositions, Club Nacional's associations with the Blancos extend further than the symbolism of their white shirts, there being an elective affinity with the party's early appeal to the rural poor and displaced (rather than foreign immigrant groups), and the club's avowedly Uruguayan origins.

These opposing club genealogies have given rise to residual fan identities, which involve a referencing of the Spanish ties of Nacional, as offset by the popular Italianization of Peñarol. The latter's supporters were disparaged with the epithet *mangare merda* (to 'eat shit' in Italian), to calumniate their ethnicity and perceived low social status (Boca Junior fans across the Rio Plata in Buenos Aires have experienced similar stigmatization). In response, these insults were refashioned by Peñarol fans into a supporter identity, in declaring themselves to be *manyas*, in songs, slogans and signatures on their black and gold appareil. In contrast, the higher socio-cultural status of the old Nacional fans is reflected in more discreet nicknames, such as the *tricolores* or the *bolsos*. The former refers to the 'three colours' in which they play: blue, white and red, which are identical to those of General José Artigas, the nationalist hero of independence, and underwrites further the club's claim to be *the* Uruguayan side.[48] The latter, meaning 'pockets', refers to the shape of the club crest. Yet, overall, the establishment of a collective Uruguayan identity by the middle of the century, meant that club affiliation on the basis of ethnicity or class was increasingly out-dated.

While the Penãrol–Nacional derby match is Uruguay's biggest, the other *clásico* involves the intense rivalry of two clubs, Cerro and Rampla Juniors, which both hail from Montevideo's Cerro district. Before the 1950s Cerro had been a town with a cultural and economic identity distinct from the capital. Its denizens were principally working class, originally employed in the old cattle industries concentrated in Cerro, with a strong ethnic flavour of eastern and southern European immigrants. The town's football passions were focused on the local team of Rampla Juniors, founded in 1914. However, as the geo-social boundaries with the old capital were broken down, so new money, industries and inhabitants entered. The rival (and initially more successful) club of Cerro was founded in 1946, and soon established itself as the more popular, working class club, drawing supporters from peripheral areas, while Rampla held on to the more central, middle class supporter groups.[49] Nevertheless, like other classic football rivalries across the world, the Cerro–Rampla derby is said now to divide families and dissolve friendships, as the sometimes violent opposition is at least as intense as that between their more illustrious rivals.

In line with other South American nations such as Argentina and Paraguay, the Uruguayan football season contains two league championships – an opening and closing one – with a play-off between the two winners to decide the top team. The teams qualifying for the Copa Libertadores must play in an end of season *Liguilla*, consisting of the play-off finalists, and the surviving four clubs from a knock-out series involving the next eight First Division teams and leading provincial sides. The emerging club of Defensor has taken best advantage of this situation. While the top two clubs fight it out for the historical prize of taking the Uruguayan championship, Defensor bide their time and seek to ensure qualification for the money-spinning Copa Libertadores. They also draw heavily on their pool of talented young players, acquired and trained as part of the club's advanced youth policy.[50] The remaining Uruguayan clubs have always been reliant on playing Penãrol and Nacional to increase their gate money. Morales found that, in the 1960s, these *clubes chicos* accrued 66–85 per cent of their spectator income from matches against *los grandes*.[51] This state of dependency remains today, such that all matches involving the big two tend to be transferred to the national stadium, the *Estadio Centenario*, to cater for demand and maximize revenues. Alternatively, the second Uruguayan *clásico*, between Rampla and Cerro, can easily be accommodated in a smaller ground, again highlighting the gulf between the top two clubs and the rest.

FOOTBALL BANKRUPTCY: ORGANIZATIONAL AND ECONOMIC ENTROPY

The financial weaknesses of Uruguayan football are immediately indicated by the fact that matches switched to the *Centenario* can struggle for attendances of above 10,000, even if the admission fee is lowered to around 10 pesos (roughly $1). Uruguayans' interest in domestic football has declined markedly. Recent surveys give the lie to the Latin American mythology of football as *pasión de multitudes*. Just over 60 per cent of Uruguayans admit they have little or no interest in football, whether in attending fixtures or watching on television. The range of explanations for this decline varies, with the most common one being a simple fall in interest. More sociological factors have been sought in the debate over television coverage of football. As well as rising in terms of live matches, the AUF attracted considerable criticism for selling broadcasting rights to the Argentinian station *T y C*. Research found that television coverage was most appealing to the less powerful social groups, particularly minors, welfare dependants and those with lower levels of education.[52]

An earlier survey of Uruguayans had given greater consideration to the question of football hooliganism. It found that around 14 per cent did not attend fixtures for reasons of personal security, with around 38 per cent blaming what trouble took place on the general *hinchadas* (fans). The atmosphere of domestic fixtures has been clouded by several recent deaths, including two murders at Peñarol–Nacional derbies, and the fatal stabbing of a fan by a 14-year-old boy following a Nacional–Cerro fixture. Nevertheless, only 5–7 per cent of respondents felt that watching football in Uruguay was more dangerous than in other specified nations (including Argentina and England), suggesting that local fans understood the real scale of their problem.[53] Equally, one may conclude that changing the atmosphere of club games will have little impact upon attendances: the malaise within the game is more deep-rooted.

Organizationally, Uruguayan football is in poor shape. The league is regularly beset by financial and administrative problems. In 1997, for example, ten AUF officials resigned rather than award points to one club to save its relegation, while referees went on strike for one week to obtain greater industrial influence. While the First Division struggles on with a dozen clubs, the lower leagues face a more onerous task; the season often starts late, while clubs regularly withdraw in mid-season after succumbing to bankruptcy. Even in terms of player recruitment, the top clubs lack a sound professional strategy. Apart from the creation of an organized scouting and coaching system at Defensor, with its effective link to the basketball club, Uruguayan clubs rely on discovering players from an informal network of 'scouts' and club associates.

A deeper structural weakness, relative to the European game, is that clubs are democratically rather than commercially organized. They are not owned as private enterprises by businessmen or institutions, but are instead run as private associations, in which the *socios* (members) pay a subscription to join the club. Membership allows the *socios* to use the club's facilities (such as the public bar, tennis courts, gym and swimming pool), as well as providing them with reduced admission fees to matches, and voting rights during the election of office bearers. The distribution of *socios* between the clubs, however, highlights the socio-economic and competitive inequalities between them. While a smaller club like Wanderers might attract 1,500 *socios* paying in the region of $100 annually, Peñarol and Nacional may each draw in 20 times that membership, with their *socios* paying up to $200 annually, according to the range of facilities that they wished to use.

Income from the *socios* is itself not enough to cover the players' wages. Club office-holders are expected to contribute some of their personal finances, but this alone cannot stave off the creditors. Without the benefaction of a rich owner to turn to, the real financial lifeblood of Uruguayan club football must come from other external sources, of which there are two: player sales and prize-money from the national team. In relation to player sales, Uruguayan clubs are known to be in a weak bargaining position, hence overseas clubs are attracted by the comparatively low transfer fees demanded for quality players. In 1997, O'Neill was signed by Cagliari for $600,000, while Recoba, a precociously gifted 21-year-old, moved to Internazionale of Milan for $2.8 million.[54]

Currently, over 400 Uruguayan players ply their trade overseas, a figure sufficient to fill the first team squads of Uruguay's First and Second Divisions. Unlike the boast of Brazilian clubs that such a diaspora is easily stemmed by unearthing yet more gifted players, Uruguay's constraining demographics ensure that migrant talents cannot easily be replaced. Even at the top clubs, the standard of play has declined dramatically, and is only arrested episodically by the discovery of young talents (quickly sold) or the return of aged, spent former superstars.

Until the 1980s the clubs' preconcern with their players' exchange values was not matched by good contractual relations. A state of industrial bondage fostered player resentment and opened the door to player agents. One entrepreneur, Paco Casal, emerged to become Uruguayan football's most powerful figure. This self-made businessman with a near mythical public persona is now the leading dealer in the football labour market, signing talented players in their early years and negotiating for them with domestic clubs, while lobbying for their transfer to Europe through his myriad contacts. For aspiring young players, therefore, Casal rather than a top football club is the 'institution' to sign for, owing to his skills in brokering higher salaries and developing professional careers.

While Casal's work has certainly improved the personal terms and status of players within Uruguayan football, his global contacts mean that their migration abroad is now positively institutionalized. Both supply and demand pressures mean that the best years of Uruguayan players are spent abroad, which does nothing to help attendances at matches at home.[55] The exodus of players has had a debilitating effect on the fortunes of the national team. Though the AUF may successfully apply to foreign clubs for the release of internationalists, the distance subsequently travelled for team meetings, as well as their short duration, limit the development of player camaraderie or playing tactics before fixtures. Hence, the decline of club and international football is intertwined. Uruguay's declining international status has hit the clubs badly, pushing them into a downward spiral of indebtedness, player sales and migration, poorer national team performances, and even lower prize money.

It is a cycle of entropy that is difficult to break. In a mirror of Latin America's political economy, Uruguayan football is on the world periphery. Its state of dependency on wealthier, more Westernized football nations also means it is caught up in the 'development of underdevelopment'. This process involves the economic 'surplus' of developing societies being transferred abroad (just as Uruguay's best players are), leading to a lack of further economic development and a furthering of global inequalities (crowds stay low, interest wanes, the clubs and national team deteriorate, so more players must be sold to meet the deficit).[56] In the powerful shape of Paco Casal, moreover, we have the effective institutionalization of this impoverishing global arrangement, one that is increasingly difficult to deconstruct and replace with a more domestically suitable footballing infrastructure. A. Klein has provided a similar analysis of baseball in the Caribbean, as US and Japanese clubs exploit and import the young 'raw materials' found in these developing nations, leaving local fans to watch only the sub-standard 'residue'.[57] The condition of Uruguayan domestic football is rather masked by the consistent competition of its top two teams in the numerous South American club tournaments. Nevertheless, there seems to be nothing that can arrest the stream of top players to better-paying clubs abroad. Finally, we may note here that A. Frank's conception of 'under-development' highlights the arrested modernization of 'developing' economies. Uruguayan football has suffered a similar retardation in terms of tactical and organizational under-development. One symptom of this process is the resort of the public culture surrounding football to regressive nostalgia or violent attitudes when assessing the national team, rather than the exploration of new tactics and playing styles that would be in accord with early Uruguayan innovation.

On occasions when players cannot be identified for sale, wage bills mount and there is a call for drastic measures. The recent financial disaster at one successful club, Sud America (of Montevideo) provides a cautionary parable for those who overstretch themselves. After winning promotion to the First Division in 1994, the team held on to a mid-table position in 1995, but soon fell into debts, owing their players some $400,000 in wages and bonuses. The AUF's bar on clubs entering tournaments in this position saw Sud America forcibly relegated to the Second Division. An attempted rescue by Diego Maradona and associates broke down, while moving the club's home games to Paysandu (380 kilometres from the capital) failed to improve gate receipts. After Sud America's withdrawal from the championship, the AUF could only advise other clubs in similar circumstances to merge and form stronger enterprises. Such recommendations could not assist one of Uruguay's big clubs, Nacional, who also owed their players $225,000. Their survival strategy was equally pyrrhic: 300 club bonds were sold to supporters, entitling them to a share of the proceeds from the players' future transfer.

The symbiosis of bankruptcy and migration has affected the grassroots of the game. In the classically proletarian culture of football, the attraction of the game to young Uruguayan players and their families has been its potential for delivery from relative economic and social poverty.[58] There are 40,000 children involved in Uruguay's *baby fútbol*, covering teams aged from around four to 16 years.[59] The potential rewards of a professional career vary hugely, with First Division salaries ranging from a meagre $400 a month to the occasional superlative sum of $5,000, depending on the elusive security of result bonuses. Yet, the charismatic and idiosyncratic skills of Paco Casal in spotting and commodifying talented young players glosses the financial allure of the game to young minds and families alike. The lucrative trip abroad is the key to their aspirations. Those able to explore football's upward option must husband their resources after retirement. The wealthiest activate their business contacts to invest their savings. Other, less gilded ex-players try to enter self-employment, by purchasing petrol stations, distribution franchises and restaurants; setting up trucking and haulage companies; or simply buying a taxi licence to trawl the streets of Montevideo's numerous *barrios*. Riskier investments are made at the capital's casinos, where fortunes are lost, but symbolically returned by the re-engagement of these ex-players as staff members.

Inevitably, young Uruguayans will seek to identify role models who might personify their aspirations and render them more tangible. Recently, the rising economic and symbolic attractions of football have seen these iconic figures emerge from more salubrious quarters than Montevideo's dusty *barrios*. For over a decade Uruguay's leading player has been Enzo Francéscoli, whose peripatetic *curriculum vita* evidences spells in France (with Racing Matra of Paris), Italy (Cagliari and Torino), and latterly Argentina (with his beloved River Plate). Francéscoli's adaptability to foreign fields and cultures owes as much to his middle-class upbringing as to his technical nursing by the Wanderers club of Montevideo. Tentatively, we may suggest that he reflects the wider and aggrandizing process of bourgeoisification within South American football, as found in other celebrated cases, such as Socrates in Brazil or Redondo of Argentina. Francéscoli's nomadic pursuit of wealth and success is also the antithesis of Varela's satisfaction with more frugal civic rewards for more definitive and glorious deeds. Within the hermeneutics of Uruguayan football, Varela's epic performances belong to a fabulous, indeed mythological past that cannot be revisited. Yet, as Hugo Batalla has argued, Francéscoli is a 'crack' player whose abilities defy easy historical periodization or contextualization.[60] He is not a 'conjunctural' player, like Varela, who emerged from the masses heroically, to deliver an historic sense of national identity for Uruguayans.

Uruguay's football dream continues to be pursued by its young players. *Baby fútbol* has produced the gifted youth team of the late 1990s, which lost to Argentina 2–1 in the World Youth Final in July 1997.

Fascinating future battles beckon both nations into the new millennium, for the latest episodes of *fútbol rioplatense*. At club level, though, the greatest of these contests are more likely to be played out as one-to-one duels in Europe, rather than at team level in the Copa Libertadores.

NOTES

The research for this essay was financed by the Carnegie Trust for the Universities of Scotland. I would like to thank my various 'informants' on Uruguayan football, in particular Roberto Elissalde, Rafael Bayce, César Aguiar, Eric Weil and José Sergio Leite Lopes. Thanks also to Gary Armstrong, David Andrews and Joe Arbena for their critical comments on an earlier draft of the paper.

1. E. Galeano, *Football: in Sun and Shadow* (hereafter *Football*) (London, 1997), p.42.
2. Ondino Viera, Uruguay manager in 1966, quoted in B. Glanville, *The Story of the World Cup* (London, 1997), pp.15–16.
3. For example, the conference papers by Rafael Bayce at the European University Institute in Florence.
4. T. Mason, *Passion of the People? Football in South America* (London, 1995), pp.8–9.
5. A. Tomlinson, 'The FIFA Story', in A. Tomlinson and G. Whannel (eds.), *Off the Ball* (London, 1986), p.88.
6. E. Galeano, *El Fútbol: a sol y sombra* (Buenos Aires, 1995), p.65.
7. M.H.J. Finch, *A Political Economy of Uruguay Since 1870* (London, 1981), p.24.
8. In 1990 Montevideo had around 1,300,000 inhabitants, while the rest of the country had a population of 1,700,000. F. Daners, 'Montevideo vs. Interior', in *Nunca más campeón mundial?*, (Montevideo, 1991), p.75.
9. T. Mason, 'Football' in T. Mason (ed.), *Sport in Britain: A Social History* (Cambridge, 1984), pp.175–6.
10. M.L. Krotee, 'The Rise and Demise of Sport: A Reflection of Uruguayan Society' (hereafter 'The Rise and Demise of Sport'), *Annals of the American Academy of Political and Social Science*, 445 (September 1979), 145.
11. J. Arbena, 'Sport and Social Change in Latin America', in A.G. Ingham and J.W. Loy (eds.), *Sport in Social Development* (Champaign, Ill., 1993), p.105.
12. J. Walvin, *The People's Game: The History of Football Revisited* (Edinburgh, 1994), p.107.
13. A less industrial, colour-based nickname is *mirasoles* (sunflowers).
14. J.L. Buzzetti, 'La Nacionalización del Fútbol', in Centro Editor de America Latina (eds.), *El Fútbol* (Montevideo, 1969), pp.5–7; E. Galeano, *El Fútbol*, p.47.
15. A. Guttmann, *Games and Empires: Modern Sports and Cultural Imperialism* (New York, 1995), pp.60–1.
16. See R. Williams, *Marxism and Literature* (Oxford, 1977).
17. E. Archetti, 'In Search of National Identity: Argentinian Football and Europe' (hereafter 'In Search of National Identity'), in J.A. Mangan (ed.), *Tribal Identities: Nationalism, Europe, Sport* (London, 1996), p.204.
18. E. Galeano, *El Fútbol*, p.64; Russ Williams, *Football Babylon* (London, 1996), pp.30–1.
19. See R. Bayce, 'Fútbol Uruguayo, Economía, Política y Cultura', in *Nunca más campeón mundial?* (Montevideo, 1991), p.42. The influence was repaid in cruel style when Uruguay crushed Scotland 7–0 at the 1954 World Cup finals in Switzerland.
20. G. Hare and H. Dauncey, 'The Coming of Age: the World Cup of France '98', in G. Armstrong and R. Giulianotti (eds.), *Football Cultures and Identities* (Basingstoke, 1999), p.47.
21. Krotee, 'The Rise and Demise of Sport', 144.
22. E. Galeano, *Football*, pp.35, 44
23. M.B. Del Burgo, 'Don't Stop the Carnival: Football in the Societies of Latin America', in S. Wagg (ed.), *Giving the Game Away: Football, Politics and Culture on Five Continents* (London, 1995), p.59.

24. W. Murray, *Football: A History of the World Game* (hereafter *Football*) (Aldershot, 1994), p.131. This did not mean that Uruguayan teams were no longer in competitive contact with European clubs. In fixtures that were played, the Uruguayans displayed a mixture of national pride and inchoate 'professionalism' that were not pretty to behold. When a Montevideo select travelled to Paris in March 1936, to play in an exhibition match, the visitors appalled spectators and officials by assaulting the opposition and abusing the referee. The Uruguayan ambassador expressed his regret to the French people (ibid., pp.32–3).

25. M.H.J. Finch, *A Political Economy of Uruguay Since 1870* (London, 1981), p.37.

26. M. Reisch, 'Alternativas', in *Nunca más campeón mundial?*, p.83.

27. J.S. Leite Lopes, 'Successes and Contradictions in "Multiracial" Brazilian Football', in G. Armstrong and R. Giulianotti (eds.), *Entering the Field: New Perspectives on World Football* (Oxford, 1997), pp.70–1.

28. My thanks to Fernando Vianna, of the University of São Paulo, for this observation.

29. J. Humphrey, 'Brazil and the World Cup: Triumph and Despair', in J. Sugden and A. Tomlinson (eds.), *Hosts and Champions: Soccer Cultures, National Identities and the USA World Cup* (Aldershot, 1994), p.69.

30. For a discussion of the dynamics of 'we' identities, see N. Elias and J. Scotson, *The Established and the Outsiders* (London, 1965).

31. B. Glanville, *The Story of the World Cup*, pp.77–8.

32. Ibid., pp.89–90.

33. E. Galeano, *El Fútbol*, p.146.

34. This continuing high public expectation is a surprise to foreigners, and goes specifically against the claim of one English journalist, that Uruguayans 'have more or less accepted their current situation, and stopped tormenting themselves about becoming world champions once again'. See J. Kelly, 'In Defence of the Realm', in J. King and J. Kelly (eds.), *The Cult of the Manager* (London, 1997), p.68.

35. See the analysis of Uruguayan football manager Oscar Washington Tabárez in *Nunca más campeón mundial?*, pp.113–24.

36. E. Hobsbawm, *Age of Extremes* (London, 1994), pp.442–3.

37. F. Morales, 'Fútbol: mito y realidad', *Muestra Tierra*, No. 22 (Montevideo, 1969), p.27.

38. T. Mason, *Passion of the People*, p.76.

39. The more important verses read:

> I don't know why I didn't shout, When I saw the ball coming,
> And you flicked it knowing, It would finish in the net.
> I don't know why, When you ran to the fence,
> A yell came up, But I bit my tongue.
> I admire you from long ago, I have your picture in the garage,
> Side-by-side with Gardel, In the changing-room.
> But sometimes I think of things, Like when I read the newspapers,
> That a goal of yours, Is ten times my salary.
> Somebody may think, That I envy your glory,
> But among the things I know, This story is very old.
> Today at the garage, I don't know what I felt,
> When I saw you again, Smiling carelessly.
> You looked at me happily, I went to clock-in as always,
> When I suddenly felt, That I was offside.
> I don't know what happened, All my workmates asked,
> When they saw the Magician [Gardel] alone, Propping up the wall.

> (Translated by Roberto Elissalde)

40. E. Hobsbawm, *Age of Extremes*, p.111.

41. See P. Mieres, 'Elecciones de 1989 en Uruguay: una interpretacion del cambio del sistema de partidos', *Revista Mexicana de Sociologia*, 52 (1990).

42. See G. De Sierra, 'La Izuierda en la Transicion', *Revista Mexicana de Sociologia*, 47 (1985); L. Stolovich, 'Los Grupos Economicos de Argentina, Brasil y Uruguay', *Revista Mexicana de*

Sociologia, 57 (1995).
43. Archetti, 'In Search of National Identity'.
44. Perhaps the nadir of this footballing 'style' was reached at the 1986 World Cup finals, in the 'Group of Death' involving Uruguay, Denmark, Scotland and West Germany. In the final group match against Scotland, with both teams looking to scrape into the second round by taking third place, Uruguay's Batista was sent off within 40 seconds for a violent tackle on the Scottish play-maker, Strachan. The game was then littered with fouls and stoppages, and concluded in a goalless draw. After the match, as Uruguayan journalists spat at the Scottish media, Scotland's officials described their opponents as 'scum', and accused Borrás of 'lying' and 'cheating'. FIFA fined the Uruguayans 25,000 Swiss francs and threatened them with expulsion if their future behaviour did not improve, though they played no further games in the tournament. The Uruguayans remained unbowed, defending their tactics and describing Batista's lunge as a 'fair challenge'. One English football writer also praised Uruguay's 10-man technical resilience against the Scots. Compare R. Forsyth, *The Only Game* (Edinburgh, 1990), pp.203–4; and B. Glanville, *The Story of the World Cup*, p.279.
45. On the key aspects of the civilizing process, see E. Dunning, 'Sport in the Civilizing Process: Aspects of the Development of Modern Sport', in E. Dunning, J. Maguire and R. Pearton (eds.), *The Sports Process: A Comparative and Developmental Approach* (Champaign, Ill., 1993), p.47.
46. See V. Duke and L. Crolley, *Football, Nationality and the State* (Harlow, 1996), p.18.
47. M. Bowden, 'Soccer', in K.B. Raitz (ed.), *The Theater of Sport* (Baltimore, 1995), p.133. The stadium was built especially for the 1930 World Cup finals, and named to commemorate the centenary of Uruguayan independence. See W.J. Baker, *Sports in the Western World* (Urbana, 1988), p.233.
48. Duke and Crolley, *Football*, p.118.
49. The differences in popularity at the two clubs is rather exaggerated by the huge differences between their respective ground capacities. While Cerro's Luis Troccoli stadium is listed as holding 40,000, Rampla Juniors are able to house only 10,000 at their Olimpico stadium.
50. J.L. González, 'Revisión Crítica al Fútbol Uruguayo', in *Nunca más campeón mundial?*, p.51.
51. F. Morales, 'Fútbol', p.25.
52. *El Observador*, 21 September 1996.
53. *El Observador*, 28 April 1996.
54. At a match I attended between Nacional and Wanderers in April 1997, Recoba scored an extraordinary goal of Maradona-type quality, running diagonally with the ball from the halfway line, round and through a string of defenders, drawing the goal-keeper and walking it into the net. My colleague Rafael Bayce informed me that the celebrating Nacional fans behind us had anticipated Recoba's exit from Uruguay, commenting that he was a 'European', and did not belong in such mediocre company. Soon after his transfer, Inter signed the Brazilian striker Ronaldo in a reported $25 million deal.
55. J. Arbena, 'Dimensions of International Talent Migration in Latin American Sport', in J. Bale and J. Maguire (eds.), *The Global Sports Arena* (London, 1995), p.104.
56. See A.G. Frank, *Capitalism and Under-development in Latin America* (New York, 1969) for the foremost statement on under-development in the 'Third World'.
57. A. Klein, 'Sport and Culture as Contested Terrain: Americanization in the Caribbean', *Sociology of Sport Journal*, 8 (1991).
58. F. Morales, 'Fútbol', p.7.
59. H. Reisch, 'Alternativas', p.87. See also R. Bayce, 'Fútbol Uruguayo, Economía, Política y Cultura', p.31.
60. H. Batalla, 'Amateurismo y Profesionalismo', in *Nunca más campeón mundial?*, p.69.

7

The Production of a Media Epic:
Germany v. Italy Football Matches

NICOLÀ PORRO and PIPPO RUSSO

One of the most hotly debated issues within the current political and sociological community is the state of health of the nation-state. In the era of globalization, and the ascendancy of unifying economic, political and socio-cultural theories, the prospects for survival of what jurists define as the optimal form of political organization are seen to be fading.

The malaise affecting the nation-state has a number of implications, which can no longer be ascribed to what J. Habermas called the crisis of legitimacy.[1] One further implication may be defined as the crisis of representation, or the increasing difficulty of the nation-state in playing the role of mediator between various different players both at home and abroad. Another implication might be defined as the crisis of unitarianism, or the growth of regional identities and their political articulation, and the increasingly confrontational relationship between regionalism and the centre.

The crisis of representation and of unitarianism are both closely linked to globalization, and represent a particular aspect of this process: the activation of 'glocal' dynamics, interweaving the cosmopolitanism of global networks with specific local realities.[2] These dynamics pit individual regions against each other within nation-states, or alternatively induce them to form supranational alliances.

As the importance of the nation-state recedes, international sporting contests appear to represent one of the last arenas of nationalism, where the nation-state is employed as a fundamental form of expression of collective identity and symbolic factor of production. Athletes' own cultural heritage and the automatic forms of expressing solidarity and conflict which they employ dominate their interactions and somehow determine their behaviour. Moreover, the persistence of these phenomena indicates the existence of an irreducible core of common loyalties.

The enduring ability of competitive sport to produce a sense of national identity in the 'local' era has been widely discussed, although we cannot enter this debate here. The goal of the present article is rather to analyse what takes place within the magic moments of an international sporting event; the symbols and images at play, the opposing models of 'Us' and 'Them' employed, and the immutable vitality of prejudice as an identifier and cognitive fact.

PREJUDICES CONFRONT ONE ANOTHER

From a cognitive point of view, prejudice operates as a decodifier for actors in a given situation. The principal characteristic of prejudice when it operates in this role, is that it is entrenched; it has functioned as a filter in real situations over a long period of time.

In international sporting events, prejudice prevails over every rational, legitimizing process, sustaining entrenched cognitive schemes. National identities preserve a vital expressive space for themselves in sporting encounters, which is denied them in other contexts. That is to say, so-called national styles, the product of different cultures, still find expression on the pitch and form a model for interpreting sporting contests which remains valid.

The 1998 World Cup, which should have been a tribute to globalization, ended up instead by reviving old footballing stereotypes and traditional rivalries. Italy, coached by Maldini, produced their traditional style of defence and counter-attack; Germany, performed their characteristically methodical game; England gave their stoical best in the gripping second round match against Argentina; naive tactics and technique scuppered the African sides once again.

Furthermore, the challenges between Italy and France, between Argentina and England and between Germany and Yugoslavia placed political, cultural and historical as well as football rivalries on centre-stage. A survey of Italian football fans carried out during the European Cup Championship in 1996 shed some interesting light on the validity of stereotypes and prejudices brought to bear in sporting contests, both regarding players' self-identification and the representation of 'Them'.[3] In answer to the question 'When you hear the term "Italian football" what comes to mind?', the most frequent reply (33.8 per cent) was the prevalence of defensive play over an attacking game. The second most frequent reply (28.1 per cent) was imagination, followed by fighting spirit (28.0 per cent) and team spirit (19.6 per cent).

In order to understand the power of stereotypes, it should be noted that the survey was carried out at the height of the Arrigo Sacchi era, the period during which the greatest attempt was made to make Italian football undergo a kind of cultural revolution.

When asked to compare Italy and Germany, respondents to the same survey saw the Italians as 'generous', 'full of joie de vivre', 'creative', 'tolerant', 'imaginative', and as possessing 'good taste 'and 'a democratic culture'. They saw Germans, on the other hand, as 'industrious', as possessing 'organizational ability' and 'discipline'. Apart from forewarning a clash between two different sporting cultures, these data demonstrate the vitality of stereotypes, and their pivotal role in the formation of identities which continue to feed off and strengthen a sense of common belonging.

ITALY AND GERMANY: TWO SEPARATE WORLDS

Of all the rivalries between different nationalities, that between Italy and Germany is one of the most entrenched. Indeed, it reflects two national characters that are diametrically opposed in many ways, and which arise from conditions that make them almost natural rivals. The stereotypes emerging from the survey cited above form virtually irreconcilable terms of reference, which have found expression in any encounter between the two national characters.

But it has been football encounters that have shown up the biggest differences between the Italian and German national characters, and which have engendered a sporting rivalry that has produced historic matches on more than one occasion. The encounter between players from different nations can be interpreted as a microcosm of political, social and cultural behaviours.[4] International football matches can be interpreted as contests between opposing and largely culturally determined styles of football. Thus when Italy plays Germany, the encounter may be viewed as a challenge between one team representing a creative but unmethodical culture which, despite their inherent lack of planning, is capable of high achievement, and another which is based on calculation, and the widespread and repeated use of strategies that favour caution over unpredictability.

When applied to the most significant games between Italy and Germany, this analysis is almost always deductively useful but, as will be seen, there are notable exceptions. One such example is the match which forms the case study of this article. As has already been noted, Italy's style of football is commonly classified in binomial terms: defence and counter-attack. Germany's, on the other hand, is traditionally described as a style based on physical strength and strong but invariably controlled attacking play. While Italy's game is seen as brilliant and improvisational, Germany's is viewed as disciplined and methodical.

These stereotypes are confirmed by some but not all of the major football encounters that took place between Italy and Germany (namely the ones during the final stages of past European Championships and World Cups). The two countries' styles of play in the 1962 World Cup game, which resulted in a 0–0 draw, fully conformed to traditional stereotypes. Italy played a defensive game for the whole match, fighting off the Germans' attack to hold them to a draw. After drawing with each other, both teams preferred not to slog it out in order to play the host country, Chile, in the next round.

However, from the point of view of the present study, the differing strategies the two sides chose in order to obtain the 0–0 result probably make the game the most interesting of the international matches between Italy and Germany. In this game, consensus prevailed over conflict and the teams drew on their tactical resources. Italy could not avoid playing a defensive game, while Germany, after a bout of inertia at the start of the match, took the initiative and went on the attack for almost the entire 90 minutes. The match provides one of the best examples of the circular mechanism whereby actors' behaviour is influenced by, and in turn confirms, stereotypes concerning the two countries' styles of play.

Another contest that played a fundamental role in the mythogenesis and symbolism of footballing rivalry between Italy and Germany was the legendary semi-final at the Mexican World Cup in 1970, which Italy won 4–3 at the end of extra time. In this game too, all the tactics and stereotypes of 'Italian' and 'German' football were to be found. Italy scored straightaway (eight minutes into the game), and spent the remainder of the match trying, unsuccessfully, to hold off the tenacious attack sustained by the Germans. During extra time, a goal-chase took place which exalted Italy's reserved 'emergency' football skills and preserved the image of German football. On that day, a rivalry was born, which has now become part of the international footballing tradition. The World Cup match played in Argentina in 1978 partly overturned existing stereotypes. To achieve a 0–0 draw, the Germans produced defensive play on a scale that has rarely been produced by Italy, while the Italian team went on the attack for almost 70 minutes, throwing caution to the wind.

In the World Cup final in Spain in 1982, Italy beat Germany 3–1, exploiting their technical skill and devastating counter-attack, which the Germans' more plodding game was unable to counter. The other two games that this article discusses both took place in the final round of the European Championships. The first, in June 1988, was played in Germany and ended in a 1–1 draw between the two sides. Both teams were going through a period of transition at the time and, for this reason, the match did not add or take anything away from their stereotypes. The second, played in England in 1996, forms the case study for this essay.

TOTAL PARITY: THE EURO '96 FIXTURE

The 1996 game resulted in a 0–0 draw, and put Italy out of the championships. After victories over the Czech Republic and Russia, Germany had already qualified for the next round, and would go on to win the cup. Italy, obliged to beat the Germans after the unexpected defeat by the Czech Republic, failed to reach the quarter-finals. But the match went down in history as the first major defeat inflicted on Italy by Germany in an official competition. The game took on a singular significance and came to represent one of the milestones in a wider confrontation between Italy and Germany that extended to the political, economic and diplomatic spheres.

The European Championships of 1996, hosted by England, took place during the critical period of European monetary union (EMU), when governments were striving to meet the convergence criteria laid down by the Maastricht Treaty. Not all countries were starting from the same position, however; some had to adopt more rigorous and cunning macroeconomic policies to meet the Maastricht criteria. Italy was one country seen as unlikely to join the single European currency, and one of the greatest sceptics in this regard was Germany. For months, the German government and public showed themselves to be extremely doubtful and frequently hostile towards the idea that Italy could turn its economy around and participate in the first wave of EMU. Indeed, Germany argued implacably for Italy's exclusion from the Euro.

Another source of friction at that time was the reform of ONU's Security Council membership. Germany put itself forward to be included in a new category of permanent members without the power of veto, and clashed with Italy, which favoured the non-aligned countries' position. This produced tension between the two governments.[5] Meanwhile, the high profile criminal trial of Nazi commander Eric Priebke was taking place in Rome, which re-opened an old but sanitized wound between the two countries.

All these factors placed Italy and Germany at odds on many fronts and formed the backdrop to the football encounter between the two countries. The prize at stake (in the encounter between the Italian team coached by Sacchi and Berti Vogts' German side) was admission to the highest reaches of European football, with Germany poised to block Italy's passage through to the next stage of the competition. Thus, the stern stance of the German government over Italy's entry to monetary union was played out on a smaller scale. In this light, the call by Franz Beckenbauer the day before the match for Italy's elimination from the European Championships assumed a curious metaphorical significance. Germany had already qualified, and the former captain and trainer of the German national team warned players not to expect an easy game against Italy and miss the opportunity to foil a dangerous opponent's bid for victory in the competition. Interpreted in tactical terms, Beckenbauer's words would seem to indicate an anti-Italian *Zeitgeist* that permeated German public opinion at the time and which sought to exclude Italy from Europe.

This context extends beyond the Italy–Germany match to other encounters between national teams where traditional and not exclusively sporting rivalry exists. These include England v. Scotland, Holland v. France and England v. Germany, according to research on the European Championships. In the first of these three matches, a centuries-old core-peripheral cleavage showed up on the pitch in a clash between local independence and the legitimate exercise of political power by central government. The second match, Holland v. France, was a confrontation between players from two multi-ethnic national teams. The British tabloid press turned the England v. Germany game into a war between two European powers, which materialized on the football field in the two sides' differing cultures of warfare.[6]

The overall picture that emerges reveals the intrinsically political nature of international football matches, and how these are affected by general semantic processes which invade the strict confines of sport and its symbolism. The conclusion to be drawn is that football can be seen to be a political forum, one that pits against each other the different mindsets that are determined by national, regional and ethnic communities. All this demonstrates the unchanging vitality of symbology and nationally determined belonging, and highlights the following paradox: at a moment in history when the nation-state is waning, nationalism seems more alive than ever, especially where it finds a sphere of expression that is consonant with their production of symbols and identities. (We propose to examine this paradox in a future study.)

A MATCH THAT DEFIES STEREOTYPING

The picture that has just been described was confirmed in the match by what will later be defined as the 'pragmatic dimension' of the event. As has already been indicated, the game was played by two sides displaying different team spirit: Germany, which had already qualified, could afford to lose, while Italy had to win at all costs and await the outcome of the other group match between the Czech Republic and Russia. This situation gave rise to 'match conditions' which did not favour the principal stereotype of Italian football: their traditional style of defence and counter-attack (*catenaccio e contropiede*).

But it was not only contingency that stopped Italy from adopting their usual tactics. A very important factor at play was the 'cultural revolution' that Arrigo Sacchi tried to bring about during his five years as Italian national coach, with mixed results. He took on the role of prophet in trying to introduce an attacking style of football that was organized down to the last detail. But supporters of the traditional style of Italian football claimed that the only result produced by Sacchi was the technical and tactical demise of Italy. So either by choice or by necessity, under Sacchi the national side did not play a single match with traditional tactics. Italy played an attacking style, despite the advice handed out by Enzo Bearzot, who had trained the national team that won the World Cup in 1982, beating Germany itself in the final. The following is an excerpt from a published interview with the old footballing guru:

> 'Germany will certainly press us. And all we must do is play them at their own game.'

> Q: 'But a draw isn't good enough, is it?'

A: 'Precisely. We'll win if we play defensively. If we go on the attack, we'll find that we can also beat them, because we're the stronger side: but we'll risk everything by doing so. If we play a defensive game, and only press them in our midfield, sooner or later we'll intercept an important pass and we'll be able to do more with the ball than they will at speed. We'll only take risks later in the game, if we don't see it opening up. But I would wait to see the opportunities after their first serious error in midfield.'[7]

The words of Bearzot almost invite Italian football to 'return to its roots', despite the fact that in the circumstances this was not really a feasible option. The analysis of the former national coach is imbued with an albeit unconscious tactical logic, based on the historic propensity of Italian football towards counter-attack and the Germans' natural tendency to press an adversary who is playing a waiting game. The tactics adopted by Arrigo Sacchi were different. Italy went on the attack for the entire game, a choice that was helped by the German midfielder Strunz being sent off, leaving Germany one player short for the last 30 minutes.

But the tactics adopted by the German team were also markedly different from their traditional game. As long as there were 11 players still on the pitch, the Germans were suddenly torn between the temptation to play a waiting game in order to eliminate a formidable foe from the championship, and the desire to honour a tradition of epic encounters. After Strunz was sent off, they closed ranks and repelled every vain attack by the Italian side. *Catenaccio* by necessity rather than choice, but in any case representing different tactics from the traditional ones of German football.

Given the conditions just outlined, the game between Italy and Germany on 19 June 1996 might be described as an 'anti-match', where national styles of football, traditions and stereotypes were turned on their heads. Such an encounter between an aggressive Italy and a defensive Germany, biding its time, had never been seen before. If the pragmatic considerations of the match are set aside, this reversal of stereotypes is stunning. For once, the cycle represented by stereotypes that reinforce the process that in turn reinforce the stereotypes was broken. The effects of this phenomenon on footballing symbolism are difficult to gauge. The established images of the two schools of football remain the traditional ones, reinforced amongst other things by the press coverage of the World Cup hosted by France in the summer of 1998.

We have already described how, under Maldini, Italy returned to its traditional game. This met with unanimous criticism from Italian commentators, who viewed it as a backward step towards an old-fashioned style of football that did not fit the modern game. The move was also criticized by foreign commentators, only too happy to dust down their critical approach to Italian football that Sacchi had seemed to have forced them to consign to history. But Germany too revealed old defects, showing themselves little able to adapt its game to the dramatic situation it faced in the match against Croatia. One goal and one man down against a technically and tactically strong opponent, the German coach Vogts brought on two strikers, leaving the side undefended. Vogts' scatterbrained strategy allowed Croatia to inflict a humiliating 3–0 defeat on Germany.

Before analysing the match between Italy and Germany, one further element, crucial to the study of the 1996 European Championships, needs to be added to the picture. That is the role played by television in the production and portrayal of this football event and television's effect on the meanings which derive from it.

FOOTBALL AS A MEDIA CEREMONY

In a well-known study, Daniel Dayan and Elihu Katz argued that television, instead of merely reporting live events, actually plays an active role in producing the events themselves.[8] Thus, television takes on a ceremonial role, administering the rules that determine the timing and means of constructing not only the technical but also the symbolic framework of the event. The authors postulate the existence of three classes of event that the televised action brings back inside the ceremonial mechanism: competitions, conquests and coronations.

Competitions are events which are characterized by conflict between two or more players to obtain a certain goal or for certain stakes. Sporting contests are one obvious example, but they are not the only kind of competition. Debates between candidates in the run-up to presidential elections provide an instance of another kind, for example. Conquests are undertakings that actors charged with arduous missions must perform in difficult, even adverse conditions. Dayan and Katz cite the Pope's visit to Poland in 1980, Sadat's visit to Israel in 1974 and man walking on the moon as typical examples of such events. Coronations are ceremonies that invest their protagonists with a unifying role and a representation of communities *super partes*, owing to their ability to mobilize collective passions and sentiments. Examples are provided by the funerals of John F. Kennedy and Princess Diana.

Dayan and Katz's threefold division of media events can be applied to top-level sporting events, albeit to differing degrees. Such events are undoubtedly competitions, but they are also conquests, because they involve environmental adversity and forces pitted against one another. They are also coronations, in which their protagonists transcend political, cultural and social differences. Precisely because it embodies competition, conquests and coronations, the televising of live international sporting events can be seen as a total media event.

According to Dayan and Katz, the communication pact which crowns the media ceremonies is made between three parties: the organizers of the events, who seek the widest possible media coverage for them; journalists, seeking to find the biggest audiences for their television networks; and the public, interested in the best possible viewing for their leisure-time investment. As has already been argued in another study, the typology of media ceremonies of the sporting kind needs to be reviewed.[9] In actual fact, the organizers and broadcasters involved in such sporting events frequently coincide. The organizers of top-level sporting events (regional and world federations) are becoming increasingly involved in the areas of production and sale of television rights.[10] In the same way, the business tycoons are acquiring teams and organizing competitions and high-level tournaments from scratch.[11] The role of master of ceremonies which television assumes, in this way sanctions its centrality to symbolic and semantic production. Television acquires sovereignty over the symbolic material contained within the sporting arena and organizes it according to its requirements.

The semantic requirements of the medium, to keep within a further typology constructed by Dayan and Katz, are tempered by two other criteria which belong to the sporting event itself. The first is a syntactic one, linked to its rules and internal dynamics (the rules of the game and its timing; within this sphere the semantic action of the medium, if excessive, causes disarray). The second is a pragmatic one, relating to the role of fate in the circumstances and course of the event (the goals, refereeing errors and red cards, in a football match; all factors from which television's semantic intervention builds a dramatic narrative).

The role of the television medium in the symbolic and semantic production of the event inspires four levels of reflection, which have already been developed as working hypotheses.[12] First, television is now the main instrument in the social construction of the great sporting event. It is television which provides an adequate narrative for sporting events, which feeds viewer expectations. Television chooses the themes and personalities it requires in order to construct its chosen narrative. Television regulates the start and finish of the sacred moments of the match. It is television that identifies the thresholds and invents authentic rites of passage from the routine to the exceptional event and vice versa.

Second, the need to produce an event through a constant process of adaptation and updating of the language and the forms and means of communication places television at the junction between events and strategies which do not always fit together easily. One need only think of the disharmonious superimposition of symbolic reasoning and commercial expediency that habitually have their epicentre in the sale of advertising space during and 'around' the event.

Furthermore, sporting spectacles are viewed by large numbers of people. Probable audience size is capable of rescheduling the major international television networks and causing commercial warfare between the competing stations, thus encouraging the pace of innovation in television. Coverage of such events is the tastiest prize for the satellite and pay-TV stations which have multiplied in recent years. It also stimulates development in television codes and formats, and even introduces synergies from outside the circuit of televised sport.

Third, the great sporting events trigger tensions within the traditional agents of socialization and call on society's frequently invisible institutional networks. Public opinion, often totally uninterested in competitive sport itself, becomes involved in a massive agenda-setting exercise. Sporting events leap out from the front pages of the newspapers, reach the television news headlines and succeed in postponing work appointments and official events. Indirectly, the sporting event indicates a latent system of preferences and values. A match that is 'narrated' by the mass-media provokes reactions and reinforces or weakens stereotypes.

In the final analysis, the construction by television of a major event represents a 'moment' that is destined to imprint itself in the collective memory, and to be recollected according to the styles and strategies used by its producers. And television coverage, which regulates our memory of the event from its start to the length of time it lasts, favours our recollection of it as truly 'epoch-making'. By stylizing social and cultural meanings and group behaviour, television condenses events as it constructs them. In some cases, it offers an interpretation of the historical and political context which differs from that of official historiography.

In the case of the European Championships, television played its role within a context characterized by a number of significant historical, political and cultural factors.

(a) The historic context was that of a Europe coming to terms with a new geopolitical reality that was strongly marked by the end of a bipolar world order, from the break-up of the Soviet Union, to the spread of a process of state building which cut across central and eastern Europe causing tensions and, in the case of Yugoslavia, civil war. The previous European Championships, held in Sweden in 1992, were deeply influenced by these geopolitical processes. Yugoslavia, already qualified and 'mutilated' by the creation of Slovenian and Croatian teams, was excluded from international sports matches, a few weeks before the start of the competition. Denmark, the side that was called in its place and whose players were already on holiday, went on to win the tournament. And a national side, that has never reappeared since, took part in the competition. The Commonwealth of Independent States (CIS) had qualified as the USSR, but only a few weeks before the collapse of the Soviet Union on 31 December 1991.

(b) Four years afterwards in England, the redesign of the continent had tangible football consequences. The multiplication of states was mirrored in the doubling of places in the elimination round (from 8 to 16). Two teams belonging to the new nation-states of central and eastern Europe (Croatia and the Czech Republic) made their debut. Most notably, the tournament ended in a repeat of the European Championship final of 20 years earlier, with the important difference that, in 1996, a united Germany took part (as opposed to only East Germany in 1976) against a Czech Republic that had emerged from the division of what, in 1976, had been Czechoslovakia. And if the 1976 final, which Czechoslovakia won, was the first high-level international football tournament to have to resort to penalties (resulting in a final score of 7–6, after the 2–2 draw at the end of extra time), the 1996 final, won by Germany, was the first to end with a 'golden' goal.

As we have already seen, the political backdrop to the 1996 European Championships was the challenge of Maastricht and the criteria for monetary union (EMU). The difficulties facing national governments in imposing EMU's strict membership rules projected a technocratic image of a future, united Europe. The curious similarity between the number of countries admitted to the single European currency in May 1998 (15) and those admitted to the second round of the European Championship in June 1996 (16) is intriguing. In the same way, it is singular that the last European tournament before Maastricht took place in the country that symbolizes Euro-scepticism: England.

(c) The cultural context was characterized by processes of European integration that were politically generated, but which received a marked fillip from the sporting arena. Just a few months before the tournament, on 15 December 1995, the European Court of Justice ruled in favour of the footballer Jean-Marc Bosman in the case brought by him against his former club, Liège. The subsequent 'Bosman ruling' established two principles: the illegality of transfer fees for out-of-contract players in Europe; and the illegality of limiting the number of European Union nationals fielded by any side in European competitions.[13] The consequences of this ruling have been exceptionally wide-reaching: the number of transfers of EU nationals from one league to another within the European Union has risen exponentially. In one sense, this produces a marked form of European integration, while in another it represents a threat to the bank of players available to the national teams.

The foregoing context forms the framework within which television constructs a narration of events. In their different ways, the four case histories examined here evince all the elements of the contexts that have been described. To recapitulate, the historical, political and cultural background, combined with certain contingencies of the medium, all contribute to the production of meaning and exert an influence on broadcasting choices.

The England v. Scotland match, already positioned semantically within a framework characterized by core–periphery conflict, was lent further drama in this regard by the IRA bomb that went off in the commercial centre of Manchester hours before the game. The effects of the bomb attack on the television coverage of the match were visible. For the first half of the game, the BBC's cameras homed in on the parts of the stadium containing the most flags and banners. It was the first contest between England and Scotland after the revival of the Braveheart myth, which through the influence of the cinema had given a new lease of life to Scottish patriotism and a new charge to the atmosphere at the match. This innocuous patriotism shown by fans was none the less eventually played down by television, as broadcasters were wary of provoking political ructions on a day that had been darkened by an act of terrorism.

This was apparent in the BBC's coverage of the Scots striker Durie's injury. Struck on the forehead by a free-kick from English defender Southgate, the television cameras rested briefly on Durie as he lay on the ground, bleeding profusely. After a second or two, they moved elsewhere, homing in on the most insignificant events, and avoiding shots of the medical team attending to the player and only filming him when he came back on the field, his head swathed in bandages. The BBC's eagerness to avoid transmitting even vaguely bellicose scenes (such as that of the combatant Durie felled in battle) might seem excessive, but none the less indicates an awareness of the central role of television in processing the flow of symbols and signs.

Similarly, broadcasting of the semi-final between England and Germany was affected by the vociferous campaign waged by the English tabloid press before the match. An editorial, published in the *Sun*, the leading English tabloid, declared a footballing war on Germany. To understand the situation forming the background to the game and the *Sun* editorial, one need only look at press cuttings from the time, both from the English and international press. The papers presented the match as yet another opportunity to re-live the past glory of the 1966 World Cup, which England won, thanks to a controversial goal scored by Hurst (footage of the game subsequently showed that the goal should have been disallowed). The match demonstrated all the characteristics of a football war, which television coverage of the event glorified.

The match possesses some particularly salient features, as it highlights the dependence of broadcasting on the political and cultural context. The BBC's television coverage exalted in the details that brought out the war-like qualities which the match assumed from the start. Above all, the censorship apparent in the England v. Scotland match was absent. Images of battle were beamed out freely. The sea of English flags fluttering in the stands, and England's devastating onslaught on the German ranks, which left Germany weakened for the final, were cause for celebration. The broadcasting of such images made a decisive contribution to the construction of a 'bellicose' match.

ITALY V. GERMANY: THE LONG MARCH TO MAASTRICHT

The television spectacle built around the contest between the Italian and German national teams was one of the must successful examples of a media ceremony associated with a sporting event. Media representation of the match was based on the use of highly effective symbolic material. It mixed the canons of sport and protocol with theatrical ones produced by an unrepeatable chance event the other high-suspense match of the preliminary round, between the Czech Republic and Russia, played in Liverpool. The first significant symbol, which television coverage of the event was based on, is tradition: Italy and Germany are two members of football's historic elite, and an encounter between the two countries mobilizes the popular imagination on the basis of long-established rivalries. And at a moment in history characterized by geopolitical change, which multiplies the number of national teams and thrusts fame upon new nations, tradition is an ever-more profitable resource to draw upon. For the television cameras, a match such as Italy v. Germany represents the preservation of strong cultural and symbolic reference points, a kind of romantic trousseau to be resorted to in times of excessively rapid change.

Another significant symbol employed in television coverage of events is represented by 'fate'. According to predictions at the start of the championship, the match between Italy and Germany, scheduled for the third and final elimination round, would have been between two teams that had already qualified for the second round. Instead, it turned into a dramatic show-down between one team that had got through and was unwilling to give anything away (Germany) and another that was facing an embarrassing elimination (Italy). These circumstances changed the course of the entire match, creating unforeseen tension, which profoundly marked television coverage of the event.

A third significant element of the game, presented as a narrative option, was linked to the 'heretical' tactical style of Arrigo Sacchi within Italian football. The football system proposed by the national coach divided football fans and arrived at its moment of trial without appeal. With its failure, came the inevitable 'symbolic burning' of the man and his approach.

The BBC coverage, as Italian television journalists reported it, focused on three symbols in turn, while weaving a narrative-symbolic thread between them. When seen on video, this reveals a remarkable internal coherence, as if it had been planned. It begins with the attention paid by players to their respective national anthems. The Germans sing along impassively, while the Italians are almost all silent, their tense faces foretelling the events of the match. The match reaches its climax in a dramatic crescendo after only eight minutes. The Italian striker Casiraghi steals the ball from the German player Sammer and flies towards the opponent's goalmouth, where he is brought down by the German goalkeeper Koepke. The action perfectly follows the advice given by Bearzot on the eve of the match: to wait for the mistakes by the German midfield and then to counter-attack. Thus the stereotypes of Italian and German football were shown to be alive and well, but ended during the course of the match, highlighting the ordeal of Arrigo Sacchi: the heretic sees a chance of salvation being offered to him through the pursuit of rigid Italian footballing orthodoxy, but fails to seize the opportunity. In any such script, the fate of the protagonist is sealed in advance. And so when Koepke blocked Zola's penalty, although 82 minutes of the game remained, a negative outcome already seemed to have been determined for Sacchi's side.

During the match, the BBC filmed Sacchi more often than Vogts, presenting him as the main protagonist in the match whatever the outcome. Almost as if to dispel the ordeal-like atmosphere, one of the two Italian journalists covering the game announced at its start that the national coach was looking for his fiftieth victory in an international match, thus trying to portray the encounter as an ordinary football event. Two different approaches to the same symbolic material were in evidence, and the 'fateful circumstances' leitmotif grew ever louder as the match wore on and the deadlock continued. The elimination of the Italian team became an increasing reality.

When Strunz was sent off, Germany went on the defensive, and the drawn-out scuffle between the two sides, followed by the television cameras, confused the events of the match even further. The final *coup de théâtre* arrived with Russia's late goal against the Czechs which would have qualified Italy, only to be followed by a Czech equalizer, that eliminated the Italian team. This seemed like an excessive drama, almost like the climax of a horror B-movie where the villain rises from the dead in one last murderous impulse, before finally expiring. Those three minutes during which Italy undeservedly seemed to have qualified represent an amazing digression in the narration of the event. The BBC coverage risked losing control of the narrative entirely, unsure whether to concentrate on the game or to focus on the scenes of jubilation on the Italian bench and among the Italian fans in the stands. When news of the goal scored by the Czech player Smicer spread, the spell was broken and tragedy returned to mark the traditional game. The broadcasters returned to determining the sacred moments of the event and exercising sovereignty over the production of meaning. Fate ran its course, Italy was eliminated from the championships and Sacchi's trial by ordeal ended badly. The event corresponded much more closely to a media ceremony than it might have seemed from the live transmission.

Tradition was used as a symbol, above all by the two Italian journalists covering the match. Their propitiatory intentions seemed crystal clear and became increasingly blatant as the match worsened for Italy. The parallel between Cabrini's mistake in the final in Madrid in 1982 and Zola's missed penalty seems obvious. Memories of the game between Italy and Germany in 1970 were revived here and there during the match, but to no positive effect. For the first time in history, the Italian national side got the worst of Germany in a game that mattered. The amulet of tradition was not enough to obtain a satisfactory result.

The battle between Italy and Germany was also played out around the arena. Before the game started, the BBC homed in on Chancellor Kohl seated in the stands. There was no sign of the Italian prime minister, Romano Prodi, a great cycling enthusiast and proudly ignorant of football. This too may have been a fateful sign. The camera-shots of supporters captured the footballing drama that created a fierce clash of attitudes. The Italian fans despaired of their side's futile attempts to attack Germany, while German fans revelled in Germany's trench-warfare tactics, delighted at the prospect of eliminating an historic rival from the competition. Towards the end, after the Czech equalizer against Russia, when the German fans began singing 'Auf Wiedersehen', the game languished and then just slipped away.

At the end of the Italy–Germany match, the BBC camera alighted on a devastated young fan wearing a black T-shirt, with the words 'Proud to be Italian' written across it. Keeping on the subject of stereotypes and those that the Italians perpetuate about the English, was this an instance of English humour or of Mussolini's perfidious Albion?

NOTES

1. J. Habermas, *La crisi della razinalità nel capitalismo maturo* (Roma-Bari, 1982).
2. R. Robertson, *Globalisation* (London, 1992).
3. See N. Porro, 'Il patriottismo catodico e come rovesciare la sindrome di Dorian Gray', in N. Porro (ed.), *L'Italia in TV agli Europei '96. Il calcio come identità e come rappresentazione* (hereafter *L'Italia in TV*) (Rome, 1997).
4. N. Blain, R. Boyle and H. O'Donnell, *Sport and National Identity in the European Media* (Leicester: Leicester University Press, 1993). Also see G.P.T. Finn and R. Giulianotti, 'Scottish Fans, not English Hooligans! Scots, Scottishness and Scottish Football' (hereafter 'Scottish Fans'), in A. Brown (ed.), *Fanatics! Power, Identity and Fandom in Football* (London, 1998).
5. P. Russo, 'Il conflitto europeo di calcio. Ovvero: un continente fra vecchie partite e nuove antagonismi', in *L'Italia in TV*, pp.187–214.
6. Ibid., also see Finn and Giulianotti, 'Scottish Fans'.
7. G. Garanzini, 'Il Segreto? Cercate lo 0–0'; interview with Enzo Bearzot, *La Repubblica*, 18 June 1996, 43.
8. D. Dayan and E. Katz, *Media Events: The Live Broadcasting of History* (Cambridge, MA, 1985).
9. P. Russo, Atlanta Fiction. 'Le Soap-Olympics della NBC', *Sport and Loisir*, II, 4 (April 1998), 67–77.
10. The most significant case is that of the Union of European Football Associations (UEFA), which has opened an agency to sell television rights for the Champions League matches.
11. The example in this case is that of the Australian-American magnate Rupert Murdoch, who organizes rugby tournaments between the Australian, New Zealand and South African national teams giving, amongst other things, shaking up to the system of dilettantism that still prevails in the sport. Another example is provided by Media Partners, an organization that aims to manage television rights more efficiently and to set up a Super League of European football.
12. The fourfold division draws on that put forward by N. Porro, 'L'evento televisivo e la costruzione del significato. Un approccio sociologico', in *L'Italia in TV*, pp.15–47.
13. See P. Russo, 'L'Europa di Bosman', *Il Mulino* 6, 97 (374) (November–December 1997), 1152–1160.

8

Fanatical Football Chants: Creating and Controlling the Carnival

GARY ARMSTRONG and MALCOLM YOUNG

The link between verse and football is as old as the game itself. How else could fans of dull or failing teams while away another tedious 90 minutes without a decent verse or two! Or luckier fans celebrate their triumphs. Blank verse and heroic couplets are chanted from Carlisle to Plymouth.

Ian McMillan, Poet in Residence to Barnsley FC, 1997

Poetry, as Ian McMillan recounts, has its roots in the spoken and the sung language, and that is why he loves the spontaneity of the match. That is what attracts McMillan's participation as a football fan; that is why it is important to explore how and why football fans chant, sing, gesticulate and dance out their obsessional support: or, just as importantly, understand when they indulge in wholesome derision of the opposition. As a dynamic part of this ebb and flow, fans create an amazing and seemingly instantaneous rhyming verse, which is set to tunes drawn from some bottomless repertoire of melodies, many of which date back 70, 80 or more years. What the social analyst is faced with in the world of chanting fandom is this problematic task of defining the emotional abstractions of a pride and a passion, and the analysis of anguish or indifference. As McMillan reminds us, language and the poetry of song is one way of moving into the analysis of the social event of football support, for the world of chanting fans pitches us into a universe which is:

- filled with a passion and a love;
- with a parallel and coexisting set of hatreds;
- with the crucial aspects of a narrow and ferociously demonstrated cultural identity;
- with an emotional commitment to events that at other times and in other circumstances would be laughable or even ridiculous.

These are not attributes to be easily measured, for they flow and circle and surface conterminously to each other, appearing and disappearing like the songs that surround them. The analysis must also encompass aspects of carnival, which – as with all carnivalesque behaviour – continuously teases and threatens the forces of authority at every turn; and is therefore always possessed of the potential for social chaos.[1]

What the researcher witnesses is obviously ritualistically embodied. Everything from the display of club favours to the choreographed method of clapping and arm waving – to the tunes used and words and songs employed, is all part of a clear ritual of support and cultural identity. Ritual demands a detailed understanding and discipline by those performing the actions, and is necessarily a repetitive construct[2] for it is in its consistent repetition that its strength lies. In the songs, dances and chants we have a dramatic social process occurring and re-occurring, consistently re-emphasizing the seriousness of play.[3]

In addition, there are aspects of a discourse of power encapsulated in what occurs. For power itself, as M. Foucault argues,[4] is an effect of the operation of social relationships between groups and individuals, and is not a unitary thing, for truly it has no essence. Moreover, there are as many forms of power as there are types of relationship, so that every group exercises power and is subjected to it. Power in the domain of football fandom is thus not simply repressive, but is also productive and reproductive. Any consideration of the fan's role, *vis-à-vis* the authorities or club officials, or police who survey fan behaviour, is therefore imbued with aspects of this exercise of power. It is in this display of power that the role of the body becomes crucial. For the exercise of power subjects bodies not simply to render them passive, but to render them active. The power of the body thus corresponds to the exercise of power over it; and in this lies the possibility of an ultimate reversal of that power. When, as in this instance, this is allied with the omnipresent potential of carnival to dislodge social norms, we can begin to see why chanting fandom always threatens the forces of social control.

Football fandom can involve such practices as painting of the body, bodily adornment with scarfs and other cultural symbols, as well as the use of the body to signify a status and position as fans chant and clap or gesture in unison. All of these kinds of practices are simply links in this melange of syntagmatic chains.[5] One link depends on and is strengthened by its adjacency to the next, such as the swaying or wave formations that sweep the grounds, even as the songs and chants tell narrative stories about events as they occur. These social processes, then, are all about the constructive and productive use of the body by those who, at other times, might well see their bodies subdued, subject to surveillance and suppressed. For at these times and in these instances power lies with them. In trying to pin down and analyse the social processes which occur when fans chant, we need also to consider the affinities between football and the masculinity of warfare; and where, once again, everyday language presents us with a way into a semantic understanding.[6] The compulsive nature to the act of following a team permits various antagonisms to well up in ways that are similar to a 'ritualized warfare'.[7] Sport and support are many things to many people but the emotional nature of intense 'fandom' can produce people, who, for the duration of the spectacle, are neither totally rational in their thinking, nor polite in their expressions.

'Fandom' activities are essentially a male domain, where male cohesion and an attributed masculinity to events are a much lauded state of affairs. Many recent moves by politicians and those authorities disturbed by such practices as chanting and singing have aimed at 'civilizing' this ritual warfare, and denying those aspects of male aggression that the drama of football has patently encompassed across the decades.[8] The vociferously pursued route to such has been to enhance a 'family atmosphere', and encourage women and children to the ground. Yet, as Katharine Viner noted in the *Guardian* (18 March 1997), the male–female ratios at the game still deny any true gender equality in the crowd make-up:

> Last week I went to see Tottenham vs Leeds, a dreary mid-table clash resulting in a sad 1–0 loss for the Yorkshire side. It would have been a miserable day out, had it not been for the half-time entertainment provided by the Leeds supporters: they took their tops off, they danced a tribal war dance, they marked their territory on the stands. We could spot only one woman in the throng, who kept her Leeds top on, but danced with the best of them. In the old days, football fans made their macho-ness known by fighting each other; today they dance topless ...

What we have to consider, then, is a collective enterprise which still offers up an identity to thousands of young men, the majority of whom gain no financial or material benefit from their obsession. Indeed, they are an audience solely seduced by an unscripted drama in which every move and countermove is open to appreciation, denial, question or ridicule. If anything *is* to be gained, it is in the emotional intensity; and this can frequently end in deep disappointment.[9]

MEN BEHAVING MADLY BUT LESS BADLY

Football support in Britain has long been one of the most obvious activities at which men have exhibited those emotions they would be reluctant to demonstrate elsewhere. In their shared enthusiasms of the match day, men can hug each other, dance together, and unashamedly sing, shriek or cry in each other's company – activities largely avoided elsewhere in their daily lives. The commentary they pursue on such occasions has not always been pure and virtuous. Grounds have therefore long reverberated to a witty, ribald and often abusive narrative directed not only at the opposing players, but often at their own team, as well as the match officials and rival fans. Throughout the history of the game 'supporters [have] never accepted the notion that the contests should be confined to the pitch'.[10] This has generated a form of what could well be described as symbolic power during which, because of their chants and skirmishes, the fans gained: 'the power to legitimate pronouncement; a power to diagnose, classify, authorize, and represent, and have this power of legitimate naming ... taken seriously ...'[11]

The result was that across these decades fights between rival fans became part of the match occasion.[12] Meanwhile, the forces of control and social order were working to their own vision of symbolic power, and had their own areas of legitimization to sustain. In their deliberations they believed that the fans who fought were also those doing most of the singing and chanting; so that almost inevitably the 'hooligan' label became related to words as well as actions. An involvement in the songs, chants, and the ribald and witty badinage thus became sufficient to generate arrests and help classify and sustain the idea of a hooligan problem.[13]

From the late 1980s, and because of a range of complex and interacting reasons – including instantaneous outside television broadcasting – football started to become *de rigueur* for middle-class pundits. Multi-nationals became increasingly keen to be associated with the game for reasons of image and profit. The result has been that football, as an event, has become impossible to avoid on television, and its ubiquity now ranges from the quiz or chat show, to the quasi-sociological documentary focusing on the game and its culture and history. In essence, the market economy and the bourgeois corporate culture that drives football, with its socially engineered need for the sanitizing influence of the all-seater stadiums, saw the game become an integral part of a style culture. This generated a proliferation of fanzines and articles in broadsheet colour supplements, and influenced a range of other strands of the media; so that mainstream publishing has looked to the 'laddish' magazine and the football novel, while cinema dabbled with the football film. Such a commercially minded world inevitably demanded that the authorities and the police combine to erase the unacceptable violence which had gone before. A blitz of surveillance and other controlling and legalistic measures, combined with the participants 'moving the goalposts' for hooligan confrontation to other arenas, more or less eradicated two decades of fighting between opposing fans inside the ground.[14] However, this left the residue of chants and choreographed gestures that had accompanied the skirmishes, for you cannot remove overnight such a highly symbolic aspect of cultural identity by wishing it away. Moreover, because of its previous identification as part of the hooligan problem, the chanting, singing and choreographed gesticulation was still seen as something needing to be addressed and prevented. The 'blandification' of the game thus seems set to continue, as global pressure to commercialize and sanitize Premier league football institutes such innovations, epitomized *par excellence* by the friendly 'family stand' sponsored by the McDonald's burger empire.

In setting out to deny these dualities, and the bias, the masculinity, and the singing and dancing, these multi-national corporations have inevitably and quickly learnt – as anthropologists doing fieldwork have also learned – that almost all peoples loathe, fear and despise the 'people next door'.[15] This inherent binary dualism uncloaked over three decades ago, when Levi-Strauss analysed aspects of the totemic mind, and argued that across all cultures 'hell is in the others'.[16] Such social differentiation is an aspect of human experience which holds huge symbolic power, and generates 'structures of feeling'.[17] These are something from which 'people evince a deep emotional commitment to and which is closely integrated with their sense of self [to] give order to their world ... [and which helps sustain] an ontological security'.[18]

Corporate success requires the avoidance of real emotional commitment or the possibility of risk or any organizational hiccup. So, it becomes crucial to eliminate the potential mayhem, but harness the vibrancy of the carnivalesque discourse at the increasingly lucrative Premier League and cup programmes (sponsored by Coca Cola and the like). Even 'approved' song sheets and 'chanting areas' have been tried as a means to remove the strong.

Yet, 'communitas' is generated during these 'anti-structural' periods in which chanting, singing and gesticulating are essentially lodged. For in this setting the subversive character of the betwixt and between state of 'liminality' allows spaces for some of the drives, the inversions and the paradigms of a counter-cultural form, and helps illuminate the postures and pedagogic reactions of the dominant structural ideology. As Victor Turner explains: 'we often find social relationships simplified, while myth and ritual are elaborated ... [and where] if liminality is regarded as a time and place of withdrawal from normal modes of social action, it can be seen as potentially a period of scrutinization of the central values and axioms of the culture in which it occurs'.[19] Turner suggests that liminality, and the marginality it produces, create a setting which generates 'an emphasis on spontaneity, immediacy, [where] the "existence" throws into relief one of the senses in which communitas contrasts with structure. Communitas is of the now; structure is rooted in past and extends into the future through language, law and custom.'[20]

The chanting, dancing fan, then, is essentially a young male who lives through a series of liminal periods within a community of like-minded others, all of whom are involved in chaotic and cascading activities which incorporate extreme elements of the carnivalesque and ritual warfare. In this the fan reaches a depth of emotion that flows from a polarity of joy on the one hand, to the alternative misery which accompanies defeat; and all the while is incorporated into a complex communal identity sustained by binary expressions of symbolic power which defines 'us' – our lads, in our favour – against 'the others' whose defeat is a priority.

The game of football and the spectator loyalties that it attracts and which sustain it provokes a spectrum of aggression and violence. As G. Finn argues on this issue, the range of potential social meanings allows considerable scope for difference and deviation.[21] Learned via a complex socialization process supporting is a milieu of quasi-violence which exists in and through an ambiguous and ambivalent moral code. At times of high intensity, Finn speaks of 'flow' experiences that make demands upon the participants. This Turnerian idea can lead to the transcendence of an individual's sense of self which makes the spectator central to the event itself. Refuting the idea of a correlation that postulates that events on the pitch determine actions off it, Finn argues instead for a whole variety of cultural meanings which can act as a guide for action. As he persuasively argues, an understanding of fandom this way may help an outsider see that what is considered 'hooliganism' is 'not dissimilar to the concerns of other supporters or of humanity at large'.[22]

Football is thus about social differentiation. It is about us against them, and their defeat. It denies egalitarian ideals, and revels in our superiority, which it sings and dances on its way to success. It denies the Christian ethic that would turn the other cheek, and rather re-emphasizes danger, victory and domination in battles against some clearly identified 'other'. In effect it is a celebration of ritual warfare that will claim victory in ecstatic song,[23] the ritual discourses of any society filter perception and dramatize reality. As an adjunct to this, we can argue that for the fan:

> the ritual process has to become a way of life, for it is made up of those cultural metaphors which persuade and project a state of being by presenting the 'truth' as already accomplished. In other words, the 'doing' or better performing of the ritual is what is critical to the accomplishment of the desired state. In a rite of passage from childhood to adulthood, for example, we know the rite itself does not cause the maturation that follows – this would occur naturally without the rite. The rite, however, is a cultural construction considered to be naturally necessary to bring about the event for which it is performed ... In doing this it carries its own justification for itself in that it 'sings its own songs'; and as the anthropologist Maurice Blok has pointed out, you cannot argue with a song![24]

Singing, dancing and chanting is therefore a self-empowering social process; for it becomes self-justifying, self-perpetuating and then succeeds, as it does, simply by deploying a ritualized control over the idea of interpreting what is true.

THE ETHNOGRAPHIC FIELD: THE CHANTS AND SONGS OF THE PARTISAN FAN

This essay is the outcome of an anthropological study of one particular group of football fans, nicknamed 'The Blades'. The sinister-sounding name of these supporters of Sheffield United FC derives from the founding of the club in 1889 in a city renowned for its steel industry. Borrowing from this heritage the club is nicknamed 'The Blades' and all United supports call themselves and each other 'Blades'. Those considered 'hooligans' also use the term 'Blades' to define themselves. When the term 'Blades' is used in this study it will refer either to all United fans or to the hooligan element – the crucial element is context. To complicate matters further, those who chant may well do so in support of their hooligan colleagues but would not consider themselves hooligans. The hooligans meanwhile will frequently join in the whole repertoire of chants sung by non-hooligans. Context is everything. Whatever their propensity to aggression or violence, all Blades share a mutual antipathy towards city rivals Sheffield Wednesday whose fans have themselves adopted the club nickname of 'The Owls'. Blades prefer the derisory firm 'Pigs' to 'Owls' and 'Owls' prefer 'Pigs' to 'Blades'. This hostility is enacted weekly at the clubs' Bramall Lane and Hillsborough grounds, respectively; it can extend beyond words and rivalry, engendering what has become, since the late 1960s, a frequently violent affair.[25]

As a public collective expression of social and cultural identity, football chants have no other modern-day equivalent. For although football crowds have chanted since the 1920s, albeit with a small and infrequent repertoire, no other sport generates behaviour parallel to that seen and heard on the terraces across the length and breadth of Britain. By the 1960s chants had become identified as an integral part of football, and had become synonymous in the public mind with the game and its younger male supporters.[26]

One suggestion for its growth in the 1960s was the evolution of a youth culture. The resulting loss of status of brass bands as a pre-match entertainment saw them replaced by a public announcement system playing pop records. These new anthems were quickly taken up on the basis of an old football cliché that 'such vocal support is worth a goal start'. Whilst footballing success has always depended on the ability of the players, the luck of the game and the run of the ball create a large measure of uncertainty and thus the chants can be said to link to these unknown yet potentially crucial factors. In such a world of latent ambiguity, singing and chanting are perfect tools to argue that influence can be created; for their veracity can never be objectively tested. However, there is no doubt that fans play a considerable part in creating the spectacle of the game, and many players have attested to the part the enthusiasm of the fans plays in sustaining team morale.

Nevertheless, measures to control the cascading nature of the metaphoric battles that football team support encompasses have long been employed. As early as 1907, Sheffield United's directors published a list of 'Do's and Don'ts' in a match programme. These requested spectators 'not to shout instructions to players, boo the referee, call for the dismissal of rival players, argue, show bad temper, or shout and be rowdy'.[27] Almost a century later things had not changed much, for the 1992 list of Ground Regulations published by the Football Association is so constraining that had these been rigorously enforced perhaps 90 per cent of any crowd would have had to be ejected or arrested. For example, regulation 15 relates that punishment will follow 'behaviour likely to cause confusion or annoyance'; while Regulation 22 promises the same for those who are a 'source of danger, nuisance or annoyance'. These, of course, are so loosely defined as to give easily stewards and the police the power to eject or arrest those they would define as being 'in breach of ground regulations'. No doubt this could encompass activity accompanying the singing, chanting and choreographed gesticulating that the partisan fan has made into something which is almost an art-form in its own right.

SINGING TO THE TEAM

Players are always seen as employees of the fans, and consequently the fans always understood it to be their duty to instruct them. So, even though they were playing for 'us', United footballers were often abused and ridiculed for their actions, which could well be influenced by the vagaries of that ambivalent thing called 'form'. However, the home fans at Bramall Lane were generally sympathetic to newcomers to the first team; and every player would have a period of around two months to win over the fans. This could be achieved in a variety of ways; by brilliant display, by an obvious innate ability, or by being a crowd-pleaser – namely through building rapport and acknowledging the fans, and showing unrestrained delight when the home team scored. The quality desired in these newcomers can be summed up by that vague entity – 'commitment', and could even be demonstrated by a player simply effecting a lot of encouraging clapping towards his team-mates, urging them on with these gestures all the while accompanied by clenching of the teeth. Any player showing this intimation of commitment was halfway to becoming popular with the fans. In the 1970s chants and songs towards individual players became increasingly popular.[28] Some other chants to certain players centred on those vaguely defined attributes of 'character' and 'talent', and related not only to the skills of a player, but to his perceived empathy with the fans.[29]

Songs and chants always presented the chance to dabble in a degree of poetic licence following the true spirit and form of a carnivalesque style. A player's reputation could well be constructed to suit the occasion. Thus, in the mid-1970s the words of 'Has Anybody Seen My Girl', a 1920s jazz song, were amended in what was a deeply ironic paeon of praise to a somewhat average centre-forward:

> Six foot two, eyes of blue
> Big Chris Guthrie's after you
> na na na na na, etc.

The fact that Guthrie was two inches shorter, had brown eyes and was said by the fans to 'have the menace of a kitten' was essential to the inverted meaning that the chant encompassed.

Certain names were chanted because their simplicity easily facilitated affective rhythms, while other players with multi-syllabic names could create a problem for the songsters. At times a player might inspire a chant simply because of an inadvertent public comment. So when, in January 1985, the United goalkeeper made a remark to the press after United lost 5–0 to a team which included three black forwards, and declared that 'keeping goal was like defending Rorke's Drift' – an allusion to the defence of a stronghold of that name in the Zulu Wars, the following Saturday saw the Blades behind his goal make repeated chants of 'Zulu, Zulu'.

Chants could be positive and encouraging, or could voice disapproval of the players. If the team was doing well, the manager's name might be introduced.[30] If the team was consistently losing games, then chants would call for the manager to go. This was the only way fans had of commenting on his signings or his team selection prowess.[31] Yet, as in all carnivals and liminal occasions, there are different foci and intentions. Fans had to be careful when voicing such opinions, for one strongly expressed could easily result in a punch from neighbouring United fans given to a different view. In these situations the 'debate' could escalate, the police might intervene; and once again these 'hooligan arrests' could be cited as proof of a growing social problem that needed further surveillance and control.[32]

CHANTS AGAINST RIVAL CLUBS AND AUTHORITY FIGURES

There is a line of thought, from those who are engaged in the exercise of socio-political control, that football should be an occasion for mutual enjoyment and appreciation between rival fans. Such a vision is unrealistic. The game and its metaphoric language is all about aggressively defeating an enemy – an 'other' – who must be shown to be inept, bungling, untalented and certain to be thrashed. The fans – pursuing a 'habitus of belief and practice'[33] – believe they have a major input in this task. The social process has always required them to be antagonistic, offensive and abusive – not only to those of their own team who fail to meet expectations but to all the opposing players. Football support is not an egalitarian spectacle, but one that demands partisan involvement; for its demands for success are such that it is fast becoming a business in which even modest failure cannot be tolerated.[34]

The way to display overt disparagement is to boo the opposition as they take the field – a normal practice at Sheffield since the 1960s. Following a calamitous decline in footballing fortunes when the club dropped from Division One to Division Four in the space of five years, opposition teams were usually considered to be 'minnows' and would receive the derisory accolade of: 'What the fuckin' hell is that?' In 1991, in an attempt to curtail this long-instituted animosity, the Football Association ordered teams to enter the pitch together, and this was often accompanied by the match disc jockey using the public address system to call fans to 'put their hands together in appreciation of both sides'. This was easily subverted, however, for the fans simply waited until half time to boo, when the teams would reappear but never together.

Since the 1970s the main body of partisan fans at the game have clearly enjoyed and been sustained by the rituals of swearing, snarling, and bellowing the cynically aggressive abuse which denies humanity to the opposition on the field, to those in an unsuccessful manager's den, and to those in power in the directors' box. Authorities at club and association level, always mindful that carnival can easily slide into chaos, have set out to defuse this abuse. One tactic they have used has been to instruct players to play down their own jubilation and celebratory rituals when a goal is scored, and thus to set an example to the crowd.[35] Players themselves, however, inevitably take a central role in this ritual warfare, and their own success at the highest level is clearly determined by an ability to humiliate the opposition both by scoring and winning, and then publicly celebrating their actions in achieving this. Thus their own interventions can incite the crowd to ecstasy or anguish. At both ends of this spectrum of elation or dejection, the fan response can cause the authorities to intervene and arrest those involved, and again swell the image of a 'hooligan' body.

Fandom is a cultural performance. This drama demands a continuous narrative of opposition that should be witty, clever, parodic, sharp, incisive, quick, and sardonically funny. A large part of the attraction of spectating is in this skilful act of denigrating others with an immediacy that draws on a Levi-Straussian *bricolage* (or cultural baggage) which assembles whatever is available to include in the abuse and ridicule.[36] This performance is made up of observations about physical appearance, about footballing abilities, and past history which is constructed into a variety of opinions that need be neither accurate or logical. The ability to manoeuvre any material into a suitable framework is part of the skill of the creativity of support or denigration. In consequence, all the immediacies of social differentiation are taken almost as stereotypes in order to create this classificatory 'otherness'; and physical features such as weight, height, lack of hair, a perceived 'foreignness', or skin colour have all been used in the process. In such a world, the instantaneous vocalization of some oppositional derision means that the more distinctive the rival player's physical appearance, the easier the chant is to sustain: 'Have you ever seen your dick?' and 'Fat Bastard' were obvious responses to observed rotundness, while long-haired players would receive chants of 'Gyppo' (Gypsy), and 'Where's your Caravan?'

Certain chants asked questions which the fans knew could not be answered, nor had much evidential legitimacy. However, innuendo and rumour would be enough to sustain a derisory calling, and managers and chairmen of rival teams were often accused of a variety of sexual misdemeanours based on such material. In January 1984 a Birmingham footballer was allegedly involved in a punch-up with his own manager, Ron Saunders, over a relationship with Saunders' daughter. A week later at Birmingham the Blades repeatedly chanted at the player:

> Shaggin' Saunders' daughter
> You should be shaggin' Saunders' daughter.

When the well-known manager Tommy Docherty saw his love life come under media scrutiny in 1984 at his Woverhampton team base, thousands of Sheffield away fans chanted: 'Who're you shaggin' Docherty?'[37] Five months later, in January 1985, Elton John, the gay pop star and chairman of Watford FC, was asked by hundreds of visiting Blades: 'What's it like to be a puff?'

Again and again opposing players would be chanted at for any incident or sexual exploit that had been usually reported in the tabloids. And as the act of denying humanity to the opposition was so intrinsic to the role of fandom, that public claim to an exemplary life would be similarly disparaged, especially if the player was known to be one who pulled strokes on the field of play. In essence they all faced abuse because they were not 'us', and our cultural identity based on this social differentiation demanded they be castigated for being of 'the other'. Being more talented and famous than those who were less able and less fit, but who could chant, was sufficient to make them the focus of the singing.

Early in the 1980s chants denigrating black players for simply being black had become increasingly associated in the public mind with football support, and earned partisan fans a status synonymous with the extremes of racism. At this time, certain grounds could indeed swell to a collective denigration based on a denial of humanity to black players, with '*Sieg Heil*' cries and Nazi salutes emanating from those with right-wing political sympathies. Though these occasions have loomed large in the collective consciousness, to the extent that fandom and racism are often seen to be synonymous, we would argue that what is occurring here is a spectrum of opposition ranging from the racist and politically motivated to the less thought out but still indefensible ritual process of differentiation between 'us' (our boys, our players, our locus and sense of place) and 'them' (their boys, their players and their origins in other places). This differentiation, well known to the participants, has been taken by those ignorant of events or wishing to impose their own morality on the football audience, to be a single overriding referent of events.

Yet the 'negative' condition of blackness like being Irish, or Scots, or Geordie, bald, hairy or overweight, and so on, can more usefully be seen as just one of a classificatory range of ways of supporting 'our' collective against whoever 'they', the other, might be.[38] As they fleetingly employ these derisory attributions, the fans momentarily enjoy a taste of the power that comes from the linguistic intimidation of an imagined and created 'other', even as their own identities are worked on. This binary situation exists in films, on television, on radio, in business (for example, the Stock Exchange in London has recently [1997] made linguistic abuse actionable);[39] and of course is part and parcel of political life.

Prolonged participant observation at Bramall Lane suggests Blades had little or no connection with overtly racial political activities. Indeed, in 1985, on one occasion when some 30 young men in a group of some 400 Blades chanted 'Nigger, nigger, lick my boots' at a winger from Barnsley, a core group of Blades (including a dozen West Indians) threatened the instigators, and in the subsequent decade such racist chanting had no part in the recorded cacophony of chanting. Politicians and certain lobbyists, of course, are not as adept as the chanters at sorting this out. And in the drift to a more authoritarian stance, the definition of racism seems set to expand even further, and become referential to everything – so that any opposition will be defined as provocative, offensive, and thus actionable. In January 1999 the Home Secretary loudly proclaimed the creation of some 29 points in yet another plan to sanitize support at the game, and to define further offences committed when fans urge on their teams, or deride any opposition.

This association in the wider public mind of football fans with hooliganism and racist behaviour has been termed by one group of researchers as the 'racist-hooligan couplet'. They sensibly explain with examples how in many instances abuse is: 'Taking place within a context where racial meanings do not "stand for" what they would outside the context of the game and the stands.'[40] The meanings of race, as the authors argue, are filtered through a discourse of being white. Their research found that racial abuse was not specific nor reserved to certain areas of the ground. Such abuse was also contextual and satisfied a variety of circumstances. The evidence of such comments forces many onlookers to express outrage which satisfies the football authorities' perception that such language and opinion are the preserve of the racist hooligan couplet. As the authors argue, the variety of schemes that have applied anti-racist missionary zeal to the ground rely 'on a morality that does little to understand the social configurations of racism'.[41]

In this world of antagonism, a fan soon realizes that certain symbolic figures, such as the police, or referee and his linesmen (or assistant referees), can be abused or denigrated without fear that fellow fans or visitors will take offence. Indeed, the situation here was similar to any carnival, where traditional authority figures often take on or are given a role reversal that denies power to those normally in charge. In this reversible world those without power on the terraces could thus make a scapegoat enemy of those visiting what is always a social drama, one that of necessity always stands apart and aside from the normal social process.

In the 1960s and 1970s chants directed at some dubious refereeing decision included:

> Who's your father, who's your father, who's your father, referee?
> You ain't got one ...you're a BASTARD
> You're a BASTARD referee.
> (to the tune of 'My Darling Clementine')

and:

> The referee's a BASTARD (*repeated three times*)
> And so say all of us.
> (to the tune of 'For He's a Jolly Good Fellow')

Physical attributes would always be called into use; so referees were derided as 'bald-headed bastards' or 'long-legged bastards', but were always 'bastards'. By the 1980s these constant accusations (apart from an occasional rendition of 'who's the bastard in the black') were becoming increasingly rare; the monitored visibility of fans in the electronically surveilled stadiums was increasingly allied to the keenness of the police to arrest those chanting such mantras. As a result, fans amended the script and chanted the short and staccato word 'cheat' as they reduced the risk of arrest, but managed succinctly to present those in power with the same dismissive message.

Prior to electronic surveillance, anonymity had served the packed terraces well across the 1960s, and allowed one of the earliest anti-police chants sung with gusto:

> Bramall Lane Coppers,
> Turn to the Kop of fear,
> With Guinness bottles whizzing
> Past your ear

You listen to the chanting far behind
The first thing that comes into your mind...
Kill the bastards! Kill the bastards!
(to the tune of 'Night of Fear' by The Move)

This was superseded when the tune became unfashionable, and in the 1970s followed by a children's rhyme was sung whenever the police (the pigs) arrested (nicked) a Blade:

Old McDonald had a farm, ee-ih-ee-ih-oh
And on that farm he had some Pigs, ee-ih-ee-ih-oh
With a nick-nick here and a nick-nick-there, etc.

At times this would be abbreviated to a single, repetitive ee-ih-ee-ih-oh, for the Blades realized the police knew what was being implied. In the late 1970s, as the police were making arrests, a chant suggesting their incompetence in the pursuit of what many considered to be a much more serious matter than their over-zealous dealings with the fans, again took its theme tune from the Latin American Anthem 'Guantanamera':

Ten thousand Coppers...
And only one Yorkshire Ripper.

This reference to a killer of some 13 women also saw the fans chant: 'You'll never catch the Ripper'; and was used as a serious indictment on outside events that the fans knew contrasted strongly with their own minor misdemeanours. In the mid-1960s the imagery had been less strident, for whenever a line of officers walked in unison along the perimeter of the pitch to take up positions, the theme tune of the 1930s 'Laurel and Hardy' comedy films – then being shown on television – would be whistled by hundreds of fans. This tune has no words, but has become an acknowledged indicator of the pomposity and incompetence that the two slapstick heroes personified; and which the fans now transferred to their enemies in the police.

OVER THERE: CHANTS ACROSS THE DIVIDES

Narration and exchange between rival factions are issues which anthropologists have examined the world over.[42] Chants recorded in the early 1970s reflected this polarization and focused on the location of the distantly positioned rival fans, and their 'otherness'. Using a Second World War tune and imagery, one popular chant was:

Over there, over there
And do they smell... (*clapping rhythm*)

Like fuckin' hell
Over there, over there.
(to the tune of 'Distant Drums')

In this era, when fans stood in physically distant 'kops' or terraces, the action of 'taking' a rival kop would always draw responses so that opposing fans who deliberately entered the 'home' terracing – the Shoreham End – would receive taunts and threats of:

– Come and have a go at the Shoreham Aggro
– You'll never take the Shoreham
– The Shoreham run from no-one.

Structural alterations in the 1970s and 1980s forced the more voluble and physical 'hooligan' element to move from favoured situations; the aim of standing or sitting close to away fans took on new import. Chants were created to respond to the fact that opposing fans now were visible and therefore individualized. Some portly rival might thus be singled out and greeted by the choir, who would taunt him:

You've never seen a salad.

or: He's fat, he's round
He bounces on the ground
Fat Bastard, Fat Bastard.

The accusers of this obese target, however, could well face arrest from one of the phalanx of police officers arraigned on three sides around the home fans. The ferocity of these arrests often contradicted the assertion that words do not break bones and in consequence, gestures became more discreet, so that rivals began quietly mimicking each other across a police-generated no-man's land. Using a variety of actions to mock and imply stupidity, the fans would wave their arms above their heads, all the while dancing, jabbing pointed fingers in the air, and slapping the top of the forehead in a gesture implying an imbecility in the opposition. Sexual innuendo was also an integral part of this performance, with each side accusing the other of being 'wankers', by using a masturbatory wrist movement at head height or in the vicinity of the groin. Occasionally, a two-handed motion would be used on an imaginary exaggerated phallus. At other times the masturbatory gesture began at the front of the forehead, signifying that the target of the abuse was a 'knobhead' – a popular insult of the moment. Perhaps the biggest insult in this exchange, however, was the double negative of purporting not to respond. Contemptuous of rivals from specific oppositional fan groups, one side would show an exaggerated disdain by ignoring their rivals' calls, or occasionally would look towards them with blank expressions accompanied by a mock-disgust shake of the head, implying an infinite sadness and superiority.

Despite these quiet gestures, the opportunity for dialogue remained a constant part of the social encounter. And if a rival team scored their fans would almost invariably break into a chant of '1–0, to which Blades (depending on the proximity of the police presence) would use the same tune to reply 'Fuck off'. These exchanges employed the tune of 'Amazing Grace' to repeat the message over and again. If, perchance, United were then to score two goals, Blades would chant '2–1', and taunt their opponents with: 'You're not singing anymore.' This, in turn, could provoke a response by the now despondent rivals, again using the tune to Guantanamera: 'Sing when you're winning ... you only sing when you're winning.'

Not all messages to rival fans offered room for such a well-matched and almost egalitarian dialogue, and some 1970s one-line chants were menacingly violent in their content:

> – We'll see you all outside
> – On the pitch (*accompanied by a surge to the front of the terracing*)
> – There's gonna be a nasty accident
> – There won't be many going home tonight
> – If it wasn't for the coppers you'd be dead
> – You're gonna get your fuckin' heads kicked in
> – You're goin' home in a Sheffield ambulance
> – Hello, Hello, Shoreham Aggro, Shoreham Aggro.

Until the increase in surveillance in seated stadiums, and the extra legalistic control practices of the mid-1980s, away games also provided a specific opportunity to taunt the home fans. One constant theme was to remind them of their alleged non-appearance at Sheffield, or a non-combativeness in those who had made the journey:

– Where were you at Bramall Lane?
– Have you ever been away?

In the early 1970s the fans of teams yet to visit Bramall Lane would be warned:

Will you come to Bramall Lane, no-oh, no-oh (*repeated 3 times*)
... get a hatchet in your brain, no-ho.
(to the tune of 'Marching Through Georgia')

By the early 1980s, for reasons outlined above, any actual physical contest usually took place hours before, or again after the match. Chants inside the ground thus became more direct in context, and increasingly made sarcastic reference to prior events:

– We thought you were hard ... we were wrong, we were wrong.
– What's it like to run at home?
– Smallest [hooligan] crew we've ever seen.
– You're just a bunch of wankers.

The jeers, whistles and gestures, such as the masturbator's wrist-jerk action of the 1970s, were added to in the 1980s, with the chant of 'You what?', and 'Do what?' being common parlance for a couple of seasons. A collective rising 'Aaaargh!' sound was also deployed to imply derision, while wolf-whistles and an effeminate high-pitched 'Oooooh!' accompanied by a limp-wristed motion was used to deny masculinity to the rivals. Ridicule was always an essential part of the verbal armoury, and meant that certain songs of the 1970s could still be used 15 years later to denigrate the opposition:

Sing something simple, you simple TWATS.
(using the tune for the 1970s BBC radio series 'Sing Something Simple')

Back to school on Monday
Does your mother know you're here?

An occasional reply in the 1970s to any threat shouted across the safety
of the fences separating the fans, was chanted in an exaggerated upper-
class accent and asked the sardonic question: 'You're Hard?' While
'Cheerio, cheerio' was used to signify that opposition fans were leaving
the ground before full time. This might be alternated with the mocking
and contemptuous cry of: 'We can see you sneaking out.'

A SENSE OF PLACE: CHANTING A REGIONAL DIFFERENTIATION

Though the game itself and the players provided rich material for a
continuous scatological dialogue, there were other themes to draw on. A
sense of regional identity, for example, which might seem insignificant
in life away from and outside the realms of football, could well be given
an enhanced significance; so that fans from market towns in rural areas
would be greeted with chants from big city Blades:

I can't read, I can't write ... but I can drive a tractor.

or: Sing when you're farming, you only sing when you're farming.

Fans from the nearby coal town of Barnsley were accused of 'Singing
only when mining.' If a team lacked any easily identifiable regional label,
Blades would use any referential crumb to make their point of
opposition, and in 1994 at Tottenham – a club with a perceived Jewish
following – they sang: 'Where's your foreskins gone?'

In 1997 a BBC television documentary on the notoriety of Millwall
supporters had included material on an individual known as 'Harry the
Dog'. On their next two visits to London, Blades chanted: 'Harry the
Dog is a Mongrel,' adding 'You can shove your reputation up your arse.'
Then, because of the alleged association of Millwall fans with right-wing
political causes, the London opposition was further advised to 'shove the
National Front party' up the same place.

In 1982 fans from Chesterfield, a town immediately to the south of
Sheffield, were recommended a similar course of action, but the
reference to a 'reputation' and the 'National Front' was replaced by

reference to the town's famous landmark of a 'crooked spire'. This same anal location was where West Ham supporters were advised to shove their fictitious supporter, the television comedy character Alf Garnett. In return, Blades were advised by various rivals as to where to shove their Yorkshire puddings and the stainless steel implements which had given the fans their name. When Derby fans – nicknamed 'The Rams' and drawn mostly from a small town in a predominantly rural county – were in opposition, a chant of 'sheep-shaggers' predominated; while a chant of 'Who hung the Monkey?' was hurled at home supporters when Blades visited Hartlepool, in remembrance of the fanciful story that during the Napoleonic wars the natives of that town had hung a shipwrecked monkey in the belief the unfortunate animal was a Frenchmen.

In the 1970s Blades would chant 'Yorkshire' when playing any team from Lancashire, and 'South Yorkshire' when playing Leeds, their West Yorkshire rivals. With any opposition from London, the cry was 'We hate Cockneys,' and 'You're the shit of London town.' Again this use of geography to define and differentiate homed in on those age-old divides of location and sense of place to make points about a cultural identity. This mode of thought provided an identical means for southerners to define themselves when they visited Sheffield, and they would use the socio-economic decline of this previously successful heavy industrial area as a way of defining their own superiority and cultural identity, to chant repetitively:

> On the Dole, On the dole
> What's it like to have no jobs?

and: One job in Sheffield, there's only one job in Sheffield.
       (to the tune of 'Guantanamera')

During the 1984 Miners' Strike, Blades would reply to these taunts by expressing support for the strikers and the miners' union leader:

> Yorkshire Miners, we'll support you evermore.
> (to the tune of the Welsh anthem, 'Men of Harlech')

> Arthur Scargill's red and white army.

and: I'd rather be a picket than a scab.

In return the southern or Lancastrian fans would respond with:

Arthur Scargill ... is a wanker, is a wanker.

Margaret Thatcher we'll support you evermore.

and: Get back to work you idle TWATS.

Messages with political overtones and especially those sympathetic to the miners' cause proved liable to provoke an arrest, and Blades would chant support for miners, well knowing the watching police might react to the sentiments. Many fans were ejected or arrested and charged with 'threatening behaviour' when chants of 'scabs' were directed at fans from the non-striking mining districts of Stoke, Derby and Nottingham. And even ten years after the strike, Blades visiting Nottingham for a match might still resort to the cry of 'Scabs' as the ultimate derogatory chant to aim at the opposition. Though support for Scargill might suggest an immutable political stance only two years before the strike, Blades had chanted: 'You can shove Arthur Scargill up your arse' at his home town fans in Barnsley. In essence, then, the chants were concerned with using material aspects of the cultural baggage or bricolage to assert the presence of 'the other', and deny them humanity and superiority.

ABSENT ENEMIES: PIGS AND ANCESTORS

The transitory element of the above chants was absent from the material used in anti-Sheffield Wednesday songs. An intra-city rivalry was the focus of an opposition that was lived and worked at throughout a fan's life; and pervaded the daily round. Derogatory songs, chants and calls were thus performed ritualistically on every occasion, even when Wednesday teams and supporters were not present.

And though United and Wednesday did not meet in a league match between 1979 and 1991 because they were in different divisions, fans of both clubs continued to chant in absentia against their rivals. In particular, songs were chanted at away fixtures as a means of impressing the listening home supporters with the venom the Blades could sustain towards the Owls (Sheffield Wednesday). Such chants had two recurrent themes: first, to express a desire to inflict violence on or humiliate their fans; and second, to rejoice in any misfortune to Wednesday's team and its players. In the 1960s a song reflected on the choices a Sheffield lad faced in deciding his loyalties, and allied this to a nostalgia for the ideals of childhood:

> When I was just a little lad
> I asked my mother what shall it be
> Shall it be Wednesday? Shall it be Leeds?
> Here's what she said to me
> Tha'll go down to Bramall Lane
> Tha'll watch Sheff United play
> They're the best team in the land
> And you'll think they're grand.
> (to the tune of 'Que Sera, Sera', a Doris Day pop song)

Choosing to be a fan of United was commonly seen as making an immediate commitment of hostility to Wednesday, and to an antagonism which had been passed down from the ancestors; as with many other tribal rites. Such a generational demand was included in the fan adaptation of 'Walk Tall', a pop song recorded by Val Doonican:

> Walk tall, walk straight, and poke a pig fan in the eye
> That's what my mother told me when I was about knee-high
> She said 'Son, be a proud man and hold your head up high
> Walk tall, walk straight, and poke a pig fan in the eye'.

Every nuance of social difference was grist to the symbolic mill in this dichotomous life of antagonism to the other Sheffield team, and even those advantages in ancillary equipment that Wednesday enjoyed were ridiculed. In this view a mid-1960s pop song was adapted to denigrate their acquisition of an electronic scoreboard and a new cantilever stand:

> Your scoreboard is crap
> Your stand's made of tin
> We'll crown all you bastards
> With bottles of gin.
> (to the tune of 'Death of a Clown' by The Kinks)

However, many of the more staccato chants were merely aimed at the whole general entity of being allied to the named opposition, and a nearly 1970s expression of contempt was the simple repetitive chant of: 'Wednesday Wednesday Wednesday ... shit, shit, shit,' while those with a more poetic bent or creative flair tended to favour:

> If I had the wings of an eagle
> If I had the arse of a crow
> I'd fly over Hillsboro' tomorrow
> And shit on the bastards below.
> (to the tune of 'My Bonny Lies Over the Ocean')

By the late 1970s, and into the early 1980s, chants contained a greater verbal menace which was often related to events outside the ground. Anticipating those confrontations, when fights between Owls and Blades became increasingly common place in the evenings after the match, Blades would sing:

> Shit on Wednesday
> Shit on the Wednesday tonight/in town.
> (to the tune of 'Roll Out the Barrel')

This tendency to be violent towards and physically humiliate Wednesday was celebrated both in the 'boot boy' fashion of the day, and the association of group identity with social space:

> Walking down Shoreham Street swinging my chain
> Along came a Pig fan and asks my name
> I kicked him in the bollocks and I kicked him in the head
> Now that Pig fan ... is Dead.
> (to the tune of 'Just One of Those Songs')

Other violent images were vocalized to the tune of a late 1950s favourite, and suggested what might occur following a chance meeting:

> I'd love to go a wandering
> Along the cliffs of Dover
> And if I saw a Wednesdayite
> I'd push the bastard over
> Valderee, Valderaa, Valderee, Valderhaa, ha, ha, ha, ha...
> (to the tune of 'The Happy Wanderer')

In the 1980s the anthem 'The Red Flag' was appropriated for a celebration of loyalties which might well have shocked those early socialists who saw it as a visionary statement of a more equal and caring society.[43]

At the first league match between the two sides in eight and a half years at Sheffield Wednesday's Hillsborough stadium on Boxing Day 1979, Wednesday trounced United 4–0. As a result of a media headline the occasion subsequently became known as 'The Boxing Day Massacre'. Blades took consolation claiming to have 'run' Owls from outside the ground; although a more accurate assessment is that there was some scuffling, and neither side could honestly claim to have 'run' their rivals. However, a week later a chant originated which was sung at almost every home or away game for the next 15 years:

Hark! Now hear, United sing
The Wednesday ran away
And we will fight for evermore
Because of Boxing Day.
(to part of the tune of 'Mary's Boy Child')

The Owls, for their part, sang the same song across the years, extolling their own ability to 'run' United, and, moreover, adopted a 1950s pop tune to remind their rivals of the 4–0 scoreline:

I've never felt more like singing the Blues
The Wednesday win ... United lose
Oh! Wednesday ... You've got me singing the Blues.
(to the tune of 'Singing the Blues' – the Owl colours)

The Blades' response was to throw the tune back at the Owls, with the words amended to encompass a violent image based on local knowledge of the particularities of support in two Sheffield districts:

I've never felt more like swingin' a pig
From Hyde Park flats to Wadsley Bridge
Oh! Wednesday ... you've got me swingin' a pig ...
As you do, As you do.

With the advent of microtechnology and 15-minute reports on radio from the early 1970s, the fortunes of the Wednesday team would be announced at United matches by anyone with a small portable. News of their fate would ripple through the Blades' contingent, and whenever the score favoured their opposition there would be immediate cheers and communal chants of 'Sheffield Wednesday fucked it up again.' Former Wednesday players, now playing for other clubs, who appeared before the United fans, would not be allowed to forget their past sins. And whenever they received the ball, or drifted close to the Blades, they would be greeted by whistles, boos and chants of 'Pig, Pig, Pig, [or] Hello, Hello ... Wednesday reject.'

The problem for analysts of this apparently divisive and deeply inculcated hatred is to realize that, regardless of the venom and violence inherent in the chants, the whole thing was socially contrived and always specifically contextual. Indeed, the record of a consistent participant observation shows that, across the years, the United fans would weekly deride Wednesday and their fans, but thousands would then go out drinking with them, or sometimes visit the homes of their rivals, because football loyalties cut across family, work-place and residence. For the vast majority, such chants, in effect, changed nothing, and meant nothing other than to reaffirm the collectivity of the Blades, who needed the Owls to define and redefine themselves and reassert their social identity in the way that secular rituals always do. When fights did occur over football loyalties as a consequence of chanting the location was more likely to be city centre bars when rival fans could and frequently would escalate hostilities.

CELEBRATING BLADES: TOTEMIC PARODY

A final category of chants celebrated the existence and the place of the Blades in working-class Sheffield society, and were drawn from a variety of sources. It seems that in their form and content they were important simply because the words and gestures were a means of showing to others that you could claim inclusion into a society that was supportive and encouraging. Knowledge thus was a part of the power of inclusion. However, we would argue that an unacknowledged element of these chants was that such chanting and performing was part of a public demonstration which made reference to the concept of fan-hooligan. For a clear knowledge of these chants and gestures confirmed the prejudices of an uncomprehending audience; and, consequently, they were used to bind the Blades together further in a cohesive social identity which presented the outside world with an incomprehensible drama of apparent violence and threat. The 1970s reflected the way this social drama was proceeding, so that, although chants of 'Sheffield ... Boot Boys' were a weekly occurrence, there were also elaborations – one of which created a mythic conversation between two famous club managers of the moment:

> Bertie Mee says to Bill Shankly
> Have you heard of the North Bank, Highbury?
> He says, 'No, I don't think so
> But I've heard of the Shoreham boot boys'.
> (to the tune of 'Just One of Those Songs')

To offset this, and to illuminate the fact that the singers understood the pretensions lying behind much of their braggardly performance, the Blades would ridicule the idealized masculinity that pervaded a large part of these macho dialogues:

> I'm a bow-legged chicken
> I'm a knock-kneed hen
> I haven't had a wank since I don't know when
> I walk with a wiggle and I talk with a squawk
> Doing the Shoreham boot walk.
> (to the tune of the 1950s pop song 'Tenessee Wig Walk')

Again the fact that the fans used any suitable material for chants was confirmed when those Blades who began following the pursuit of 'taking ends' and 'running their boys' borrowed from socio-political events in the early 1970s, and set themselves up in a chanted (but pale) reflection of the IRA, by giving birth to an SRA (the Shoreham Republican Army).[44]

Other songs with no obvious football connection were also used to these ends of showing knowledge and partisan membership of the group. A version of 'Falling in Love with You', an early 1970s Andy Williams ballad, was taken up on the terraces.[45] Another more up-tempo chant even crossed over from the 1940s, when an old Bing Crosby number – 'You Are My Sunshine' – appeared on packed terraces.[46] Despite their universality and American origins, these two tunes were appropriated by the United fans as being *theirs*, as if to say they had made them football relevant and brought them into the ground. As a result they would boo any other fans who tried to use them.

Other activities used to create a spectacle and to confuse rival fans were employed, and explained away in a deprecating manner as 'acting daft'. Celebration of a United goal, although always a matter for jubilation, would sometimes be acclaimed with a level of euphoria that was over-done simply because it was understood that rival fans would be further cowed and subdued by the spectacle. This ecstatic demonstration was known as 'Going Barmy', or doing 'the Headless Chicken', or the 'Dip', or the vividly metaphoric 'doing t' can o'maggots' – a close parallel of what the thousands packed together must have resembled during these chaotic celebrations.

Other chants were almost a self-parody of stereotypical attributes that were allegedly the province of the northern, working-class male. Throughout the 1970s one regular anthem was sung by hundreds of very young men, most of whom had hardly tasted beer, nor had yet dated a woman:

> Shoreham Boys we are here wo-oh, wo-oh (*repeated 3 times*)
> ... shag your women and drink your beer
> wo-oh oh oh oh oh oh.
> (to the tune of 'Marching Through Georgia')

Another parodic chant took its imagery from a television advert for 'Hovis' bread. This had used a pre-war industrial setting, with a young boy speaking in a strong regional accent about the virtues of the product and his home town, somewhere in deepest Yorkshire; and accompanied by a brass band playing the slow movement from the Dvorak's 'New World Symphony'. Southern team supporters seized on this imagery and would hum the tune in mockery. Blades, anticipating such mockery, adopted the tune as their own, and thus prevented their rivals from gaining a slight advantage in the totemic rites that were the games of social one-upmanship.

An alleged capacity for strong beer consumption by Northern working-class males also became the subject for self-ridicule and parody.[47] And, the heterosexual attractions said to be on offer in Sheffield were also expounded in song.[48] Indeed, in this male collectivity the appearance of women was always worthy of comment, and sexist comments would be shouted at women employed to promote the match sponsor's product and at the occasional policewoman. The solitary repetitive chant sung to the old hymn tune, 'Bread of Heaven' of 'Get your tits out for the lads' might also incorporate wolf whistles.

In complex ways, then, chants fed a sense of identity to fans, and those songs and chants with no overt message about the club or the game were as much a part of providing an identity to 'the lads' as the most virulent anti-Owl message. What the noise and the emotion helped create was a simple paradigm of social endeavour that varied on the mood of the moment. At away games the chanting was dictated by the numbers who travelled. On 'derby' occasions against Wednesday the chants tended to be single-minded and aimed at the rivals. On the last away game of the season the match was always an occasion for 'a good sing', and the carnival atmosphere was often enhanced and encouraged by fans in fancy dress 'acting daft' in ways described above. That said, there was no critical density required to initiate a chant. Eight Blades might sing with as much fervour as 800, but location was important. A low roof and an enclosure which packed fans together produced more concentrated noise than those occasions when the fans were loosely collected on some open-air terrace. No two matches ever saw the same repertoire used, and away fixtures often produced more chanting with fewer numbers, simply because regular followers were the most devout fans, and the most knowledgeable. Moreover, the result of the game did not always affect the chanting. Blades usually would go quiet if the team was losing, but on many occasions they would chant non-stop to signify strength in a hopeless defeat. As with all Blade activity, inside and outside the ground, chanting was an action accomplished without high-level organization and leadership.

CARNIVAL CURTAILED AND CRIMINALIZED: SEATING AND SURVEILLANCE

By the early 1990s what we have identified as a carnivalesque activity had been the norm at football grounds for over 25 years. In the 1980s certain songs and chants began to be accompanied by the waving of a range of inflatable artefacts whose use swept the English grounds.[49] These huge bananas, inflatable fish and the like were quickly deemed inappropriate by the authorities, and banned by some clubs, with their use being proscribed by certain police forces. Stalks of celery waved at Chelsea in the 1980s reappeared at Gillingham and the authorities reacted by subjecting supporters to turnstile celery searches. Five fans, aged between 16 and 19, were banned from the ground after being caught on CCTV for 'chucking celery'.[50] The club's Safety Officer revealed the new corporate desire of these football family occasions to be one in which 'docile bodies' reigned supreme, for as he answered a media enquiry: 'We've still got 4,900 standing at the ground and I was beginning to see a lot of undue movement in the crowd as people were jumping around while singing this [celery] song.'

Large inflatables never took off at Bramall Lane, but red balloons were the rage for a couple of seasons (1991–94), and began when a United fan bought 5,000 and gave them to turnstile operators to hand to the fans before the 1991 Sheffield derby. Fans then brought red balloons to matches over the next three years, although the police tried to prevent this by searching and confiscating them at turnstiles. Police also prevented fans entering the ground with, or displaying, banners and union flags with the club name or the word 'Blades' written on. Those market-driven forces that were fast propelling the game towards a homogenized, family affair argued that such items could obstruct the view of other 'customers', or could obstruct the advertising hoardings so essential to the corporate mind if they were draped around the ground. Business was thus setting out to dictate what favours the fans or customers could or should not carry.

Powerful marketing corporations which have now made football such a huge business and extended its impact well beyond the match day and into the clothes shops, the clubs stores, the video retailers and the like, together with surveillance and controls operated by the police and the football authorities have largely achieved what we would term 'the enslaving violence of the agreeable'.[51] Their product is now to be presented to the 'customer', with a consistency and an unquestioned conformity being the order of the day – as if the 'McDonaldization' of wider society must continue to gallop unquestioned across British society.[52] Today the match-day customer must be protected from social pollution as he/she consumes the commodified leisure experience, and be controlled by panoptical CCTV surveillance whose aim is to standardize behaviour and make the audience react in predictable and in preordained ways. As stated persuasively by anthropologist Mary Douglas:

institutions systematically direct individual memory and channel perceptions into forms compatible with the relations they authorize. They fix processes that are essentially dynamic, they hide their influence, and rouse our emotions to a standardized pitch. Add to this that they endow themselves with rightness and send their mutual corroboration cascading through all levels of our information system.[53]

In other words, football decrees that those who are now allowed to attend its functions display the institutional mind necessary to overcome individual thought, to straitjacket intellects and bodies. A purified community of compliant customers is thus considered essential to sustain this multi-million pound business, and holding that image is more important than its fans. For its ultimate aim is to create mutually appreciative consumers, who display no trace or hint of social differentiation or prejudice towards some socially-created opposition.[54]

Clearly there is a cost to this process. For though the authorities tinker with some of the links in these complex syntagmatic chains which have been built around football support over decades, events do not always follow the market prediction. The symbolic world that football fandom is all about is not one that will always react in ways the market might decree. On match day Bramall Lane may now be more silent than it has ever been, but things are not always as clean and neat as they appear. The price of admission in comparison to income has made the game unavailable to many previous fans – and those who can afford entry are told where to sit even when space is available elsewhere; and are then stewarded, disciplined and punished if they do not. Yet, already in this brave new clean and antiseptic world the clubs have found they are having to orchestrate chanting, or even play chants over the tannoys to provide the passion and atmosphere that has all but vanished from these all-seater customer castles.

As Umberto Eco might argue 'we are giving you the reproduction so you will no longer face any need for the original'.[55] However, cultural forms are not so easily created, nor existing ones subdued or proscribed, and at Bramall Lane in January 1997 the DJ's tannoyed urgings to 'Come on you fans, and sing; and not just when there's a goal' saw his demands subverted. As true commentators on the bizarre socio-economic process that football has become, the Blades easily moved into their liminal role as the street-wise court jesters of society who comment on the antics of those in power. Their response denied the pristine purity of the corporate image which, since 1981, has seen the club logo incorporate the message of being 'The Family Club', for on hearing that rivals Wednesday were losing, they reminded everyone that: 'Sheffield Wednesday's fucked it up again.' This was not a message the authorities wanted to hear. And, we would argue you deny such symbolic logic and symbolic power at your peril, for this may well contradict some official version of reality.

Academic analyses of football chants have tended to suggest these subverting chants are vehicles for expressing nationalism, regionalism and socio-political antagonism; and at times there are traces of such concepts in the songs. However, chants are more than that. For we believe they can be read as vehicles to dramatize and exaggerate a cultural identification that uses gender and social differentiation to create tension, to provoke nostalgia, to show endurance in the face of defeat, to provoke ridicule, and to provide intimacy.[56] These are cascading social processes that use and intertwine themes of sex, death, gender, a sense of place, social history, group identity, love and hate; and in which a constructed world of 'real' men is contrasted with ambiguous and weak ones. We can therefore argue that spectators turn into true social participants in the game by becoming narrators encompassed in these transgressions of etiquette. But this freedom is being curtailed as the consumer-led world of football seeks to deny the consumer a say in the past.

Thus, we face a future of conflict because carnival can consist of the pleasures achieved by subordinates who oppose the established. Carnival combines elements of excess, laughter, degradation and offensiveness, to produce an 'egalitarian second world' lying outside and beyond that preferred by officialdom.[57] Carnival produces disrespect, and with this a 'Radical opposition to the illegitimately powerful, to the morose and the monological.'[58] Thus, with their chants directed at players and powerful officialdoms, football fans ridicule the self-important and self-regarding guardians of propriety. Such performances therefore reproduce notions of 'Plaisir and Jouissance' where 'Plaisir' is the cultural enjoyment which enforces the ego, whilst 'Jouissance' is a violent pleasure that dissipates cultural identity to the point of discomfort, and which unsettles the subject's relationship to language and representation; 'our pleasures then come from both experiencing the consistency of self-hood and its collapse'.[59] Such fan participants are involved in the 'guerrilla activity' of resistance. Exhibiting 'tenacity, trickery, and guileful ruse', they consistently resist the authoritarian forces of the media, the judiciary, and the police by small incursions that continuously deploy ways of cheating the social constraint.[60]

From the 1960s social attitudes have become increasingly liberal towards sexuality, the body and language. The exception, it would seem, is when words are used by football fans. Whilst some chants may contain obscenities, they constituted, arguably, the only point at which ordinary spectators could at times exert opinion and perhaps influence the club. Others contain words which are meant to be offensive by attributing feminine characteristics and general incompetence to men. Such accusations dressed up in imagery and metaphor are part of a decades-old ideology, a collective conscience, which will not disappear simply because politicians pass new laws to criminalize such opinions. The demonization of such fandom occurred in parallel with Thatcherism, with its denial of the concept of society and disdain for any form of display of collective working-class culture. Since the 1980s successive administrations have pursued the idea of an individualized, privatized, bourgeois mentality and seem to find collective displays of cultural solidarity to be incomprehensible and threatening. It is not coincidental that the police have pursued all-seater stadiums and encouraged family unit participation, so that the traditional macho football supporter is confined to individual seating that destroys the old terrace culture. This mirrors the political denial of any collective activity which has the potential to represent an alternative vision of how things might be. Today the paying match-day consumer is promised a commodified leisure experience for the family that will not require him or her to think or worry about any form of 'pollution' from the unsightly.[61] Controlled by panoptical CCTV surveillance, the aim is to make discipline automatic, behaviour is normalized, with the audience reacting in a manner predictable to the point of docility. That seen as detracting from the norm produces a ranked and separated hierarchy of individuals, as the body itself becomes the site where power is exercised and the 'deviant' arrested and criminalized. All the time, the authorities assure us of their righteousness in defeating the icon of evil – The Hooligan.

NOTES

The authors are extremely grateful for the helpful comments on an earlier draft that were offered by Gerry Finn and other referees. The authors are, respectively, a partisan follower of Sheffield United ('The Blades') (GA), and an uncommitted native of Newcastle who occasionally reads newspaper reports on Newcastle United ('The Magpies' or 'Toon Army' (MY). The data on chants and songs are mostly taken from the fieldwork records of GA, and, except where mentioned, relate to events at Bramall Lane, the home of Sheffield United.

1. For the application of carnival to football, see R. Giulianotti, 'Scotland's Tartan Army in Italy: The Case for the Carnivalesque', *Sociological Review*, 39, 3 (1991), 503–27; R. Giulianotti, 'Football and the Politics of Carnival: An Ethnographic Study of Scottish Fans in Sweden', *International Review for the Sociology of Sport* 20 (1995), 191–224.
2. V. Turner, *The Ritual Process* (Chicago, 1969).
3. V. Turner, *Fields and Metaphors: Symbolic Action in Human Society* (New York, 1974). See also V. Turner, *From Ritual to Theatre: The Human Seriousness of Play* (New York, 1982).
4. A. Sheridan, *Michel Foucault: The Will to Think* (London, 1980), pp.218–20.
5. C. Levi-Strauss, *The Savage Mind* (London, 1966). Perhaps Edwin Ardener has shown most complete potential of the terms 'paradigmatic' and 'syntagmatic' chains, taken from the Saussurian school of linguistics, and from Jakobson. These chains have what Ardener describes as a 'transactional' quality, allowing semantic or metaphoric understandings that have an ascriptioned programme of meaning or value to the user. These, he argues, are socially apprehended, having been generated in a multi-dimensional space. In the circumstances here, the passion and the joy, or the pain and despondency of the game, are linked and encompassed by the transactional nature of the wearing of the favours, the body paint, the gestures, the songs, and the whole gamut of being at the match with others who are singing and chanting in unison; and this generates a linear syntagmatic chain of such events that creates paradigmatic meanings and values for those who are socially involved with them. See E. Ardener, 'The New Anthropology and its Critics', *Man* 6, 3 (1971), 449–67. H. Chapman (ed.), *Edwin Ardener, The Voice of Prophecy and Other Essays* (Oxford, 1989).
6. M. Crick, *Exploration in Language and Meaning: Towards a Semantic Anthropology* (London, 1976).
7. C. Bromberger, 'Fireworks and the Ass', in S. Redhead (ed.), *The Passion and The Fashion: Football Fandom in the New Europe* (Aldershot, 1993), p.133.
8. The Football Association, in conjunction with private business sponsorship and senior police officers, began a campaign to attract more women into football grounds from the mid-1980s. The government-commissioned Popplewell Report published in 1986 considered that women's role in football crowds was 'essential' but did not explain which women or why. Later, in 1990, the Taylor Report after the 1989 Hillsborough Disaster recommended that women be encouraged to football grounds as a means of altering the behaviour of some of the men therein. The fairer sex was idealized in terms that defined them as the opposite of brutish men, and a process was begun which saw the promotion of virtue epitomized by femininity and motherhood attempt to cleanse the polluted site that was the working-class, male-dominated football ground.
9. As Bromberger points out, the 'dramatic qualities' of the game equate with those 'genres of theatrical production' which provide a unity of time, space and action. This favours a communion between spectators and players. But of course in a theatrical production we always know the tragedy will end in tragedy, and that the love story will have a happy ending. At the match, however, the anguish of never actually knowing how it will end is what gives the whole drama an extra emotional dimension. C. Bromberger, 'Fireworks and the Ass', p.117.
10. R. Holt, *Sport and the British: A Modern History* (Oxford, 1989).
11. P. Bourdieu, *Language and Symbolic Power* (Cambridge, 1991).
12. J. Hutchinson, 'Some Aspect of Football Crowds Before 1914', in *The Working Class and Leisure* (Conference Papers) (Brighton, 1975). T. Mason, *Association Football and English Society: 1883–1915* (hereafter *Association Football*) (Brighton, 1980). J. Fishwick, *English Football and Society 1910–1950* (Manchester, 1989). G. Finn, 'Football Violence: A Societal Psychological

Perspective' (hereafter 'Football Violence'), in R. Giulianotti, N. Bonney and M. Hepworth (eds.), *Football Violence and Social Identity* (London, 1994).

13. G. Armstrong, *Football Hooligans: Knowing The Score* (hereafter *Football Hooligans*) (Oxford, 1998).

14. G. Armstrong and M. Young, 'Legislators and Interpreters: The Law and Football Hooligans', in G. Armstrong and R. Giulianotti (eds.), *Entering The Field: New Perspectives in World Football* (Oxford, 1997). See also G. Armstrong and R. Giulianotti (1997), 'Avenues of Contestation: Football Hooligans Running and Ruling Urban Spaces', Working Paper in Sport and Leisure Commerce, University of Memphis.

15. N. Barley, *The Innocent Anthropologist* (Harmondsworth: Penguin, 1986).

16. C. Levi-Strauss, *The Savage Mind* (London, 1966).

17. R. Williams, *The Long Revolution* (Harmondsworth, 1964).

18. I. Loader, 'Policing and the Social: Question of Symbolic Power', *British Journal of Sociology*, 48, 1, 1–8.

19. V. Turner, *The Ritual Process*, pp.155–6.

20. Ibid., pp.99–100.

21. G. Finn, 'Football Violence'.

22. Ibid., p.114.

23. G. Lienhardt, *Divinity and Experience: The Religion of the Dinka* (Oxford, 1961).

24. M. Young, *In The Sticks: Cultural Identity in a Rural Police Force* (hereafter *In The Sticks*) (Oxford, 1993), pp.161–2.

25. G. Armstrong, *Football Hooligans*.

26. This has been noted by P. Marsh, E. Rosser and R. Harré, *The Rules of Disorder* (London, 1978). In recent years compilations of football songs have proved a commercial success, see L. Bulmer and R. Merrills, *Dicks Out! The Unique Guide to British Football Chants* (Kent, 1992); A. Thrills, *You're Not Singing Anymore* (London, 1998).

27. T. Mason, *Association Football*.

28. The favourite of the decade repeated some two decades later, in a nostalgic recall of earlier times:

> Well we ain't got a barrel of money
> But we've got Woodward and Currie
> And wi' Eddie Colquhoun
> Promotion is soon – U-ni-ted
> (sung to the tune of 'Side-by-Side', a pop song of the early 1950s).

29. Perhaps the most frequent chant heard in many grounds in the 1980s was one borrowed from the Latin American pop song 'Guantanamera', with a player's name being repeated after an opening line. For example:

> One Tony Currie
> There's only one Tony Currie
> One Tony Currieee...
> There's only one Tony Currieee.

In the 1984–85 season one team member received the continually repeated chant of 'Joe, Joe, Joe, Joe...' whenever he scored or flattened a rival; especially if he then ran close to groups of Blades in the crowd and acknowledged them with a wave or a wink.

30. One message – in which the more polite in the crowd substituted the word 'damn' for the word 'fuck' – went:

> We're on the march wi' Basset's Army
> We're *not* going to Wembley
> But the Blades don't give a fuck
> Cos' we know we're staying up
> Cos' United are the greatest football team
> (to the tune of 'Ally's Dream' – the Scottish World Cup Squad Song, 1978).

(The reference here to 'staying up' relates to the constant relegation problem United faced between 1990 and 1994.)

31. In 1986 the constant chant of 'Porterfield Out' was believed to have achieved the desired result when the chairman sacked manager Ian Porterfield.

32. How 'big' a problem football hooliganism is will always provide a careful analyst with a phenomenological problem. However, for those who wish to avoid deeper reasoning and debate, comfort can be drawn from the annual release of arrest and ejection figures from the Football Intelligence Unit. This public relations exercise always guarantees a lot of media coverage based on the numbers presented compared to the previous year. Nobody seemingly asks for a breakdown of what changes are proffered (if any) or how many defendants are subsequently found guilty. Nobody to our knowledge has even analysed such figures in the light of the expansion of the 'hooligan-related' legislation or as a consequence of a new morality imposed on football in the past 15 years.

    Between 1996 and 1998 the Metropolitan Police pioneered in two London football grounds a technique that combined covert video surveillance with covert listening devices with a view to arresting those suspected of using 'foul and racist' language. Selecting individuals beforehand, the police placed tiny microphones adjacent to their seat and focused the camera on them, thereby recording sound and vision. The stated aim of police was to gain evidence to prosecute 'racist' football fans (*Evening Standard*, 6 October 1997). One technique not publicized by the Met. saw them locating an undercover police officer wired with listening devices adjacent to suspected racist fans. The failure of this operation at a North London ground was not made public.

33. P. Bourdieu, *Outline of a Theory of Practice* (Cambridge, 1977). P. Bourdieu, *In Other Words: Essays Towards a Reflexive Sociology* (Stanford, 1990).

34. One third of the league management were sacked or had their contracts terminated because they were unable to provide a winning formula in season 1997–98.

35. Instruction in the form of edicts to players to be modest in the goal-scoring celebration has come from the European governing body UEFA since 1974; the English FA since 1980, and from the world governing body FIFA since 1984.

36. M. Young, *In The Sticks*, p.112.

37. The famous Tommy Docherty, when manager of Manchester United in the late 1970s, attained a notoriety beyond his tactical prowess when it was discovered he was having an affair with the wife of the club's physiotherapist. At many away games the home fans would use this fact in their chants in an attempt to embarrass the visiting manager. Years later, when managing other teams, the affair still provided rival fans with ammunition.

38. M. Young, *In The Sticks*, pp.234–71.

39. In July 1996 one of the top traders in the Futures and Options Exchange of the London Stock Exchange was fined £500 by the Exchange for 'foul, abusive and embarrassing language' directed towards another member of staff. The trader's racist abuse towards a black 'floor observer' was considered severe by colleagues and therefore brought a reprimand. In an informative article covering the case, a reader learned that fines of around £50 were levied each month to traders for various transgressions, ranging from swearing to fighting on 'the pit' of the floor's trading area. Various interviewees spoke of a racist and aggressive work culture fostered by the needs of acquisitive capitalism. Fellow traders spoke of how dealing in millions of pounds created a stressful situation in which aggression and racism were manifested. *The Independent*, Business Section, 15 August 1996.

40. L. Back, T. Crabbe and J. Solomos, 'Racism in Football, Patterns of Continuity and Change', in A. Brown (ed.), *Fanatics! Power, Identity and Fandom in Football* (hereafter *Fanatics!*) (London, 1998), pp.71–86.

41. Ibid., p.86. For further highlights/comments on this issue see P. Dimeo and G. Finn, 'Scottish Racism, Scottish Identities. The Case of Partick Thistle', in A. Brown (ed.), *Fanatics!*; and P. Dimeo and G. Finn, 'Racism, National Identity and Scottish Football', in B. Carrington and I. McDonald (eds.), *Racism in British Sport* (London, 1999).

42. Bailey, for example, describes verbal contests amongst the Doludoi of Bisipora: '... words, unlike sticks and stones, do not break bones. The contest was conducted through an endless series of confrontation ... encounter, challenge, and assertion [and these] were met by counter-

challenge and counter-assertion ... Points are scored by the quality of the gauntlet and the dexterity and style with which it is flung down.' F. Bailey, *Strategems and Spoils: A Social Anthropology of Politics* (Oxford, 1968), pp.91.

43. The anthem of socialism had a most uncomradely message:

> Forever and ever
> We'll follow our team
> Sheffield United, they are supreme
> We'll never be mastered
> By the Wednesday bastards
> We'll keep the red flag flying high.

44. With the pseudo-creation of a paramilitary organization came a song of celebration:

> Aye Aye Aye Aye
> Shoreham Republican Army
> Wherever we go, we fear no foe
> 'Cos we are the S.R.A.

This was sung to the melody of a Mexican folk song from around the 1930s called 'Ceilito Lindo' (beautiful little heaven), and which was translated into an American popular song some 20 years later. Now it was to become a chanted song in Sheffield some 20 years further on. One aspect of this is worthy of comment, for the fact remains that Latin American melodies are consistently used in these carnivalesque proceedings; and perhaps thus make some sort of oblique comment on the understanding of the Latin American tendency to equate football and its spectacle with music and the carnival. Around the mid-1980s, for example, Newcastle fans took the music of the Conga, and allied it to a paeon of praise to a newly acquired Brazilian player, all the while making another oblique comment on the recently fought Falklands War; and all in a few lines:

> Oh we've got Mirhandina
> He's not from Argentina
> He's from Brazil
> He's fucking brill... (*repeated ad infinitum, just as in the Conga*).

45. The ballad was meant to show the depths of love a man had for a woman. It was appropriated here to declare an individual's love for the entity called Sheffield United FC:

> Wise men say
> Only fools rush in
> But I can't help
> Falling in love with you
> Take my heart
> Take my whole life too
> But I can't help falling in love with you...
> United...United...
> (to the tune of 'Falling in Love with You').

46. Why any specific tune appears is hard to say, but one consistently puzzling factor is how these young men suddenly present a verse to a tune that to all intents and purposes has drifted from the airwaves and the public consciousness some decades earlier. Thus, generations of Blades sang a song which was played on the airwaves decades before they were born. This fact did not matter because the words were part of an oral tradition:

> You are my sunshine
> My only sunshine
> You make me happy

When skies are grey
You'll never know just
How much I love you
Please don't take my sunshine away.

47. A chant surviving from the 1970s, and sung in pubs before the match a dozen years later by the older Blades, ran:

All the Blade Men love their gravy [beer]
All the Blade Men love to spew
'Cos when you've had a triple gallon [24 pints]
It's the natural thing to do
Nice 'n greasy, goes down easy
And it comes up just the same
So if you see a fellow spew, it's the natural thing to do
Call him a 'Blademan' – 'cos that's his name
(to the tune of 'All the Nice Girls Love A Sailor').

Another chant with similar sentiments was the most popular for over 18 years beginning in 1982:

You fill up my senses
Like a gallon of Magnet [local beer]
Like a packet of Woodbine's [strong cigarettes]
Like a good pinch of snuff
Like a night out in Sheffield
Like a greasy chip butty
Like Sheffield United, come fill me again
(to the tune of John Denver's 'Annie's Song').

48. One ditty the Sheffield Tourist Board did not use went:

Sheffield is wonderful
Oh Sheffield is wonderful
It's full of tits, fanny and United
Oh Sheffield is wonderful
(to the tune of 'When the Saints Go Marching In').

49. S. Redhead, *Sing When You're Winning* (London, 1986).
50. In 1987–88 Chelsea fans began waving sticks of celery, singing a bizarre sexual chant that had little or nothing to do with the game:

Cel-er-y, Cel-er-y...
If she don't come
I'll tickle her bum
With a stick of celery
(*Guardian*, 11 February 1986).

51. P. Bourdieu and J. Passeron, *Reproduction in Education, Society and Culture* (London, 1977).
52. G. Ritzer, *The MacDonaldisation of Society* (London, 1994).
53 M. Douglas, *How Institutions Think* (London, 1987), p.92.
54. And yet, when the police denied Sunderland fans a presence at a Newcastle derby game in the 1996 season, it was not the match that was reported on in the media the next day, but the unbalanced support of 36,000 Newcastle fans, which meant any Sunderland effort went unrewarded by crowd participation. As the match reports concluded, the game became an irrelevance in the light of the long periods of utter silence and the strange one-sided lack of conflict and apposition engendered.
55. U. Eco, *Travels in Hyper-reality* (London, 1986), p.19. Eco's argument was exemplified in

December 1995 when the Arsenal club were so concerned their multi-million pound all-seater stadium was lacking in atmosphere, that, in the absence of fans singing, they introduced a 'singing section' to the former North Bank terracing. Ideally, this becomes authorized singing, with chants and songs the authorities approve and provide in their song sheets.

56. E. Archetti, 'Argentinian Football: A Ritual of Violence', *International Journal of the History of Sport*, 9, 2 (August 1992), 219–21.

57. M. Bakhtin, *Rabelais and His World* (London, 1984).

58. R. Stam, 'On the Carnivalesque', *Wedge*, 7 (1982), 47–55.

59. S. Moore, 'Getting a Bit of The Other: The Pimps of Postmodernism', in R. Chapman and J. Rutherford (eds.), *Male Order: Unwrapping Masculinity* (London, 1988), p.191.

60. M. De Certeau, *The Practice of Everyday Life* (Berkeley, 1984), pp.18–26.

61. In 1997 Bristol Rovers FC implemented a 'no swearing' terrace at their Memorial Ground. Citing complaints about bad language from the occupants in the newly-built corporate hospitality boxes, the club threatened to ban language miscreants from the ground if found guilty of using expletives. This new morality was not just reserved for spectators. In November 1998 the assistant manager of Sheffield United FC was arrested in the middle of a match by a WPC policing a game at Queens Park Rangers. His crime was to use swear words when shouting at his own players. Held in custody for six hours he was bailed to return to the police station a month later whereupon he was cautioned but not charged with any offence.

The ludicrous impositions at times crossed national frontiers. In June 1998, shortly before the World Cup began in France, police in the North London district of Camden issued a warning to those who would be watching the matches live on televisions in pubs. In what was termed a 'zero tolerance' campaign aimed at stamping out any racist or 'xenophobic' chants, plain-clothed police officers were to be deployed in licensed premises to seek out breaches of the Race Relations Act. In what must rank as one of the most surreal acts of policing in the history of the Metropolitan Police, undercover officers watched groups of young men shouting at television screens following football events up to 900 miles away in the anticipation that they would in their chants offend foreign nationals who may happen to be in, or passing, the premises.

9

Soccer in Japan: Is *Wa* all you Need?

JOHN HORNE

Much of the sociology and social science of sport has been focused on sport in the West. This is especially so with respect to the study of association football (soccer). Debates about globalization have widened the scope of the sociology of sport and revealed the importance of considering sport in non-Western societies. This essay considers soccer in Japan in the light of an examination of the most influential discussion of team sport in Japan – Robert Whiting's depiction of 'samurai style' baseball. Three main questions are considered: why did baseball and not soccer become the national team sport; what factors lead to the emergence of professional soccer in the 1990s; and what are the prospects for soccer in Japan?

INTRODUCTION

Although the recorded history of football (soccer) and baseball in Japan dates from more or less the same time (the 1870s), it has been the latter that has become the pre-eminent team sport, both at high school and professional levels until recently. Western observers of Japanese culture and society have often emphasized its distinctive qualities.[1] In sports literature, too, the exotic and non-Western elements of Japanese sport and physical culture – especially the creation of a *do* or 'way' of practising the martial arts and 'samurai baseball' – has been stressed. So influential has this been that the 'samurai baseball' perspective has provided the lens through which a number of articles about sport in Japan written in English have been filtered. Here it is argued that this approach to sport in Japan is ultimately inadequate for understanding the growth and development of football since the 1990s and an alternative model is suggested. The essay begins with a brief consideration of Whiting's approach to baseball in Japan. The subsequent account of the recent development of professional soccer (*sakka*) in Japan will highlight similarities and differences between baseball and soccer in the light of these observations.

BASEBALL IN JAPAN

The modern era of professional Major League baseball in Japan (hereafter JML) began in 1936 with a seven-team league. Although three more teams were added prior to the 'Pacific War', regular season play was suspended in 1945.[2] Play was allowed to resume under American occupation in 1946 and from 1950 the current two-league system was introduced. Today there are six teams in both the Central League (CL) and the Pacific League (PL). Since 1966 the leagues have had a 130-game schedule compared with the 28 Major League teams in the USA which play a 162-game season.[3] In terms of live attendances and television viewing figures, baseball remains very popular in Japan. Most teams are owned by major corporations, and most have serious mass media interests. In the CL the Giants are owned by *Yomiuri Shimbun*, Japan's leading daily newspaper. The Giants are regularly on television, have the largest crowds – averaging over 50,000 per home game – and are supported by approximately 60 per cent of Japanese baseball fans. The Seibu Lions of the PL have been owned since 1979 by Seibu Tetsudo, a prominent land and property development company with interests in railways and department stores, but previously have been known as 'Crown Lighter Lions' (1977–78). Orix Blue Wave came into existence when the 'Orix Braves' were taken over by a rental company in 1991. Behind the impressive averages, at the other end of the scale are teams such as Nippon Ham Fighters and Lotte Orions. Whilst the former (who, as their name suggests, are sponsored by a meat-processing company) share the stadium in Tokyo with the Giants, they have one-tenth the number of regular supporters and are rarely covered on television. Lotte are owned by a Korean chewing gum and confectionery company and again rarely get much media coverage.

In addition to professional baseball, a regular feature of the Japanese sports calendar is the National High School Summer Baseball Championship which has been sponsored annually by the *Asahi Shimbun* since 1915. Arguably of equal significance to this were the initial encounters between Japanese and American baseball teams at the end of the nineteenth and beginning of the twentieth century. The development of *besuboru* ('baseball') in Japan – normally referred to in

Japanese as *yakyu*, a phrase meaning 'field ball' derived from the combination of Chinese Kanji characters – was given a big stimulus at the end of the last century when Japanese school teams beat American sailors. In this respect, amateur baseball quickly gained a central role in defining modern Japan's national identity, as well as a distinctive place in its sports tradition.[4]

Since the late 1970s American writer Robert Whiting has been the chief proponent of the notion that a distinctive 'samurai style' of baseball has developed and is played in contemporary Japan. The key features of his argument can be summarized as follows.

At both High School and professional levels, Japanese baseball involves the inculcation of a *bushido* spirit (or the 'way of the warrior' or samurai) through a strict training regime which promotes endurance, *gutsu* ('guts') and *seishinshugi* ('spiritedness') – sometimes referred to as 'death training'. Whiting argues that the Japanese baseball coaching tradition places a stress on anti-individualism and the importance of group/team harmony, or *wa*, through adherence to beliefs such as 'the tall tree catches the wind' and 'the nail that sticks out will be hammered down'. Hierarchical manager–coach–player relations exist in baseball clubs, which elevates the position of manager almost to a god, and subordinates players within a system of control similar to a 'total institution', which covers not just the regular season, but also the close season and life outside of baseball too. A style of play distinctive to Japanese baseball – sometimes referred to as 'mechanical baseball' – consists of distinctive tactics, such as the persistent use of safety plays and the so-called 'sacrificial bunt'. Media coverage remains important for the spread of this view of Japanese baseball, and includes not just the extensive coverage of professional baseball, but also the national high-school championships and the highlighting of the importance of the psychological confrontation between *pitcha* and *batta*, similar to that in sumo bouts, in match commentaries. In the 1970s a distinctive baseball 'star system' developed, involving the differential treatment of *gaijin* ('foreign', especially American), foreign–Asian (especially Korean or Chinese), and Japanese players.[5]

Whiting's view is to be found extensively in academic and journalistic treatments of Japanese baseball.[6] His ideas have been widely documented in Japan and have come to shape a Japanese view of its own distinctiveness. Yet as Roden, amongst others, argues, Whiting's 1976 essay can also be seen as a contemporary example of the patronizing cultural relativist approach to Japanese involvement in baseball; an approach which has been utilized in order to maintain 'the national integrity of the sport' for Americans since the first defeat at the hands of Japanese schoolboys at the beginning of the century.[7] Whilst it is possible to read Whiting as providing some important insights into the Japanese approach to a Western sport, it is important to maintain some distance from interpreting all Japanese sports in the same way. It is important to recognize that the characteristics of any sport are shaped by specific moments of social, political and economic development. Hence Whiting's analysis first developed in the wake of the 1964 Tokyo Olympics and at the time when a particular management regime was having success at Yomiuri Giants – the Giants won every championship for nine straight years, from 1965 to 1973. Known as the 'V9 Giants', the Yomiuri sponsored team came to represent the emergence of Japan as an economic superpower.

Whiting's analysis of 'samurai style baseball' would suggest that, in Japan's sporting culture, there has been little room for players who stand out for their individuality – the sort of player needed to help out in a crisis on the football pitch. He cites one *gaijin* baseball player, Reggie Smith, who remarked, 'There is very little anticipation on the part of the players during games.'[8] Hence in baseball, even when foreign coaches have tried to encourage players to think for themselves, they have often been seen by team managers as a threat and rejected. It might be suggested that in football this situation would not occur. Because of the influence of South America and Europe, more freedom would be allowed. Certainly, on the face of it foreign managers in the J. League have been able to dictate tactics, and many Japanese football players have been allowed to let their hair grow long, or even dye it, like their foreign team-mates. Whiting acknowledges that rebels have existed in Japanese baseball. Arguably, in several ways football in Japan marks a new departure. As we will show in the next section of this essay, football in Japan has its own specific history.

A BRIEF HISTORY OF FOOTBALL IN JAPAN

Football has developed in Japan in terms of both national club competitions and involvement in international representative matches since the beginning of the twentieth century. Although football has not become a compulsory subject in the school physical education curriculum, it was in teacher training that it originally developed. The earliest significant mention of football involves Commander Douglas of the British Royal Navy, who is recorded as playing and teaching football in a navy school in Tokyo in 1873.[9] From 1900 football was taught at the Tokyo Teachers' Training College and played by some students at Tokyo University. Graduates taught football all over Japan in middle and high schools. In 1917 the Japanese Amateur Sports Association (JASA) was formed under the control of the Ministry of Education (*monbusho*) as an umbrella organization for all sports, although it was not until 1921 that the Japan Football Association (JFA) was launched. Nevertheless a schools football championship began in 1918 with three school teams representing Osaka, Nagoya and Tokyo. Now called the High School National Championship, the competition still continues. The English Football Association presented a trophy to the Tokyo Teachers' Training College in 1919 and after the JFA was launched in September 1921, the first 'All Japan' (national) football tournament began. Later this trophy became known as the 'Emperor's Cup', because the Emperor had attended a match.

Like many other national football organizations, the JFA joined FIFA, the world governing body of football, before the English FA in 1929. In 1936 a Japanese team entered the Olympic championship for the first time at the Berlin Olympiad. The team defeated Sweden 3–2 in one match with a side that included one Korean. Another Korean was also included in the squad sent to Berlin. In the same year, the team *All Seoul* won the Emperor's Cup. Football was played at the Meiji Games but the cup donated by the English FA was requisitioned by the military in the late 1930s. After the war, football was (re-)introduced into the school curriculum during the US Occupation, while other traditional sports and physical activities remained proscribed. The JFA rejoined FIFA in 1950 and joined the newly formed Asian Football Confederation (AFC) in 1954. In the same year, Japan entered the FIFA World Cup qualifying competition for the first time and played the Republic of Korea twice in March: Japan was defeated 5–1 and drew 2–2, with both matches played in Tokyo.

The 1960s were a very important decade for the growth of soccer in Japan. A German, Dettmar Cramer, was appointed as manager of the national team in 1960. In November of that year the team were defeated yet again by Korea in a World Cup qualifying game played in Seoul, 2–1. Yet in 1964, at the Tokyo Olympics, the Japanese team, having beaten

Argentina 3–2, reached the quarter-finals of the football competition. In 1965 the 'Japan Soccer League' (JSL), featuring company teams, was launched. Initially there were large attendances at what was essentially a form of industrial recreational welfare. It was the first proper national football league. Three years later a further success saw Japan take the bronze medal (third place) and the 'fair play' award at the Mexico Summer Olympics in 1968.

During the 1970s there was a failure to capitalize on the developments in the previous decade, although interest in soccer was sustained for the dedicated through the JSL and the hosting of international events such as the FIFA World Youth Championships (1979). In 1981, the first Toyota Cup match – between the leading European and South American club sides – was held in Tokyo. As Japan failed to qualify for the Mexico World Cup in 1986, a committee was established to consider the development of professional football in Japan, and in 1990 the establishment of a Japan Professional Soccer League (J. League) was announced.

It has been argued elsewhere that the most valuable way of understanding the development of sport in Japan is to consider the way that political and economic élites have utilized it to secure international recognition for Japan.[10] A brief sketch such as this still begs the question, however, why did baseball and not soccer become the leading team sport in modern Japan? A number of suggestions have been put forward. J. Watts suggests that there may be a cultural explanation for it. After E. Ohnuki-Tierney he suggests that the foot has long been regarded as an unclean body part in Japan (except in purified arenas, such as the *kemari* court) and hence has not been associated with positive attributes.[11] Whilst there may be something in this account, it is not generally regarded as a sufficient explanation.

Watts also suggests that sport forms a part of cultural diplomacy and, as Japan was more under the sphere of influence of the United States of America from the 1920s, it was highly likely that it would play one of the United States' sports. As we have noted, there is a suggestion that football went out of favour with the military government in the late 1930s. This may have been because it was closely associated with the colonized Koreans, whose All Seoul team actually won the All Japan ('Emperor's Cup') trophy in 1936. Soon after the Berlin Olympics later that year, the military requisitioned the trophy which had been donated to Japan by the English Football Association. However, baseball too was

'Japanized' at this moment, with foreign 'loan words' being replaced by Japanese terms. The other moment when soccer might have become more popular – during the 1960s – coincided with the V9 Giants success.

Two further influences may have been responsible for baseball's relative success in establishing itself as the leading team sport in Japan. From the beginning of the twentieth century institutional and professional élites have favoured baseball over football. Tokyo, Waseda, Keio, Hosei, Meiji and Rikkyo – the élite universities in Tokyo – formed the 'Big Six'. Football was only taken up by Tokyo and Tokyo Teachers' Training College (in the present day, part of Tsukuba University). Hence students entering élite professions, such as law and economics, and political office preferred baseball to football. Additionally, media and commercial interests, also strongly composed of graduates from the 'Big Six', have come to favour baseball. Professional baseball in Japan has essentially become a commercial activity with close ties between media interests and clubs. (The Yomiuri Giants best exemplify this connection.)

JAPANESE FOOTBALL IN THE 1990s

From the mid-1990s successful Japanese involvement in international soccer has increased. In 1995 Japan won the Dynasty Cup in Hong Kong, the Japanese women's team reached the quarter-finals of the Second FIFA Women's World Football Championship, held in Sweden, and at the World University Games (Universiade) held in Fukuoka, Japan won the football championship. The following year FIFA allocated the hosting of the 2002 World Cup Finals to both Japan and South Korea, and Japan beat Brazil, 1–0, at the Summer Olympic Games held in the United States. The women's team took part in the Olympics for the first time. In 1997, the JFA announced the opening of the 'J.Village', a training facility for the national squad, in Fukushima, and Japan qualified for the finals of the FIFA World Cup finals for the first time.

In 1998 Japan played at the FIFA World Cup finals held in France, but failed to qualify for the later stages of the competition. Underpinning this sequence of relative successes has been the launch of the J.League in 1993.

The transformation brought about by the launch of the J.League in May 1993 has been discussed elsewhere.[12] Watts suggests that the distinctiveness of the J.League is that it involved an attempt to market soccer in the same way as a new improved consumer product would be – through a *shinhatsubai* strategy (literally, 'new improved product'). It also sought to refocus Japanese people's identification on their home town (*furusato*) or at least place of consumption, as opposed to their company and place of occupation (production). To do this a number of criteria were attached to J.League membership. As one of the criteria for joining the J.League was possession of a stadium of at least 15,000 capacity that could also be turned into a community-based sports centre, from the outset this meant that local authorities would also be involved. In addition each J.League team would have to adopt a clear youth policy with links with schools and the local community.[13]

The number of J.League teams was originally ten and this grew until 1998 when there were 18 J.League teams. Table 1 shows how the J.League line-up evolved from May 1993 to the start of the sixth season in March 1998.

TABLE 1

THE JAPAN PROFESSIONAL FOOTBALL LEAGUE (J.LEAGUE) LINE-UP, 1998

Club	Main Sponsors	City
Verdy	Yomiuri Nippon (press, TV)	Kawasaki
Marinos	Nissan (motors)	Yokohama
Antlers	Sumimoto Metal, Kashima	Kashima
JEF United	JR East (rail) Furukawa Electric	Ichihara, Chiba
Urawa Reds	Mitsubishi (motors)	Urawa
Sanfrecce	Mazda (motors), Hiroshima	Hiroshima
Gamba	Matsushita Electric ('Panasonic')	Suita, Osaka
AS Flugels	All Nippon Airways (ANA), Sato Kogyo	Yokohama/ Kyushu
Shimizu S-Pulse	Shizuoka (TV)	Shimizu
Grampus Eight	Toyota, Tokai Bank	Nagoya
Bellmare Hiratsuka[a]	Fujita	Hiratsuka
Jubilo Iwata[a]	Yamaha	Iwata
Cerezo Osaka[b]	Yanmar,Capcom,Nippon Ham	Nagai, Osaka
Kashiwa Reysol[b]	Hitachi	Kashiwa
Kyoto Purple Sanga[c]	Kyocera	Kyoto
Avispa Fukuoka[c]	Fuokoka-shi, Sanyo Shimpan	Fukuoka
Vissel Kobe[d]	Not available	Kobe
Consadole Sapporo[e]	Not available	Sapporo

[a]from 1994; [b]from 1995; [c]from 1996; [d]from 1997; [e]from 1998.

Sources: *World Soccer* (May 1993), 4–5; (January 1994), 54; (December 1994), 51; (January 1996), 44; (October 1998), 59; Asahi Shimbun, *Japan Almanac 1993* (Tokyo, 1993) p.36; Yano-Tsuneta Kinenkai, *Nippon 1993/94: a charted survey of Japan.* (Tokyo, 1993) p.30; *J.League Official Guide* (Tokyo, 1997), p.151; *Sportsworld Japan* (March–April 1998), 24–7.

In the first three seasons of the J.League all clubs played each other four times on a home and away basis, in two stages. Hence the 'Suntory' first stage ran from mid-March to mid-July and the second 'Nicos' stage from mid-August to mid-November. In contrast to British and most other European leagues, if scores were level after full-time, a period of 30 minutes extra time was played. If the game was still tied, the result was determined by a penalty kick shoot-out, as happens in the World Cup finals. Watts suggests that this enabled the element of 'showdown', found in sumo and baseball, to be incorporated into football. Teams received three points for a win of any kind. From the 1995 season teams losing a penalty shoot-out were awarded one point.[14] With the gradual expansion of numbers of teams in the J.League and hence the potential number of competitive games per season increasing, the J.League was reorganized for the 1996 season. The two-stage system was abandoned in favour of a single format with two (home and away) meetings each season. A break in the summer of the 1996 season enabled the national under-23 team to compete in the Atlanta Olympics. In 1997 and 1998 the two-stage format of the J.League was resumed and the league expanded from 16 to 17 and then 18 teams.

At the end of the 1998 season economic conditions resulted in the merger of two J.League teams – Yokohama Flugels and Yokohama Marinos.[15] Hence only one team (Consadole Sapporo) was relegated to compete in the new 'J2' Division in 1999. Yomiuri, sponsors of Verdy Kawasaki, withdrew their support. Expensive foreign players were released by clubs as a result of a new J.League regulation limiting the size of all senior squads to 25 – part of an economy drive in the light of declining live attendances and media interest. From 1999, two J.League divisions have been created – J1 and J2 – out of the existing J.League teams and the semi-professional company teams in the old Japan Football League (JFL). There are now 16 teams in the J1 Division and 10 teams in the J2 Division, with promotion and relegation between them.

Another change introduced from 1999 has been the dropping of the penalty shoot-out as a way of deciding tied matches in the J.League. For the first time since its creation the J.League will permit drawn games. Ties have been technically allowed in JML baseball for some time, although normally most baseball matches do end in a win-loss result.[16] From 1999, three points are awarded for a win in the ordinary 90 minutes of play; two points are awarded for a win in extra-time through the scoring of a 'golden goal' (i.e. the first goal scored in the 30-minute extra-time period); and one point is awarded to each team for a draw after 120 minutes' play. In a commitment to consistency, the J.League has announced that this points system will apply for at least three years.[17]

Since its inception only four teams have won the overall J.League championship: Verdy Kawasaki (1993 and 1994); Yokohama Marinos (1995); Kashima Antlers (1996 and 1998) and Jubilo Iwata (1997). Whilst Verdy, Marinos and Jubilo are based on former company teams (Yomiuri, Nissan and Yamaha), Kashima have been heralded as an example of the local authority/local employer partnership that best exemplifies the J.League principles.

Table 2 shows average attendance figures by stage, and the number of games played, compared with Japanese Major League (JML) professional baseball. Whilst some questions about the accuracy of attendance figures may be asked, baseball clearly remains the most popular live spectator sport in Japan. It is worth noting, however, the way that averages mask individual variations. In baseball, the Central League figures are swollen by the presence of the ever-popular Yomiuri Giants whose average attendance per home game was 53,864 in 1995 and 53,800 in 1996. Leaving aside the Giants, the lowest average gate in the

TABLE 2

J.LEAGUE AND PROFESSIONAL BASEBALL ATTENDANCES, 1993–97

Season	J.League		Professional baseball	
1993	1st stage	16,876	Central League	n/a
	2nd stage	19,077	Pacific League	n/a
	Total average (180 games)	*17,976*	Average (260 games)	*n/a*
1994	1st stage	19,679	Central League	n/a
	2nd stage	19,517	Pacific League	n/a
	Total average (264 games)	*19,598*	Average (260 games)	*n/a*
1995	1st stage	16,724	Central League	31,573
	2nd stage	17,120	Pacific League	24,733
	Total average (364 games)	*16,922*	Average (260 games)	*28,153*
1996	(two-stage system dropped		Central League	31,300
	due to Olympic Games)		Pacific League	22,800
	Total average (240 games)	*13,353*	Average (260 games)	*27,050*
1997	1st stage	10,611	Central League	33,100
	2nd stage	n/a	Pacific League	24,700
	Total average (364 games)	*10,131*	Average (260 games)	*28,900*

Sources: *J.League Guide* (Tokyo, 1997) p.86; *Japan Almanac 1997* (Tokyo, 1996), p.268; *Japan Almanac 1998* (Tokyo, 1997), p.276; *Japan Almanac 1999* (Tokyo, 1998), p.276; *World Soccer* (October 1997), 67; *World Soccer* (February 1998), 41.

Central League was still a very respectable 19,900 enjoyed by Hiroshima Toyo-Carp. Whilst the J.League has started to develop its 'star' teams – Verdy, Marinos, Kashima, Jubilo, and so on – they have not yet got such audience 'pulling' power as the Giants.

One of the biggest issues facing the J.League has been the decline of average crowd sizes, after an initial boom in the first three years. As can be seen in the table (Table 3) in the 1997 season, average attendances dropped by close to 3,000. In 1998, with the creation of play-offs to see who stayed in J1, the added incentive for all J.League teams to play for maximum points, and with qualification for the FIFA World Cup in France by the national team, there was some improvement in spectator figures at soccer matches, but the greater attraction of professional baseball continued to be a talking point in much of the Japanese media during the year.[18] Towards the end of 1998 serious economic problems began to emerge for a few of the J.League teams. Unlike baseball, where individual clubs negotiate their own television deals, the J.League co-ordinates all media contracts on behalf of its members. Each club's income is thus derived from gate money, individual sponsorship deals and the J.League redistribution of any surplus generated during the year. Whilst the surplus amount available for redistribution by the J.League halved between 1994 and 1998, the main problem for Flugels and Verdy was that their main sponsors withdrew support.

TABLE 3

J.LEAGUE: INCOME (YEN MILLION), SURPLUS AND ATTENDANCES, 1993–98

	1993	1994	1995	1996	1997	1998
Income from:						
TV rights	1,093	2,190	2,214	1,207	2,056	1,905
Sponsors	2,310	2,961	3,799	4,681	4,106	4,028
Merchandise	3,601	3,588	2,099	934	473	324
Surplus income*	6,147	7,647	7,364	5,385	5,128	3,831
Average attendance	17,976	19,598	16,922	13,353	10,131	11,982
Home games	18	22	26	15	16	17
J.League Teams	10	12	14	16	17	18

*As a non-profit organization, after running costs (office rental, human resources, and so on) any economic surplus (profit) is redistributed to each of the J.League member teams.

Source: Nihon Keizei Shimbun (or Nikkei), 21 November 1998, 3.

If it is not through *wa* alone but a combination of social, political and economic factors that sport develops and continues to flourish, what conditions permitted football to develop in Japan in the 1980s and 1990s? Undoubtedly the 'bubble' economic conditions of the late 1980s and early 1990s created the conditions in which *mecenat* (private sponsorship of cultural activities, including sport) was made possible and became more acceptable in Japan.[19] In addition, *kokusaika* ('internationalization') became a dominant ideal as Japan sought wider international relations outside of the American sphere of influence. As the World Game, it became more likely that association football would gain greater support in Japan at this moment. The emphasis in the J.League rules of membership on developing links with local communities related to another dominant ideal of the last two decades in Japan, the creation of *furusato* ('hometown'). Finally, as Watts suggests, the strategy of marketing football as *shinhatsubai*, or a new, improved product, just like facial cream or shampoo, certainly encouraged a soccer boom in the first three seasons.

It has been argued elsewhere that, as a site of leisure, the football stadium can be seen as a 'decompression' chamber from the world of time–space compression, but the growth of soccer in Japan is also related to attempts to manage economic, demographic and urban change.[20] Soccer has been manipulated by different interest groups to accommodate new demands and initiate new ways of thinking. The 'internationalization' of the J.League is exemplified by the team names, and the composition of teams, players and managers and playing styles. J.League team names are a mixture of European languages – especially English, Spanish, Italian, German – and Japanese. All the teams that have joined the J.League since 1994 have composite names such as Bellmare Hiratsuka, Cerezo Osaka, and Kashiwa Reysol. Kyoto Purple Sanga derives its name from the colour associated with the Japanese royal family (for many centuries resident in Kyoto) and *sanga*, a Buddhist term in sanskrit for 'friends united'. Avispa Fukuoka were known as 'Fukuoka Blux' before promotion to the J.League, when the name was altered because 'Blux' – which stood for 'Brave Lads with Ultimate X' – sounded too much like 'Brooks' when pronounced in Japanese, an athletic wear company with no relationship to the team. Vissel Kobe (so named after 'the Vi(ctory Ve)ssel') bear the legend 'Vissel Kobe 1995' on the team badge. Unlike previously promoted teams neither Kyoto Purple Sanga nor Avispa Fukuoka were based on a former company club with an illustrious past.

J.League teams have also reflected the internationalism of football through the adoption of different playing styles mainly as a direct result of the composition of their squads – especially the nationality of their managers and players. Hence Kyoto were hailed as a Brazilian team in their first season (although this did not prevent them from establishing the record for losing the most consecutive J.League matches), Fukuoka and Marinos have been seen as Argentinian, and JEF United Ichihara and Sanfrecce Hiroshima played a European style game in the early seasons. Interestingly, the attempt to mould a team into a particular national style of play has not always worked. On appointment to Jubilo Iwata in 1997, new manager Felipe declared: 'I am converting this team from European to Brazilian football.'[21] A few months later he resigned, complaining that the Japanese players did not 'take the game seriously enough'.[22]

Arsène Wenger, currently manager of Arsenal in the English Premier League, managed Nagoya in 1995 and 1996, and was voted manager of the season in 1996. His success with Nagoya, and more recently with Arsenal, plus the triumph of the French team at the 1998 World Cup finals, has enhanced his reputation even further in Japan. It was on his recommendation that another Frenchman, Philippe Troussier, the manager of South Africa's team at the 1998 World Cup finals, was appointed as manager of the Japanese national team in August 1998.[23] In these and other ways football in Japan sustains its image as the 'world game'.[24]

THE FUTURE OF FOOTBALL IN JAPAN

Will the J.League last? One of the slogans adopted by the J.League was: 'A 100 year project.' At the start of the 1999 season the J.League adopted another one: 'A happier nation through sport.' The decline in attendances after 1995 has led some commentators to view the J.League's slogans to represent rather over-optimistic ambitions. Added to this fall in interest, in 1998 came the folding of Yokohama Flugels, a change in sponsors for Yomiuri, the previously noted decline in revenue, and an early return from France 1998 for the national team. It is important to put these developments in perspective, however.

In 1998 Japan qualified for the World Cup finals for the first time – a notable achievement. Adjustments have been made in terms of economic outlay in the J.League: first-team squad size has been reduced to a maximum of 25 players and the number and size of salaries payments to foreign players have been scaled down too. It could also be argued that the J.League is now attracting a more realistic level of interest and support than in the over-hyped initial three years. As the figures show, attendances rose in 1998. Furthermore it is clear that there are now some hardcore football fans in Japan.

Such developments are forged in the midst of contradictory forces. The mass mediation of football plays possibly the most important role in its reception. With respect to football in the societies of Asia and the Pacific, Murray suggests that television coverage of the game has played an ambiguous role: 'The acquisition of TV sets by formerly impoverished peoples has brought the world game to tens of millions of Asians, and so encouraged some interest in football, but playing highlights from the best leagues in the world, most notably Italy's Serie A, has shown up the local product to be somewhat woeful by comparison.'[25]

In 1997 the launch of the Japan Sky Broadcasting Company (JSkyB) – a joint venture between Rupert Murdoch's News Corporation and Softbank Corporation, run by Masayoshi Son – brought English Football Association Premier League games from BSkyB, the British satellite television company that JSkyB was modelled on, direct to Japanese subscribers.[26] From 1998, renamed SkyPerfecTV, Rupert Murdoch's company has had to compete with several other satellite companies operating in Japan. The adoption of satellite television has seen an explosion of sports channels offering live matches and time-delayed recordings (i.e. 'as if live') from the major European football and rugby leagues. The impact of this development on Japanese, and other Asian, sports cultures, their players and supporters, will need further research in the future.[27]

Baseball remains televised by terrestrial and satellite companies on a regular basis, including the National High School Championship. Interest in baseball – both JML and ML – has been maintained by the success of Nomo Hideo and other Japanese players in ML baseball.[28] The ML has gained more exposure in Japan through the success of Nomo and this has created further opportunities for commercial exploitation through the advertising and marketing of ML goods. In 1998 interest in the JML was further enlivened through the success of Yokohama Baystars, who won the Championships after winning the Central League for the first time in 38 years. One of the aims of the launch of the J.League was to broaden the pool of Japanese soccer players. In the 1960s and 1970s there was a handful of good players, but a large supporting cast was lacking. In the 1980s, however, more young Japanese began to play soccer than baseball at school and in university. Some of these young players have begun to make their presence felt in the national team and with this the opportunities to be signed by clubs outside of Japan have increased. The creation of local heroes doing well abroad may be one way in which Japanese football may hope to emulate JML baseball. It might enable the J.League to retain supporters and possibly stimulate more demand for football.[29]

Since 1995 the print media have not covered soccer in so much detail and the television channels have reduced the amount of J.League soccer in their schedules. The FIFA decision to ask Japan to co-host the 2002 World Cup finals with South Korea, and the associated restructuring of plans which reduced a potential 15 host sites in Japan to only 10, also dented optimism in football in 1996. Yet as Japan's road to the World Cup finals in 1998 was full of twists and turns, a feeling of nervous anticipation was shared by almost half the Japanese television viewing public; indeed, a 50 per cent viewer rating was recorded during the World Cup qualifying match with Iran on Sunday, 16 November 1997 as the game entered the 'golden goal' period. That Japan achieved the desired result with seconds of extra time remaining places the event alongside many in the history books of football – including the fact that four years earlier Japan had failed to qualify for USA 1994 by a last-minute equalizer goal (known in Japan as 'the tragedy of Doha'). The qualification of the national team for the FIFA World Cup finals for the first time in history brought an increase in media attention in 1997, and not surprisingly television audiences for the 1998 World Cup were high. Japan's matches against Argentina and Croatia had audience ratings over 60 per cent – the highest for any sporting event in the 1990s and the sixth highest recorded since television programme ratings began in 1962.[30] It also generated considerable consumer demand for the new digital television receivers and video-recorders with satellite tuners. NHK (the Japan Broadcasting Corporation) estimated that new subscribers to its satellite broadcasting service grew by 60 per cent in June as television coverage of the 1998 World Cup in Japan was greater than for any previous finals.

Writing soon after the launch of the J.League in 1993, J. Horne and D. Jary suggested that there were several strong influences at work which might help professional soccer to succeed in Japan.[31] One of these was that there were differences in the role of sport in defining national identity in the United States and Japan. In the former, identity has been defined primarily in terms of distinctively 'American' sports: in Japan, identity has been defined only in part through distinctive sports, and an adaptive, 'syncretic' cultural tradition, including the adoption of foreign sports, existed. Football in Japan, like soccer in the United States, has had to compete with other national team sports. In the United States, these are principally baseball, gridiron football and basketball, whilst in Japan, although sumo is described as the 'national sport', the main spectator team sport remains baseball, at both professional and high-school levels. Although it has been suggested that the Japanese have a cultural tendency to celebrate the 'nobility of failure', a problem for those seeking to establish soccer in Japan is that no one wants to back a loser indefinitely. This is a problem for soccer, unlike baseball, where there really is a 'world series' and competition takes place with other nation states.[32] In some respects the use of alternative cultural vehicles – including sports and physical contests such as baseball and sumo – to gain national dignity and a sense of cultural identity is safer.

Whilst much has been made of the politics behind the decision to allow co-hosting of the FIFA World Cup finals in 2002, it is the case that Japan (and Korea) have the chance to put on a great spectacle, which will make the game even more popular in Asia. Individual stars, such as Nakata Hidetoshi, will increase interest in the game at all levels in Japan. Of course these developments are not without problems – the dominance of the European and South American core football leagues on television contrast with the local spectacle; in a move that could be positive or negative for the development of the J.League, the International Management Group (IMG) are major sponsors of the newly formed Yokohama team. Nevertheless, an adequate understanding of sport in Japan, as elsewhere, requires more than just a cultural approach like that adopted by Whiting. To tell the tale so far involves recognition of the role of social, economic and political developments in shaping the development of sport. To investigate these interrelationships further will require a combination of ethnographic, institutional and political economic analyses.[33]

NOTES

This essay primarily relies upon desk-based research, whilst a brief visit to Japan at the start of the seventh J.League season in March 1999 enabled observations and further interviews with officials to be carried out. I want to acknowledge the assistance of my Japanese acquaintances who have helped me collect information, in some cases translated it, and subjected my impressions to critical comment. Small sections of the study update material first published in '"Sakka" in Japan', in *Media, Culture and Society*, 18, 4 (1996). In this essay some monetary values are expressed in yen, some in pounds and some in US dollars. A billion, following American and Japanese convention, is regarded here as one thousand million. In March 1999, 1 US dollar = 118 Yen and 1 GB pound = 192 Yen. Finally, following Japanese convention, family name precedes the given name of Japanese authors and football players.

1. W. May, 'Sports', in R. Powers and H. Kato (eds.), *Handbook of Japanese Popular Culture* (Connecticut, 1989), pp.167–95.
2. B. Maitland, *Japanese Baseball: A Fan's Guide* (Rutland, Vermont and Tokyo, 1991).
3. I. Horowitz, 'Betto-san and the White Rat: Evaluating Japanese Major League Baseball Managers Vis-a-Vis Their American Counterparts' (hereafter 'Betto-san and the White Rat'), *International Review for the Sociology of Sport*, 30, 2 (1995), 166.
4. D. Roden, 'Baseball and the Quest for National Dignity in Meiji Japan' (hereafter 'Baseball and the Quest'), *American Historical Review*, 85, 3 (1980), 511–34.
5. R. Whiting, *The Chrysanthemum and the Bat: Baseball Samurai Style* (New York, 1976); R. Whiting, *You gotta have wa* (New York, 1989).
6. B. McPherson *et al.*, *The Social Significance of Sport* (Illinois, 1990), p.22; *Guardian*, 4 March 1986, 21; *The Economist*, 28 September 1995, 152.
7. 'Baseball and the Quest', 532.
8. R. Whiting, *You gotta have wa*, p.320.
9. The main sources for this sketch of the history of football in Japan are: Asami, Toshio (1997) 'The Korea-Japan Co-Hosting of the 2002 FIFA World Cup: Trends and Perspectives for Japanese Football', a presentation at an 'International Scientific Symposium on the 2002 FIFA World Cup', Korean Alliance for Health, Physical Education, Recreation and Dance (KAHPERD), Seoul, Republic of Korea, December; an interview with Derek Bleakley of the Japan Organizing Committee for the 2002 FIFA World Cup Korea/Japan (JAWOC), Tokyo, March 16 1999; an interview with Takahashi Yoshio, Research Center for Health, Physical Fitness and Sports, Nagoya University, 18 March 1999; and J. Watts, 'Soccer *shinhatsubai*. 'What are the Japanese Consumers making of the J.League?' (hereafter 'Soccer *shinhatsubai*'), in D.P. Martinez (ed.), *The Worlds of Japanese Popular Culture: Gender, Shifting Boundaries and Global Cultures* (Cambridge, 1998), pp.181–201.
10. J. Horne, '"Sakka" in Japan', 527–47.
11. *Kemari* was an antecedent of football introduced into Japan from China in the eighth century and unlike football was played in a sacred (hence cleansed) location. On culture and pollution in Japan see E. Ohnuki-Tierney, *Illness and Culture in Contemporary Japan* (Cambridge, 1984) and E. Ohnuki-Tierney, *The Monkey as Mirror* (Princeton, 1987).
12. J. Horne, '"Sakka" in Japan'; J. Watts, 'Soccer *shinhatsubai*'; J. Sugden and A. Tomlinson, *FIFA and the Contest for World Football* (hereafter *FIFA and the Contest*) (Cambridge, 1998).
13. The old company team 'Japan Soccer League' was officially wound up in March 1992 and a replacement ('Japan Football League'), for company teams was formed with two divisions and less stringent regulations than the J.League. In 1994 the JFL became one division, effectively the 'J.League Second Division'. Because of the regulations regarding J.League membership only Associate Members who met them have been able to be considered for promotion. Hence during its existence (1992–1998) two teams that won the JFL (Honda and Tokyo Gas) were not allowed to join the J.League because of the regulations regarding stadium size.
14. *World Soccer* (April 1995), 45.
15. In their last ever match before merger on 1 January 1999, Yokohama Flugels won the Emperor's Cup. After the decision to merge with Yokohama Marinos, Flugels fans immediately organized petitions and began fundraising. Supporters of Flugels have helped to rebuild the team and

attracted individual sponsors and eventually financial support from IMG, the multinational sports media company. Renamed Yokohama FC, and managed by Pierre Littbarski, the team is allowed to compete in the new national amateur/company team 'Japan Soccer League'. If the team finish in the top four places in 1999 they may be able to gain promotion to 'J2' in 2000.

16. I. Horowitz, 'Betto-san and the White Rat'.
17. *World Soccer* (October 1998), 46.
18. *The Nikkei Weekly*, 19 October 1998, 10.
19. I. Sayama, 'Soccer – The Limit of the Japanese Society and the Bitter Reflection of its Possibility', in *Proceedings of How Sport can Change the World*, International Conference, The Japan Society of Sport Sociology, Ritsumeikan University, Kyoto, Japan, 26–28 March 1997, pp.46–52 (in Japanese).
20. J. Horne, '"Sakka" in Japan'.
21. Quoted in *World Soccer* (April 1997), 48.
22. Quoted in *World Soccer* (August 1997), 48.
23. *World Soccer* (October 1998), 46.
24. *The J.League Official Fans' Guide* for 1999 features a mixture of writing in English and Japanese, as does the 'Official Matchday Progam' available at J.League matches. The author witnessed the mixture of English and Japanese at a Nagoya Grampus Eight home match in March 1999 where the pre-match entertainment was conducted by an English-speaking disc jockey playing such familiar tunes as 'Let's get ready to rumble' and acts such as Gary Glitter and Fat Boy Slim.
25. B. Murray, 'Cultural Revolution? Football in the Societies of Asia and the Pacific', in S. Wagg (ed.), *Giving the Game Away: Football, Politics and Culture on Five Continents* (London, 1995), p.140.
26. *The Nikkei Weekly*, 30 December 1996/6 January 1997, 9.
27. *SportsWorld Japan* (August 1998), 6.
28. H. Hajime, 'Can Nomo change "Yakyu" to Baseball? – Impact of Major League Baseball on Japanese Baseball Fans' (unpublished paper presented at the North American Society for the Sociology of Sport Annual Conference, Sacramento, California, 1995).
29. This appears to have happened with 21-year-old Nakata Hidetoshi, Asian Football Confederation Player of the Year and the star of the Japanese team at France 98. Following the World Cup, Nakata signed a five-year contract with Perugia in the Italian Serie A. After scoring twice on his debut against Juventus sales of his Perugia number seven shirt boomed in Japan. In 1999 most of the soccer magazines available in Japan continue to follow Nakata's exploits in great detail, including one called *Calcio*, purely focusing on the Italian game.
30. *World Soccer* (September 1998), 59.
31. J. Horne, and D. Jary, 'Japan and the World Cup: Asia's First World Cup Final Hosts?', in J. Sugden and A. Tomlinson (eds.), *Hosts and Champions: Soccer Culture, National Identities and the USA World Cup* (Aldershot, 1994), p.179.
32. I. Morris, *The Nobility of Failure: Tragic Heroes in the History of Japan* (New York, 1975).
33. J. Sugden and A. Tomlinson, *FIFA and the Contest*.

10

French Football after the 1998 World Cup: The State and the Modernity of Football

PATRICK MIGNON

It is difficult now to discuss the modernization of French football without evoking the image of French success in the 1998 World Cup; both the successful organization of the tournament and the victory of the French national side could be considered as evidence of modernity. In some respects, modernization requires the acceptance of competition, the capacity to mobilize different resources to achieve specific goals, and the means to be efficient. The youth training scheme which produced most of France's victorious international players or top coaches is a study in this modernity. So too is the tournament organization, consisting of efficiency in the organization of numerous matches, the public transportation system, policing measures and even in the ticketing, which produced a wide price range that resulted in full stadiums even for matches of little importance. Of course, all of these processes have attracted criticism but the display of some modern virtues is undeniable; paradoxically, those reflected the traditional *savoir-faire* of the State.

Yet, the other side to the World Cup for French football has been the return of most internationalists to their English, Italian or Spanish teams, and it has led to a new exodus of young players to these foreign leagues. As a result, France is transformed 'into a Bulgaria' in the view of the leading French coach Guy Roux. Football in France today also has other concerns: the management of ultras; the issue of hooliganism and security; worries about the violence around amateur and grass-roots football; the relationship between football and social and urban policy issues. (Decision-making around the future of the Stade de France illustrates these particular concerns.)

This essay seeks to explain the incomplete professionalization and commercialization of French football. The common sense meaning of modernization, as an obedience to market forces, is broadened to include a possible integration with democratic values. Here the uniqueness of French football, which still allows the active role of the State via political regulation to be important, could have some impact upon the future development of football in Europe.

THE NEW BULGARIA

After the glory of the World Cup, the hard reality of club football returned. In August, proposals for a European Super League demonstrated to new football supporters in France that the major clubs wanted to reorganize football. Olympic de Marseille and Racing Club de Strasbourg were involved, but Paris Saint-Germain was reluctant. The project provided an opportunity for a new wave of football administrators to express their visions of modern football, free from regulation by the State or football's governing bodies, the Ligue Nationale de Football (LNF) and the Fédération Française du Football (FFF).[1] Financially, players' wages could be reduced, while television money could be redistributed among the professional clubs themselves. Arsenal, AS Roma and, above all, Manchester United, and its potential purchase by BSkyB, had become the models to emulate. Some comparisons easily demonstrate the difference between France and the big football nations.

First, if success in European competition is a sign of sporting and economic strength, France belongs to a lower division. There have been only two successes in European finals (Marseille in the 1993 European Cup and Paris Saint-Germain in the 1996 Cup Winners' Cup), although many clubs have played in other finals. Prior to the 1990s French clubs and players were seen as lacking the competitive spirit necessary to win major competitions, owing to the relatively weak indigenous football culture. Latterly, that interpretation has changed: the physical, technical and moral qualities of French players are no longer responsible but the weakness of French football economics is blamed instead.

In a recent Deloitte and Touche report,[2] the only French club in Europe's top 20 clubs was Paris Saint-Germain, in thirteenth place, but only because it counts the transfer values of players in its annual turnover, unlike the others. France's other wealthiest clubs, Marseille or Monaco, could be considered to be at the same economic level as Leeds or Everton in England. Before discussing why investment in French clubs is very low, we should examine some of the more dramatic aspects behind their relative impoverishment. The most popularly identified reason for the weak state of French club football concerns the transfer of the top young players to foreign clubs. Consequently, one reason for the poor domestic support for the national side before the 1998 finals was the supporters' lack of familiarity with these players. Many French football followers viewed the expatriate players as mercenaries who should not be involved in the national team.

Previously, some highly talented French players left for Italy or Spain, such as Ben Barek and Bonifaci at Torino, and Raymond Kopa and Muller at Real Madrid, during the 1960s. But since the introduction of the professional game in the 1930s, France has mainly been an importer of players, from South America, Eastern Europe and, of course, Africa. The situation changed slightly after the Spanish World Cup in 1982 with the departure of Michel Platini and then, in the 1990s, Jean-Pierre Papin, Didier Deschamps, Eric Cantona, Marcel Desailly, David Ginola and Zinedine Zidane among others. These players were almost big stars, but still below Platini and Kopa in status; even Zidane was not entirely established as a 'great' when he left Bordeaux for Juventus. But then we have the likes of Boghossian, Cauet, Laigle, Dutruel and Bonissel who were solid professionals but not exceptional footballers, at least not in the sense that French players are valued abroad for their creative genius. One could add to this list even less celebrated players like Blanchard, Sanchez, Ziani, Saha and Domi. For them, the experience of playing football abroad was less to do with financial rewards, but more a means towards self-improvement (although their recruitment was an acknowledgement of the quality of French youth training).

However, the most dramatic aspect of this continuing exodus of players is the youth of many of them. Jérémie Aliadiere was 16 years old when bought by Arsenal, who also purchased Patrick Vieira, David Grondin and, above all, Nicolas Anelka; players under 18 also moved to Inter (Sebastien Frey) and Milan (Samir Beloufa). This process reflects the failure of French football to prevent young players leaving for richer clubs. Player wages reflect the inequalities: the best paid French players like Zidane earn an estimated 29 million French francs a year in Italy; Fabien Barthez and Laurent Blanc earn around 11 million francs in the French league.[3] A key reason for some of the difference lies in the tax structure. In 1996, on a salary of 100,000FF a month, French clubs paid an additional 55,100FF to the State and then the players paid 15,937FF for insurance and 34,130FF in income tax, leaving them 49,933FF. In

Italy, players retained 56,800FF in net income; in England, they kept 62,400FF.[4]

French football is further impoverished by the contracts between French and foreign clubs that provide for the transfer of young players overseas. Hence, Saint-Etienne has a contract with Arsenal, Nantes is exploring a similar scheme with Tottenham, and Nice has been bought by the President of AS Roma. Cannes, which reared Zidane and Vieira, as well as Micoud and Frey, have been courted by Spanish and Italian clubs. Recently, Nice and Cannes have examined a merger under the authority of Nice's new Italian president.

Finally, this dramatic trend damages French football's capacity to buy and retain foreign players. Traditionally, African, Argentinian, Brazilian and Yugoslavian players went to play in France, but they now stay only a year or two (as did George Weah and Leonardo), or they go directly to Spain, Italy and Germany, leaving only lesser players for the French market, such as Simone or Ravanelli. Two exceptions during the 1998–99 season were Okocha and Worms at Paris Saint-Germain, but the latter is set to return to Germany. These reasons explain why some say that France has become the new Bulgaria or Yugoslavia of European football.

THE FRENCH FOOTBALL COMPROMISE

To explain more fully the lack of money within French football, we must examine the structure of club budgets. During the 1970–71 season, French First Division clubs turned over a total of 37.5 million francs (approximately 3.7 million pounds sterling), of which 81 per cent came from admission charges to the spectators. Local authorities provided another 18 per cent, and only 1 per cent came from sponsorship. For the 1997–98 season, the total revenues were 3.2 billion francs. Now 25.1 per cent of income came from television rights, 10.8 per cent from local authorities, 19.7 per cent from sponsorship, 19.7 per cent from spectators and 20.2 per cent from transfers.[5] The figures reflect the strong development of the French football economy, but at a more modest level than in Italy or England. In addition, there remains the unusual influence of local authority revenue. The budget reflects the compromise between public and private investments in French soccer, but public authority subscriptions to French football clubs will be suppressed by a new law intended to bring about conformity with

European Union regulations from 1 January 2000. What we have to recognize here, therefore, is the cultural difference between the state of football culture in France and more 'rational' financial mechanisms within football elsewhere.

The fact that big clubs draw the biggest support also helps to explain the relative poverty of the French game. During the 1960s, inadequate income made many venerable and famous professional clubs revert to amateur status. These included Rouen, Red Star, Le Havre, Sète, Alès and Roubaix. Player wages had risen just as attendances declined. These clubs became amateur because of public indifference. In 1964 the gate revenue at one Tottenham Hotspur match in London was the equivalent of a full year's revenue at Rouen, then in the French First Division. Average attendances tell a similar story: only the 1987–88 season could match the high attendances of the 1950–51 season of 11,000 spectators a game. Even the increased average attendance of 16,000 for 1997–98 (maybe 20,000 for the 1998–99 season) leaves French football lagging well behind English or Italian attendance levels.

In 1997–98 Paris Saint-Germain (PSG) had the highest attendance with an average of 36,700 spectators (and 41,400 for the first part of the 1998–99 season with 20,000 season ticket holders); Marseille had only 28,200 spectators on average but this attendance was in a stadium undergoing refurbishment. (This season, average attendance is more than 50,000 with 40,000 season ticket holders.) But the average attendance in relation to capacity is also interesting. Marseille attains 88 per cent occupancy and PSG 85 per cent, however Strasbourg, sponsored by the IMG, part of the Mark McCormack group, and one of the main supporters of a European Super League, only has an average of 17,200 spectators, with an occupancy rate that is merely 48 per cent. These generally positive attendance figures, however, are very recent, and may still reflect match results rather than faithful support. They are also limited to a few clubs. Hence, one question is whether sufficient clubs have worked seriously to attract spectators beyond the few hundred season ticket holders that characterize the support of most French clubs.

This year, some big clubs have been bought by media investors. Olympique Lyonnaise is owned by Pathé, Bordeaux by CLT–UFA, and Canal Plus is the main owner of PSG, and Adidas own Marseille. But what is astonishing is the 'modest' investment put into the clubs. For example, Pathé has put 'only' 100 million francs into the Lyon club; a sum much less than AC Milan or Lazio will spend on one player. Big investors, like

Renault, are often said to prefer to subsidize amateur teams in France because professional clubs are too risky a form of investment.

The role of merchandising in revenue-raising at French clubs is also limited in comparison to other European nations. On average, only 4 per cent of income comes from this source, but there is considerable variation, especially between Marseille and Lens and the rest of the clubs. Certainly, it is a new phenomenon to see French people dressed in football shirts and to find club shops selling goods to supporters. For a long time, only a few shops near to the stadiums sold a limited range of football-related products. A similar narrow vision is shown by the failure of leading clubs to locate and retain young players. For example, one source of jokes has been the inability of Paris Saint-Germain to develop training centres, which led to the failure to recruit gifted players like Thierry Henry, Wiltord, Trezèguet, all of whom hail from the Paris area but were signed first by Monaco or Rennes. The Anelka case is a little bit different: he was at PSG and Arsenal's financial offer was very important, but the club management were still unable to convince the player that he could have a positive footballing future at the club.

French clubs are so weak in Europe, because football culture is not as important in France as elsewhere.[6] Some reasons are cultural, such as the importance of Jacobin and republican ideology: others are structural, such as the lack of big cities that are able to build big football audiences. There is also a lack of professionalism in club management which, for example, limits consideration of merchandising or fails to adapt the treatment of young players to new European regulations like the *Bosman* ruling. In addition, there is the effect of the public–private compromise which, for a long time, meant that presidents and their staff did not need to invest in clubs: access to local authority money was easy, and there were legal prohibitions on gaining financial returns from football clubs and general sports activities. Conversely, the new wave of French club managers want to be real entrepreneurs. Yet we must recognize the importance of public authority intervention in football.

THE PUBLIC AND THE MODERNIZATION OF FRENCH FOOTBALL

France's unusual situation stems from the role of the State and public intervention in football.[7] Sports entertainment is generally seen as an essentially private realm. From a legal standpoint, sport institutions are regulated by private law: therefore they 'own' the entertainment every time they organize sports events. Sports organizations receive income from events by negotiating exclusive broadcasting deals with a television channel; they are also responsible for the expenses. However, sport activities are often promoted and developed by the State, with France granting the strongest role for public authority intervention in sport of all the Western countries.

As a result of the Act of 16 July 1984, French competitions which award local or national titles to athletes are treated as providing a public service, reflected in the transfer of State powers to the sports federations. The Ministry of Youth and Sport delegates the organization and regulation of football to the FFF, and to the LNF for activities within professional football. Moreover, most sports facilities belong to the municipalities. In football, with the exception of Auxerre which owns its stadium, all stadiums are owned by local authorities. They are part of the public domain and clubs which receive subsidies from the local authorities simply use these local facilities. Money for clubs and sports associations from the local authorities and the State is channelled through sports' governing bodies and other public institutions like the National Fund for Sports Development, financed by the National Lottery. For the 1998 World Cup, the clubs were not required to pay for stadium modernization.

French republican law ensures that it is the State that is responsible for the improvement of the general well-being of citizens and for efforts to integrate all citizens into the nation. One law dating back to the 1920s obliges the municipalities to offer sporting recreation. Public intervention in sport is legitimized through its promotion of solidarity, health and education. For example, during the government of the Front Populaire, when the Socialist party came to power, numerous stadiums were built and subsidies were given to various sporting associations. In the early years of football professionalism, club presidents were instructed to ask the local authorities for finance to assist the local team in addition to any money that came from rich benefactors. During the 1960s sports policy became an integral element of the Welfare State and was also aimed at gaining international success and prestige. The policy was mainly directed towards the Olympic Games, and therefore amateur sports like athletics or swimming, but gradually it encompassed football too.

The importance of public money to football is shown by the crisis in French football during the 1960s, when average attendances fell below

8,000. Small or middle-sized cities were no longer able to invest in professional football, owing to their own demographic and economic decline. However, the renewal of French football during the 1980s was directly influenced by football clubs again being able to obtain money from city councils, as France increasingly became an urban society. Furthermore, new decentralization laws granted more autonomy to local authorities, making football and sport in general, as well as both popular and high culture, central to civic strategies. Victories or good performances in European competitions, it was believed, could allow even the smaller, less well-known cities to become famous. Saint-Etienne's successful performances in European football inspired Le Havre and Lens, cities with similar problems of industrial decline; the local authorities in Auxerre, a town of nearly 30,000 citizens, invested heavily in football 'to be put on the European map', with the intention of attracting investors, and creating local pride and solidarity. Paris and Marseille had their own specific motives, but these did include the search for a wider civic profile and to attract local development projects.

At the State level, we can see the result of the public intervention in the 1970s reorganization of French football. In the 1950s the French State created a category of civil servants known as the 'directeurs techniques nationaux' (DTN) to help sports' governing bodies develop their sports. Aimed first at Olympic sports, this system was widened to include all sports, even professional ones. Consequently, sporting governing bodies represent a balance of power between clubs, associations and the State. The DTN is the guarantor of good sporting development, nationally and internationally, while sport federations obtain State funding in proportion to their number of members; membership often being strongly associated with success in international competition.

These reforms are the source of French football's current success. State intervention was a force for modernization in two senses. First, it aimed to improve technical skills but also to enhance social justice and social mobility; second, it promoted a more economically rational and efficient brand of club management. The first reform transformed the players' contracts. Before 1968 players were tied to their clubs until the age of 35. They could leave the club before this age only if the club's owner agreed to a transfer. After 1968 the time period for the contract was specified: players were able to sign for other clubs once their contract had ended. This change was a consequence of the political demands of the 1968 social movement. For the first time, professional players were to be allowed the same principle of worker autonomy as other employees. The new contracts favoured player mobility and created the possibility of ambitious clubs assembling more successful teams.

Another change occurred at the start of the 1970s in the shape of a new league set-up with four divisions and local championships. The new pyramid structure linked all clubs, professional and amateur. Previously, there had been only two professional divisions with no route from the amateur leagues to the professional divisions. Theoretically, the new structure allowed any club to progress to the top but, since the 1993–94 season, all clubs playing in the Second Division must be, or become, professional. The Third Division includes a mixture of amateur and professional teams. These measures allowed ex-professional clubs to regain their professional status, while enabling new, unknown clubs to reach the highest level, as in the case of Auxerre. Aspirant and ambitious clubs were now able to sign players of good standard for free, once their contracts had finished.

The most important reform came in 1974 with the compulsory creation of training centres at any club that sought professional status. At the same time, the Institut National du Football was founded in Vichy, to train the national team and to prepare forty 16-year-old players for a professional career. The institute was switched later to Clairfontaine. In Vichy, as in Clairfontaine, the DTN was responsible for a large staff of qualified coaches who worked locally with young people, supervised the organization of football training in France (for example, the structured system of youth development) at professional or amateur clubs, and oversaw the qualification of future coaches. The results are well known today through the dramatic exodus of young players from France.

However, the production of skilled young players enabled French clubs to get good returns from a modest investment. In the 1976 Saint-Etienne European Cup final side, with the exception of two foreign players, all players had been produced by the club's youth policy. At a time when limited money from television or new investors was arriving in football, the training centres allowed clubs to develop good, affordable teams. Further, the regular arrival of young players at clubs provided a good incentive to resist wage inflation, which, of course, still remains the case. The continuous arrival of young players feeds not only the foreign clubs but also domestic ones, at each level, from professional to amateur. As a result the 'young' push the 'old' out of the first team, so that the 'old' move and become leading figures at young, ambitious amateur clubs.[8]

All of these changes helped to bridge the gap between the golden years of Stade de Reims (between 1955 and 1962) in European tournaments and the barren years until 1975. Then that was followed by renewed success for French football at international level. There were the successes of Saint-Etienne between 1975 and 1981, then Nantes, Bordeaux and the comeback of Parisian football with Paris Saint-Germain in the 1980s, then Marseille or Monaco in the 1990s, as well as the honest World Cup performance in 1978, the glorious semi-final achievement in 1982 and lesser glory in 1986, culminating in winning the 1998 World Cup. These results show that French football is successful today. But why does it remain so poor and why is uncertainty and disharmony associated with French football?

L'association loi 1901 versus the PLC

The idea of sport as a public service is linked to the idea that football clubs have to help produce citizens of the republic. The organization of football clubs is based on the 'l'association loi 1901', the French law that established freedom of association: French citizens became legally entitled to group together to undertake any collective activity. The law applied to parties, unions, cultural, social or educational groups – and to the new sports clubs which were appearing in France at the end of the nineteenth century. Administrators of social organizations were elected and under the control of members who were able to express their views at general meetings. But under the 1901 law, these associations need to be non-profit-making: the administrators could not profit personally from the activities of the society and no dividends could be distributed to members. Until the 1920s the movement towards professionalism was of little importance: football clubs were not intended to make money but were instead a space for the expression of local and political sensitivities. Catholics had their football clubs, while socialists too had their teams. Later, in the 1930s, when the discussion of professionalism was on the agenda, the legal requirements of the 1901 law of association were not seen to be an obstacle. Until the end of the 1970s football was the business of local personalities who saw it as a means of making local and national reputations for themselves. The legal status of the professional clubs as non profit-making reflected the nature of club professionalism:

club management was an act of goodwill, patronage or, most rationally for some, a business advertisement. The law did not prevent clubs from paying players or coaches, or from picking up local authority subsidies or from obtaining generous private patronage. Players were not particularly expensive, at least until the 1960s. Professional sport was not perceived as a source of social mobility among the working or lower-middle classes. The French professional player, more often than not semi-professional, usually had a middle class background, such as being a student, for whom football was an agreeable and lucrative pastime, a kind of 'vie de bohème'.

However, from the 1950s professional football increasingly became a working-class job. But right up to the 1960s it was not unusual to see talented players choosing to remain amateur, thereby adding to their salaries, possible benefits and bonuses from their grateful club president, who was also their factory boss. The situation was transformed by the decline of traditional industries which had financed the first generation of professional clubs. That led to the emergence of new players for whom football was a way to escape job insecurity and financial hardship. 'Les événements' of 1968 led to new contracts and new ambitions. And, from the 1980s, new entrepreneurs arrived, determined to invest in football.[9] Football can now be increasingly equated with money.

To face football's new economic circumstances, the State decided in 1984 to change the legal regulation of professional clubs. A law, known as 'loi Avice', named after the Minister for Youth and Sport, decreed that clubs with a turnover of over 2.5 million francs must become an SAOS or an SEM. To become an SAOS (Société anonyme à objet sportif) the club remains as an association, affiliated to the FFF, and it must retain at least 33 per cent of the capital, though other investors can come in. For example, Bernard Tapie, when at his peak, created an SAOS in Marseille with financial 'partners' like Panasonic, Adidas or Credit Lyonnais. In PSG, Canal Plus, the pay television company, owns 49 per cent of the club. The SEM (Société d'economie mixte) introduces local authorities into the club structure. The local authority owns 50 per cent of the capital, with the association again retaining 33 per cent.

Both kinds of limited company ensure that the club association retains considerable power. The 33 per cent ownership is sufficient to be a blocking minority, and could prohibit investors from receiving any dividends. That is, of course far from the creation of a real SA (Société anonyme) or PLC that is floated on the stock market, but that will be sought by those who would wish to go further in the economic rationalization of football. But in the context of the early 1980s, and the discovery of football's economic potential, these new business arrangements have allowed the big names in sport equipment or media to intervene directly in French football.

Direction nationale de contrôle de gestion

Before explaining the changes in French football management that underlie the present conflicts, we have to examine another feature of the game, namely its financial regulation by the Direction nationale de contrôle de gestion (DNCG) established in 1991. This body is made up of independent financial experts who have to analyse the accounts of all professional clubs to make sure they are financially balanced. If they are not, it has the right to prohibit any new spending, for example the buying of new players, which could cause a further imbalance. It can also relegate a club which is 'in the red' or ban it from competition for the season. There were two reasons for the creation of this body: first, local authorities argued strongly that professional football was becoming too expensive and that there were no controls on expenditure; and second, there was a political reaction to a long series of football scandals during the 1970s and 1980s. A mixture of football ambitions and personal greed led club presidents to take dubious, even illegal actions to fulfil them. For example, Roger Rocher, Saint-Etienne's president during the glorious 1970s, was jailed, as were Daniel Hechter, president of PSG, and Claude Bez, president of Bordeaux. Offences included double-ticketing scandals, fictitious loans or fees, and illegal payments to family members; others were guilty of the non-payment of taxes. Bernard Tapie was jailed for match-fixing, accounting frauds and tax evasion. His club, Marseille, was relegated to the Second Division and went bankrupt in 1995, before being bought, first partly by the local authorities as an SEM, then by a newcomer, Roger-Louis Dreyfus, boss of Adidas.

Against this backdrop the influence of the DNCG has been impressive. In 1991 the total debt of First Division clubs was 451 million francs, with total assets set at 363 million. State initiative has transformed debt-ridden clubs from being paternalist, irresponsible and short-term in management thinking to financially balanced organizations with a more rational view, even if this is most evident only for some big clubs. Nevertheless, if today French clubs are financially clean and players technically good, it is largely because of State intervention channelled through the actions of the FFF and LNF. From another perspective, however, one can say that the prolonged weakness of French professionalism is largely due to the influence of the State, which also hinders initiatives from being taken by the clubs, and thus stops French club football from reaching the top. At least this is what the new wave of football managers claim.

A New Football Landscape

A new wave of club directors appeared during the late 1980s to take a more active role in French club football, thus defining a new football economy. They saw football as a universal sport and, at the same time, a universal market. From this new perspective, French football is significant when it has an impact abroad and can then promote French products or when French football audiences can be seen as a target audience for marketing.[10]

In addition, just as Taylorism has come to an end and companies are looking for new methods of management, the vocabulary of sport, and especially that of collective sport, serves to mobilize company staff around themes of competition and organization in the context of a free market. In this metaphor, individuals must be strong, and stand up for themselves if they are to become established within the company, and so in society itself. Football can be adopted by companies as a means of creating staff solidarity around their projects. However, the sport is also an external means of communication, used to promote the fame of brands or new entrepreneurs. With the end of 30 years of unsurpassed economic growth and prosperity, French companies needed to turn towards new markets and sought to gain strong positions against their international competition. Sport provides them with the instrument to achieve those ends.[11]

Thus, new, rich investors appeared in the early 1980s: Jean-Luc Lagardère and Matra-Hachette at Matra Racing; Bernard Tapie Holding at Olympique Marseilles; Canal Plus at Paris Saint-Germain (PSG). And, in the 1990s, Pinault, with the second biggest financial fortune in France, arrived at Rennes, and IMG-McCormack at Strasbourg. With the entry of these newcomers, the structure and organization of the most important clubs has followed the SAOS model. For example, Marseille was, during Bernard Tapie's golden years, part of a holding company in which one found the club, television sports interests, and the Adidas company and agency for the marketing of sport events. Canal Plus became the principal stockholder in PSG which, in an attempt to emulate Real Madrid, has been transformed into a multisports club by buying basketball, volleyball and handball clubs. But between 1985 and 1995 football could be seen as a kind of lawless Wild West. Bernard Tapie or other lesser known presidents fell because of fraud or mismanagement. Big investors like Matra-Hachette left football quickly, unable to understand that large amounts of money were not by themselves guaranteed to deliver an efficient and successful team.

Now the situation is different. Some club presidents have taken advantage of the DNCG regulation to build a sound management structure. Besides the old style managers and presidents, alongside the world of small business and local personalities, people are entering football from business schools, even from the ENA (Ecole nationale d'administration)[12] and from multinationals. Networks of local firms have been created to produce a stable income from sponsorship money. A strong support (and a basis for strong, merchandising income) has been mobilized. Youth training policies have been developed; some clubs have even given coaches sufficient time to build a successful team for national or international success. Bordeaux, Lyon, Lens, Montpellier, Auxerre or Metz, or the patient comeback of Saint-Etienne, provide examples. These cities are middle-range, indeed, sometimes really small places (like Auxerre). Some clubs are located in de-industrializing or still rural areas. But some of them have such a strong local and national support, as for Lens and Saint-Etienne, that they can count on income from merchandising and outside investors. Yet these clubs operate at different financial levels. In bigger cities, like Lyon or Bordeaux, or clubs with reputations, like Marseille, the adoption of similar policies has allowed the local club to attract the really new big investors, the media groups and sports events organizers.

Another important influence for change came with the end of the State monopoly on television and the creation of several independent channels. Football has become a commodity in the competition between media stations. In 1974 there were barely 10 hours of football per year on the French channels; now, it is more than 500 hours and it can draw some of the largest television audiences. Competition for the broadcasting of large football events has produced a lot of money for clubs, which has changed the pattern of recruitment of new players and has promoted the more spectacular staging of matches, as well as having led to increased excitement for spectators. But the competition for television money has made some clubs vulnerable in the event of sporting failure. That vulnerability gave television companies leverage when they decided to invest in football clubs. When Canal Plus decided to buy shares in PSG, the television company determined it would organize the spectacle of PSG football matches. Canal Plus would raise money for the club from television revenues, but the company would also broadcast the games and so control the costs of television rights, and the development of pay television. The same role is taken by CLT–Ufa and Pathé in their clubs.

However, current investment in French football by television companies is rather modest in comparison to elsewhere, and certainly when compared to the BSkyB bid for Manchester United. The reason is that, for the moment, all new investors are waiting for two assurances. First, they want to be sure that football does really attract such a big market of viewers. For the moment, there is some doubt. Television audiences for the Champions' League have discouraged TF1 which owns the rights, while interest in the start of pay per view for the national championship has also been disappointing. Kiosk, the Canal Plus channel which offers pay television, attracts only between 7,000 and 11,000 viewers on average per match. One problem for French football is that the national team is the greatest attraction. There is less interest in the clubs, except sometimes when they represent France in European club competition. In addition, in anticipation of even bigger changes in football culture, such as greater economic liberalization of the game, many potential investors are delaying entry. Clubs may then become real public limited companies which can enter the stock exchange and pay dividends to shareholders. They may be able to negotiate direct contracts with television channels. Economic change may also lead to a lowering of the additional social costs of player wages.

The Big Debate: Who is to Rule French Football?

The most powerful French clubs include PSG and Marseilles, both of which are members of G14. Powerful French clubs as a group participate in a lobby called the Club Europe, which includes PSG, Bordeaux, Marseilles, Lens, Nantes, Strasbourg and Lyon, and they are represented by UCPF (Union des clubs professionnels de football). These clubs want less taxes on clubs and wages; they want the right to become real SAs or PLCs and to float on the stock market; they want to be acknowledged as the owners of the football spectacle, and to take all the economic rights that result from their involvement in the organization of games. Furthermore, they seek to establish ownership over the use of any image from the matches, in terms of television highlights or merchandising, and to have the right to negotiate directly with the channel of their own choice for the broadcasting of their own games.

The big clubs challenge the LNF's monopoly on the management of television rights. They accuse the League and its president, Noël Le Graët, of selling the championship cheaply to Canal Plus (750 million francs compared to 1.6 billion francs in England). They complain that the television income is distributed too fairly among French professional clubs. Their alternative distribution would risk a growing gap between rich and poor clubs.

Who then should lead French football? The League has been delegated powers by the FFF, and represents the State. As a result, the league guarantees that football is seen to be a public service, and ensures the unity of all levels of professional football. The League enforces the application of State directives. Its present legitimacy arises from making sure that professional football is on a good footing. Given its achievements, the league attempts to take advantage of income for all clubs by monopolizing the revenue from merchandising revenues. Because it represents egalitarianism, and insists on the implementation of State policy, which meant new spending and new responsibilities for the clubs, it attracts some hostility from the UCPF. But, for the same reasons, the league does truly represent smaller clubs in the First and Second Divisions. These clubs are concerned by recent changes, for good reasons (e.g. fairness and fiscal equity) and bad reasons (e.g. the market threat to bad club management).

Another involved party is the Ministry of Youth and Sport, and the Minister, Marie-Georges Buffet. As a member of a left coalition and the Communist Party, Mme Buffet is very critical of the spirit of capitalism in sport and sees herself as a guardian of sport and football as a public service. More generally, she is a strong champion of State regulation and its power of intervention. So, when she took her position as minister, she stopped all negotiations on the tax states of professional athletes that would have lowered the social tax paid by their employers or their own personal taxation. She was also hostile to the creation of a Super League and to developments that would privilege the richest clubs. For the same reason she is hostile to clubs being listed on the stock market. She is also against the Pasque decree that public subsidies be withdrawn. Instead,

Buffet argues for the continuation of this form of investment, for example in projects of public interest associated with football, such as the improvement of youth training centres in general education. She is in favour, at the European level, of sport being treated similarly to cultural matters and not being simply subject to market forces. European sport should promote fairness and all levels of sport should be respected and supported. Buffet proposes that there be some kind of regulator like a European DNCG.

But the future of football in France remains unclear. Will it follow the British model as the big clubs hope, or will it remain a form of republican compromise? Political factors like M.-G. Buffet's departure from her ministerial position could play a disproportionate role in decision-making. Football is a political issue, but of limited interest for the society as a whole and more important to particular political personalities. Yet, football could play, in a humble way, an interesting part in making changes in French society.

MEANINGS OF MODERNIZATION

Modernization is everywhere and touches everything. In France it means different things and functions at different levels. It means opening the country to more international influences, the rationalization of public expenditure, greater economic efficiency – and in the sporting world too; but it also implies a new relationship between the public sector and its users. It requires the end of paternalism, a new sense of individual and collective responsibilities, the development of new forms of knowledge and the ability to master technological innovations. Modernization has two main dimensions: the economic rationalization of all human activities, which suggests a move to the free international market and promotion of the idea that the market will regulate itself for the good of everybody; but modernization also suggests an increasing ability of individuals to express themselves, to master their life and their environment, and to play their part in decision-making. Modernization in society confronts various problems, and resolves these problems by breaking with tradition or non-rationalized ways of acting. For this reason, we may debate if the market is the only solution to these problems. That question is especially pertinent to sport, which emphasizes the need to win fairly, and which expects to contribute to a better society. Yet, the importance of the State may be an obstacle to autonomy, not as a restraint on the free market, but as a restraint on change in the relationship between the State and its citizens, and on the development of a broader participatory democracy.

Modernization and Security: French and European Policies

The security issue first emerged in France because of fan hooliganism. There was also, as in England after Hillsborough, concerns over safety issues following the Furiani disaster in Corsica when a stand collapsed, killing several spectators. Here the focus remains on the role of the State in reforming some security practices but these issues also highlight the limits to State intervention. The State helped to rationalize how football clubs managed safety and security issues, but State intervention failed to provide sufficient innovative ways to deal with security problems associated with football or urban life.

If we view football hooliganism as a social problem which expresses social dysfunction, different countries distinguish themselves by their more or less systematic policies and the balance between different kinds of regulation. Policies contain an admixture of repression and/or prevention, State control, 'spontaneous' societal control, or self-regulation by the groups that are seen as responsible for the problem.

In Europe, there are two general policy approaches. A Southern model (Italy, Spain) describes and regulates hooliganism as a public order problem mainly for the police, but also identifies an ambiguous political role for supporters' organizations in finding solutions, which reflects the power of clientelism and strong fan associations in football in these societies. A Northern model (Germany, England, Holland and Belgium) views hooliganism in a wider context, mixing repression, social prevention, and changes in clubs' commercial policies.

If we compare English and German policies, we can say that English policy is a compromise between market regulation (the modernization of football grounds, producing all-seater stadiums, the growth of season ticket holders and an increase in prices that transforms the demographic characteristics of spectators who can now afford to attend), changes in policy (CCTV, intelligence and 'low profile policing, high profile stewarding'), and recognition of the potential role of supporters' organizations and of clubs in their communities (via Football in the Community schemes).

In Germany, the 'Sport and Security' policy provides a framework for action. At the local level, police, cities and regional authorities, football clubs and social workers co-operate and work with the *Fan Projekts* initiative. Belgium and Holland, with their Fan Coaching initiatives, which attempt to provide football clubs with a sense of social responsibility, can be seen as very close to the German model.

These two policies have different aims. German policy emphasizes risk reduction (containing hooliganism within a part of the stadium), while English policy pursues eradication (the elimination of even bad conduct, not only violence). Although they aim to address different aspects of the problem, both are coherent and systematic policies.

A French Policy?

The French approach is different. A year before the World Cup, France was far from having any concerted initiative, as in Germany. There was no sharing of responsibilities between police and clubs, as in Holland. There was no simple attempt to adapt methods to help ease the problem, as in Belgium. The situation was very distant from the kind of policing employed in England during Euro '96. France was closer to the southern policy approach, but unprepared. Yet, things changed.

The 1993 report by M. Swiners-Gibaud, endorsed by the Ministère de l'Intérieur, examined incidents between police (CRS) and supporters during the Paris Saint-Germain–Caen match on 28 August 1993. The report noted:

- The lack of CCTV to monitor crowd incidents;
- The failure of clubs to take responsibility for, and plan for, safety and security issues;
- The resistance of local authorities to improve security and safety at stadiums;
- The bad image of supporters and the ignorance of fan culture among clubs and football institutions;
- The strong antagonism between supporters and club administrations;
- The inappropriate police control strategies, which were too inflexible compared to the kind of acts committed by French hooligans;
- The resulting increased tension between supporters and police;
- The lack of an intelligence agency for football hooliganism;
- The need for training and specialization of police officers in charge of the management of supporters.

The report could have had an effect similar to that of the Taylor Report in England. In the light of the critical conclusions in the report, what did happen in France?

A law, the so-called Alliot–Marie law, was passed on 6 December 1993. This law expanded an earlier one of July 1984, which makes provision for penalties for certain acts when committed in sport grounds. In its content, the new 1993 law is not really different from UK laws that set punishments for alcohol abuse, violent conduct, possession of weaponry, the stirring up of racial hatred, and so on.

A committee on security, safety and supporter policy issues has been established by the FFF and the LNF. This committee initiated the drafting of stadium regulations on spectator conduct, the establishment of security officers at each club, the installation of CCTV systems, and the regulation of announcers and broadcast information in the stadiums. This committee, in association with others in the football authorities, monitors the implementation of FIFA and UEFA rules on, for example, approved stadium capacities for international games or seating requirements. LNF has created a 'fair play' competition to reward the most sporting club support. Generally, LNF's attempt to improve the morality of football clubs, by improving club management or by punishing bad conduct among club executives, could be seen as another way of improving the good behaviour of supporters by creating a climate of fair play and good sporting behaviour.

Some clubs have taken initiatives to promote good relationships with ultras supporters or to improve stewarding. By doing so, they have followed up, and sometimes anticipated, a directive from the Ministère de l'Intérieur (9 December 1994) which reaffirmed that clubs had legal responsibility for security and safety inside the sports grounds, with the police being responsible for supporters outside and serious disorder inside. Paris Saint-Germain, for example, have expanded their stewarding and have initiated schemes similar to Belgium's 'fan coaching'. They have also created a supporters' department, hold regular meetings with ultras' associations and have set up socio-educational activities with the toughest fan groups. Similarly, at Le Havre, supporters help young, unemployed or disabled people and players work with communities in different areas of the city. And, for the police, there are now training programmes on hooliganism and security.

But all these initiatives do not constitute an agreed system because, as yet, there is no common understanding of the problem and, consequently, no agreement on common action. Locally, some clubs and local authorities are reluctant to set up CCTV, or to develop stewarding or even to apply the law that bans alcohol consumption or advertisements inside sport grounds. There continues to be confusion over the identification of supporters and hooligans and some clubs are reluctant to establish relationships with supporters' associations. Generally, it is thought that security and safety work is not a real and worthwhile investment. Around the Parc des Princes, the police are still much too evident and much too numerous, despite a dominant discourse that 'troublemakers are only a small minority'. The situation is paradoxical: the problem is said to be very serious, but each group 'does what has to be done' and then simply blames the 'others' (police, judges, clubs, and so on) for not doing what is required of them!

The list of complaints and complainants is long. Grievances may centre on the individual's institution. Inside the police, some talk about an overly hierarchical institution which stifles initiative; police transfer rules which hinder the development of good knowledge of the local football scene; or there are rivalries between different kinds of police units, according to their specialization in public order and judicial matters. The grievances may focus on other actors in the security system: for police or club executives, the justice system is too slow; for judges, police do not apply proper judicial procedures; there is too the prefect who may want to cover himself against any criticism on issues of police resources; then the clubs may be seen as only pursuing short-term policies, or even of wanting to protect their own supporters.

THE WORLD CUP: A MISSED OPPORTUNITY?

French fan violence is less serious than in England. It should be easier to do what the English did, and remove fences, reduce the police presence, and set in train other measures as required, such as: the use of CCTV, the creation of a national intelligence agency, the specialization of staff in security and hooliganism, the professionalization of stewarding and staff in football clubs, and the establishment of links between clubs, local authorities and supporters' associations. More generally, France could seek to develop a national policy to tackle all of these issues within the long-term development of professional French football.

The seriousness of the hooligan issue differs across European societies. There has been no extreme and routine violence in France as in England or Italy, but there remain issues for French football to face. Some are evidently on the security side. The established popular success of football and the general emergence of ultras groups bring the risk of increased tensions. The return of Marseille to the First Division, the increased number of derby matches, the French success in European competition and the development of top flight football clubs in and around Paris, all have potential security implications, as does the building and location of the Stade de France. The 1998 World Cup brought the arrival of English, German and Dutch supporters, but there were also supporters from Eastern Europe, from the Maghreb and Africa, and all kinds of mobilization and counter-mobilization of fan groups was evident. These arrivals meant that there were security issues, and public order concerns, as well as matters to do with border control or international police co-operation.

The World Cup meant that the whole world looked at France: the image of fences around the playing arena and of security police (CRS) usually displayed around the Parc des Princes would have dissatisfied those who participated in Euro '96 in England. But international competition cannot be limited to the sporting event, it is also a matter of national image. The location of the new stadium raised issues to do with city suburbs and social integration, because the massive stadium for the final was built in Saint-Denis, one of the most deprived areas in northern Paris. For this reason, the World Cup should have been a stage on which to establish a new vision for football, the management of football passion and its positive role in socialization and national integration.

This hope was held by the Comité français d'organisation (CFO) in charge of the technical and commercial side of the competition. For its president, Michel Platini, the Cup had to be seen to be a celebration. The organization of the tournament was to be an opportunity to introduce a new style in French crowd management. The CFO intended to adopt English methods and decrease police inside and outside the stadiums, increase stewarding, and even, with some hesitation, remove fences from around the grounds. The intention was to produce something similar to Euro '96 in England in terms of ambience and policing. But in February 1998 the Minister of the Interior decided not to remove the fences. Instead, the World Cup in France was to be about CCTV, stewarding and a strong police presence: risk would be minimized, the control maximized. No longer, it seemed, was the celebration of football to be the dominant aim. Finally, however, the decision was taken to remove the fences. None the less, this hesitation underlines the uncertainty over strategy and responsibility in decision-making and French football.

The Vicious Circle in France

The problem is the influence of professional cultures which makes co-operation, or simply even discussion, difficult. There is an emphasis on short-term policy by the clubs (security costs too much, the objective is performance next season) and even a culture which seeks to avoid confrontation with the more enthusiastic and faithful supporters. There are the strong financial, and sometimes political, links between clubs and local authorities. As a result, the clubs claim that the local authorities should pay for security, but then the local authorities reverse this argument. In the football authorities, the executives are at the same time judge and judged (i.e. presidents of clubs judge themselves). It is now normal to feel that nothing can change. In the face of football hooliganism, the most suitable explanation of inaction is derived from Michel Crozier;[13] football becomes a system in which there is no precise knowledge of facts and no real determination of shared responsibilities. So, in the absence of knowledge of hooliganism and in a situation of uncertainty of the exact seriousness of the hooligan problem in France, police retain their capacity to define the situation to suit their own ends. They can argue that, if they do not persist with their established approach, the situation will deteriorate. Clubs can persist in their own reality and claim policing is too expensive, the problem is not serious, and so many policemen are not required. Equally, the clubs can refuse to remove the fences, arguing that their removal would truly make the situation worse.

Paradoxically, this uncertainty becomes a comfortable situation because it removes any sense of clear and specific responsibility from the actors. In this context, the removal of fences is certainly unpopular among those in charge of football because it would presuppose a common diagnosis of the nature and seriousness of fan violence. It would define an objective (risk reduction) and an agenda for the implementation of actions to meet that objective. Technical and judicial conditions could then be applied, and a clear determination of shared responsibilities and financial contributions could be made.

Yet in football, as in other fields, there is a tendency to await decisions from above. So, FIFA or UEFA can determine general safety regulations, or the European Union can decide on the links between football clubs and public money. Conversely, the State can take the lead, and establish a consensus, as in Germany, or a political dispute, as in England under the Thatcher government. The 1997 General Election changed the government in France, and that did lead to an amended policy. The question of fences was reviewed and, during the Tournoi de France (in June 1997), there was an experiment with the policing of matches. Despite the apparent success, 1998 saw hesitancy over the issue. Then the final decision for removal of fences was made by the government in order to conform with FIFA requirements.

In the Shadow of the Stade de France

Despite the vacillation over the removal of fences, the less security conscious approach has worked fairly well. One of the results of the World Cup has been the generalization of this approach to the domestic championship. A lot of problems remain around club management, and the management of clubs' relationships with supporters and their own commercialism. Club–supporter relationships are still defined by questions of policing, paternalism or clientelism, but some things have been learned. It is now recognized that it was possible to differentiate between hooligans and ordinary supporters. Some wondered if these lessons could be applied to the important issue in France of urban disorder, which is especially problematic in Saint-Denis, the location for the new Stade de France.

The Stade de France is typical of the uniquely French view of sport. The stadium expresses the tradition of *grands travaux*, the stadium is big after the style of the New Library or the Louvre's Pyramid. Its scale is intended to address France's international reputation for hosting a global event. But the stadium is also about urban regeneration, and is an instrument of planning policy. The location of the Stade de France became a choice between Melun and Saint-Denis and a choice between two ideas of urbanization. The decision in favour of Saint-Denis was for a locality in an area of deprivation. The area was characterized by high unemployment, high delinquency, very low qualifications by local youngsters and the lowest school achievements. It had the lowest average income for the whole Paris area. It also had a substantial immigrant population. So the stadium was to be built there to change the image of the area. The building work would create jobs and the operation of the stadium would be a source of permanent employment. Additional housing was also included in the project.

The new stadium and the World Cup have been of great symbolic significance in Saint-Denis. There was a peaceful atmosphere in the tough neighbourhood and around the stadium. The French victory led to a great and joyous multicultural demonstration on the night of 12 July 1998. But very soon hard reality returned, especially around football matches. The Saint-Denis district championship had to be cancelled for three weeks in April 1999 because of violence in and around football grounds. The reasons are well known: poverty, low expectations, racism, and the rise of communitarianism among football teams organized around ethnic origins.

But there has also been a failure in football. The game has not faced up to its own responsibilities. There has been a continued lack of insight, and of foresight, by people responsible for sport policy at local or State level. Violence today is, in part, the result of a failure to adapt sports structures and the ideology of sport to changed times and to the new populations in the suburbs of the major cities. Sports clubs often not only failed to meet the expectations of the young people they attracted, but they taught young players bad habits, such as cheating. By insisting on competition, small clubs become socially selective rather than mechanisms for social inclusion. Formed by local élites, the clubs often failed to be open to new social groups coming from the new populations. Jealous of the social power of some clubs, local authorities were in any event unable to accept social organizations which would not come under their control or follow their guidance.

Football authorities and football clubs have been too Republican and too Coubertian: they believed that sport alone was sufficient to promote good moral values. They were in the limited sense too sporty: they thought that sport had no connection to other aspects of popular culture. And the State has made the same mistake too: often it appears to forget that it has a Ministry that is for *both* Youth and Sport. So, although State and public subsidies have had a positive effect at high levels of French football, public intervention has been much too inadequate when football is located in its widest social context, and placed against a backdrop of serious social disadvantage.

NOTES

1. The Ligue nationale de football (LNF) manages and represents the interests of professional football, the Fédération française de football (FFF) oversees all of French football and represents its interests in UEFA and FIFA.

2. Summarized in *4-4-2* magazine, January 1999.

3. *France Football*, 27 April 1999.

4. Figures given by UCPF (Union des clubs professionnels de football), November 1996.

5. Figures cited in the paper come from *LNF Infos*, the monthly magazine edited by the Ligue nationale de football.

6. See Patrick Mignon, *La Passion du football* (Paris, 1998), and in English, Patrick Mignon, 'New Supporter Cultures and Identity in France: The Case of Paris Saint-Germain', in R. Giulianotti and J. Williams, *Game without Frontiers: Football, Identity and Modernity* (hereafter *Game without Frontiers*) (Aldershot, 1994), and Patrick Mignon, 'Fans and Heroes', in H. Dauncey and G. Hare, *France and the 1998 World Cup: The National Impact of a World Sporting Event* (hereafter *France and the 1998 World Cup*) (London, 1999).

7. Dauncey and Hare, *France and the 1998 World Cup*, contains several good chapters on these issues.

8. For an analysis of the player market, see Jean-François Bourg and Jean-Jacques Gouguet, *Analyse économique du sport* (Paris, 1998).

9. For an analysis of French football professionalism, see Alfred Wahl, *Les Archives du football: sport et société en France, 1880–1980* (Paris, 1989) and Alfred Wahl and Pierre Lanfranchi, *Les Footballeurs professionnels en France des années trente à nos jours* (Paris, 1995).

10. See Michel Raspaud, 'From Saint-Etienne to Marseilles: Tradition and Modernity in French Soccer and Society', in R. Giulianotti and J. Williams, *Game without Frontiers*.

11. See Alain Ehrenberg, *Le Culte de la performance* (Paris, 1991).

12. The new general director of PSG is an ENA graduate.

13. Michel Crozier, *L'Acteur et le système* (Paris, 1977).

Old Visions, Old Issues: New Horizons, New Openings? Change, Continuity and Other Contradictions in World Football

RICHARD GIULIANOTTI
and GERRY P.T. FINN[1]

CREOLIZATION: LOCALIZATION THROUGH GLOBALIZATION?

Globalization has too often been presented as an extraneous force which ensures the imposition of universal homogeneity. While there are strong structural factors that do influence social and cultural relations within football, it is important to recognize that the game functions, like any other form of popular culture, within a structural relationship to other institutions that may be described as having some 'relative autonomy'. Moreover, the consequences of globalization, and the social responses of specific cultural groups and communities to global sporting forms, are neither monochrome nor predetermined. While major transnational corporations and political élites may seek to impose particular forms of global cultural identity and practices upon specific localities, the targets on whom this change is to be imposed do have some scope for agency and, thus, choice, in terms of how they play and organize their sports.

B. Houlihan has neatly summarized the different structural forms and consequences of sports globalization by proffering a useful, classificatory approach.[2] He is sceptical about the complete explanatory power of conceptualizations of globalization that emphasize a simplistic and overly-econocentric Marxist position, notably that offered in cruder versions of cultural imperialism or Americanization. Both of these positions simply posit that global cultural forms such as sports are passively internalized within the target society as a consequence of the exertion and expression of colonial power.

Houlihan draws upon U. Hannerz's notion of creolization[3] to emphasize how targeted societies may actively redefine the legal, political and normative framework within sports to fit their own local, pre-existing conditions. Instances of creolization highlight the structural relative autonomy of sport as popular culture, and reflect the continuous processes of negotiation with, sometimes resistance to, social élites from within and without the specific sporting territory.[4]

One shortcoming of the creolization position, as it is advanced by Houlihan, is its initial acceptance of relatively fixed senses of time and space. This difficulty enables a meaningful discussion to begin regarding the specific locality in which the globalization of sport takes place, but it does run into some problems when explaining the diachronic processes of creolization. For example, it is geographically and historically meaningful to use taken-for-granted notions of national identity and the nation-state to examine the globalization of sport. However, the long-running consequences of globalization are such that it is increasingly difficult to talk accurately about anything 'national' in a singular or all-inclusive way. That is especially evident in the case of sport. Indeed, the very history of sport reveals a continuing dialectic between the local and the global.

The essays in this volume emphasize the 'creole' aspect of football culture throughout the world. As these studies explain, the institutional and social responses to the shared global culture of football do identify commonalities but equally highlight important differences, most notably in relation to the production of specific senses of local, ethnic or national identity. Indeed, one consequence of globalization is, ironically, to offer new means by which social differences can be displayed and reasserted or reconstituted, or, in a false and illusory sense of the reversal of time, returned to in the guise of historical re-enactment and the re-invention of tradition.[5]

FOOTBALL, THE NATION AND NATIONAL IDENTITY

Undoubtedly, sport is one of the key mediums within popular culture that can be used in an attempt to produce and reproduce senses of national identity. As the modern, 'national' game in Europe and South America, football has provided the most important setting within popular culture in which symbols and discourses of national identity may be displayed and mediated through mass communication.

Historically, as we have noted, the game's global diffusion throughout the late nineteenth and early twentieth centuries went hand-in-glove with the formation of senses of national identity and nationalism. By the outbreak of the Second World War, football internationals or national cup finals had become crucial sites for the popular reproduction of dominant forms of national identity. These fundamental, state-centred rituals came to conjoin the national flag, the national anthem, the nation's top players and the nation's VIPs. Football thus provides the pretext through which the 'imagined community' of fellow nationals may be reached and unified, via the match's mediation on television, radio or on print. Similar nation-building projects through football continue throughout the world[6] but can meet special difficulties in the face of local ethnic and linguistic complexity in the same nation-state.[7]

In a Durkheimian vein, it can be argued that, by staging major football tournaments, the nation-state can assist its corporate and cultural image overseas, and transform its diffuse citizenry into a community of hosts. Effectively the nation utilizes the tournament so that it becomes the vehicle for the projection of a social representation[8] of the state. The national football team's chances of winning, and certainly of performing well,[9] are much increased, and the 'nation' can itself participate in making a success of the tournament by attendance at matches of low-appeal and by arranging local festivities in association with tournament matches. Staging the World Cup has been significant for football in the United States and France, and is intended to be for Japan and Korea too.[10] The financial benefits and powerful political symbolism to be gained through the association with the tournament is well recognized by national ruling élites. Japan and South Korea each spent $100m in successfully wooing FIFA's decision-makers so that the World Cup would be located there in 2002. Intense lobbying and skilful politicking for the 2006 finals has involved political, financial and football leaders from England, Germany, South Africa and those ranked as outsiders from other countries in Africa and South America. Staging the tournament can also serve to legitimize a specific state model of political administration. The 1998 World Cup finals, for example, reaped the obligatory profitable reward for the French state, while highlighting the efficacy of France's unusually large, public sector involvement in player coaching and club subsidies.[11]

However, while political leaders have long sought to mobilize the nationalist potential of the game to their advantage, their record of success is not clear-cut. South American nations provide obvious case studies of how fascistic politicians and military governors attempted to inculcate a 'false consciousness' among the masses.[12] Sport was at the core of the ideological projects of Peron and the later military junta in Argentina. Yet we learn much about the limited successes of these political strategies when we examine the collective Argentinian memory (or amnesia) of their two victories at the World Cup finals. Many Argentinians still celebrate the technical skills of the side which hosted and won the 1978 tournament under the auspices of the junta. But most will more readily recall or discuss the side that took the 1986 tournament in Mexico; it is Maradona (rather than Galtieri or Peron) who is most favourably associated and credited with football success.

In Brazil and in Uruguay, a similar differentiation is made between successful national footballers and the military regimes that sought favour from football fervour. In a pioneering study, J. Lever considered the politically soporific nature of football within Brazilian society, but later concluded that no simple, functional relationship merged the state with this realm of popular culture.[13] Indeed, we can easily locate counter-evidence that highlights the potential of football spaces for facilitating political protests or other expressions of social disharmony. Football fan violence in Latin America has often dramatized a deep public unease or antagonism towards political élites or the quasi-paramilitary forces of social control.[14] Moreover, the relationship between football identities and constructions of nationalism may be even more accurately portrayed if it is reversed. In other words, it is within the affective space of major football fixtures and events that we can find the initial constructions of expressive forms of non-sanctioned nationalism or national identity: football offers the same opportunity for the expression of societally disapproved ethnic or local identities too.[15]

E. Gellner argues that the formation of national identity requires strong institutional support from the national mass media and a national educational system.[16] Football is a staple feature of everyday cultural production within these institutions, and therefore serves to underwrite deeper constructions of national identity. However, the response to these top-down social forces has been the near-simultaneous recognition of the creation of another site for the potential display of resistance. Among British sports, football has been the most important vehicle for the expression of alternative social identities. Yet, increasingly it is football that assumes a privileged position within the sports curriculum of schools at the expense of other sports, such as cricket in England. The game is a pivotal part of the scholastic subcultures among male (and increasingly female) school pupils and college students. That is despite the evidence that shows the appropriation of football for service in counter-cultural resistance.

None the less, it is now almost banal to point to the strong nexus between the mediation of football matches and the formation and reproduction of national identity. Newspapers have long been 'reversible' in the sense that they can be read from back-to-front, beginning with the football and ending with more 'serious' issues.[17] The proliferation of outlets for the electronic media enhances our routine interaction with sports and football, as part of the incessant 'background noise' of everyday life.[18] Collectively, media analysis of major international fixtures and the conduct of football celebrities provides us with some insight into the debates that surround national social values and ethics, and political and cultural relations with other societies. From a historical perspective, analysis of the media coverage surrounding international football matches tells us much about the changing relations between the two nations in political, economic and cultural terms.[19]

SOCIAL DIFFERENCE AND SOCIAL STRATIFICATION WITHIN THE FOOTBALL NATION

Evidently there is no simple, direct relationship between football culture and national identity. While political and cultural élites try to employ the game to promote common senses of national identity, football will facilitate the reproduction of social inequalities and the popular expression of conflict and difference. Football is certainly an important venue for the production, reproduction, but also contestation, of forms of social exclusion. In the United States, football has become a post-industrial, white, suburban sport that is seen to exclude African-Americans and other disadvantaged groups.[20] In Japan, the profound inequalities experienced by those of Korean descent are further reflected within the developing football culture.[21]

These reflections of strong forms of social stratification mirror the early experiences of large disadvantaged populations that sought to participate more fully in their specific national cultures through football. In the United Kingdom and continental Europe, the struggle to legalize professional football was essentially a long battle between the working-class practitioners and spectators at football matches, and the hegemonic élites that clung to the amateur ethos that only they could afford. In Latin America, the participation of non-white players in top-flight football matches (including internationals) was staunchly resisted by the white élites that had financial and juridical control over the game.[22] Since the 1930s we have been more able to speak of football culture as a 'game of the masses' in both Europe and in South America. Yet, the intensification of inequalities and poverty over the past 30 years now means that international football players in Argentina, Brazil, Chile and elsewhere are increasingly unlikely to be drawn from the 'favelas' and 'misery villages'. The basic prerequisite for a successful career is a healthy and energetic body, not malnutrition in infancy or drug consumption in adolescence. Chronic problems in the socio-economic structure now underpin this increasing disenfranchisement of displaced and socially disadvantaged classes from football too.[23]

So the professed universalism and multiculturalism of the football world belies the complexity of power relations between different ethnic groups within specific national settings. At a worldwide level, football is a conduit for the expression and practice of racism and other forms of ethnic intolerance. In Australia, the contrasting policies of assimilation or multiculturalism fail to neutralize the strong traditional animosities between ethnic groups drawn from different parts of southern Europe.[24] In South America, football continues to be underpinned by racialized forms of social stratification. In England, the attempt to reduce racism within football's major institutions and spectator cultures fails to keep pace with the emergence of black footballers on the field.[25] In Scotland, the rhetoric of 'sectarianism' is used to deflect attention from the social reality of the nature of ethnic and racialized division.[26] In Italy, quasi-racial ideologies permeate the *mezzogiorno* division of north and south, while more subtle forms of racial categorization pervade the popular imagination when relating international fixtures to European politics. And in France, while multiculturalism seemed to be celebrated with victory in the World Cup, we should not forget the street riots that marked the start of the tournament, involving young, disenfranchised Parisians of North African extraction who had been effectively excluded from the commodified jamboree.[27] Racism is a serious question across Europe, one that European football has not only been slow to address, but one which still awaits a sustained and powerful rebuttal.[28]

Gender and generation represent two other points on the sociological compass of social stratification, and football culture plays its part in their realization at the everyday level. Football is undoubtedly a 'modern' game, that is a product of modernity, and so its articulation is heavily genderized. As a traditionally 'male' sport, football provides a space in which dominant forms of masculinity are constructed and reproduced. We may point here to the aggressive or quasi-violent culture of football, in playing and spectating terms, as evidence of a hegemonic form of masculinity.[29] Yet we should not ignore, as has often been the case, the cultural variations on this masculine identity, or indeed those principles of masculine ontology that challenge or mock aggression or violence.

Football 'artists' like Maradona, Johnstone or Zidane are certainly able to 'look after themselves' and gallant enough to seek to humble their opponent's masculinity with deceptive ball-play or dribbling. But these iconic figures also exhibit exceptional grace and style, an aesthetic that is far from the simple physicality of some of their contemporaries, and which allowed them to move safely beyond the reach of lumbering opponents with malice in mind. Football fans especially appreciate these players, even when they may not represent some supposed ideal of footballer body types. Yet fan chants may also mock those (usually lesser players, but sometimes opposing fans too) who fail to conform to a typified male body shape that is svelte and muscular.[30] Adding further complexity to the matter is that these detectors of deviance can themselves be corporeal deviants, who are full participants within a fan carnivalesque which accommodates physical diversity through boisterous and playful ridicule.[31]

It is significant that cultural differences in masculinity are reflected in different styles of play. In the small nation of Uruguay, a pragmatic playing style that blended different influences with immense success has now resorted to a more aggressive, classically masculine approach as the players fight to preserve their glorious football heritage.[32] And, in Argentina the debate over 'traditional' or 'European/modern' play actuates different notions of national, masculine identity.[33]

With the gradual increase in the social and economic power of women, female participation in football has risen, though the degree of penetration of this male enclave varies. Greatest headway has been made within the new football nations, especially the United States where the proportion of female players is remarkably close to their wider social presence; unfortunately this apparent gender equality overcomes neither racism nor social class division.[34] In the United Kingdom, the number of female players has risen, but more noticeable has been the pressure within football's 'Culture Industry' to draw women with sizeable disposable incomes into the grounds. Consequently, more traditional male practices – such as chanting or swearing – have been legally circumscribed.[35]

Conversely, relatively little attention has been paid to the future gerontological profile of football. The commercial boom within world football has often entailed a passionate sweeping out of tradition from within the game's culture, including a dramatic change in its now idealized target audience. The endeavour to portray football as a clean, modern, vibrant object of cultural consumption means that most signs of the old days carry negative connotations (decrepit grounds, hooliganism, less merchandising) and are thus suppressed or critically redefined. Yet, while football has always been defined professionally as a 'young man's game', the near obsession with youth, novelty and change means that a growing proportion of the game's traditional support in Western countries begins to feel no longer wanted, and even excluded.[36] This subtle ageism is certainly apparent in British football stadiums, where fan demographics are skewed towards those aged under 35 years.[37] The emphasis on youth and novelty has also become deeply troubling for many former football celebrities who are required to slip into obscurity before they have sufficient maturity or even time to understand the nature of their fame.[38]

DECONSTRUCTING THE NATION: TRANSNATIONAL FOOTBALL CLUBS?

The paradoxes and contradictions of the interactions of processes of globalization, identity formation, localization and commodification are neatly exemplified by a club from the past as it looks to the future. In Scotland the Irish and Catholic background to the formation of Glasgow Celtic has been regularly interpreted from within Scottish football as being incompatible with a Scottish identity. One result has been what some have perceived to be the vilification of Celtic players in the national side by sections of Scotland fans.[39] Local prejudice persists in attributing a narrow, even dangerous, identity to the club and its supporters. Yet this was a club that set out to appeal across national boundaries: to be a Scottish club with an Irish heritage. It was literally to be a *Celtic* club that would transcend the national boundaries of Scotland and Ireland, ironically then located in one state.[40] As one of the first examples of a football club representing a diaspora, Celtic provides an intriguing historical case study of one form of transnational identity and its reception.

It is more than ironic then that Celtic is now intent on marketing itself as another *modern* 'transnational' club, thereby following the approach of Europe's leading teams in maximizing their share of football's global marketplace. Worldwide networks of supporters' clubs now double as a matrix of outlets for merchandise, such as seasonally adjusted clothing and colourful paraphernalia, to serve consumers on the continent, in the Far East, across North America and throughout the antipodes. Clubs recruit and control an international array of labour on an ever-greater scale, assembling their teams from all parts of the world in the same way that cars are constructed from imported parts.

Global football enterprises like Arsenal, Manchester United, Roma and Ajax have contracted smaller clubs in other nations to refine and enskill those players that have potential before, if successful, the players are fully integrated within their superteams. In financial and symbolic terms, these transnational clubs have outgrown their national associations, in much the same way that Microsoft or General Motors dwarf the economy and polity of developing and small developed nations. Yet the owners of AC Milan, Bayern Munich, Manchester United *et al.* face the same juridico-political problems of Bill Gates in dealing with the nation-state's institutions: regulation, taxation and authorization of their business practices.

The most direct conflict between the clubs and the national associations centres on the growing number of international fixtures. Clubs consistently protest that they foot the real bills for national football's international division of labour: clubs pay player transfer fees and huge salaries for élite professionals, as well as ancillary medical, insurance, transport and subsistence expenses. National football associations do not provide proper payment to players nor compensation to clubs for the temporary employment of this scarce labour resource. Yet the national associations are legally empowered by FIFA to have first call on these professionals, excepting those players who have declined selection or report themselves ill. The legal foundation of the G-14, consisting of most of Europe's richest clubs, threatens to switch the balance in the clubs' favour and weaken the organizational powers of the

national associations and the national leagues.[41] This development will
have dramatic consequences for less prestigious leagues, and in the case
of South American leagues will intensify the haemorrhage of ever-
younger players to European clubs.[42]

The greater number of fixtures for international teams, the result of
the increase in competitive global and continental fixtures, threatens to
relocate inequalities between core and peripheral football markets to the
level of international selection too. The more powerful European clubs
employ large squads of players from different continents. Despite the
use by some clubs of regular labour rotation, 'crack' players that are
recruited from peripheral countries might be encouraged to naturalize
their citizenship, thus preventing any lengthy or awkwardly timed
absences from domestic league competition. For example, young
Australian players joining English clubs have been pressurized to use
their British genealogy to represent one of the Home Nations (whose
matches do not usually clash with domestic competition), rather than
regularly return at inopportune moments to the southern hemisphere
for internationals. More commonly, when they do take long-haul flights
home to play matches, these crack players lack energy, fail to practice
well together, and struggle to perform effectively as a team. For example,
though Uruguay's contemporary condition of having over 400 players
abroad attests to a culture of football excellence, a listless national side
consistently fails to qualify for the World Cup finals.[43]

CORPORATIONS VERSUS NATIONS: THE TRANSNATIONAL
ASPECT OF NEW FOOTBALL 'LOYALTIES'

The transnational dimension of the football industry has other impacts
that serve to dislocate a sense of national identification. At club level,
although there remains an orientation towards football support that sees
it in terms of an irreversible, fatalistic attraction,[44] there appears to be an
increased abandonment of local connections and loyalties by fans who
turn to follow the more successful or glamorous teams that are given
greater exposure in the media. The Norwegian football experience does
show that this process is not new and can lead to dual support, in which
there is an allegiance to a locally-based team as well as to a bigger and
glamorous 'transnational' team, based elsewhere and operating in
another football league.[45] Nevertheless, even at international level, we
find that routine identification with one's own nation (and its individual

'stars') is increasingly replaced by following other national teams that consist of players made 'familiar' by the global football media and transnational merchandising companies.

This process of transnational identification is particularly apparent among 'new' football consumers, such as in the Far East and North America, or among new middle-class or young female spectators in the United Kingdom. In Sydney, Singapore or San Francisco, no urban stroll is complete without sighting a Manchester United shirt or the Brazilian number 10 of Ronaldo (and Nike). In Japan, for example, following a losing side is not going to establish anybody's social kudos.[46] In such instances, football support is no longer an 'end' in itself, but a medium for the consumer to buy safely and successfully into global popular culture. Within this cultural logic, the new football consumers can truly exercise their 'distinction' from others by getting to the centre of this global cultural form, most obviously by paying heavily to attend the World Cup finals. There is at the World finals a growing trend to represent this new supporter relationship with the players as one rooted in an active reification of celebrity and lifestyle, effectively a reflection of the personal achievement of the fan-as-consumer, rather than that of the fan necessarily as bearer of a national identity.[47]

While the battle of players and teams represents football's more traditional form of contest, the matches and tournaments also dramatize the clash of corporate signifiers: Nike v. Adidas, Coca-Cola v. Pepsi, Mastercard v. Visa. The integrity of the game – in its philosophical sense – is lost in a sea of corporate signs, thus following the experience of North American sports. The relative success or failure of these signs is determined by the mediated story of the individual superstars, the signifiers' referents. Certainly, the actual 'use value' of these players is closely scrutinized, specifically as to how effective they are in their match performance. Yet, the fetishized exchange value of the players is increasingly important: how much personality and 'style' they display on and off the pitch; how much they may be worth on the transfer market or in salary terms; and now, how much they may be worth as a result of these external business interests too.[48]

This partial deconstruction, and more significant displacement, of the truly national within international football may have less invidious consequences for the new football nations than for the older ones. Giulianotti has argued elsewhere that football's continuing globalization has seen it expand greatly in 'post-national' contexts.[49] In Japan,

Australia and the United States, football does not constitute the 'national sport', and so has not yet been expected to play a central part in the construction of a nationally unifying culture and set of symbols. Hence, the post-national strength of soccer has been founded, initially, on its seizure by relatively marginal groups within the wider society. In Japan, female involvement in the fan culture is noticeably strong, and can be contrasted with the more masculine baseball culture that emerged after the Second World War.[50] In Australia, soccer has been particularly strong among ethnic minorities of southern European extraction.[51] In the United States, soccer is hugely popular in terms of participation, especially among women, but it does not have the crucial institutional support in the mass media and the educational system traditionally enjoyed by baseball, American football and basketball.[52] That raises questions about the future for post-national sports at the advantaged margins of a society. It is that sense of marginality that provides the present niche-market appeal for soccer in these locations: equally, the marketing of that selective image of the marginality of soccer hinders even more the development of mass-market appeal. This equilibrium seems unstable, yet any seeming movement forward might signal, not dynamism, but a lurching fall to failure.

Consequently, for the moment at the élite level in these nations, the future of the young soccer culture is strongly dependent upon effective international 'trade' if domestic leagues are to survive. Financially, the fledgling Australian league requires an improvement in World Cup qualification performance to bring it out of danger. The Japanese and the United States professional leagues rely heavily on the recruitment of overseas stars, notably from Europe and especially South America, to improve the skills and performances of local teams. Both have stronger civic and commercial backing than in Australia, but still require to perform well at international level to cement their reputations (and to establish their right to World Cup qualification through what are viewed as less competive regional sections).

Culturally, however, these new football nations seem to nourish the wider ambition that the game may become a force for the demonstration and celebration of multiculturalism within a society where a range of national and cultural identities might interact directly and peacefully with each other. Football in America was a marginal game practised by immigrants from the United Kingdom, southern Europe and Latin America before it was taken up by the aspirant middle classes. In

Australia, the ethnic segregation of soccer may seem to have been supplanted by greater Anglo-Celtic involvement and strong coverage of the national league by ABC television, the state-funded broadcaster. The semiotics of football *qua* multicultural sport are routinely displayed in television advertisements for the world game's major sponsors (Coca-Cola, Adidas, Nike): the aim is to signify how these transnational companies are a normative mirror of football's universal reach and competitive meritocracy. Yet, close examination of the labour practices of these sportswear and clothing manufacturers reveals that the semiotics of the use of football in this context can be deconstructed to identify football with the notions of ruthless competition, economic domination, and global exploitation.

Globalization in relation to the labour process involved in sports clothes manufacturing describes little more than the exploitation of cheap labour markets and a return to sweatshops as the means of production. One associated, highly lucrative market for sportswear manufacturers has been the production of university sportswear and leisure clothing which, because it incorporates the university logo, provides a slice of the profit to the university itself. Recognition of the appalling labour conditions under which this apparel, like other sportswear, is produced has had a damaging effect on the image of the companies, and their university partners, in the United States. Across college campuses the United Students against Sweatshops (Usas) have organized campaigns, including 1960s-style direct action, against the manufacturers and against the college administrations that entered into agreement with them. One positive outcome has been that more universities are now being forced to insist that their contract with the manufacturers includes clauses on labour rights and the independent monitoring of working conditions. Unless football authorities and clubs insist on some similar arrangements, this involvement with the sports clothing industry will give football the wrong image: the relationship will act as a signifier of football and global exploitation, rather than an image of football and global equality.

Despite the numerous examples of football reflecting social division rather than celebrating social diversity, this much proclaimed rhetoric of equality and justice around the image of football can be given some support. Yet, even in examples of its apparent success lie the demonstration of the clear limits to the universality of football. Unsurprisingly, any example also demonstrates the inevitable inability of football to step outside of society and constitute independent arenas of equality and human justice. FIFA's first World Cup winners – Uruguay – borrowed heavily upon the local British for their highly successful playing style, and drew their players from the ethnic melting-pot of Montevideo.[53] A positive European message also emerges from France;[54] the recent World Cup victory drew millions of fans of European, African and Polynesian extraction on to French streets, to celebrate the diverse origins of their 'home' side. Yet in Uruguay and France, the national team has become almost a football refuge for spectators alienated from a locally impoverished club competition as a result of the globalization of football player markets. And there is also the evidence from France, before this flush of mutual, and inevitably briefly shared, celebration, of that earlier demonstration by North African French of their sense of exclusion. Marketing plays on football which present the illusion of universal appeal are no more than marketing ploys to attract the universal consumer, who bears little relationship to the mass of humanity.

HOOLIGANISM, FAN CONTROL AND THE NEW FOOTBALL CONSUMERS

Spectator violence continues to be a recurring concern of the football clubs, the game's governing bodies and the mass media. Hooliganism has also been a dominant issue within academic debates on football, most obviously within the United Kingdom, but there is little benefit in rehearsing these arguments here.[55] A major development of the 1990s has been the political and social recognition throughout Europe and Latin America that fan violence is not primarily an 'English' problem, and that its strong subcultural properties usually preclude 'non-hooligan' fans being targeted by violent supporters. Indeed, within the hooligan groups themselves, there is an increasing impact of globalization, and the creation of global (rather than national) hooligan practices and styles. For example, the 'casual' style of expensive sportswear and designer clothing was imported to the United Kingdom from the continent in the late 1970s, transplanted into the local football context by hooligans, and then delivered back to northern European football fans. Meanwhile, a more obviously competitive relationship exists between hooligan formations at the national level, especially English, Scottish, Dutch and German 'casuals'.[56]

The debate on spectator violence needs to be located within the wider context of contemporary football's political economy. The 'official culture' within football grounds has been transformed since the late 1980s, especially in the United Kingdom, through the construction of new all-seated stadiums, the raising of ticket prices, the targeting of female spectators and families, the use of stricter codes of conduct that are enforced on fans by stewards and police officers, and by the intensified 'hype' surrounding matches in the mass media and in pre-game festivities. Endeavours by football's marketing people to reach new consumers, notably among the wealthier and more 'respectable' social classes, receive significant blows when outbreaks of fan violence occur at national and international levels. One concern is that the overt marginalization of hooligan groups within the grounds will provide a covert impetus for squeezing out more participatory (and perhaps less respectful) fans too.

It is important not to confuse the participatory behaviour of young fans with actual violence.[57] Indeed, this confusion might hasten the present trend which has seen the decline in the irreverent songs and participatory chants of the United Kingdom football fan. Already young supporters are less likely to engage in the subcultural practices of singing. Equally it is true that young supporters are now much less likely to be involved in episodic violence (at least in the ground) than they were during the 1970s and 1980s. The confusion of singing and chanting with violence seems to arise from the confusion over the linguistic usage of the term aggression, to which is added a lack of clarity over what constitutes violence. Participation in aggressive and dismissive chanting is not to be equated with football violence in any of its forms.[58] None the less, there is the danger that new legal regulations surrounding football in England and Wales might actually prohibit singing in the new stands.[59]

The increased cost of attending redeveloped, all-seated grounds has reduced the scope for informal association of supporters, the vital conditions for a singing fan culture.[60] Football songs and chants need to have a humorous aspect to survive their first public airing.[61] Giulianotti introduced the concept of the 'carnivalesque' to explain the informal organization of football crowd behaviour, in which collective participation in singing and chanting is a core cultural element. The decline of singing reflects the gradual demise of the culture of fun and laughter created by crowd participation within football grounds. Laughter, it should be noted, has its serious side: a side that emanates from an aged folk culture of which the culture of singing at football matches has been a latter-day variant. According to Rabelais, 'Laughter has a deep philosophical meaning ... the world is seen anew, no less (and perhaps more) profoundly than when seen from the serious standpoint.'[62] Through the humour of singing and the general banter, which at its best in matches can seem almost to attain Socratic heights, the tragicomedy of a superstar who has wasted a penalty, or the equestrian aesthetics of a centre-back's tackling, can be richly appreciated. Instead, new developments ensure that the fan practices within older football cultures become less distinct from those in the newer football societies, such as Japan and the United States. Audiences there consist of those who largely spectate: they are predominantly viewers with relatively limited football biographies.

Changes in the class structure of post-industrial societies will inevitably affect the demographics and practices of football crowds. The rise of a media-literate, service sector stratum that has also been called the 'new middle class' has had an impact upon spectator cultures. Fan cultures have always crossed class divides, but this strata brings to bear its expertise in group organization, marketing, personal and collective self-expression, mobilization of resources, and the use of new technology on fan culture itself. That has helped some fan groups to be even more articulate and less strictly tied to football's institutions. So there has been a growth in independent supporters' associations. There has also been the development of the football fanzine industry in the United Kingdom, which has spread across mainland Europe. Other fan groups have headed off the football industry's extraction of spectator expenditure by transforming their supporter identities into a trademark. The 'Tartan Army' of fans that follows the Scotland team to fixtures home and away now find themselves with a trademarked name which is controlled by a handful of supporters. Most spectacularly, the strongly football-influenced culture of English cricket fans, known as 'England's Barmy Army', functions under the auspices of a trading company that has an extensive portfolio of clothing and supporter paraphernalia.

These diverse activities do show fans attempting to take greater control of fandom and its practices. The range of activities, however, does also demonstrate the range of responses to the new commercialism of European football. Some fan actions demonstrate a co-operative and collective effort to represent and work with, and for, their fellow supporters. Others show entrepreneurial flair and seize a commercial opportunity ahead of the sports industry. They do so for their own personal advantage and reward. Some activities, such as some of those involved in the fanzine movement, occupy the middle ground. The complex responses hint at one, often neglected, truth: football fandom is complex, complicated and very diverse. It is only the sport that can bring the diversity of football fans together, sometimes in rare moments, in the common communion of an intensely emotional feeling.[63]

THE NATIONAL AND GLOBAL MEDIA

However, the timing of when these supporters come together in celebration of sport is increasingly determined by the interests of television broadcasting companies. Uncertainty over timing, even of the date, of future matches is now part of the price paid by committed supporters for television investment in football: but the price paid by the television companies is substantial. Revenue from satellite and cable television has been the major catalyst for world football's financial growth. As late as the mid-1980s football club chairmen remained distrustful of television's influence on the game, fearing that televised fixtures or regular highlights of games would have a singularly adverse effect on attendance figures. However, the arrival of media deregulation and new broadcasting technology encouraged most national leagues to enter negotiations with independent satellite stations. As a result, by the mid-1990s all major Western European and Latin American associations had entered into deals that allowed subscription-based channels to broadcast several live league fixtures each week.

In England, the new income from satellite television transformed the game's finances. In 1978, the four-division Football League had earned £9.8 million from a four-year highlights deal with the BBC. In 1992 a five-year deal with BSkyB netted £304 million for the 20 club Premier League in return for 300 live matches.[64] A new £670 million deal between the two parties was agreed for a four-year period in 1997. Similar investments in football have been made by media giants such as TyC (South America), Fininvest (Italy), Bertelsmann and the Kirch Group (Germany), and Canal Plus (France). While these media corporations seem initially to be tied to national contexts, they do share an underlying commitment to minimize competition between each other, preferring instead to develop new technology together with a view towards maximizing the size of football's economic pie. The developments have been vindicated by FIFA's sale of World Cup television rights. For the 1998 tournament, FIFA earned £84 million in deals with free-to-air stations. For the 2002 and 2006 tournament, FIFA's marketing arm has controversially sold the rights for £1.16 billion to satellite broadcasters who narrowly outbid the free-to-air companies.

The attraction of football for satellite stations is its capacity to deliver relatively large subscribing audiences of several million viewers. Moreover, the development of pay-per-view (PPV) services and multi-channel digital television foretells a scenario in which all top league fixtures may be viewed on the basis of individual, match-by-match subscription. PPV was first introduced in France with only moderate success, although the relatively weak supporter culture there suggests far greater success for major European football markets.[65]

Satellite broadcasting of fixtures has weakened the national links between football fixtures, television and the fan audiences, but has enhanced continental and global ties. In nations like the United Kingdom, France and Italy, the pursuit of commercial television by football associations weakened the national links between the domestic game and state broadcasting companies. Moreover, the switch from 'free-to-air' to subscription broadcasters fragmented the national audience, producing only a small minority of households that could watch the televised games, which thus had a deleterious effect on football's supposed capacity to unite a disparate 'imagined community'. Meanwhile, viewer access to 'foreign' football leagues has increased on both free-to-air and subscription television.

During the early 1990s European football associations had regularly complained to UEFA that satellite companies were flouting the existing broadcasting rules that banned the beaming of a 'foreign' fixture into their nation while any domestic league football was being played. With the lifting of that prohibition, satellite television viewers in the United Kingdom soon found themselves with a choice of Scottish, English, Italian or German live football on Sunday afternoons. Invariably, the more modest European leagues struggle to withstand the appeal of the top world players in other nations. Meanwhile, the arrival of PPV ensures that all but a handful of 'protected' fixtures will be increasingly expensive to watch, privileging an armchair audience with the wealth and technology to obtain their reception.[66] Yet the globalization of the electronic media does enable migrants and cultural cosmopolitans to reenact their national ties with the imagined community at home by watching matches with their compatriots in pubs or private surroundings at unusual hours of the day. Nevertheless, the kinds of deal that are brokered between the national associations and the media companies will reflect the political and economic complexion of that society.

In Western Europe, the powerful associations can extract immense income from the satellite stations; in smaller European nations, the income is far less, with live televised matches more frequently rescheduled to complement, rather than compete with, other domestic matches. In Latin America, the influence of the mass media is far stronger and the negotiating power of the football authorities much weaker. Television there is able to secure long contracts to televise football and takes the dominant role in the organization of the football calendar. Ironically, in the seemingly post-national settings of Japan, the United States and Australia, the long-term success of the relatively new football league tournaments is strongly dependent upon negotiating a national broadcasting deal. That will ensure that, in these ambivalent settings, football gains the television exposure that could educate locals and help elaborate and develop a football culture in these societies.

Yet, although national football leagues do need television to aid their growth and development, television also poses problems for the sport. PPV and satellite television income will probably provide a major threat to the long-term stability of the national leagues. Current satellite deals are negotiated by the leagues, which in England and Italy do provide for a relatively equitable distribution of income between the member clubs. However, some of the top clubs in France, as well as those in Holland, have begun to explore the possibility of acquiring a greater share of television revenues on the basis of their greater audience share.[67] Ideally, Europe's G-14 clubs[68] would look to negotiate their own television deals with broadcasting corporations, as well as develop the technological basis for creating their own digital television station. Such measures will exacerbate the deepening of structural inequalities between clubs that play within the same league system, and erode the 'uncertainty of outcome' in an increasing number of fixtures. In England, Scotland, Italy and Spain, it has already become increasingly difficult for smaller provincial clubs like Nottingham Forest, Aberdeen, Sampdoria or Zaragoza to mount a genuine challenge for their domestic championships. A devalued domestic league in these nations provides the powerful clubs with a much stronger case for their participation in Europe-wide competition instead, which could become a self-fulfilling prophecy.

The changes made to EUFA club tournaments throughout the 1990s have also led to domestic competition becoming devalued. The European Champions' Cup became the Champions' League in 1992: the quarter and semi-final rounds were replaced with competition in a league format to determine the two finalists. The move from traditional cup knockout removed the risk of elimination and guaranteed greater income to successful clubs. This increased financial reward made it even more imperative that clubs gained access. For a few seasons, AC Milan had problems in finishing high enough in Italy's Serie A to qualify for European competition. That led Berlusconi (the club's owner, controller of Fininvest, and former leader of Italy's right-wing political bloc) to propose a simple solution. The richest European clubs would simply break away, and reward themselves for their organizational initiative by awarding themselves certain inclusion, regardless of playing performance, in their own new European Super League.

This threat led EUFA to offer a compromise to the leading clubs, whose participation in European tournaments was a source of considerable income to EUFA as well as to themselves. Entry to the tournament was now extended to clubs that finished second in the most powerful leagues, which were also located in the countries that provided the biggest income from television companies. The danger of even being knocked out was also reduced by delayed entry to the competition for some of these national representatives. And, for the champion clubs still unfortunate enough to be knocked out in what were now called preliminary rounds, there was even a back-door entry to the EUFA Cup.

From season 1999–2000, the format of the Champions' League has become even more friendly to the richest clubs. Now the top six rated national leagues each gain three or four qualifiers; two clubs from each league are allowed direct entry into the league stage, and the others are required to play in only one qualifying round. Again there is the consolation of an entry into the later rounds of the EUFA Cup for clubs that fail in this qualifying round. Another nine nations also gain multiple entries of two clubs. Again there are different entry points, with guaranteed access for some into the EUFA Cup if they are unsuccessful in the qualifying rounds for the misleadingly still titled 'Champions' League. These arrangements, and the demise of the European cup tournament for national cup winners, will further diminish domestic competitions. Now FIFA is to run the World Team Championship for the leading clubs from continental tournaments from around the globe. As this tournament will clash with some domestic competitions, even participation in it is bound to add to the devaluation of national club competitions.

CONTRACTS AND PLAYERS

Contractual arrangements between players and clubs historically gave clubs very considerable power over players. Increasingly, players have won more legal rights, which has served to strengthen their hand in negotiations with the clubs, but which has, because these clubs can offer bigger financial inducements to join and the prospect of greater playing success, made the richer clubs even stronger in playing power. England offers an illustrative example. The contracts that bound footballers had been a source of legal dispute for much of this century.[69] In 1961 the maximum wage set for footballers was abolished. Then, in 1963, the 'retain and transfer' contractual system was considerably modified as a result of George Eastham's court victory over Newcastle United, on grounds of 'restraint of trade', when the club refused to transfer him. Arnold judged that these regulations had until then 'probably help[ed] to equalise playing standards between clubs',[70] but that these constraints on the rights of players were unjustifiable. In 1977 the transfer system was amended once again, introducing 'freedom of contract'. Now players were able to move between clubs, subject to a transfer fee which, if clubs were unable to agree, was determined by an independent tribunal. By the end of 1986 football competitions in England were being dominated by élite clubs to a greater extent than ever before.[71]

More recently there has been the *Bosman* ruling,[72] which ruled in favour of free movement across national boundaries in the European Union, and ended transfer fees at the end of contracts to allow this movement to occur. That meant that rather than being transferred between clubs, players could now negotiate directly with clubs and seek substantial signing fees for themselves. No longer did the player's former club receive any recompense when an out of contract player moved to another club.[73]

This ruling has not ended the transfer market. However, it has brought about marked modifications to how it operates.[74] Clubs that are aware of a player's intention to move on now try to cash in on the player's market value before his contract ends. However, some players simply sit tight so that they can ensure that any end-of-contract payments go to them. Others agree some compromise deal with the club over the proposed transfer fee and the arrangements for their own signing-on fee, the timing of the move, and the choice of new club. None the less, transfer records continue to be set for the purchase of players still in-contract and buying clubs seek to put players on longer-term contracts. The contractual changes do advantage élite players. They are now much more able to determine their own playing career. These changes also benefit the élite clubs. It is to the élite clubs that élite players are most attracted in terms of both financial inducements but also probable playing success.

CO-OPERATION AND COMPETITION

Yet mention of the role of probable success identifies perhaps the biggest contradiction in competitive football: probable playing success is contrary to the production of good football which depends on a certain level of uncertainty of outcome. Successful football competition requires that clubs *co-operate* to produce good *competition*.[75] Indeed, this necessary contradiction means that clubs cannot allow strong competition to be diminished if good quality football is to result. Ironically, it is this very contradiction of co-operation and competition that seems to lie, often unrecognized, alongside these interlocking processes that seem to be leading to weakened internal domestic competition along with the simultaneous search for more lucrative and strong competition on a more continental or global basis.

Historically, football clubs have represented some sense of community, difficult as that notion can be, and have allowed a representation of that social identity[76] to be put on display. Social identities are neither fixed, nor frozen, but are a consequence of the social dynamics of intergroup exchange.[77] In a metaphorically shrinking world, and in a world of changing geopolitical structures and units, new expressions of social identity are as inevitable now (though as unpredictable in form) as they were when they emerged in the past. Some transformations in the soccerscape[78] reflect these global and local changes: others seem to be the consequence of the efforts of market-driven football clubs and authorities to maximize their income. The first set of changes will be accompanied by different expressions of social identities which will lead to new identity contests associated with football, running alongside other, longer-standing differences that have imposed social meaning on football contests: the second set of changes is more likely to lead to contestation over the very identity of football itself. But here the essential contradiction between competition and co-operation can only be resolved by the recognition that it is the latter that must be granted priority in the field of sport.

Co-operation is required to initiate and maintain competition, which is then bounded by the requirements that co-operation be maintained, or the competition itself will fail. That recognition might mean that Bourdieu's plea for a new universalist model of sport need not go unheard.[79] Recognition, followed by the proclamation, of the primacy of co-operation in sport might serve to illustrate that the very future of our common humanity lies in the combination of our varied social identities in co-operative effort. Such a philosophy could help teach sporting lessons to football identity contestants around the globe. Perhaps it would then be possible to make the necessary moves towards the inclusive, but pluralist, models of society that so many commentators seem to find so inconceivable. Rather than sport being seen as an extension of war by other means, perhaps it would be this social representation of harmony in diversity that could be sported in metaphor instead,[80] or is this speculation simply too utopian even for Bourdieu's future sporting vision?

NOTES

1. The order of names used here is again intended to indicate the shared responsibility for both the whole collection and the jointly contributed chapters.
2. B. Houlihan, 'Homogenization, Americanization, and Creolization of Sport: Varieties of Globalization', *Sociology of Sport Journal*, 11 (1994), 356–75.
3. U. Hannerz, 'Cosmopolitans and Locals in World Culture', *Theory, Culture and Society*, 7 (1990), 237–52.
4. See, for example, A. Klein, 'Sport and Culture as Contested Terrain: Americanization in the Caribbean', *Sociology of Sport Journal*, 8 (1991), 79–85.
5. Fragments of this process can be detected in Giulianotti's contribution to this collection. On occasions this last element in fleshing out some sense of social identity ranges from the serious to the burlesque: see G.P.T. Finn and R. Giulianotti, 'Scottish Fans, not English Hooligans! Scots, Scottishness and Scottish Football' (hereafter 'Scottish Fans'), in A. Brown (ed.), *Fanatics! Power, Identity and Fandom in Football* (hereafter *Fanatics!*) (London, 1998), pp.193–4.
6. See, for example, Porro and Russo in this collection.
7. See, for example, Vidacs in this collection.
8. See R. Farr and S. Moscovici (eds.), *Social Representations* (Cambridge/Paris, 1984) for further discussion of the psychosociological status of social representations.

9. The host nation qualifies by right. That also allows the national side the luxury of being able to forego short-term competitive demands and prepare for the finals themselves. In addition, all that is encapsulated by the notion of 'home' advantage also helps explain the usually relatively successful display of home nations even when they fail to win the tournament itself.

10. In this collection, see Andrews, Mignon and Horne, respectively, for essays on football in the United States, France and Japan.

11. See H. Dauncey and G. Hare (eds.), *France and the 1998 World Cup: The National Impact of a World Sporting Event* (hereafter *France and the 1998 World Cup*) (London, 1999) for a full discussion of the interrelationship of the 1998 tournament and the French state.

12. See Alabarces and Rodríguez in this collection.

13. J. Lever, 'Soccer: Opium of the Brazilian People', *Trans-Action* 7, 2 (1969), 36–43. See also the later work: J. Lever, *Soccer Madness* (Chicago, 1983).

14. E. Archetti and A. Romero, 'Death and Violence in Argentinian Football', in R. Giulianotti, N. Bonney and M. Hepworth (eds.), *Football, Violence and Social Identity* (London, 1994).

15. In this collection, see for example: Hughson; Finn; Armstrong and Young.

16. E. Gellner, *Nations and Nationalism* (Oxford, 1983).

17. S. Hall, 'The Treatment of Football Hooliganism in the Press', in R. Ingham (ed.), *Football Hooliganism: The Wider Context* (London, 1978).

18. A. Blake, *The Body Language* (London, 1996).

19. See Porro and Russo in this collection; also Finn and Giulianotti 'Scottish Fans', for the case of Scotland and England.

20. See Andrews in this collection.

21. H. Nogawa and H. Maeda, 'The Japanese Dream: Soccer Culture towards the New Millennium' (hereafter 'The Japanese Dream'), in G. Armstrong and R. Giulianotti (eds.), *Football Cultures and Identities* (London, 1999).

22. J.S. Leite Lopes, 'Successes and Contradictions in "Multiracial" Brazilian Football', in G. Armstrong and R. Giulianotti (eds.), *Entering the Field: New Perspectives in World Football* (hereafter *Entering the Field*) (Oxford, 1997).

23. See Alabarces and Rodríguez in this collection.

24. J. Hughson 'Football, Folk Dancing and Fascism: Diversity and Difference in Multicultural Australia', *Australian and New Zealand Journal of Sociology*, 33, 2 (1997), 167–86.

25. See S. Orakwue, *Pitch Invaders: The Modern Black Football Revolution* (London, 1998). Also see in A. Brown, *Fanatics!*, L. Back, T. Crabbe and J. Solomos, 'Racism in Football: Patterns of Continuity and Change' and B. Carrington, '"Football's Coming Home", But Whose Home? And Do We Want It? Nation, Football and the Politics of Exclusion'.

26. See Finn in this collection. Also see P. Dimeo and G.P.T. Finn, 'Scottish Racism. Scottish Identities: The Case of Partick Thistle', in A. Brown, *Fanatics*; P. Dimeo and G.P.T. Finn, 'Racism, National Identity and Scottish Football', in B. Carrington and I. Macdonald (eds.), *Racism and British Sport* (London, forthcoming).

27. See H. Dauncey and G. Hare (eds.), *France and the 1998 World Cup* for further discussion.

28. See U. Merkel and W. Todorski (eds.), *Racism and Xenophobia in European Football* (Aachen, 1996).

29. See G.P.T. Finn, 'Football Violence: A Societal Psychological Perspective', in R. Giulianotti *et al.*, *Football Violence and Social Identity* on violence and aggression in football.

30. See Armstrong and Young in this collection.

31. Ibid. See also R. Giulianotti, 'Scotland's Tartan Army in Italy: The Case for the Carnivalesque', *Sociological Review*, 39, 3 (1991), 503–27; R. Giulianotti, 'Football and the Politics of Carnival: An Ethnographic Study of Scottish Fans in Sweden', *International Review for the Sociology of Sport* 20 (1995), 191–224.

32. See Giulianotti in this collection.

33. E. Archetti, 'In Search of National Identity: Argentinian Football and Europe', in J.A. Mangan (ed.), *Tribal Identities: Nationalism, Europe, Sport* (London, 1996).

34. Andrews in this collection; also see D. Zwick and D. Andrews, 'The Suburban Soccer Field: Sport and America's Culture of Privilege', in G. Armstrong and R. Giulianotti (eds.), *Football Cultures and Identities* (London, 1999).

35. See Armstrong and Young in this collection.

36. Ibid.
37. For example, see R. Giulianotti, 'Putting the Dons on the Spot: The Aberdeen Football Questionnaire' (unpublished M.Litt. thesis, University of Aberdeen, 1992).
38. See M. Gearing, 'More than a Game: The Experience of being a Professional Footballer in Britain', *Oral History* (Spring 1997), 63–70.
39. R. Boyle. '"We are Celtic Supporters...": Questions of Football and Identity in Modern Scotland', in R. Giulianotti and J. Williams (eds.), *Game without Frontiers: Football, Identity and Modernity* (Aldershot, 1994).
40. See, for example, Finn in this collection.
41. See Mignon in this collection.
42. See Giulianotti, and Alabarces and Rodríguez, in this collection.
43. See Giulianotti in this collection.
44. Susan Condor and Mark Levine, Department of Psychology, University of Lancaster have carried out some fascinating but, as yet, unpublished research into how supporters see their relationship with football clubs.
45. For example, see the Norwegian experience in which there is support for an English team and a local Norwegian team: M. Goksøyr and H. Hognestad, 'No Longer Worlds Apart? British Influences in Norwegian Soccer', in G. Armstrong and R. Giulianotti (eds.), *Football Cultures*. There can also be historical and cultural links that lead to a sympathy for clubs in the same league. An example, a link which is now disappearing, was the perceived common Protestantism of Heart of Midlothian in Edinburgh and Glasgow Rangers. See H.K. Hognestad, 'The Jambo Experience: An Anthropological Study of Hearts Fans', in *Entering the Field* (Oxford, 1998). However, support for one club can more commonly be accompanied by support for another club in the same country when clubs are located in different leagues. Will the greater economic disparities and the emergence of élite clubs within the top European leagues lead to an extension of this style of 'support' so that it becomes common to support two teams in the same league: a 'big' élite team for vicarious glory and television interest and a smaller, local, club for more 'traditional' reasons?
46. See Horne in this collection.
47. A possible illustration of this development comes in anecdotal evidence that, in parts of Scotland, the Jamaican team, and especially their technicolor garb, was very popular with hash smokers! This intriguing example indicates continuing potential counter-cultural resistance within this form of spectator affiliation too.
48. The relationship between sponsor and player can also produce negative publicity. The uncertainty over Ronaldo's selection for the 1998 World Cup final, and the even bigger uncertainty over the back-stage manipulations, did not cover Nike in Ronaldo's glory. Instead there were rumours that Nike's main concern was that an unfit player should still play! See Dauncey and Hare (eds.), *France and the 1998 World Cup*, pp.134, 196.
49. R. Giulianotti, *Football: A Sociology of the Global Game* (Cambridge, 1999).
50. H. Nogawa and H. Maeda, 'The Japanese Dream'.
51. J. Hughson, 'Australian Soccer: "Ethnic" or "Aussie" – The Search for an Image', *Current Affairs Bulletin*, 68, 10 (1992), 12–17.
52. D. Andrews, R. Pitter, D. Zwick and D. Ambrose, 'Soccer's Racial Frontier: Sport and the Suburbanization of Contemporary America', in G. Armstrong and R. Giulianotti (eds.), *Entering the Field*.
53. See Giulianotti in this collection.
54. See Mignon in this collection.
55. See E. Dunning, P. Murphy and J. Williams, *The Roots of Football Hooliganism* (London, 1988); R. Giulianotti *et al.* (eds.), *Football Violence and Social Identity*; G. Armstrong, *Football Hooligans: Knowing the Score* (hereafter *Football Hooligans*) (Oxford, 1998).
56. R. Giulianotti, *Football: A Sociology of the Global Game*.
57. See Armstrong and Young in this collection.
58. See Finn in R. Giulianotti *et al.* (eds.), *Football Violence and Social Identity*.
59. G. Armstrong, *Football Hooligans*.
60. G. Armstrong and R. Giulianotti 'From Another Angle: Police Surveillance and Football Supporters', in C. Norris, J. Moran and G. Armstrong (eds.), *Surveillance, Closed Circuit*

Television and Social Control (Aldershot, 1998).

61. Armstrong and Young in this collection.
62. M. Bakhtin, *Rabelais and His World* (Massachusetts, 1965), p.66.
63. Finn in Giulianotti *et al.* (eds.), *Football Violence and Social Identity*.
64. S. Szymanski and R. Smith, 'The English Football Industry: Profit, Performance and Industrial Structure', *International Review of Applied Economics*, 11, 1 (1997), 135–53.
65. See Mignon in this collection. See also J. Eastham, 'The Organization of French Football Today', in Dauncey and Hare, *France and the 1998 World Cup*, pp.58–78.
66. Some estimates placed the projected PPV charge for individual fixtures as high as £10 or £12 meaning that a club like Manchester United could pull in up to £50 million from PPV coverage of one match purchased by around 4 million subscribers worldwide.
67. See Mignon in this collection.
68. The G-14 clubs are believed to be potentially the top clubs in terms of financial turnover and are a financial élite of aspirant European super-clubs.
69. See E. Grayson, *Sport and the Law* (London, 1988) and S. Wagg, *The Football World: A Contemporary Social History* (London, 1984).
70. T. Arnold, 'Rich Man, Poor Man: Economic Arrangements in the Football League' (hereafter 'Rich Man, Poor Man'), in J. Williams and S. Wagg (eds.), *British Football and Social Change: Getting into Europe* (Leicester, 1991), p.53.
71. Ibid., pp.58–9.
72. This has been described as 'the notorious *Bosman* ruling' by P. Bourdieu, 'The State, Economics and Sport', *Culture, Sport, Society*, 1, 2 (1998), 17. Bourdieu is correct in the sense that the ruling was the result of the application of free-market economics to football clubs and players. However, as the clubs already possessed many 'liberal' economic rights for their own use, there was justice in the extension of similar economic rights to players. None the less, Bourdieu's substantial criticism is well made.
73. As the *Bosman* ruling focused on cross-border European Union transfers, some leagues at first retained an internal transfer market for out of contract players. That is now ended, though in some countries there remain regulations which require recompense for the loss of players under a certain age. H. Moorhouse has recently tried to explore the effects of the transfer market in England, especially in relation to the common belief that clubs in the lower division clubs gained from transfers. Sadly he has neglected the work of Arnold ('Rich Man, Poor Man'), despite having a paper in the very same collection himself, and Moorhouse consequently ignores the previous history of change to this system. Indeed, Arnold had himself already noted that lower division clubs did not gain from the transfer market as a result, he implies, of the changes that had been made by 1963. Unfortunately, Moorhouse presents analyses (either by himself or more commonly he recounts other analyses) that are after the dates by which the traditional, unchanged transfer system *might* have had some general redistributive effect. Moorhouse is correct to re-emphasize that the recent contemporary transfer market was not generally a measure for redistribution of football income within countries. However, there is insufficient evidence to see how the general pattern does operate. Nor is there, despite Moorhouse's certainty about the gains to smaller external leagues, clear evidence for that claim yet. Nor does the present evidence allow any examination of the interesting suggestion that individual clubs pursued different income-generating polices with respect to the transfer system. Arnold's own evidence (with Beneviste) suggests that selling players was an undesirable short-term financial strategy, even among lower league clubs, rather than an accepted and welcome policy. However, see H.F. Moorhouse, 'The Economic Effects of the Traditional Transfer System in European Professional Football', *Football Studies*, 2, 1 (1999), 90–105. Moorhouse recently reviewed the collection which included Arnold's essay: H.F. Moorhouse, 'Ending Traditions: Football and the Study of Football in the 1990s', *International Journal of the History of Sport*, 15, 1 (1998), 227–31.
74. There is a need for a good systematic study of the effects of these modifications. At present most accounts are necessarily impressionistic.
75. See Arnold, 'Rich Man, Poor Man', also see S. Tischler, *Footballers and Businessmen: The Origins of Professional Soccer in England* (London, 1991).
76. Some commentators do still appear to have problems with the notion of social identity too, but

see Finn in this collection.

77. See, for example, D. Abrams and M.A. Hogg, *Social Identity Theory: Constructive and Critical Advances* (London, 1990) or R. Brown, *Prejudice – Its Social Psychology* (Oxford, 1995).

78. See R. Giulianotti, *Football: A Sociology of the Global Game* (Cambridge, 1999).

79. Bourdieu, 'The State, Economics and Sport', p.21.

80. G.P.T. Finn, 'Communal Contacts and Soccer: Conflict and Conciliation', invited paper to the 'International Symposium on Youth, Soccer, Violence, Society', University of California at Santa Barbara (1994). See also Finn in this collection. The culture of quasi-violence associated with football can in some circumstances be transformed into a celebration of football and social diversity (see Finn, in Giulianotti *et al.*, *Football Violence and Social Identity* and see Finn and Giulianotti, 'Scottish Fans'), but also see Armstrong and Young in this collection.

Select Bibliography

Local Contests and Global Visions:
Sporting Difference and International Change
Richard Giulianotti and Gerry P.T. Finn

G. Armstrong and R. Giulianotti (eds.), *Entering the Field: New Perspectives in World Football* (Oxford, 1997)

G. Armstrong and R. Giulianotti (eds.), *Football Cultures and Identities* (Basingstoke, 1998)

A. Brown (ed.), *Fanatics! Power, Identity and Fandom in Football* (London, 1998)

P. Dimeo and G.P.T. Finn, 'Scottish Racism, Scottish Identities: The Case of Patick Thistle, in A. Brown (ed.), *Fanatics! Power, Identity and Fandom in Football* (London, 1998)

G.P.T. Finn, 'Multicultural Antiracism and Scottish Education', *Scottish Educational Review*, 19 (1987)

G.P.T. Finn, 'Sectarianism and Scottish Education', in T.G.K. Bryce and W. Humes (eds.), *Scottish Education* (Edinburgh, 1999)

G.P.T. Finn, 'Social Identities and Comparative Visions', *The Psychologist Bulletin of the British Psychological Society*, 7 (1999)

R. Giulianotti, *Football: A Sociology of the Global Game* (Cambridge, 1999)

R. Giulianotti and J. Williams (eds.), *Game without Frontiers: Football Identity and Modernity* (Aldershot, 1994)

R. Giulianotti, N. Bonney and M. Hepworth (eds.), *Football Violence and Social Identity* (London, 1994)

I. Taylor, 'Soccer Consciousness and Soccer Hooliganism', in S. Cohen (ed.), *Images of Deviance* (Harmondsworth, 1971)

A Tale of Two Tribes: Expressive Fandom in
Australian Soccer's A-League
John Hughson

K. Hetherington, *Expressions of Identity: Space, Performance, Politics* (London, 1998)

J. Hughson, 'Is the Carnival Over? Soccer Support and Hooliganism', in D. Rowe and G. Lawrence (eds.), *Tourism, Leisure, Sport: Critical Perspectives* (Sydney, 1998)

J. Hughson, 'Soccer Support and Social Identity: Finding the "Thirdspace"', *International Review for the Sociology of Sport*, 33, 4 (1998)

J. Hughson, 'The Bad Blue Boys and the Magical Recovery of John Clarke', in G. Armstrong and R. Giulianotti (eds.), *Entering the Field: New Perspectives on World Football* (Oxford, 1997)

M. Maffesoli, *The Time of the Tribes: The Decline of Individualism in Mass Society* (London, 1996)

P. Marsh, *Aggro: The Illusion of Violence* (London, 1978)

P. Marsh, E. Rosser and R. Harre, *The Rules of Disorder* (London, 1978)

D. Matza and G.M. Sykes, 'Juvenile Delinquency and Subterranean Values', *American Sociological Review*, 26, 5 (1961)

D. Moore, *The Lads in Action: Social Process in an Urban Youth Subculture* (Aldershot, 1993)

G. Noble, S. Poynting and P. Tabar, 'Youth, Ethnicity and the Negotiation of Identities', paper presented to the Australian Sociological Association (TASA) Annual Conference (Hobart, 1996)

Contextualizing Suburban Soccer: Consumer Culture, Lifestyle
Differentiation and Suburban America
David L. Andrews

D.L. Andrews, R. Pitter, D. Zwick and D. Ambrose, 'Soccer's Racial Frontier: Sport and the Segregated Suburbanization of Contemporary America', in G. Armstrong and R. Giulianotti (eds.), *Entering the Field: New Perspectives on World Football* (Oxford, 1997)

F. Delgado, 'Major League Soccer: The Return of the Foreign Sport', *Journal of Sport and Social Issues*, 21, 3 (1997)

J. Sugden, 'USA and the World Cup: American Nativism and the Rejection of the People's Game, in J. Sugden and A. Tomlinson (eds.), *Hosts and Champions: Soccer Cultures, National Identities and the USA World Cup* (Aldershot, 1994)

S. Wagg (ed.). 'The Business of America: Reflections on World Cup '94', *Giving the Game Away: Football, Politics and Culture on Five Continents* (Leicester, 1995)

D. Zwick and D.L. Andrews, 'The Suburban Soccer Field: Sport and America's Culture of Privilege', in G. Armstrong and R. Giulianotti (eds.), *Football Cultures and Identities* (London, 1999)

Scottish Myopia and Global Prejudices
Gerry P.T. Finn

G.W. Allport, *The Nature of Prejudice* (25th Anniversary Edition) (Reading, MA, 1979)

C.G. Brown, *Religion and Society in Scotland since 1707* (Edinburgh, 1997)

S.J. Brown, '"Outside the Covenant": The Scottish Presbyterian Churches and Irish Immigration', *Innes Review*, 42 (1991)

R.J. Finlay, 'Nationalism, Race, Religion and the Irish Question in Interwar Scotland', *Innes Review*, 42 (1991)

G.P.T. Finn, 'Racism, Religion and Social Prejudice: Irish Catholic Clubs, Soccer and Scottish Society – I The Historical Roots of Prejudice', *International Journal of the History of Sport*, 8, 1 (1991)

G.P.T. Finn, 'Racism, Religion and Social Prejudice: Irish Catholic Clubs, Soccer and Scottish Society – II Social Identities and Conspiracy Theories', *International Journal of the History of Sport*, 8, 3 (1991)

G.P.T Finn, 'Sporting Symbols, Sporting Identities: Soccer & Intergroup Conflict in Scotland and Northern Ireland', in I.S. Wood (ed.), *Scotland & Ulster* (Edinburgh, 1994)

G.P.T. Finn, '"Sectarianism" and Scottish Education', in T.G.K. Bryce and W.M. Humes (eds.), Scottish Education (Edinburgh, 1999)

G.P.T. Finn, 'A Culture of Prejudice: Promoting Pluralism in Education for a Change', in T.M. Devine (ed.), *Scotland's Shame? Bigotry, Sectarianism and Catholicism in Modern Scotland* (Edinburgh, 2000)

Football in Cameroon: A Vehicle for the Expansion and Contraction of Identity
Bea Vidacs

W.J. Baker and J.A. Mangan, *Sport in Africa, Essays in Social History* (London, 1987)

R. Clignet and M. Stark, 'Modernisation and Football in Cameroun', *The Journal of Modern African Studies*, 12 (1974)

R. Cohen, 'Ethnicity: Problem and Focus in Anthropology', *Annual Reviews of Anthropology*, 7 (1978)

L. Fair, 'Kickin it: Leisure, Politics and Football in Colonial Zanzibar, 1900s–1950s', *Africa*, 67 (1997)

Louise de la Gorgendière, K. King and S. Vaughan (eds.), *Ethnicity in Africa: Roots, Meanings and Implications* (Edinburgh, 1996)

Jean-Claude Kodo-Ela and A. M. Masika, *Il était une fois andhellip; les Lions Indomptables du Cameroun* (Yaoundé, n.d.)

J.A. Mangan (ed.), *Tribal Identities: Nationalism, Europe, Sport* (London, 1996)

P.M. Martin, 'Colonialism, Youth and Football in French Equatorial Africa', *International Journal for the History of Sport*, 8, 1 (1991)

H.M. Mokeba, 'The Politics and Diplomacy of Cameroon Sports: A Study in the Quest for Nation-Building and International Prestige' (unpublished PhD thesis, University of South Carolina, 1989)

P.N. Nkwi and B. Vidacs, 'Football: Politics and Power in Cameroon', in G. Armstrong and R. Giulianotti (eds.), *Entering the Field: New Perspectives on World Football* (Oxford, 1997)

S. Tsanga, *Le Football camerounais des origines à l'indépendence* (Yaoundé, 1969)

J. Vincent, 'The Structuring of Ethnicity', *Human Organization*, 33 (1974)

Football and Fatherland: The Crisis of National Representation in Argentinian Football
Pablo Alabarces and Maria Graciela Rodríguez

P. Alabarces and M.G. Rodríguez, *Cuestión de Pelotas. Fútbol. Deporte. Sociedad. Cultura* (Buenos Aires, 1996)

E. Archetti, 'Argentina and the World Cup: In Search of National

Identity', in J. Sugden and A. Tomlinson (eds.), *Hosts and Champions: Soccer Cultures, National Identities and the USA World Cup* (Aldershot, 1994)

E. Archetti, 'Estilo y virtudes masculinas en El Gráfico: la creación del imaginario del fútbol argentino', *Desarrollo Económico. Revistas de Ciencias Sociales*, 139, 35 (1995)

E. Archetti, '"And Give Joy to my Heart": Ideology and Emotions in the Argentinean Cult of Maradona', in G. Armstrong and R. Giulianotti (eds.), *Entering the Field: New Perspectives on World Football* (New York, 1996)

V. Dini (ed.), *Te Diegum, Genio, sregolatezza and baccettoni* (Milan, 1991)

A. Ehrenberg, 'Estadios sin dioses', *Revista de Occidente*, 134/135 (1992)

P. Lanfranchi (ed.), *Il calcio e il suo pubblico* (Naples, 1992)

M. Maffesoli, *El tiempo de las tribus* (Barcelona, 1990)

A. Scher and H. Palomino, *Fútbol: pasión de multitudes y de elites* (Buenos Aires, 1988)

M. Varela, *Los hombres ilustres del Billiken. Héroes de los medios y la escuela* (Buenos Aires, 1994)

Built by the Two Varelas: The Rise and Fall of Football Culture and National Identity in Uruguay
Richard Giulianotti

G. Armstrong and R. Giulianotti (eds.), *Football Cultures and Identities* (Basingstoke, 1998)

G. Armstrong and R. Giulianotti (eds.), *Entering the Field: New Perspectives in World Football* (Oxford, 1997)

E. Galeano, *Football: In Sun and Shadow* (London, 1997)

R. Giulianotti, *Football: A Sociology of the Global Game* (Cambridge, 1999)

A. Klein, 'Sport and Culture as Contested Terrain: Americanization in the Caribbean', *Sociology of Sport Journal*, 8 (1991)

M.L. Krotee, 'The Rise and Demise of Sport: A Reflection of Uruguayan Society', *Annals of the American Academy of Political and Social Science*, 445 (1979)

T. Mason, *Passion of the People? Football in South America* (London, 1995)

F. Morales, 'Fútbol: mito y realidad', *Muestra Tierra*, 22 (Montevideo, 1969)

W. Murray, *Football: A History of the World Game* (Aldershot, 1994)

Various editors, *¿Nunca más campeón mundial?* (Montevideo, 1991)

The Production of a Media Epic:
Germany v. Italy Football Matches
Nicolà Porro and Pippo Russo

D. Dayan and E. Katz, *Media Events. The Live Broadcasting of History* (Cambridge, MA, 1985)

N. Elias and E. Dunning, *The Quest for Excitement* (Oxford, 1986)

J. Habermas, *Legitimation Crisis* (London, 1973)

J.M. Hoberman, *Sport and Political Ideology* (Austin, TX, 1984)

E. Menduni, *La televisione* (Bologna, 1998)

N. Porro, *Identità Nazione Cittadinanza. Sport, società e sistema politico nell'Italia contemporanea* (Rome, 1995)

N. Porro (ed.), *L'Italia in TV agli Europei '96. Il calcio come identità e come rappresentazione* (Rome, 1997)

P. Russo, 'Atlanta Fiction. Le Soap-Olympics della NBC', *Sport and Loisir*, 2, 4 (1998)

P. Russo (1997), 'L'Europa di Bosman', *Il Mulino*, 6, 374 (1997)

L.A. Wenner (ed.), *MediaSport* (London, 1998)

Fanatical Football Chants: Creating and
Controlling the Carnival
Gary Armstrong and Malcolm Young

E. Archetti, 'Argentinian Football: A Ritual of Violence', *International Journal of the History of Sport*, 9, 2 (1992)

G. Armstrong, *Football Hooligans: Knowing the Score* (Oxford, 1998)

G. Armstrong and R. Giulianotti (eds.), *Entering the Field: New Perspectives in World Football* (Oxford, 1997)

L. Back, T. Crabbe and J. Solomos, 'Racism in Football, Patterns of Continuity and Change', in A. Brown (ed.), *Fanatics! Power, Identity and Fandom in Football* (London, 1998)

P. Bourdieu, *Language and Symbolic Power* (Cambridge, 1991)

C. Bromberger, 'Fireworks and The Ass', in S. Redhead (ed.), *The Passion and The Fashion: Football Fandom in the New Europe* (Aldershot, 1993)

R. Holt, *Sport and the British: A Modern History* (Oxford, 1989)

S. Redhead, *Sing When You're Winning* (London, 1986)

Soccer in Japan: Is *Wa* All You Need?
John Horne

J. Horne and D. Jary, 'Japan and the World Cup – Asia's First World Cup Finals Hosts?', in J. Sugden and A. Tomlinson (eds.), *Hosts and Champions: Soccer Cultures, National Identities and the World Cup* (Aldershot, 1994)

J. Horne, '"Sakka" in Japan', *Media, Culture & Society*, 18, 4 (1996)

W. May, 'Sports', in R. Powers and H. Kato (eds.), *Handbook of Japanese Popular Culture* (Connecticut, 1989)

H. Nogawa and H. Maeda, 'The Japanese Dream: Soccer Culture towards the New Millennium', in G. Armstrong and R. Giulianotti (eds.), *Football Cultures and Identities* (London, 1999)

D. Roden, 'Baseball and the Quest for National Dignity in Meiji Japan', *American Historical Review*, 85, 3 (1980)

J. Sugden and A. Tomlinson, *FIFA and the Contest for World Football* (Cambridge, 1998)

J. Watts, 'Soccer *shinhatsubai*. What are the Japanese Consumers Making of the J. League?', in D.P. Martinez (ed.), *The Worlds of Japanese Popular Culture: Gender Shifting Band Cultures* (Cambridge, 1998)

R. Whiting, *The Chrysanthemum and the Bat* (New York, 1976)

R. Whiting, *You gotta have wa* (New York, 1989)

French Football after the 1998 World Cup:
The State and the Modernity of Football
Patrick Mignon

Jean-François Bourg and Jean-Jacques Gouguet, *Analyse économique du sport* (Paris, 1998)

M. Crozier and E. Friedberg, *L'Acteur et le système. Les contraintes de l'action collective* (Paris, 1977)

H. Dauncey and G. Hare (eds.), *France and the 1998 World Cup: The National Impact of a World Sporting Event* (London, 1999)

J. Eastham, 'The Organisation of French Football Today', in H. Dauncey and G. Hare (eds.), *France and the 1998 World Cup: The National Impact of a World Sporting Event* (London, 1999)

A. Ehrenberg, *Le Culte de la performance* (Paris, 1991)

P. Mignon, *La passion du football* (Paris, 1998)

P. Mignon, 'Fans and Heroes', in H. Dauncey and G. Hare (eds.), *France and the 1998 World Cup: The National Impact of a World Sporting Event* (London, 1999)

M. Raspaud, 'From Saint-Etienne to Marseilles: Tradition and Modernity in French Soccer and Society', in R. Giulianotti and J. Williams, *Game without Frontiers: Football, Identity and Modernity* (Aldershot, 1994)

A. Wahl, *Les Archives du football: sport et société en France, 1880–1980* (Paris, 1989)

A. Wahl and P. Lanfranchi, *Les Footballeurs professionnels en France des années trente à nos jours* (Paris, 1995)

Old Visions, Old Issues: New Horizons, New Openings? Change, Continuity and Other Contradictions in World Football
Richard Giulianotti and Gerry P.T. Finn

D. Abrams and M.A. Hogg, *Social Identity Theory: Constructive and Critical Advances* (London, 1990)

G. Armstrong and R. Giulianotti (eds.), *Entering the Field: New Perspectives in World Football* (Oxford, 1997)

G. Armstrong, *Football Hooligans: Knowing the Score* (Oxford, 1998)

G. Armstrong and R. Giulianotti (eds.), *Football Cultures and Identities* (Basingstoke, 1998)

T. Arnold, 'Rich Man, Poor Man: Economic Arrangements in the Football League', in J. Williams and S. Wagg (eds.), *British Football and Social Change* (Leicester, 1991)

H. Dauncey and G. Hare (eds.), *France and the 1998 World Cup: The National Impact of a World Sporting Event* (London, 1999)

G.P.T. Finn, 'Faith, Hope and Bigotry: Case-Studies in Anti-Catholic Predjudice in Scottish Soccer and Society', in G. Walker and G. Jarvie (eds.), *Sport, Leisure and Scottish Culture* (Leicester, 1994)

G.P.T. Finn, 'Football Violence: A Societal Psychological Perspective', in R. Giulianotti, N. Bonney and M. Hepworth (eds.), *Football, Violence and Social Identity* (London, 1994)

R. Giulianotti, *Football: A Sociology of the Global Game* (Cambridge, 1999)

R. Giulianotti, 'Scotland's Tartan Army in Italy: The Case for the Carnivalesque', *Sociologica Review*, 39 (1991)

Notes on Contributors

Pablo Alabarces is Professor and Researcher in the Faculty of Social Sciences at the University of Buenos Aires, Argentina. His book *Cuestión de Pelotas: Fútbol, Deporte, Sociedad, Cultura* (with María Graciela Rodríguez) was published by Editorial Atuel of Buenos Aires in 1996. His other research interests include media studies and social theory. He is currently working towards the completion of his doctorate and co-ordinating a sports research network in Latin America.

David L. Andrews is Associate Professor in the Department of Human Movement Sciences and Education at the University of Memphis. He teaches and researches on a variety of topics related to the critical analysis of sport as an aspect of contemporary popular culture.

Gary Armstrong is Lecturer in Criminology and Sociology at the University of Reading, England. He completed his doctorate at the Department of Anthropology, University College, London in 1996. He is author of *Football Hooligans: Knowing the Score* (Berg, 1998); and *Blade Runners: Lives in Football* (Hallamshire Press, 1998). He is co-editor (with Richard Giulianotti) of *Entering the Field: New Perspectives in World Football* (Berg, 1997); *Football, Cultures and Identities* (Macmillan, 1999); and *Oppositional Cultures in World Football* (Berg, forthcoming).

Gerry Finn is Reader in the Department of Educational Studies in the University of Strathclyde, Glasgow. He completed his doctorate in social and developmental psychology at the University of St Andrews in 1979. He teaches and researches on a variety of topics around social development, human social behaviour and education. His main research interests are concerned with intergroup behaviour and prejudice in education, sport and society.

Richard Giulianotti is Senior Lecturer in Sociology at the University of Aberdeen, Scotland, where he completed his M.Litt in Social Research Methods and PhD in Sociology. He is author of *Football: A Sociology of the Global Game* (Polity, 1999); editor of *Sport and Social Theorists* (Macmillan, forthcoming); and co-editor (with Gary Armstrong) of *Entering the Field: New Perspectives in World Football* (Berg, 1997); *Football, Cultures and Identities* (Macmillan, 1999); and *Oppositional Cultures in World Football* (Berg, forthcoming).

John Horne lectures in the Sociology of Sport and Leisure in the Department of Physical Education, Sport and Leisure Studies at the University of Edinburgh, Scotland. He is co-author (with Alan Tomlinson and Garry Whannel) of *Understanding Sport* (1999) and co-editor of *Sociology of Sport and Leisure: Current Alternatives* (1995, published in Japanese). His research interests include the development of sport in Japan, minority ethnic group involvement in sport and leisure in Scotland, and structuration theory.

John Hughson is at present Principal Research Fellow in Cultural Studies at the University of Wolverhampton, England. He is currently on leave from the University of New England, Armidale, Australia. He has published in the area of sports fandom with particular reference to collective ethnic identities.

Patrick Mignon holds a research post in the Sociology Department of the Institut national du sport de l'éducation physique, Paris, and teaches on popular culture at the University of Paris-IV. A member of the editorial board of the review *Esprit*, he is the author of numerous articles on the sociology of football fans in England and France, and also wrote the book *La Passion du football* (Odile Jacob, 1998). He is currently working on the transformation of sports culture in relation to popular culture in France.

Nicolà Porro is Associate Professor in Sociology at the University of Cassino, Italy. Previously he taught Political Sociology at the University of Roma La Sapienza and Sociology of Media at the University of L'Aquila. Among his published works are *L'Imperfetta Epopea* (Clup, 1989); *Identità, Nazione, Cittadinanza* (Seam, 1995); with P. De Nardis and A. Mussino (eds.), *Sport: Social Problems, Social Movements* (Seam, 1997) and *L'Italia in TV Agli Europei '96* (Rai-Eri, 1997).

Marìa Graciela Rodríguez is Lecturer and Researcher in the Faculty of Social Sciences, University of Buenos Aires, Argentina. She is co-author (with Pablo Alabarces) of *Cuestión de Pelotas: Fútbol, Deporte, Sociedad, Cultura*, and has published numerous articles in books and journals, including *Contratexto* and *The International Journal of the History of Sport*. Her main research interests are in the relationship of sport to popular and political culture.

Pippo Russo is a doctoral candidate in Political Sociology at the University of Florence. His thesis is a detailed examination of Talcott Parsons' political theory.

Bea Vidacs is at the City University of New York Graduate Center. She carried out 19 months of anthropological fieldwork in Cameroon on the social and political significance of football.

Malcolm Young obtained a doctorate in social anthropology at the University of Durham following a 33-year career in the British police force. He is also the author of two monographs: *An Inside Job* (Oxford, 1991) and *In the Sticks* (Oxford, 1993); and has written widely on policing, power, dress and gender.

Abstracts

Local Contests and Global Visions:
Sporting Difference and International Change
by Richard Giulianotti and Gerry P.T. Finn

Association football is the global sport. There seem to be contradictions between the processes involved in the globalization of the sport and its perceived origins in, even reliance upon, its local roots. There can be little doubt that much of the present social significance of soccer lies in its capacity to embody aspects of local cultures. None the less, although football does represent cultural features back to specific societies in locally significant ways, the sport simultaneously reflects globally relevant, common themes around social identity and inter-group relationships, including forms of inclusion and exclusion, that operate at local, national and international levels. This introduction foreshadows some of the main themes that emerge in the relationship of football to the societies in the six different continents that are discussed in this special issue.

A Tale of Two Tribes:
Expressive Fandom in Australian Soccer's A-League
by John Hughson

The essay connects Maffesoli's term neo-tribes with Matza's term subterrranean values in an examination of contemporary parochial (expressive) football fandom. The particular case study is Australian soccer's A-League. Two distinct forms of expressive fandom are identified in association with both the traditional 'ethnic' clubs and the new 'one team city' clubs. It is contended that these groups are usefully considered as neo-tribes that pursue subterranean values through an affective commitment to the support of their team. The essay suggests that all forms of ethnic identity paraded on the soccer terrace must be examined in terms of the meaning held for participants. Accordingly, the English identity expressed by a current group of supporters from Perth should not be dismissed as an unfortunate re-emergence of colonialist chauvinism. To do so forecloses an important discussion of what 'being English' means to some people in Australian suburbs and how neo-tribal expressions of Englishness are produced in social forums such as the soccer stadium. Australian soccer sociologists and cultural researchers can learn more from listening to these voices than from putting their hands to their ears.

Contextualizing Suburban Soccer:
Consumer Culture, Lifestyle Differentiation and Suburban America
by David L. Andrews

This study examines the location, nature and influence of soccer within the contemporary American suburb. It focuses on the phenomenal rates of soccer participation among suburban youth. Following a genealogy of soccer within the United States, the discussion draws connections between soccer and the broader societal forces that shaped post-war suburban America. It is argued that soccer is now an important feature of the competitive, socially differentiating, and highly stylized lifestyles, through which individuals seek membership of the valorized suburban middle class.

Scottish Myopia and Global Prejudices
by Gerry P.T. Finn

'Sectarianism' is used to describe the ethnic divisions between Protestant Scot and Catholic Irish in Scottish football. Murray's pioneering historical study of Rangers and Celtic adopts a 'realist' theory of prejudice: majority prejudice is justified by the actions of the minority. Consequently, Murray examines the history of Celtic to the neglect of Rangers in support of his thesis that the anti-Catholicism of Rangers was 'caused' by Celtic. This common 'realist' belief has sustained a culture of ethnic division in Scotland. Recently, Moorhouse, in a self-contradictory piece, argues not only that sectarianism is no longer a concern for Rangers and Celtic supporters, but also simultaneously supports Rangers fans' claims that Celtic and their supporters give offence by retaining Irish associations and by supposedly supporting the actions of the IRA in Northern Ireland. When academics can be so disturbingly wrong there can be no surprise that Scotland's media persistently misrepresent and misinterpret 'sectarianism' too. But 'sectarianism' is itself a coy term which obscures any real understanding of the processes of racialization and ethnic division in Scotland and ignores international parallels elsewhere.

Football in Cameroon:
A Vehicle for the Expansion and Contraction of Identity
by Bea Vidacs

The essay examines how football in Cameroon both creates and breaks down boundaries: local level teams recreate local identities, even at the expense of more overarching ones, while the national team has the capacity to create the 'imagined community' of the nation and, on an even higher level, of engendering a pan-African consciousness. These two processes coexist and have to be analysed in conjunction with each other. On another plane, football plays an innovative role in the lives of its practitioners. It provides an avenue for the creation of loyalties and linkages which fall outside the traditional trajectories of people's lives and has the potential to bring about a true crossing of boundaries.

Football and Fatherland:
The Crisis of National Representation in Argentinian Football
by Pablo Alabarces and Maria Graciela Rodríguez

From very early times in Argentina, football has provided a strong focus for the representation of nationality. A series of international successes and a list of football 'heroes' combined to provide an epic narrative in which football made an important contribution to the 'invention of a nation'. Starting from the populist experience of the first Peronism, in the 1940s, the relationship between football (sport) and nationality became strong, with a visible climax in the '80s and '90s through the appearance of the 'Maradona saga'. Today, the globalization of the football stage coincides with the crisis of national representation through Argentinian football. The crisis seems to be conterminous with an infinite expansion of football in the daily agenda of the Argentinian public, which cuts across gender and class. Yet there is a fracture in the imaginary representation of Argentina evoked by their national team. Soccer therefore appears to be the only medium capable of developing epic nationalism in times of conservative neopopulism; yet soccer seems unable to produce it.

Built by the Two Varelas: The Rise and Fall of Football Culture and National Identity in Uruguay
by Richard Giulianotti

The essay draws upon recent research that examines football and national identity in Uruguay. Uruguay's contribution to the early history of world football, in winning the World Cup twice and being crowned Olympic champions in 1924 and 1928, is momentous. So too is the game's function in helping to formulate a strong sense of national identity among its disparate peoples. The Uruguayan success at the 1950 World Cup finals provided a mythological construction of national identity, as embodied by the victorious captain, Varela. However, within the modern football setting, demographics and historical burdens have weighed heavily against this nation of barely three million people. Poor results and negative tactics often reflect Uruguay's turbulence off the field in political and economic terms. The game's most important impact upon Uruguayan identity may be psychosocial. Although all the objective indicators point to an upturn in Uruguay's future prospects, its citizens are the most pessimistic and insecure of all Latin Americans: the decline in football fortunes provides the most profound cultural index for this sense of decay. The essay locates these structural and psychological changes within a discussion of Uruguay's global relations, specifically its state of dependency upon larger (football) economies.

The Production of a Media Epic: Germany v. Italy Football Matches
by Nicolà Porro and Pippo Russo

The study deals with the broadcasting strategies adopted by television and other mass media in order to produce and/or to emphasize the meanings of the main football matches between Germany and Italy since 1970. Adopting a qualitative content analysis, the football matches are interpreted as narrative scripts and as Weberian strategies of meaning (charismatic identification, traditional ceremony, legal-rational 'modern' competition). A survey of television spectators stresses a set of underlying conflicts, prejudices and stereotypes emphasized by history and political issues. Both the qualitative analysis and the survey data assist in understanding the syntax, semantics and unforeseeable pragmatics of these media sports events. The three main acts of this epic construction (the exciting World Cup semi-final in Mexico City in June 1970; the 1982 World Cup final in Madrid; and the match held in Manchester during Euro '96), are located in a sequential history. The crucial match in 1970 can be considered as the making of a rivalry and the beginning of a sort of media dialectic of revenge and redemption. The match works in Italian social imagery as a sort of founding myth, as reinforced by the script on the *conquest* and the *coronation* (the World Cup final in 1982) and by the last challenge played in Manchester 1996 (Germany–Italy 0–0: the unsuccessful *competition*), which led to the elimination of Italy from the European Championship. The latter event is analysed as a powerful political metaphor (the miniaturization of the 'Maastricht battle') and, at the same time, as an example of broadcasting strategy and sophisticated narrative techniques.

Fanatical Football Chants: Creating and Controlling the Carnival
by Gary Armstrong and Malcolm Young

This essay examines a hitherto unexplored dimension of football, specifically the songs and chants of football supporters. Football chants reflect strong senses of regional and local pride among working-class supporters, as well as serving to establish particular notions of masculinity within the male football crowd. An anthropological analysis identifies ways in which chants are replete with lewd expression, combining elements of the tragic and the comic. The analysis draws heavily upon over 15 years of research with football crowds in England and Wales, primarily among fans of one of the world's oldest football teams, Sheffield United. The targets and imagery of fan chants and songs have changed over the decades: the often haphazard nexus of these fan airs to popular forms of music, both mainstream and obscure, is described. Ironically, the confusion between participatory fan styles and aggression has led to the effective outlawing of expressive fandom at a time when the marketing of football trades on the 'passion' and 'atmosphere' of games, as part of an overall 'entertainment' package.

Soccer in Japan: Is *Wa* All You Need?
by John Horne

Much of the sociology and social science of sport has been focused on sport in the West. This is especially so with respect to the study of association football (soccer). Debates about globalization have widened the scope of the sociology of sport and revealed the importance of considering sport in non-Western societies. This essay considers soccer in Japan in the light of an examination of the most influential discussion of team sport in Japan – Robert Whiting's depiction of 'samurai style' baseball. Three main questions are considered: why did baseball and not soccer become the national team sport; what factors lead to the emergence of professional soccer in the 1990s; and what are the prospects for soccer in Japan?

French Football after the 1998 World Cup: The State and the Modernity of Football
by Patrick Mignon

French football can be described as a field of action in which there is too little precise knowledge of relevant facts and no real shared responsibilities for action. That is why it is so difficult to change things. These difficulties can be illustrated by examining how the State and the football authorities have tried to deal with issues of ground safety and security. The relationship between clubs, State and local authorities is problematical. Here the modernization of French football seems to mean two things: cutting the allocation of public money granted to football clubs, and stimulating public debate on different sporting issues. The organization of the World Cup in France introduced changes in French football and new European regulations make others compulsory. Examination of these different, sometimes new, public issues surrounding French football reveals some of the complexity of the meaning of modernization in relation to French football.

Old Visions, Old Issues: New Horizons, New Openings?
Change, Continuity and Other Contradictions in World Football
by Richard Giulianotti and Gerry P.T. Finn

Some key issues surrounding the contemporary processes of globalization within football are explored. The 'creolization' of football culture enables specific communities or nations to play the game in a manner that reflects local meanings, customs and social hierarchies. Football has been employed by nation-states to represent a sense of national identity, but this 'function' has met with internal resistance, and is made ever more problematical by the new global football economy. Modern football clubs double as 'transnational corporations' which challenge the centrality of the nation-state in football; transnational fan loyalties are also emerging, particularly in the new consumer markets targeted by the game's burgeoning commercial departments. Established football fans now find themselves in an ambiguous position: the informal, carnivalesque atmosphere is increasingly policed out of grounds, though some supporter groups have found a political or financial niche within the new market order. Latterly, the most powerful institutional actors have been Europe's largest clubs, the global football body FIFA, and private broadcasting networks such as BSkyB, TyC and the Kirch Group. Football's legal and financial liberalization has enriched the world's élite professionals, but has also undermined the co-operative effort required to maintain the uncertainty of outcomes on which national sport has traditionally been based. Good quality football, in the sense of meaningful competition, depends on this co-operation: is it simply utopian to believe that this recognition could contribute to more positive social relations between different communities?

Index